Poverty and Welfare in Guernsey
1560–2015

Poverty and Welfare in Guernsey
1560–2015

Rose-Marie Crossan

THE BOYDELL PRESS

First published 2015
The Boydell Press, Woodbridge

ISBN 978 1 78327 040 8

The Boydell Press is an imprint of Boydell & Brewer Ltd
PO Box 9, Woodbridge, Suffolk IP12 3DF, UK
and of Boydell & Brewer Inc.
668 Mount Hope Ave, Rochester, NY 14620–2731, USA
website: www.boydellandbrewer.com

A catalogue record for this book is available
from the British Library

This publication is printed on acid-free paper

Printed and bound in Great Britain by
TJ International Ltd, Padstow, Cornwall

MIX
Paper from
responsible sources
FSC® C013056

In memory of my father
Ted Taylor, 1930–2008

Contents

Illustrations

Plates 1 and 2 courtesy of the Priaulx Library, Guernsey; Plates 4, 6, 7 and 10 courtesy of Guernsey Museums & Galleries (States of Guernsey) 2015; Plates 3, 5, 8 and 9 courtesy of the Island Archives Service, Guernsey, and Plate 11 by kind permission of Michael Deane at deanephotos.com.

Acknowledgements

I owe my thanks to Dr Darryl Ogier for his encouragement of this project and to Gillian Lenfestey for sharing her insights on the Town Hospital. I am also grateful to Anna Baghiani for forwarding information on Jersey, to Brian Bonnard and Colin Partridge for answering queries about Alderney, to Dr Richard Axton for supplying information on Sark, and to the staff of Guernsey's Island Archives, Priaulx Library, Museum Service and Greffe for their professional assistance. My greatest debt, however, is to my husband, Jonathan Crossan, whose unfailing support I am sure I do not deserve.

Rose-Marie Crossan
Guernsey, June 2015

Abbreviations

Acte	*Acte des Etats*[1]
Billet	*Billet d'Etat*[2]
IA	Island Archives, Guernsey[3]
O in C	Order in Council
Ord	Ordinance of the Royal Court
PL	Priaulx Library, Guernsey
PP	Parliamentary Papers
SPCK	Society for Promoting Christian Knowledge
TNA	The National Archives, Kew
TSG	*Transactions of La Société Guernesiaise*

[1] Acts of the States, Orders in Council and Ordinances issued prior to 1950 will be referred to by their date, and, unless otherwise stated, will be found in the published volumes held at the Priaulx Library. Post-1950 legislation will be found online at www.guernseylegalresources.gg.

[2] *Billets d'Etat*, which contain the agenda and supporting material for States meetings, will be referred to by the date of the meeting for which the Billet was compiled, and will be found in the bound volumes held at the Priaulx Library.

[3] Records in the custody of the Island Archives will be referred to by their date followed by the Archives' reference code for the document concerned.

Conventions

Dates before 1752 are Old Style but adjusted to a year beginning 1 January. Translations from the customary French of Guernsey's pre-twentieth-century records are my own and are provided without reproduction of the original, except in cases of unresolved ambiguity. Guernsey parishes are referred to by the English version of their names, and those prefixed 'St' are rendered with a terminal 's' unpreceded by an apostrophe.[1]

Note on currency

Before the nineteenth century, the currency used in Guernsey was the French *livre tournois* (divided into *sols* and *deniers*). Where a sterling equivalent is required for the purposes of this book, sums in *livres tournois* will be converted at the standard eighteenth-century London rate of fourteen to the pound.[2]

After the French government replaced the *livre tournois* with the franc in the early nineteenth century, the *livre tournois* was superseded in most local contexts by the Guernsey pound. Prior to 1921, the Guernsey pound was worth 19s 2½d sterling. After that date, it was fixed at parity with sterling. No attempt will be made to convert Guernsey currency into sterling, and unless otherwise stated, all sums in pounds and pence relating to local affairs from the early 1800s to 1921 are in Guernsey values.[3]

---

[1] This practice is not universal. It is followed here to reflect current spoken usage, where the final 's' has effectively become accreted to the names (as in the British towns of St Albans and St Andrews). Note that the parish of St Peters is also known as St Peter-in-the-Wood (or Saint-Pierre-du-Bois).

[2] The local rate varied, with £1 worth up to 22 *livres* at some points in the 1700s (P. Raban, 'War and trade in the mid-eighteenth century', *TSG*, 22 (1986), p. 160).

[3] For more detail on local currency, see S. Carey Curtis, 'The currency of Guernsey in historical times' (Guernsey pamphlet, n.d.), PL; *Clarke's Monthly Illustrated Journal*, October 1872, pp. 37–9; J. Marr, *The History of Guernsey: The Bailiwick's Story* (1982; Guernsey, 2001 edn), pp. 439–42.

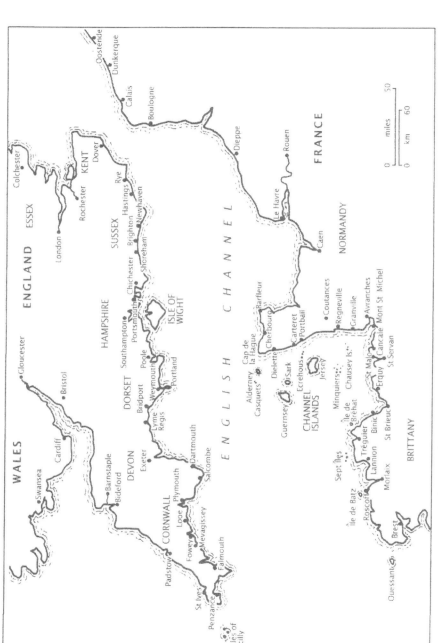

Map 1 Channel Islands and adjacent French and English coasts

Map 2 Parishes of Guernsey

Introduction

The history of poor relief in England and Wales has been well studied, receiving almost continuous academic attention since the early twentieth century: from the Hammonds, Webbs and Dorothy Marshall in the 1910s and 1920s, through Mark Blaug, J.S. Taylor, Peter Dunkley and Michael Rose in the 1960s and 1970s, to Paul Slack, Keith Snell, Steven Hindle, Steven King (and many others) from the 1980s to the present day.[1] For Scotland, the corpus of work is relatively more modest and more recent. Rosalind Mitchison laid the foundations for modern Scottish poor law studies in the 1970s, and her work has subsequently been added to by such scholars as Robert Cage, Ian Levitt, Andrew Blaikie and John Stewart. Irish poor law studies also began modestly and comparatively late. However, they have expanded rapidly since the late twentieth century, with notable contributions by Helen Burke, Virginia Crossman, Peter Gray and, most recently, Mel Cousins.

By contrast with Great Britain and Ireland, the history of poor relief in the offshore Crown Dependencies has been neglected, for none have attracted the attention of academic welfare historians. Nor has much work been produced by local historians. Jersey has been the subject of a 200-page study by a retired local schoolteacher,[2] but there are no comparable surveys of either Guernsey or the Isle of Man. All that exists on the welfare history of both of these islands are one or two articles in local studies journals, and chapters or sections in books on more general subjects.[3]

But perhaps there is good reason for such scant attention. Why, after all, should an island such as Guernsey, measuring just over twenty-four square miles, merit an extended analysis of its welfare arrangements? And could such arrangements hold

---

[1] For references to the work of these scholars and others mentioned in this paragraph, see bibliography.

[2] M. Phillips, *Poor People* (Jersey, 2001). Mrs Phillips' book focuses primarily on the experience of poverty in Jersey, as also on the history of Jersey's General Hospital and events leading to the passage of Jersey's 1951 Insular Insurance Law.

[3] In respect of Guernsey, the historiography is as follows. Articles: M. Brock, 'La maison des pauvres, St Peter's', *Quarterly Review of the Guernsey Society*, 18 (1962), pp. 4–6, and T.F. Priaulx, 'Les pauvres', *Quarterly Review of the Guernsey Society*, 21–4 (1965–8), pp. 32–5. Sections in books: C.J. Ribton-Turner, *A History of Vagrants and Vagrancy and Beggars and Begging* (London, 1887), pp. 457–65; D.M. Ogier, *Reformation and Society in Guernsey* (Woodbridge, 1996), pp. 25–31, 158–73; G. Stevens Cox, *St Peter Port, 1680–1830: The History of an International Entrepôt* (Woodbridge, 1999), pp. 106–8; R.-M. Crossan, *Guernsey, 1814–1914: Migration and Modernisation* (Woodbridge, 2007), pp. 149–60.

any interest for readers without local ties? The following paragraphs will propose a justification for the undertaking.

To begin with, despite its small area, Guernsey has supported a disproportionately large population for most of recorded history. In past centuries, this arose partly from the island's climate and fertility, and partly from the trading activities of its capital, St Peter Port. As early as the Iron Age, St Peter Port, a sheltered haven on Guernsey's east coast, offered a useful stopping-off point to vessels sailing up from Biscay into the Channel. The trading settlement which established itself along its shore gradually expanded over time, and, by the eighteenth century, had become, by contemporary standards, a major town. In 1700, there were only fifty towns in the whole of Britain with a population of over 2,000.[4] With some 4,350 inhabitants in 1727, St Peter Port was directly on a par with such English county towns as Warwick and Lincoln.[5] Many similarly sized towns (notably Dorchester, Oxford, Shrewsbury and York) have already provided the subject for important welfare studies.[6] If size is a criterion, then the arrangements of Guernsey's substantial community should be of at least as much interest as these.

An even more pertinent justification for a welfare study of Guernsey, however, lies in the realm of politics and culture. Although the Channel Islands were allied to England from the thirteenth century, they fell outside Westminster's jurisdiction and evolved their own unique laws and institutions. They also retained strong linguistic and cultural ties with France well into the modern era. Against this mixed politico-cultural background, questions arise as to the influences which might have moulded Guernsey's welfare arrangements, and a survey of the insular system might make an interesting addition to the field of comparative welfare history. Significantly for our context, one strand of comparative studies has focused strongly on differences between the English poor laws on the one hand, and continental welfare regimes on the other. Among the many eminent scholars who have written in this vein are Joanna Innes, who has drawn contrasts between English and European welfare at the level of public policy formation,[7] and Peter Solar, Peter Lindert and Larry Patriquin, who have emphasised the English/continental welfare 'dichotomy' in studies relating to economic development.[8]

---

4   C.W. Chalklin, *The Provincial Towns of Georgian England* (London, 1974), p. 5.
5   For population figures, see Stevens Cox, *St Peter Port*, p. 164; Chalklin, *Provincial Towns*, p. 18.
6   Dorchester in David Underdown's *Fire from Heaven: Life in an English Town in the Seventeenth Century* (London, 1992); Oxford, Shrewsbury and York in Alannah Tomkins', *The Experience of Urban Poverty, 1723–82: Parish, Charity and Credit* (Manchester, 2006).
7   Professor Innes's essays on this subject include 'State, church and voluntarism in European welfare, 1690–1850', in H. Cunningham and J. Innes (eds), *Charity, Philanthropy and Reform in Europe and North America, 1690–1850* (Basingstoke, 1998); 'The state and the poor: eighteenth-century England in historical perspective', in J. Brewer and E. Hellmuth (eds), *Rethinking Leviathan: The Eighteenth-Century State in Britain and Germany* (Oxford, 1999); 'The distinctiveness of the English poor laws, 1750–1850', in D. Winch and P. O'Brien (eds), *The Political Economy of British Historical Experience, 1688–1914* (Oxford, 2002).
8   P.M. Solar, 'Poor relief and English economic development before the industrial revolution', *The Economic History Review*, 48 (1995), pp. 1–22; P.H. Lindert, 'Poor relief before the Welfare State: Britain versus the Continent, 1780–1880', *European Review of Economic*

An alternative strand of writing on comparative welfare has, however, taken issue with the starkly polarised nature of this perspective. Steven King, in particular, has contended that 'wide chronological and spatial variation ... characterised England as surely as it did France or the Netherlands'.[9] More recently, Professor King has proposed a typology for categorising European welfare regimes at regional rather than national level.[10] In this context (and germane to our subject), he has identified peripherality as a possible 'organising principle', discerning a number of 'common-alities' which suggested that 'there was something about being "peripheral" that created distinctive welfare regimes'.[11]

An analysis of Guernsey can contribute to all aspects of these studies. Adopting the first perspective, we might, for instance, enquire whether affinities with France resulted in welfare patterning more typical of that country than of England. Adopting the second perspective, we might examine whether Guernsey's periph-erality produced a 'distinctive' effect on its welfare, and seek to locate the island on King's typological spectrum. Finally, in a combination of both perspectives, we might investigate the extent to which Guernsey belonged to the 'British welfare family' at all, and, if so, whether there were other peripheral members with whom closer affinities existed than with England.

Guernsey's political autonomy has not only resulted in institutions which are unique to the island; it has also produced an abundance of records suited to the genesis of a 'history from below'. One such source, hitherto little exploited, is the compendious Town Hospital collection, unearthed as recently as the 1980s, which contains hundreds of ledgers, registers, daybooks, logs and other documents relating to indoor and outdoor relief in St Peter Port. This is the chief source on which this study will draw. Heavy use will also be made of the day-to-day records of the island's ten parishes, since welfare was primarily a parochial affair. Thirdly, in an effort to document the increasing involvement of central insular institutions, extensive refer-ence will be made to records generated by the island's Royal Court and States.[12]

This book is divided into four sections. The first will set out the context for the welfare study, with chapters covering Guernsey's governance, economy and social structure. The second section will mark the beginning of the welfare study proper. Its opening chapter will trace the evolution of a parochial welfare system in Guernsey after the Reformation; its second chapter will concentrate solely on outdoor relief, analysing its administration from c.1750 to c.1950, and its final chapter will attempt to evaluate the welfare contribution of public relief relative to that of private charity.

History, 2 (1998), pp. 101–240; L. Patriquin, *Agrarian Capitalism and Poor Relief in England, 1500–1860* (Basingstoke, 2007).

[9]   S.A. King, 'Poor relief and English economic development reappraised', *The Economic History Review*, 50 (1997), pp. 365–6.

[10]   S.A. King, 'Welfare regimes and welfare regions in Britain and Europe, c.1750s to 1860s', *Journal of Modern European History*, 9 (2011), pp. 57–63.

[11]   King, 'Welfare regimes', pp. 52–3; see also S.A. King and J. Stewart (eds), *Welfare Peripheries: The Development of Welfare States in Nineteenth and Twentieth Century Europe* (Bern, 2007), pp. 22–31.

[12]   For the respective roles of parishes, Royal Court and States, see Chapter 1.

In the third section of this book, the focus will turn to indoor relief. Using St Peter Port's workhouse (the Town Hospital) as an exemplar, the four chapters in this section will investigate all aspects of indoor life and policy between the eighteenth century and World War I.

Lastly, to conclude the welfare study, the fourth section of this book will survey twentieth-century innovations, charting in detail the assumption of welfare responsibilities by the States, and examining the process whereby parish relief was transformed – not without acrimony or contest – into the States-administered social security system which exists today.

I
Context

1

Governance, Economy, Society

Governance

Until the thirteenth century, the Channel Islands shared a common history with north-west France.[1] It is thought that they became part of the Roman Empire at the same time as Gaul, and were inhabited after the fall of the Empire by a Gallo-Roman population under the Frankish monarchy.[2] In the 900s, the Islands and adjacent Cotentin peninsula were absorbed into the territory of the Dukes of Normandy. Duke William's conquest of England in 1066 brought no change to the Islands, which continued to be governed as part of Normandy as before. In 1204, however, the Islands were politically severed from the Norman mainland when John, king of England and duke of Normandy, lost the continental portion of his duchy to the French king. The Islands gained strategic value as stepping-stones between England and John's remaining continental possessions, and he and his successors contrived by various means to secure their allegiance.[3] An important way in which insular sympathy was won lay in the decision of post-1204 monarchs to respect the Islands' existing law and institutions, and to allow them to govern themselves, under royal supervision.[4]

After a period of instability, the Islands were recognised by the 1259 Treaty of Paris as part of Henry III of England's continental territories.[5] Five years previously, Henry had granted them to his son, the future Edward I, 'in such manner that the said lands … may never be separated from the Crown'.[6] The Islands thereafter remained possessions of the English Crown but were never incorporated into the Kingdom of England (nor, later, into the United Kingdom). Subsequent monarchs issued charters guaranteeing Islanders' customs and privileges, and granting them

---

[1] This chapter addresses similar ground to that covered in the preliminary chapters of my *Guernsey, 1814–1914: Migration and Modernisation* (Woodbridge, 2007). Readers familiar with that book might wish to proceed to Chapter 2.

[2] H. Sebire, *The Archaeology and Early History of the Channel Islands* (Stroud, 2005), p. 109; A.H. Ewen, 'The Breton Myth', *TSG*, 21 (1982), p. 199.

[3] J.A. Everard and J.C. Holt, *Jersey 1204: The Forging of an Island Community* (London, 2004), p. 115.

[4] Everard and Holt, *Jersey 1204*, pp. 155–65, 187–8.

[5] D.M. Ogier, *The Government and Law of Guernsey* (Guernsey, 2005), p. 2.

[6] J. Loveridge, *The Constitution and Law of Guernsey* (1975; Guernsey, 1997 edn), p. 1.

further privileges. Among these were autonomy in tax matters, freedom of trade with England, immunity from the jurisdiction of English courts, and exemption from military service outside the Islands.[7]

By the late 1200s, the local administrations of Jersey and Guernsey were each headed by a Bailiff with ultimate responsibility for the administration of justice in the king's court.[8] These acted under a joint Warden appointed by the English king to uphold the wider interests of the Crown.[9] The two Bailiwicks in time embarked on divergent courses. By 1469, Edward IV had granted each a separate charter of its own.[10] By 1478, each Bailiwick had its own Warden.[11] The Bailiwicks eventually became completely sundered, and their political, legal and administrative structures assumed different, though related, forms.[12]

While the Bailiwicks enjoyed considerable autonomy, English sovereigns maintained the right to legislate directly for them by Order in Council through exercise of the Prerogative. This was commonly used in medieval and early modern times. After the seventeenth century, as the king's personal power waned, much Channel Island business came to be settled by committees of the Privy Council or individual government ministers, even though the Islands were not represented at Westminster.

In the eighteenth century, this state of affairs raised the issue of the wider powers of Parliament to legislate for the Islands. The fact that these powers had never been defined gave rise to friction. In the eyes of English jurists, all that was required for Acts of Parliament to have force in the Channel Islands was that the Islands should be expressly mentioned in the Acts. Insular authorities never accepted this view, contending that Acts could not apply until transmitted by Order of the King in Council and formally registered by the Islands' Royal Courts.[13] The number of occasions when Acts were imposed on the Islands against their will was, however, minimal. The position was never explicitly resolved, but Westminster gradually came to the view that – given the Islands' lack of parliamentary representation – intervention should not be undertaken without serious reason. Hence the constitutional convention evolved over the nineteenth century that legislation should not be extended to the Channel Islands without their prior consultation and consent.[14]

Prior to the nineteenth century, Governors appointed to the Islands by the Crown were frequently absentees. In 1835, the office of Governor was abolished in Guernsey, and its powers devolved to the Lieutenant-Governor who henceforth always resided locally.[15] Besides acting as intermediary between British and insular

---

[7]   For the substance of charters, see T. Thornton, *The Charters of Guernsey* (Bognor Regis, 2004).
[8]   Everard and Holt, *Jersey 1204*, p. 155.
[9]   Wardens were also known as Keepers or Captains, and later as Governors.
[10] T. Thornton, *The Channel Islands, 1370–1640: Between England and Normandy* (Woodbridge, 2012), p. 60.
[11] Thornton, *Charters*, p. 46
[12] The Bailiwick of Jersey comprised only Jersey and adjacent reefs, but the Bailiwick of Guernsey also included the islands of Alderney, Sark, Herm and Jethou.
[13] R.P. Hocart, *An Island Assembly: The Development of the States of Guernsey, 1700–1949* (Guernsey, 1988), p. 1.
[14] G. Dawes, *Laws of Guernsey* (Oxford, 2003), p. 20.
[15] Ogier, *Government and Law*, pp. 104–5.

authorities, his responsibilities were chiefly military. He was in overall command of the garrison and militia. He had a right to address the States (which required his consent to convene), but he had no vote in that assembly. After the close of the Napoleonic Wars, the influence of Governors and Lieutenant-Governors over insular affairs progressively declined.

During the period with which we are concerned, Guernsey's government and administration fell into three tiers. Much basic work was done at parish level. Guernsey's ten parishes each possessed a body elected for life by the *Chefs de Famille* (adult male ratepayers) known as the *Douzaine*.[16] Among other things, this body was responsible for assessing and levying parochial taxation and apportioning parochial expenditure. At the apex of parish structure were the two Constables, elected by the *Chefs de Famille* for overlapping terms of one to three years.[17] As well as being responsible for public order, the Constables also acted as parish treasurers and executive officers of their *Douzaines*, and, until 1844, they had seats in the States as representatives of their parish.[18] Owing to their exercise of these functions, Guernsey's parish Constables – held in 'much reverential awe by the lower orders' – were of considerably higher rank and status than their nominal counterparts in England.[19]

At island-wide level, most day-to-day work of law and administration was performed by the Royal Court. The Court was composed of the Bailiff, who was appointed by the Crown, and twelve Jurats (or magistrates), elected for life. It had jurisdiction over criminal and civil law within Guernsey. Its members, most of whom were not legally trained, were sole judges of law as well as of fact.[20] In its administrative capacity, the Royal Court had wide-ranging ordinance-making powers on matters of internal domestic regulation which it could (and, until the mid-1800s, frequently did) exercise without reference to the States.[21]

The highest tier of local government was the States, which was essentially an expanded version of the Royal Court, to which were added representatives of the parishes. It has been suggested that this body, first recorded by name in 1538, might have originated in the Court's need to gauge the wider community's views on matters of collective concern.[22] Meetings of the States were convened by the Royal Court until 1776 when this function passed to the Bailiff alone.[23] Since 1844, the composition of the States has evolved incrementally through a series of five

[16] *Douzeniers* were twelve in number in all parishes aside from the Vale, which had sixteen, and St Peter Port, which had twenty (between 1844 and 1948, St Peter Port also had an additional forty-eight 'cantonal' *Douzeniers*, serving on four subsidiary *Douzaines*).
[17] From 1736, St Peter Port also had four 'assistant constables' dealing exclusively with policing matters (Ord, 4.10.1736).
[18] Normally only one Constable from each parish would be present at any given States' meeting (Hocart, *Island Assembly*, pp. 2–4).
[19] W. Berry, *The History of the Island of Guernsey* (London, 1815), p. 122.
[20] Until 1964, when the Jurats' competence as judges of law was removed (Ogier, *Government and Law*, p. 65).
[21] Hocart, *Island Assembly*, p. 109.
[22] Ogier, *Government and Law*, p. 20. See also Hocart, *Island Assembly*, p. x.
[23] Berry, *Island of Guernsey*, p. 229.

reforms.[24] However, for a long period before 1844, the assembly consisted, in its deliberative capacity, of thirty-two members: the twelve Jurats of the Royal Court, ten parish Constables, eight parish Rectors,[25] the *Procureur* (a Crown-appointed law officer corresponding to the English Attorney-General), and the Bailiff, who as well as presiding over the Court, also presided over the States.[26]

Well into the 1800s, the States met only a few times yearly to consult on matters deemed beyond the domestic regulatory scope of the Royal Court. However, the States themselves had no ordinance-making powers, and their decisions could be given force only by ordinances of the Royal Court. That said, ordinances could not be used for any States-originated *projets de loi* (proposed laws) which embodied new taxes or major judicial innovations, since such laws required the approval of the King in Council. These *projets* had therefore to be forwarded for the Privy Council's consideration, and, when royal sanction was given, they acquired the status of Orders in Council. Orders in Council emanating from States' *projets* were few in the early nineteenth and preceding centuries but became increasingly common as changing economic and social conditions broadened and deepened the legislative role of the States. One consequence of this was to reduce the power and influence of the Royal Court. This reduction was, however, gradual, and it was not until 1948, when the Court's ordinance-making powers were transferred to the States, that the States finally achieved a complete monopoly of legislative power.[27]

In matters of finance, aside from some defence costs, Guernsey was self-sufficient.[28] Before the nineteenth century, all-island (as opposed to parochial) expenditure was mainly funded through harbour dues and import duties.[29] These revenues were controlled by the States, which also intermittently levied a property-based general tax to finance major projects such as road-making.[30] In 1813, the States were compelled to boost their revenues with a new income stream when they took over maintenance of sea defences from the parishes. This took the form of the *impôt* (a duty on locally sold spirits which was first levied in 1814).[31] As routine spending for all-island purposes mounted (from 1825 the States contributed

---

24 These reforms took place in 1844, 1899, 1920, 1948 and 2004.
25 Eight Rectors for ten parishes because, until 1859 and 1867 respectively, St Sampsons/the Vale, and Torteval/the Forest each formed one living.
26 The States also had an elective role. In this capacity, as the 'States of Election', the body comprised all the above, plus the ten other parish Constables and entire *Douzaines* of each parish. Its functions as such were to elect the Jurats and the Sheriff (an official responsible for executing Court judgments) and, from 1844, to approve applications for the levying of island-wide taxes (Hocart, *Island Assembly*, p. 3).
27 Ogier, *Government and Law*, p. 40.
28 The British government, which was responsible for the island's defence and foreign affairs, paid the expenses of the British garrison as well as the construction and maintenance costs of some of Guernsey's fortifications. It also partially funded the insular militia.
29 For a summary of dues and duties, see Hocart, *Island Assembly*, pp. 7–9. From 1780, there was also a tax on inn-keepers.
30 General taxes, a bone of contention, were only levied on thirty or so occasions between 1660 and 1920 (Hocart, *Island Assembly*, pp. 9, 10, 92).
31 Hocart, *Island Assembly*, p. 25.

towards schools, sewers and street maintenance),[32] the States grew more reliant on the *impôt*. Later extended to cover imported wines, beers and tobacco, the *impôt* became the States' single most important revenue source until the introduction of income tax in 1919.[33]

Until the twentieth century, however, by far the majority of community needs were funded not at insular but at parish level. Records survive from the late 1600s of parochial taxes being levied for the upkeep of churches and graveyards, for the billeting of soldiers, and for the construction and maintenance of schools and coastal fortifications. After the introduction of poor rates in the eighteenth century, the combined tax revenue of Guernsey's parishes rose to exceed that of the States. In 1780, for instance, States' revenue amounted to 12,250 *livres tournois*, or about £875 sterling, while in St Peter Port alone 6,000 *livres tournois* were raised for the poor and 8,000 *livres tournois* for other parochial needs, making a total of £1,000 sterling.[34] The balance improved somewhat in the States' favour after the introduction of the *impôt*, but this still made the parishes, and particularly St Peter Port, a force to be reckoned with. Guernsey's governance during the eighteenth and nineteenth centuries is thus characterised by a degree of tension, not only between the parishes and the States but also among the parishes themselves, as rural parishes vied with St Peter Port to exert control over all-island structures.

Economy

Guernsey being better situated on maritime trade routes than Jersey, St Peter Port was the Channel Islands' leading harbour from at least the Middle Ages.[35] By the late thirteenth century, hundreds of vessels were calling in each year on voyages between northern and southern Europe.[36] A sizeable harbour-side settlement grew up, and, in 1309, when Guernsey's main market was moved to St Peter Port from the Castel parish, the settlement became recognisably a town.[37] A Papal Bull of 1481 which effectively made the Channel Islands neutral in wartime gave a fillip to St Peter Port's traders, and by the 1580s, Guernsey-owned vessels were sailing to Newfoundland

---

[32] Hocart, *Island Assembly*, p. 53.

[33] Hocart, *Island Assembly*, p. 96.

[34] 28.10.1780, IA, AQ 1003/03; 28.3.1781, IA, AQ 0964/01.

[35] C. Platt, *A Concise History of Jersey: A New Perspective* (Jersey, 2009), p. 30.

[36] W. Stevenson, 'The Middle Ages, 1000–1500', in A.G. Jamieson (ed.), *A People of the Sea: The Maritime History of the Channel Islands* (London, 1986), p. 43.

[37] Note, however, that St Peter Port continued to be run as a parish while retaining a distinct rural fringe (comprising in the mid-1800s a mile-wide semi-circular band to the north, west and south of the built-up area, with 14 per cent of St Peter Port's houses situated in its rural portion). The area around St Sampsons' harbour acquired a semi-urban character in the nineteenth century, but St Peter Port remained the island's only true town (G. Stevens Cox, *St Peter Port, 1680–1830: The History of an International Entrepôt* (Woodbridge, 1999), pp. 12, 50; J. Duncan, *The History of Guernsey* (London, 1841), p. 288).

and local merchants were acting as middlemen in Anglo-French trade.[38]

To begin with, Guernsey's home-grown exports were minimal: dried and salted fish; small amounts of agricultural produce. This changed somewhat in the late sixteenth century, when a stocking-knitting industry grew up. The industry lasted until the mid-eighteenth century, initially exporting mainly to France and subsequently to England.[39] Described as 'a poor man's alternative to unemployment', it was a putting-out industry controlled by local merchants who distributed wool among the lower ranks and paid a piece rate for finished articles.[40]

In the 1680s, privateering was added to St Peter Port's repertoire when the Channel Islands lost their neutrality on the accession of William III.[41] Although this risk-fraught activity did not contribute as much to Guernsey's economy as trade,[42] local shipowners engaged in it in each successive war, their occasional spectacular gains outweighing equally dramatic losses.[43]

Arguably, the most important effect of privateering was to establish St Peter Port as a depot for luxury goods subject to high duties in England. Prize cargoes of spirits and tobacco captured by Guernsey's earliest privateers had attracted buyers from among the smuggling fraternity of south-west England, and, as a result, merchants and shipowners were encouraged to continue importing these commodities in peacetime. They stored them in purpose-built warehouses, repackaging and decanting them into portable containers for the smugglers, who found their provisioning trips conveniently short.[44] By the 1730s, Guernsey was one of the main suppliers of contraband to south-west England. After 1765, when Manx activities in this line were curtailed by the British government, and before the rise of continental supply bases such as Flushing and Dunkirk, Guernsey and Alderney became the principal depots for contraband bound for the whole of Britain and Ireland.[45]

The need to continue sourcing luxury goods also gave a fillip to insular participation in the wider carrying trade, and capacious warehousing built to store such goods allowed the town to develop a more respectable role as depository and bulk-breaker for dutiable commodities destined for legal entry into Britain before the

[38] D.M. Ogier, *Reformation and Society in Guernsey* (Woodbridge, 1996), pp. 37–8; J.C. Appleby, 'Neutrality, trade and privateering, 1500–1689', in Jamieson (ed.), *A People of the Sea*, p. 59.

[39] Exports to France declined steeply from the mid-seventeenth century, when the French imposed a punitive duty on imported stockings (Appleby, 'Neutrality, trade and privateering', p. 87).

[40] P. Raban, 'War and trade in the mid-eighteenth century', *TSG*, 22 (1986), p. 156; Stevens Cox, *St Peter Port*, p. 54.

[41] J.S. Bromley, 'A new vocation: privateering in the wars of 1689–97 and 1702–13', in Jamieson (ed.), *A People of the Sea*, pp. 109–47.

[42] A.G. Jamieson, 'The return to privateering: Channel Island privateers, 1739–83', in Jamieson (ed.), *A People of the Sea*, p. 172; Stevens Cox, *St Peter Port*, p. 48.

[43] These wars were the Nine Years War (1688–97), the Wars of the Spanish Succession (1702–12) and Austrian Succession (1739–48), the Seven Years War (1756–63), the War of American Independence (1776–83) and the French Revolutionary and Napoleonic Wars (1793–1815).

[44] Berry, *Island of Guernsey*, pp. 268–84.

[45] A.G. Jamieson, 'The Channel Islands and smuggling, 1680–1850', in Jamieson (ed.), *A People of the Sea*, pp. 195, 203–5.

introduction of the bonding system. By the mid-eighteenth century, local ships were bringing in wine, brandy and textiles from France; rum from the West Indies; tobacco from Maryland and Virginia; and they were also trading with Newfoundland and Africa.[46] So extensive was St Peter Port's eighteenth-century trade that a modern-day historian has ranked it 'one of the principal commercial entrepôts in the Atlantic economy'.[47]

All this created employment opportunities – for porters, carriers, boatmen, sailmakers, blockmakers, ropemakers, ship carpenters, blacksmiths and, above all, for the coopers who made the small wooden barrels into which cargoes were decanted and repacked, and for the tobacco workers who processed imported raw leaf. Some 700 coopers were working in the town by the late 1700s.[48] In 1800, a visiting Customs Commissioner counted fifteen tobacco and snuff factories employing no less than 'one thousand of the poorest Men, Women and Children'.[49] To this we must also add seafarers. Guernsey's fleet quadrupled from thirty-two vessels in 1701 to 112 in 1803. Peacetime crewing requirements ranged from a couple of hundred in the early days to about a thousand at the end of the period. They reached almost double this number during wartime bouts of privateering.[50]

Eighteenth-century wars also significantly boosted the number of uniformed men in St Peter Port, which added to the profits which the town's retail and service sectors already derived from seafarers. Numbers of servicemen reached unprecedented levels after 1780 when the garrison strength was increased, and they rose still further in the 1790s when a naval squadron was stationed at St Peter Port and various foreign regiments were quartered in the island.[51] One assessment put garrison numbers alone at 5,903 in 1798.[52] Military and naval inputs combined with maritime trade led to a peaking of Guernsey's economy in the early 1800s.

As commercial and industrial activities were tightly concentrated in town, St Peter Port may be said to have profited most from the Georgian boom. This is not, however, to say that Guernsey's rural parishes reaped no benefit. A mid-eighteenth-century document reported that farmers from these parishes sold some £22,000 sterling worth of cider, butter, eggs, poultry, fish, vegetables and livestock in St Peter Port in 1758.[53] Nevertheless, Guernsey's countryside was geared to a system of agriculture whose main object was self-sufficiency. The sale of surplus produce in town was thus merely a valuable sideline. Most farms were diminutive and owner-occupied

---

[46] G. Stevens Cox, *The Guernsey Merchants and their World* (Guernsey, 2009), p. 7.

[47] Stevens Cox, *St Peter Port*, p. 23.

[48] Stevens Cox, *St Peter Port*, pp. 52–3, 59.

[49] TNA, T 64/153.

[50] A.G. Jamieson, 'Channel Island shipowners and seamen, 1700–1900', in Jamieson (ed.), *A People of the Sea*, pp. 34–78; Stevens Cox, *St Peter Port*, pp. 44, 79.

[51] Stevens Cox, *St Peter Port*, pp. 58, 106; A.G. Jamieson, 'The Channel Islands and British maritime strategy, 1689–1945', in Jamieson (ed.), *A People of the Sea*, p. 225.

[52] T.W.M. De Guerin, 'The English garrison of Guernsey from early times', *Transactions of the Guernsey Society of Natural Science and Local Research*, 5 (1905), pp. 80–81.

[53] *The Case of the Town Parish versus the Nine Country Parishes respecting a Change in the Rates and Representation, appointed to be heard before the Committee of the Privy Council at 11 o'clock, on Thursday April 26, 1759* (Guernsey, 1843), PL, pp. 23–4.

(Guernsey had no large landowners and no tradition of renting). The largest farms were rarely over twenty-five acres, and the average no more than five.[54] The first time holdings were counted was in 1851, when Guernsey's twenty-four square miles were found to contain just under 800 farms, virtually all of them worked by their owners.[55] Until the twentieth century, these were essentially mixed farms, producing cereals, vegetable crops and cider apples, and rearing small numbers of livestock. Cattle were always important, because of their marketable produce, but specialisation in dairying was a twentieth-century phenomenon.

The lack of large landowners and the small size of farms owed much to Guernsey's system of modified partible inheritance, whereby all of a deceased person's sons and daughters were entitled to a share of his real property, although the eldest son received most, including the family house.[56] On smaller holdings, younger siblings' shares could prove uneconomic, and they might choose to part with them to the oldest brother. Some would then leave the countryside to seek a living elsewhere.[57] As a nineteenth-century observer remarked, 'these small farms cannot possibly support all that are born on them'.[58]

Those left behind in the country parishes comprised the principal heirs with their more substantial holdings, and a proportion of their less well-off brethren who nevertheless invariably held some scrap of land, supplementing what they could grow or rear with intermittent day labour for better-off neighbours; by fishing if they lived near the coast; or through the exercise of a trade. 'With scarcely any exception, every man has a cottage and some land of his own', a journal commented in the 1830s, 'and if it be not sufficiently large to subsist his family, he makes up the difference by working at his trade, either as a mason, or a carpenter, and sometimes as a fisherman'.[59] Thus the landless rural proletariat that was such a feature of eighteenth- and nineteenth-century England was almost completely lacking in Guernsey.[60]

St Peter Port's Napoleonic heyday was short-lived. Guernsey's involvement with smuggling had attracted the displeasure of the British government. In a report to the Treasury in 1800, Customs Commissioner William Stiles estimated that smuggling from Guernsey and Alderney injured the Revenue 'to the enormous amount of one million pounds per annum'.[61] In 1805 and 1807, the Westminster parliament passed anti-smuggling Acts encompassing the Channel Islands, and effectively

[54]   T. Quayle, *A General View of the Agriculture and Present State of the Islands on the Coast of Normandy subject to the Crown of Great Britain* (London, 1815), p. 249; Duncan, *History of Guernsey*, p. 288.

[55]   PP 1852–3 LXXXVIII. See also Conclusion, n. 3.

[56]   For more on inheritance, see P. Jeremie, *On Real Property and Taxation in Guernsey* (Guernsey, 1841).

[57]   S. Lewis, *A Topographical Dictionary of England*, 4 vols (London, 1831), 2, p. 273; R.P. Hocart, *Guernsey's Countryside: An Introduction to the History of the Rural Landscape* (Guernsey, 2010), p. 43.

[58]   Letter from 'H.A.M.', *Tait's Edinburgh Magazine*, 4 (1839), p. 432.

[59]   *The Guernsey and Jersey Magazine*, 2 (1836), p. 127. See also H.D. Inglis, *The Channel Islands*, 2 vols (London, 1834), 2, pp. 48–50.

[60]   Quayle, *General View*, p. 283.

[61]   TNA, T 64/153.

put an end to this activity.[62] As a result, many of St Peter Port's leading merchants withdrew from business, sold off their ships and their warehouses and invested the proceeds in government securities.[63] This withdrawal, combined with the end of the Wars and reduction of the garrison, gave a check to the economy, with particularly adverse effects on St Peter Port's middling and lower social strata.

Nevertheless, St Peter Port's ex-merchants were far from poor, and the majority of them remained resident in the town.[64] From the early 1820s, they were joined by British half-pay officers, ex-colonials and retired professionals drawn by the town's growing reputation as a place where one might live 'genteelly' on a fixed income.[65] The presence of this relatively affluent contingent stimulated demand for housing, goods and services and, by the late 1820s, the urban economy was beginning tentatively to pick up.

This period also saw something of a resurgence in shipping. The rump of merchants who did not retire in the post-smuggling period turned their sights south and built up a successful carrying trade between Europe and such places as Cuba, Brazil and Uruguay.[66] This trade was gradually lost to other nations from the 1840s, but shipowners maintained the size of their fleet by monopolising niche markets such as the Azores fruit trade and the Costa Rica coffee trade.[67] During the 1840s and 1850s, island-registered vessels also took an increasing share of the local inshore trade. Guernsey's nineteenth-century shipping industry peaked in the 1860s, when it directly employed around 1,200 seamen.[68] The gradual move from worldwide into inshore carrying was, however, a sign of decline. Insular shipowners had neglected to invest in modern steam technology and iron ship construction, with the result that, during the 1870s and 1880s, their wooden sailing ships were displaced from the worldwide market. Guernsey's ageing vessels continued to operate in inshore waters for a few years more, but to a progressively declining extent. Such was the speed of the decline, that, by the end of the nineteenth century, shipping had lost almost all its significance to the insular economy.

While it endured, however, Guernsey's shipping industry had sustained an important terrestrial offshoot in the form of shipbuilding. Between 1815 and 1880, fourteen major firms and a handful of smaller builders had produced nearly 300 ships in yards along the east coast, most of them ocean-going vessels for Guernsey's worldwide carrying trade.[69] Shipbuilding and its parent industry shipping were manpower-intensive industries, so that, for a while around mid-century, they

---

[62] Jamieson, 'Channel Islands and smuggling', p. 195.

[63] Duncan, *History of Guernsey*, p. 262.

[64] The value of St Peter Port ratepayers' real and personal property was assessed at over £3,000,000 sterling in 1830 (F.B. Tupper, *The History of Guernsey and its Bailiwick* (1854; Guernsey, 1876 edn), p. 524).

[65] Tupper, *Guernsey and its Bailiwick* (Guernsey, 1854 edn), pp. 432–45.

[66] Duncan, *History of Guernsey*, p. 261; Tupper, *Guernsey and its Bailiwick* (1854 edn), p. 444.

[67] A.G. Jamieson, 'Voyage patterns and trades of Channel Island vessels, 1700–1900', in Jamieson (ed.), *A People of the Sea*, pp. 381, 399–400.

[68] 26.1.1865, IA, AQ 44/05.

[69] E.W. Sharp, 'The shipbuilders of Guernsey', *TSG*, 27 (1970), p. 492.

collectively provided work to more islanders than any other sector outside farming. It was fortunate for Guernsey's economy that, by the time of their demise, the island's quarrying sector had grown to such a size that it was able to replace them in this role.

The stone trade had begun in a small way in the eighteenth century, when granite from the northern parishes of the Vale and St Sampsons was shipped to towns such as Southampton for street paving. However, it was macadamisation, invented at the end of the Napoleonic Wars, which provided the main impetus to the nineteenth-century growth of Guernsey's stone trade.[70] Demand for hard-wearing Guernsey granite grew rapidly under this stimulus, providing a livelihood to many skilled and unskilled workers – particularly after 1847, when contractors supplying London gained the right to have the stone, which had formerly to be broken within twenty miles of the metropolis, cracked before leaving the island.[71] A statistical return submitted to the Home Office that year showed that Guernsey possessed ninety-seven quarries.[72] The stone trade continued to grow for the rest of the century, and peaked just before World War I. Then, like the entrepôt business, the carrying trade and the shipbuilding industry before it, it fell inexorably into decline.

Happily, yet another revenue-earner was ready to replace quarrying as the island's economic mainstay. This new sector was commercial horticulture, which had been slowly expanding over the past four decades. It had grown out of farming, which, although not hitherto the largest cash-earner, had nevertheless always occupied the island's largest workforce.

Before the 1860s, although a substantial quantity of local farm produce was sold in St Peter Port, very little had been exported beyond Guernsey's shores. A minor exception were the small consignments of hot-house grapes intermittently sent to England from the eighteenth century.[73] In the late 1860s, exports of these grapes were boosted by new steamer berths in St Peter Port harbour together with new facilities for onward rail transit to the wholesale market in Covent Garden.[74] This stimulated the introduction of other commercial crops whose early production under glass was facilitated by Guernsey's mild climate. As early as the 1870s, Guernsey's small farmers began to build greenhouses on their land, and, in the 1880s and 1890s, large numbers of industrial-scale 'vineries' were established by local and non-local entrepreneurs. The focus of farming shifted decisively from subsistence to the market. The rural population began to increase as land became more remunerative and employment opportunities opened up outside St Peter Port and the quarrying parishes. From the 1890s, tomatoes became the island's main horticultural

---

[70] Macadamisation created road surfaces by building up layers of compacted broken stone. This is not to be confused with tarmacadam, a later invention consisting of stone or slag bound with tar.

[71] *Comet*, 4.2.1847.

[72] TNA, HO 98/88.

[73] P.J. Girard, 'The Guernsey grape industry,' *TSG*, 15 (1951), pp. 126–44.

[74] Hocart, *Guernsey's Countryside*, p. 74.

export and, in the early twentieth century, a trade in bulbs and flowers also developed.[75] The principal destination for all these products was the United Kingdom. This, together with the end of self-sufficient farming, meant that Guernsey was now more economically dependent than ever on its neighbour to the north.

As quarrying declined, horticulture was complemented by tourism in sustaining Guernsey's economy until World War II. After the hiatus of Occupation, both sectors resumed strongly in the mid-1950s, stimulating population growth and a building boom. Conditions then remained reasonably buoyant until the oil price shocks of the 1970s began to reduce growers' profits by raising the cost of heating fuel. The industry suffered further from competition with Dutch horticulturalists benefiting from cheap North Sea gas. Finally, changes in transport economics led to the undercutting of Guernsey produce on United Kingdom markets by imports from such distant places as Israel and even Kenya. The same factor also led to the decline of tourism. By the late twentieth century, Guernsey's horticulture and tourism had dwindled into insignificance.

Nevertheless, in a pattern repeated more than once since the eighteenth century, there was an emerging replacement. In the early 1960s, banking was becoming increasingly globalised, and major players were experimenting with offshore locations to maximise tax efficiency. A handful of merchant banks, mainly from the United Kingdom, set up operations in Guernsey (and Jersey) as a means of sidestepping high onshore taxes and restrictive regulation: Kleinwort Benson in 1963, Hill Samuel and Co. in 1964, N.M. Rothschild and Sons and Hambros Bank in 1967. These mainly provided services to United Kingdom expatriates abroad and to the tax refugees who had come to the Islands from Britain following the introduction of capital gains tax in 1965.[76] At that time, the Channel Islands were subject to the 1947 United Kingdom Exchange Control Act. After the rescheduling of the sterling area in 1972, they benefited from inclusion in a select band of five rescheduled territories outside the United Kingdom, which led to further banks relocating to the Islands from descheduled areas such as Bermuda and the Bahamas. The Islands also benefited from Protocol 3 of the 1972 United Kingdom Treaty of Accession to the Common Market, by which they were deemed onshore Europe for the limited provisions of the trade regime, but offshore Europe for financial and other services.[77] When the United Kingdom lifted exchange controls altogether in 1979, Guernsey's finance sector was sufficiently mature to attract banks and finance companies from all round the globe. This initiated a sustained and unparalleled period of expansion.

As at 2014, the finance industry was Guernsey's largest economic sector, generating about 40 per cent of Guernsey's gross domestic product and directly

---

[75] E.A. Wheadon, 'The history of the tomato in Guernsey,' *TSG*, 12 (1935), pp. 338–50; P.J. Girard, 'Development of the bulb and flower industry in Guernsey,' *TSG*, 13 (1939), pp. 284–97.

[76] R.A. Johns and C.M. Le Marchant, *Finance Centres: British Isle Offshore Development since 1979* (London, 1993), pp. 59–60.

[77] Johns and Le Marchant, *Finance Centres*, pp. 55–6.

employing 21 per cent of its workforce.[78] The early twenty-first-century situation offers interesting parallels with Guernsey's Georgian boom. In both cases, fiscal autonomy allowed Guernsey to provide facilities to non-islanders seeking to circumvent taxation elsewhere. In the Georgian case, this proved contingent on the United Kingdom's good will. Over the past 300 years, each of Guernsey's major branches of trade has endured about a century. History suggests that finance, too, will have its term. The local economy has now expanded to such an unprecedented extent, however, that it is unclear whether any alternative would be adequate to sustain it at its current level.

Society

Demography

The earliest date for which we have a reasonably solid population estimate for Guernsey is 1615. Basing himself on the number of houses in the island, F.B. Tupper, a nineteenth-century historian, calculated a figure of 7,342, of which some 35 per cent were resident in St Peter Port.[79] In 1727, an island-wide headcount was taken, and Guernsey's population had risen to 10,256 with St Peter Port's share at 42 per cent.[80] Another estimate/count in 1800 showed a further increase to between 18,000 and 19,000, with St Peter Port accommodating at least 55 per cent.[81] Aside from a brief post-Napoleonic drop, the population of both St Peter Port and the island as a whole continued to grow throughout the nineteenth century. St Peter Port accommodated more than all other parishes combined until 1891, when growth in the country parishes outstripped the increase in the town parish, and St Peter Port's share dropped to 48 per cent.[82] St Peter Port's population ceased growing altogether in 1901, when it peaked at 18,264.[83] Then, through the effects of war and emigration, the town parish lost a tenth of its inhabitants between 1911 and 1921. Country parishes also sustained a population loss, and Guernsey's total population fell from 41,823 in 1911 to 38,283 in 1921, an overall drop of 9 per cent.[84] St Peter Port never recovered from its losses, and its population has since

---

[78] *Billet*, 24.3.2015, appendix 1, p. 12; States of Guernsey, *Guernsey Financial Services: A Strategy for the Future* (Guernsey, 2014), p. 41.

[79] Tupper did not give a precise source for the number of houses, but it appears to have derived from a contemporary militia census (Tupper, *Guernsey and its Bailiwick* (1854 edn), p. 227). Robert Montgomery Martin used the same data in his *History of the British Colonies*, 5 vols (London, 1835), 5, p. 470.

[80] Stevens Cox, *St Peter Port*, p. 164.

[81] The Royal Court, which undertook this exercise at the request of visiting Customs Commissioner William Stiles, numbered the 'permanently settled' at 16,155, and estimated temporary residents at '2,000 or 3,000', most of whom would have lived in St Peter Port (Royal Court to William Stiles, 15.12.1800, Greffe, Royal Court Letter Book 1).

[82] PP 1893–4 CVII.

[83] PP 1903 LXXXIV.

[84] *Census 1911: Islands in the British Seas* (London, 1913); *Census 1921: Jersey, Guernsey and Adjacent Islands* (London, 1924).

stabilised at about 16,500. However, by 1931, Guernsey's population as a whole had resumed its growth, and, at 42,388 in 1948, it was higher than it had ever been.[85] The upward trend has since continued. With expansion in the finance industry, Guernsey's population increased by over 10 per cent in the decade 1981–90.[86] In 2012, it stood at just over 63,000.[87]

Separate population figures are unavailable for St Peter Port in 2012, but in 2001 it accommodated just 28 per cent of islanders.[88] In the eighteenth century, by contrast, it was thronged in comparison with the countryside, and single-hand-edly generated almost the entirety of Guernsey's population growth. The number of town parishioners more than tripled between 1700 and 1800. In the early 1700s, this growth was mostly down to a high birth rate and natural increase, but natural increase was supplanted by migration in the second half of the century, as a consid-erable stream flowed into town from Guernsey's country parishes, and immigrants also came from across the sea to work in the developing entrepôt.[89]

Rural in-migration to St Peter Port declined sharply in the nineteenth century, but immigration from outside the island persisted at a significant level until World War I. In the seven decennial censuses between 1841 and 1901, non-natives accounted for an average of 25 per cent of Guernsey's civilian population. St Peter Port always accommodated a majority of these incomers, but its share declined from 85 per cent in 1841 to 60 per cent in 1901.[90]

Nineteenth- and early twentieth-century immigrants to Guernsey were a mixture of English, Irish, other Channel Islanders, and French. English and Irish migrants consistently predominated. They were at their most numerous in the census of 1851, when a stream of refugees from depression-stricken south-west England initi-ated c.1816 was joined by refugees from Ireland's mid-nineteenth-century famine. In the 1851 census, migrants from England and Ireland comprised 78 per cent of Guernsey's civilian non-natives and 21 per cent of the island's total population. Some 80 per cent of these English and Irish were based in St Peter Port.[91]

In the last third of the nineteenth century, immigration from England and Ireland declined, but immigration from France increased as Breton peasants fled their own agricultural depression. By 1901, the English/Irish share of Guernsey's migrant cohort had declined to 47 per cent and the French share had risen from 6 per cent in 1851 to nearly 20 per cent, so that the French now accounted for about a fifth of non-natives and a tenth of total population.[92] A majority of late nineteenth-century French migrants settled in the rural parishes, where they found work in the stone

---

[85] *Billet*, 21.4.1948.

[86] States of Guernsey, *Report on the 2001 Guernsey Census* (Guernsey, 2002), p. 20.

[87] States of Guernsey, *Guernsey Facts and Figures, 2013* (Guernsey, 2013), p. 50.

[88] States of Guernsey, *Report on the 2001 Guernsey Census*, p. 12.

[89] Stevens Cox, *St Peter Port*, pp. 64–7, 82–5, 86–8.

[90] R.-M. Crossan, *Guernsey, 1814–1914: Migration and Modernisation* (Woodbridge, 2007), p. 70.

[91] Crossan, *Guernsey, 1814–1914*, pp. 93, 107.

[92] Crossan, *Guernsey, 1814–1914*, p. 124.

trade and horticulture.[93] As a result of this phenomenon, the rural parishes' share of the migrant cohort increased from 15 per cent in 1841 to 40 per cent in 1901.[94]

Outward emigration of native islanders does not seem to have taken place on any scale until the first decade of the nineteenth century, when Westminster's imposition of anti-smuggling Acts provoked an initial exodus.[95] After this time, however, large-scale overseas emigration became a firmly entrenched part of insular life. Censuses between 1841 and 1901 show that, at the same time as large numbers were entering the island (an average of at least 5,000 per decade), almost equally large numbers were leaving it, attracted by the same opportunities in North America and Australasia that were drawing their contemporaries from all over Europe.[96] Were it not for the constantly self-replenishing supply of youthful immigrants bearing children in the island, Guernsey's nineteenth-century population growth would have been considerably less: throughout much of the Victorian era, some two-thirds of the island's population were aged under 35.[97]

A large contingent of nineteenth-century emigrants were male. This, combined with the fact that female immigrants outnumbered male immigrants at this time, and seafaring detained many men at sea, produced unbalanced sex ratios. In every nineteenth-century census, females markedly outnumbered males in the island as a whole, but the lack of males was always excessively pronounced in St Peter Port, which (excluding the garrison) never had a ratio of more than seventy-four males per 100 females in the thirty years between 1841 and 1871.[98] As we will see later, this had major implications in the welfare arena.

Social and political structures

For much of the period under consideration, St Peter Port and the country parishes had differing social and political complexions. In the countryside, widespread property ownership and the lack of large landowners obviated 'extremes of wealth and poverty'.[99] Jurat Thomas Le Retilley observed in 1846 that even those occupying the upper echelons of rural society were, comparatively speaking, 'persons of very limited means'.[100] A Guernsey farmer's way of life was necessarily characterised by frugality whether he worked five acres or twenty-five. William Berry commented that a 'mediocrity, rather bordering on poverty' overspread the countryside.[101] However, while no great gulfs existed in rural society, it was still strongly hierarchical. Distinct social layers were kept separate in what one writer has described as a 'caste system'.[102]

---

[93] Crossan, *Guernsey, 1814–1914*, p. 125.
[94] Crossan, *Guernsey, 1814–1914*, p. 281.
[95] See section on 'Peaks and troughs of distress', Chapter 2.
[96] Crossan, *Guernsey, 1814–1914*, p. 60.
[97] Crossan, *Guernsey, 1814–1914*, p. 77.
[98] Crossan, *Guernsey, 1814–1914*, pp. 76–7, 208–9.
[99] P. Jeremie, *On Parochial and States Taxation in Guernsey* (Guernsey, 1856), pp. 83–4.
[100] *Second Report of the Commissioners appointed to enquire into the State of the Criminal Law of the Channel Islands* (London, 1848), p. 254.
[101] Berry, *Island of Guernsey*, p. 299.
[102] P.J. Girard, 'Country life and some insular enterprises of the late 19th century', *TSG*, 19 (1972), p. 89.

It was from the owners of more substantial holdings that rural ratepayers, Constables and *Douzeniers* were exclusively drawn. Smallholders who fished or laboured did not normally pay rates and were thus excluded from voting at parish meetings and holding parochial office. Country-dwellers saw participation in parish affairs as a badge of social pride, and each parish had its elite tier of office-holding families who monopolised parochial power well into the twentieth century.[103]

In stark contrast with their mid-nineteenth-century rural counterparts, nearly three-quarters of St Peter Port's adult residents owned no real property at all.[104] A chasm separated the property-owning minority from the throng of artisans, shopkeepers, servants and labourers beneath them. Since parochial affairs were the prerogative of the propertied, very few of St Peter Port's mid-century artisans, and none of its labourers, would have qualified to vote in parish assemblies and elections. Only adult male ratepayers had the vote, and the 543 identified in 1843 by Richard Hocart left 86 per cent of urban adults unenfranchised.[105]

Reference to social groups known as the 'Sixties' and the 'Forties' was a commonplace of Victorian writing on Guernsey.[106] It is between these two groups that the upper rungs of St Peter Port society are said to have been divided in the late eighteenth and early nineteenth centuries. The labels, dating from the opening of St Peter Port's Assembly Rooms in the late eighteenth century, stemmed from the number of families notionally assigned to each group. The 'Sixties' corresponded to the leading mercantile families; the 'Forties' to what we may call the commercial bourgeoisie, whom the 'Sixties' regarded as their inferiors, and whom they excluded from the Rooms. In the eighteenth century, St Peter Port's 'Sixties' dominated the Royal Court, and rural Jurats were few – Richard Hocart names just three between 1777 and 1810.[107] As well as supplying most eighteenth-century Bailiffs, Crown officers, militia colonels and island-born Rectors, the 'Sixties' also enjoyed a monopoly of St Peter Port's prestigious parochial offices.[108] By the 1820s, however, the ranks of the town *Douzaine* had been penetrated by the 'Forties' and, from the 1840s onwards, urban parochial administration was mainly in the hands of the commercial bourgeoisie.

As the nineteenth century progressed, the fortunes of old 'Sixties' families diminished, and many in later generations left for England or the Empire to earn a living in army, church or medicine.[109] These would often return to Guernsey in retirement and serve their turn as Jurats, but increasingly they lacked the command of French needed for the Court, whose business was transacted in that language.[110] From the 1870s, therefore, the ranks of Jurats were more frequently leavened with

[103] T.F. Priaulx, 'Secular parish administration in Guernsey', *Quarterly Review of the Guernsey Society*, 21–4 (1965–8), pp. 50–51.
[104] PP 1852–3 LXXXVIII; 8.3.1854, IA, AQ 0966/01.
[105] Hocart, *Island Assembly*, p. 34; PP 1844 XXVII.
[106] Inglis, *Channel Islands*, 2, pp. 63–4; H. Boland, *Les Iles de la Manche* (Paris, 1904), pp. 133–5.
[107] R.P. Hocart, 'Elections to the Royal Court of Guernsey, 1821–1844', *TSG*, 19 (1979), p. 496.
[108] Hocart, 'Elections to the Royal Court', p. 496; Stevens Cox, *St Peter Port*, p. 15.
[109] D.T. Ansted and M.A. Latham, *The Channel Islands* (London, 1862), p. 552.
[110] See article on 'Les places vides' in *Le Baillage*, 30.1.1892.

French-speakers from the countryside. Most rural Jurats had gained their experience in parochial office. Their presence probably reinforced rather than relieved the conservative cast of late nineteenth-century Royal Courts.

It was during the second half of the nineteenth century that the Court began to yield its political dominance to the States. The States reform of 1844, while not introducing any directly elected members, brought six St Peter Port *Douzaine* representatives into the States. These made their presence felt, but any liberalising influence they might have had was counterbalanced by the predominantly conservative Jurats, Rectors and rural *Douzaine* representatives. It was only after 1900, when another States reform introduced nine ratepayer-elected 'Deputies', that radically new voices at last began to be heard and tentative progress made on social issues.[111]

Even so, those in Guernsey who did not pay rates remained unenfranchised at all political levels until 1920. In this year, a further reform of the States extended the suffrage for States elections to non-ratepaying men over 20 and non-ratepaying women over 30 who were British subjects and had lived in Guernsey at least a year.[112] This important reform also doubled the number of States' Deputies (now styled 'Deputies of the People') to eighteen, and permitted women to sit in the States for the first time.[113] Notwithstanding the change in States' suffrage, however, non-ratepayers continued to be denied the vote in the parish.

By this stage, 'Sixties' and 'Forties' alike had been eclipsed by a newly influential cohort of businessmen and growers, many of them non-native, whose focus was neither narrowly urban nor rural but encompassed the whole of the island.[114] Some of these gained seats in the States without prior experience of parochial office, side-stepping the conservative influence of the parish and hastening social reforms. Such reforms further eroded the parishes' power base, so that, by the time non-ratepayers finally gained the vote at parish level in 1963, the parochial tier of government had become all but irrelevant.[115]

Political and social factors such as these had an important bearing on the development of welfare provision in Guernsey, in that they influenced how and to whom assistance was dispensed. So, too, did economic and demographic factors, which determined when and by whom assistance was sought. Before entering into the detail of provision, however, the next chapter will focus on need. It will attempt to gauge the extent of poverty in Guernsey, to map peaks and troughs in distress over time, and to draw comparisons with communities elsewhere.

---

[111] Hocart, *Island Assembly*, pp. 43–4, 72–3.
[112] O in C, 13.10.1920.
[113] Hocart, *Island Assembly*, p. 96.
[114] Boland, *Les Iles de la Manche*, pp. 134–5.
[115] O in C, 29.8.1963.

2

Poverty

General considerations

Poverty in its most basic sense may be characterised as a shortage of the resources required to satisfy life's three fundamental needs: sustenance, shelter and warmth. This is the kind of poverty which exists in parts of the developing world today, and it is also what most people in the past would have conceived of as poverty. Until the twentieth century, there was a broad acceptance in western society that some degree of poverty of this sort was a permanent and ineradicable fact of life: 'the poor you will always have with you'.[1] This was linked to the conventional Christian belief in a divinely ordained hierarchy in which the ranking of people into different stations was regarded as God's will.

In medieval and early modern times, the poor were everywhere in evidence. A majority of those who lived on the land produced only just enough to feed and clothe their families. Unfavourable environmental factors made survival in certain parts of Europe (such as the Scottish Highlands or the French Massif Central) persistently more challenging than in others, but peasants everywhere fared harshly, and a single poor harvest could bring disaster. Neither were living standards any better in Europe's medieval and early modern towns. Wages paid to urban workmen were pegged to bare subsistence needs, and they had to endure periodic worklessness as well as a frequently pestilential environment.[2]

By the eighteenth century, England was exceptional among its European peers both in the amount of its national wealth and its progress from peasant subsistence to agricultural and industrial capitalism.[3] This did not, however, translate into significant improvements for labouring families. Survival-level wages continued to be accepted as normal, and while these might just fulfil a family's physical needs, they also precluded savings. Without a margin in reserve, any of life's vicissitudes, be it illness, injury, death of a spouse, failing sight or an extra mouth to feed, could plunge a family into difficulties overnight. The loss of work in a slump or

---

[1] Mark 14:7.
[2] For an overview of rural and urban conditions in pre-modern Europe, see C. Lis and H. Soly (trans. J. Coonan), *Poverty and Capitalism in Pre-Industrial Europe* (1979; Brighton, 1982 edn) and R. Jütte, *Poverty and Deviance in Early Modern Europe* (Cambridge, 1994).
[3] G. Himmelfarb, *The Idea of Poverty: England in the Early Industrial Age* (London, 1984), p. 51.

bad weather might bring a whole household into insufficiency. For family members too sick or disabled to contribute to their keep there was little to spare, and there was nothing to call upon when, as inevitably happened, one grew too old to work oneself.

As the economy developed and the amount of money potentially available for wages increased, many British social theorists adduced arguments as to why it was positively essential they stayed low. Bernard de Mandeville famously asked: 'when men show such an extraordinary proclivity to idleness and pleasure, what reason have we to think that they would ever work, unless they were obliged to it by immediate necessity?'[4] If men were paid more than was strictly needed to keep their families alive, they would either fritter it away in drink, stop work until the wolf was once more at the door, or absorb the excess by having more children. Poverty was hence both socially and economically necessary.[5]

Commentators of the later eighteenth century expanded on this by formulating a distinction between poverty in general and a subset of it which they called 'indigence'. According to the Scotsman Patrick Colquhoun, poverty was 'that state and condition in society where the individual has no property but what is derived from the constant exercise of industry in the various occupations of life'. 'Indigence' was what arose when individuals – the old, the sick, the handicapped, lunatics – were prevented by incapacity from exercising that resource and had nothing to fall back on. Attempting to palliate poverty in general was undesirable as it might weaken work incentives. Only the indigent needed help.[6]

At this time, government at both national and local level was 'small' by today's standards, and it was felt to be impossible, as well as inappropriate, to raise the large sums required to underwrite security for all. There was a small-scale parochial relief system, but many theorists of Colquhoun's school felt that mutual schemes such as box clubs should take the lead in minimising indigence, and they also held the view that, if and when indigence did take hold, the burden of support should principally be borne by private charity.[7] Many of the poor had recourse to mutualism and charity, but these were unequal to the task of providing a comprehensive safety net. Charity was random and unsystematic. Until the twentieth century the private/mutual insurance and pension sectors remained underdeveloped, and the weekly premiums they required made them inaccessible to those on low and irregular incomes.

The passage of time brought some improvements in workmen's wages, especially in England. Between 1790 and 1900 the real earnings of the average English worker increased two and a half times.[8] However, the starting point had been abysmally

---

4   B. de Mandeville, *The Fable of the Bees* (1723; London, 1724 edn), p. 211.
5   Himmelfarb, *Idea of Poverty*, pp. 41–51.
6   P. Colquhoun, *A Treatise on Indigence* (London, 1806), pp. 7–8. Other influential commentators thinking along these lines included Jeremy Bentham, Thomas Malthus, David Ricardo and Frederick Eden (Himmelfarb, *Idea of Poverty*, pp. 154–5).
7   Himmelfarb, *Idea of Poverty*, p. 76.
8   J. Burnett, *A History of the Cost of Living* (1969; Aldershot, 1993 edn), p. 257.

low and there remained many who were under- or unemployed.[9] The historian Peter Laslett has contended that the 'abolition' of poverty in Britain, in its age-old fundamental sense, came about 'suddenly between the late 1930s and late 1940s'.[10] Economic growth certainly played its part in this but it was by no means the only factor. The political enfranchisement of lower income groups over the late nineteenth and early twentieth centuries had made them an electoral force to be reckoned with. As a result, traditional views as to the ineradicablity of poverty came to be revised. Taxation of the propertied was increased, and wealth was redistributed in order gradually to extend the public safety net.[11] In Britain, the process began with Lloyd George's social security innovations in the first decade of the twentieth century and culminated after World War II in the foundation of the welfare state. The extent to which the post-war welfare settlement constituted a truly unprecedented social transformation cannot be underestimated. It was a phenomenon which occurred at a similar time throughout most of western Europe.

A modern welfare state has been characterised as one 'which defines as an essential part of its role the maintenance of a reasonable standard of life for all its citizens ... A society in which government is expected to ensure the provision for all of not only social security but also a range of other services – including health, education, housing – at a standard well above the barest minimum'.[12] The result of the post-war welfare revolution was that millions of people achieved 'better health, housing, clothing and diet ... than at any period in the past', and that 'these improvements ... were most marked in the working classes'.[13]

In twenty-first-century Britain, as elsewhere in western Europe, poverty is rarely of the absolute, life-endangering variety experienced in past generations. It has become essentially a relative matter. The sociologist Peter Townsend set out the standard definition of relative poverty in the late 1970s, when he suggested that people can be said to be poor 'when they lack the resources to obtain the types of diet, participate in the activities, and have the living conditions and amenities which are customary ... in the societies to which they belong'.[14] A study at the turn of the millennium found that 17.2 per cent of United Kingdom households could be considered 'poor' in that they lacked four or more of these popularly perceived 'essentials'.[15] A study which focused solely on Guernsey at about the same time found that 16 per cent of insular households might be viewed as 'poor' in this

---

[9] One has only to read Robert Tressell's account of working-class life in a southern English town around 1906 to be reminded of its enduring harshness (R. Tressell, *The Ragged Trousered Philanthropists* (1914; Ware, 2012 edn).

[10] P. Laslett, *The World We Have Lost – Further Explored* (1965; Cambridge, 1983 edn), p. 253.

[11] British government spending increased by about 500 per cent between 1900 and 1955 (Burnett, *Cost of Living*, p. 302).

[12] M. Cousins, *European Welfare States: Comparative Perspectives* (London, 2005), p. 6.

[13] J. Burnett, *A Social History of Housing, 1815–1970* (1978; London, 1983 edn), pp. 273–4.

[14] P. Townsend, *Poverty in the United Kingdom: A Survey of Household Resources and Standards of Living* (Harmondsworth, 1979), p. 31.

[15] D. Gordon et al., *Poverty and Social Exclusion in Britain* (York, 2000) reworked in J. Bradshaw and N. Finch, 'Overlaps in dimensions of poverty', *Journal of Social Policy*, 32 (2003), p. 517.

sense.[16] In terms of the basic requisites of food, shelter and warmth, however, their disadvantages bore no comparison with the stark physical wretchedness of some of their forebears. It is to an investigation of the nature of poverty in Guernsey's past that we shall now turn.

Poverty in Guernsey

Insights into the preoccupations which exercised Guernsey's early modern ruling caste can be derived from the laws which they passed.[17] That serious poverty was an everyday fact of life seems evident from ordinances concerning begging, which survive in number from the 1530s.[18] Ordinances protecting food supplies indicate that hunger, too, was an ever-present threat, with laws passed to prevent the engrossment of essential foodstuffs and prohibit grain exports in times of dearth.[19] Under- and unemployment were further problems highlighted by sixteenth-century legislation. Ordinances sought to palliate them by providing for the workless to be compulsorily apprenticed or taken into service by better-off members of the community.[20]

Darryl Ogier has described Guernsey in the 1570s as suffering 'economic and commercial problems' and 'a degree of unrest'.[21] In this, the island was not unusual, for the sixteenth century was a time of dislocation for Europe in general. Aberrant weather and repeated harvest failure led to famines and epidemics in many countries, in addition to which much of the continent was in religious turmoil. Many of the measures enacted by Guernsey's Royal Court were therefore almost identical to measures being enacted all over Europe at this time.[22]

All the above-mentioned ordinances concerned the whole island, so ostensibly they shed no light on the balance of poverty between town and country. We do, however, know that in early modern Europe generally, country people in difficulty would gravitate towards the towns.[23] The repeated insistence of Guernsey's sixteenth-century begging ordinances that islanders should only be allowed to beg in their own parishes suggest that such a phenomenon might also be occurring here.[24]

---

[16] D. Gordon et al., *Anti-Poverty Policies – A Range of Possible Options for Guernsey* (Bristol, 2002), p. 31.
[17] The records of Guernsey's Royal Court survive from the late 1520s (D.M. Ogier, *Reformation and Society in Guernsey* (Woodbridge, 1996), p. 9).
[18] Those, for instance, of 1.10.1537, 20.1.1589, 21.1.1598.
[19] Ords, 6.10.1533, 3.10.1535, 15.5.1568.
[20] Ords, 13.9.1566, 20.1.1589, 21.1.1598.
[21] D.M. Ogier, *The Government and Law of Guernsey* (Guernsey, 2005), p. 83.
[22] Lis and Soly, *Poverty and Capitalism*, pp. 84–5.
[23] J. Walter and R. Schofield (eds), *Famine, Disease and the Social Order in Early Modern Society* (1989; Cambridge, 1991 edn), pp. 27, 52, 223.
[24] For example, ord, 1.10.1537.

The country parishes

Population estimates from 1615 for the rural portion of Guernsey show about 5,500 people existing on some 13,000 acres of land.[25] This would make about two and a half acres per person. In 1709, Daniel Defoe calculated that three acres of good English land would feed one man for a year.[26] Guernsey's farmland was fertile and its climate benign. It had the supplementary resource of the sea, and adult men made up only about a quarter of its population.[27] Despite all this, the 1615 figure suggests a rural population perilously close to the margin of sustainability. Gregory Stevens Cox has suggested that earnings from stocking-knitting after the late 1500s allowed more people to subsist in the countryside than would otherwise have been possible.[28] However, the knitting industry underwent a crisis in the 1650s, when it lost a large proportion of its French markets through the imposition of a duty on imported stockings.[29] On top of this came the bad weather and food shortages recorded by a local diarist in the 1650s and 1660s, which mirrored similar conditions Europe-wide.[30] A local petition to the English parliament in 1652 described rural parishioners as living in 'extreme poverty'.[31] In 1657, the first of a series of ordinances was passed which sought to restrict the inflow of country-dwellers into St Peter Port.[32] The limits of rural sustainability had evidently been reached, and excess population vented itself in town, which, as a trading centre, was seen as offering better chances of survival than the land.

The rural situation appears to have deteriorated still further in the first half of the eighteenth century. The 1720s again saw poor harvests and food shortages in Guernsey, as all over Europe.[33] By the 1740s, stocking-knitting, though it had surmounted the mid-seventeenth-century crisis by transferring its exports to England, was in terminal decline, described by contemporaries as 'so sunk' that knitters earned just pennies a week.[34] Rural sustainability was again under acute stress,

[25] Population estimates from R. Montgomery Martin, *History of the British Colonies*, 5 vols (London, 1835), 5, p. 470. Land area from 1899 Ordnance Survey of Guernsey (less 300 acres reclaimed from the sea in 1803 and a further deduction for non-rural St Peter Port).

[26] D. Defoe, 'Review of the state of the English Nation', 36 (25 June 1709), in J. McVeagh (ed.), *Defoe's Review*, 9 vols (London, 2003–11), 6, p. 194.

[27] Montgomery Martin, *British Colonies*, 5, p. 470.

[28] G. Stevens Cox, *St Peter Port, 1680–1830: The History of an International Entrepôt* (Woodbridge, 1999), p. 81.

[29] J.C. Appleby, 'Neutrality, trade and privateering, 1500–1689', in A.G. Jamieson (ed.), *A People of the Sea: The Maritime History of the Channel Islands* (London, 1986), p. 87.

[30] G.E. Lee (ed.), *Note-Book of Pierre Le Roy, Guernsey* (Guernsey, 1893), pp. 21, 33, 35; Jütte, *Poverty and Deviance*, p. 31.

[31] J. Jeremie, *An Historical Account of the Island of Guernsey* (Guernsey, 1821), p. 44. Jeremie suggests that the turmoil of the Civil Wars may have had detrimental effects on farming. During the Wars Guernsey's principal fortification, Castle Cornet, held out for the king, while the rest of the island espoused the parliamentary cause.

[32] Ord, 1.4.1657 (IA, AQ 0988/01). This prohibited town parishioners from providing lodgings to poor rural parishioners on pain of maintaining them if they fell into need.

[33] S. Woolf, *The Poor in Western Europe in the Eighteenth and Nineteenth Centuries* (London, 1986), p. 8.

[34] 18.11.1741, St Peter Port Délibérations des Chefs de Famille, 1715–79, PL.

and the movement of the poor into St Peter Port reached worrying proportions. A document dating from 1759 complained in strident terms that the town was 'over-burdened', its streets 'crowded by the poor of the country'.[35]

The 1759 document contained an in-built bias. It was intended to rebut the idea that St Peter Port should pay a higher share of insular general taxation, and may thus have overstated the rural influx. In order to assess what proportion of country-dwellers the desperate might have comprised, we must seek a more objective source. The earliest point for which we have any useful evidence is 1766, and even then only for one parish. In that year, Guernsey's grain supplies ran out before the harvest. St Saviours' poorest parishioners were hungry and without food, and its *Douzaine* decided to give them a cash hand-out so that they could buy enough to fill their stomachs. The number of such persons was found to be 128.[36] Taking St Saviours to contain about 865 people in 1766, this gives a proportion of some 15 per cent.[37] These 128 people will, moreover, not have included St Saviours' very poorest, who by this time would have been consigned to the rural workhouse. The sizeable proportion at risk of real hunger is not surprising when holdings were so small. Even in a good year, five to ten acres would only just have covered a family's food needs, and a large proportion of rural families survived on less than this. Such families would have scant opportunity to garner stores or accumulate cash against bad harvests, and these were frequent in the eighteenth century.[38]

Evidence, however, suggests that the mid-1700s marked the high tide of modern rural poverty in Guernsey. With St Peter Port's maritime sector distinctly on the rise in the second half of the century, the rural situation seems gradually to have eased. In particular, an escalating demand for crew supplied an exit for rural parishioners at sea, reducing numbers of surplus hands as well as opening a conduit for cash remittances to those who remained. Moreover, as the town grew more prosperous, so the market increased for the produce of those remaining on the land. This greatly improved the chances of a viable living for those with the smallest holdings – anyone with a cow, for instance, might make as much as £10 per year from butter.[39] In a further turn of the virtuous circle, as demand grew from merchants for new houses in St Peter Port, so more work also became available to rural tradesmen. At about this time also, the stone export trade got under way in the Vale and St Sampsons, which afforded rurals yet further cash-earning opportunities as quarrymen. By enhancing the poorest country-dwellers' cash-earning powers, all these factors broadened the

---

35   *The Case of the Town Parish versus the Nine Country Parishes respecting a Change in the Rates and Representation, appointed to be heard before the Committee of the Privy Council at 11 o'clock, on Thursday April 26, 1759* (Guernsey, 1843), PL, pp. 9–10, 19.

36   27.7.1766, IA, AQ 0116/02.

37   No population figure exists for 1766, but 865 marks a mid-point between headcounts taken in 1727 and 1800 (for numbers, see Stevens Cox, *St Peter Port*, p. 164).

38   Woolf, *The Poor in Western Europe*, p. 8.

39   In the late eighteenth century local butter sold at 1s per lb and milk from one Guernsey cow yielded on average 5lb of butter a week (Montgomery Martin, *British Colonies*, 5, p. 489). Those too poor to buy a cow could rent a beast from wealthier farmers (R.P. Hocart, 'Jean Guille of St George: an extended view, 1711–1721', *TSG*, 26 (2008), p. 404).

margin of survivability in the rural parishes. By the turn of the nineteenth century, there would have been far fewer rurals than previously without some cash in reserve to buy food in a bad harvest.

In the short term, perhaps the most palpable effect of these improvements was to diminish St Peter Port's burden of rural refugees. After 1806, that burden diminished still further when mass departures for North America set a precedent for long-distance migration, which henceforth became the favoured rural option.[40] By 1851, natives of the country parishes comprised no more than 8 per cent of the town parish's population.[41]

Nevertheless, at no time in the nineteenth and early twentieth centuries was life for Guernsey's poor countryfolk either easy or comfortable. Ingrained parsimony kept rural wage rates low. In 1830, John Jacob cited typical rates for a day's labour of 1s with meals and 1s 6d without, which meant that a labourer might take home as little as 6s for a full week's work.[42] In 1833, the average weekly wage of a farm labourer in south-west England was 8s 9d.[43] As late as 1910, greenhouse hands in Guernsey's country parishes earned between 15s and 17s a week, whereas the average Devon farmworker received 19s 4d.[44] Well into the twentieth century, moreover, many rurals were still only semi-employed, precariously combining short-term jobs with spells of fishing and other activities on their own account.[45]

St Peter Port

In Guernsey's countryside, 'wealth' principally took the form of real property – land and buildings. In St Peter Port, commerce facilitated a greater diversification of assets: sailing vessels; stock in trade; personal valuables of all kinds; government securities and other investments. Unlike the land, which was finite, trade also permitted unlimited accumulation of assets. Over time, this brought about an enormous disparity between urban and rural wealth. In 1757, St Peter Port's parishioners were taxed on assets collectively valued at approximately £613,820 while all the rural parishes could muster between them was £290,200.[46] However, urban assets were concentrated in few hands, and the vast majority of parishioners had little but their skill and muscle-power to live on. This left them dangerously exposed not only to the periodic grain shortages which drove up the price of their daily bread but also to the intrinsic ebb and flow of trade. In addition to this, a range of social problems

---

[40] A.G. Jamieson, 'The Channel Islands and overseas settlement, 1600–1900', in Jamieson (ed.), *A People of the Sea*, pp. 281, 286; R.-M. Crossan, *Guernsey, 1814–1914: Migration and Modernisation* (Woodbridge, 2007), p. 226.

[41] Crossan, *Guernsey, 1814–1914*, p. 209.

[42] J. Jacob, *Annals of Some of the British Norman Isles Constituting the Bailiwick of Guernsey* (Paris, 1830), p. 224.

[43] A.L. Bowley, 'The statistics of wages in the United Kingdom in the last hundred years, Part one, agricultural wages', *Journal of the Royal Statistical Society*, 66 (1898), p. 704.

[44] *Star*, 24.12.1910; G. Finch, 'The experience of peripheral regions in an age of industrialisation: the case of Devon, 1840–1914' (unpub. PhD thesis, Oxford University, 1984), p. 319.

[45] *Billet*, 28.4.1926.

[46] *Case of the Town Parish versus the Nine Country Parishes*, p. 39.

impinged particularly on the town. We will now look in depth at specific factors generating and exacerbating urban poverty.

Lone women and single-parent families

We saw above that Guernsey's fleet employed large numbers of seamen, with totals exceeding 1,000 in the late 1700s and mid-1800s. Demand for seafarers was at times so high that it could not be satisfied by natives alone. A mid-eighteenth-century source identifies non-native seamen arriving to crew St Peter Port vessels as engendering particular problems:

> the many sailors who come into this island, especially in time of war, some-
> times to the number of fifteen or twenty hundred, is another very great and
> inevitable burden to this town. For many of them have married and do daily
> marry in this town, and afterwards either die at sea, or desert the island and are
> never heard of, leaving their wives and children upon this parish.[47]

Analysis of the St Peter Port parish church ('Town Church') marriage registers bears this out. These show that mixed native/non-native marriages accounted for 38 per cent of all marriages between 1750 and 1814, and that, in an astonishing 92 per cent of these mixed marriages, it was the grooms, not the brides, who were from outside.[48]

After 1814, sailors' widows and cast-offs began to be joined by large numbers of sailors' wives also left alone for protracted spells. Guernsey-based seamen engaged in the South American trade were frequently away 'nine, twelve, fifteen, eighteen months, and perhaps two years'.[49] In 1851, for every 100 women aged over 20 in St Peter Port, there were only sixty-three men of similar age.[50] The parish also contained a sizeable juvenile contingent: nearly a third of its population was aged 15 and under in 1851. About a third of all households and a fifth of those containing children were headed by lone women. Their prospects were not favourable. Women's work opportunities were more limited than men's, and their earning power when in work as much as 50 per cent lower.

Many soldiers from St Peter Port's large wartime garrison also married locally and added to the stock of widows, orphans, deserted wives and children. A further problem stemmed from soldiers who brought, or were followed, into the island by dependent women and children from outside, for whom military authorities took no responsibility. In 1807, the Lieutenant-Governor numbered these dependants at 1,000.[51] Most were not accommodated in barracks but found lodgings wherever they could, and, if death or accident befell their man, they were left to shift for themselves. Difficulties also arose when regiments departed, as no transport arrangements were made for dependants. St Peter Port's *Douzaine* was still pleading with

---

[47]   *Case of the Town Parish versus the Nine Country Parishes*, pp. 9–10.
[48]   Town Church marriage registers (microfilm), PL.
[49]   *Comet*, 14.3.1836.
[50]   Population data in this section are based on the 1851 enumerators' books (microfilm, PL) and
       exclude the garrison. For detailed analysis, see Crossan, *Guernsey, 1814–1914*, pp. 51, 208–10.
[51]   Stevens Cox, *St Peter Port*, p. 65.

the Board of Ordnance to include wives and children in transport arrangements as late as 1819.[52]

Retired soldiers caused further complications. The number of military pensioners settling in Guernsey increased after the Napoleonic Wars. Some were officers, but by far the majority were from the rank and file. Commissioners sent to the island by the British government in 1846 learned that there were about 300 military pensioners in Guernsey, mainly in St Peter Port, and most of them on tiny pensions of just a few pence a day.[53] Problems arose when these retired soldiers started families. To qualify for a pension, they were obliged to have served at least twenty years; thus, most were not in the first flush of youth.[54] If they sickened or died, this again left widows and orphans unprovided for.[55]

Migrants

Military pensioners were just one aspect of the problem posed by migrants in general. Although wealthy incomers were generally welcome, attitudes to poorer migrants were more ambivalent. It was freely acknowledged that such migrants were often among the poorer urban residents: 'the most necessitous class', as the St Peter Port *Douzaine* put it.[56] Sometimes, their poverty was viewed in a positive light. A States committee of 1846 saw it as 'a source of profit, since without the throng of labourers arriving from all over to seek work, the cost of labour would be infinitely higher than it is today'.[57] But it could also be viewed negatively. A St Peter Port parish committee had a few years earlier railed against 'that mass of strangers arriving here with their large families and accepting reduced wages, which then deprives natives of the work they need for their support'.[58] Sir Edgar MacCulloch, a serving Bailiff of Guernsey, in his contribution to C.J. Ribton-Turner's 1887 *History of Vagrants and Vagrancy*, attributed the 'pauperism' which he felt had increased since the beginning of the century fairly and squarely to strangers. 'Guernseymen', he remarked,

> are thrifty, and in many instances will bear with great privations rather than apply for parish relief, but it is not so with strangers. They soon get demoralised by the temptation afforded by the cheapness of spirits, and, neglecting their children, these grow up in habits of idleness, and often end in becoming paupers and chargeable.[59]

[52] 11.11.1819, IA, AQ 0965/01.
[53] *Second Report of the Commissioners appointed to inquire into the State of the Criminal Law in the Channel Islands* (London, 1848), p. 153.
[54] P. Thane, *Old Age in English History: Past Experiences, Present Issues* (Oxford, 2000), p. 241.
[55] *Second Report of the Commissioners*, p. 153.
[56] 29.5.1833, IA, AQ 0965/02.
[57] Report of the States' Stranger Relief Sub-Committee (*Billet*, 17.6.1846).
[58] 19.12.1832, IA, DC/HX 135–03.
[59] C.J. Ribton-Turner, *A History of Vagrants and Vagrancy and Beggars and Begging* (London, 1887), p. 464. On p. 465, Ribton-Turner acknowledges that 'the whole of the account of Guernsey is due to the kindness of Sir Edgar MacCulloch'.

MacCulloch took no account of strangers' lack of local support networks and their resulting greater reliance on public relief sources. Neither did he acknowledge that their precarious situation may have enhanced the temptations of alcohol. His words must therefore be seen as coloured by a degree of xenophobic prejudice. Nevertheless, in raising the relationship of poverty with drink, Edgar MacCulloch was far from alone. It was an issue that came up repeatedly in connection with Guernsey's poor, both migrant and native. As such, it requires analysis in a section of its own. What follows is focused specifically on St Peter Port, but broadly applicable to other parishes as well.

Drink

'It is well-known that the prevailing sin of the Island is drunkenness', a States member observed in 1828.[60] The assembly was discussing the need for special facilities to punish petty criminality, arising in particular from excessive alcohol consumption among the poor. The coupling of poverty with drunkenness and misconduct was aphoristic among British social theorists in the nineteenth and previous centuries. As Gertrude Himmelfarb observed, there was hardly a commentator 'who did not associate drink … with poverty and pauperism, immorality and crime'.[61]

In eighteenth-century St Peter Port, alcohol formed a large part of the business of the upper classes, and they had a vested interest in seeing that it flowed freely. Edgar MacCulloch's own family's fortune had been derived from it. The number of liquor outlets registered in St Peter Port rose from ninety-seven in 1764 to 115 in 1780.[62] The low price and accessibility of spirits also led at around this time to the widespread substitution of spirits for weaker potations as the workman's daily drink.[63] St Peter Port's *Douzaine* observed in 1780 that 'spirituous liquors' had completely superseded cider and beer. They also reflected that this had harmed many poor families and increased the burden on the rates. Nevertheless, profits from sales must have outweighed any rate rises, for the *Douzaine* failed to persuade the parish's merchants to pledge their support for a new tax the States were proposing to levy on spirit consumption.[64]

Thirty-four years later, the States resurrected the measure, and this time they succeeded in their purpose. In 1814, the first ever *impôt* on locally sold spirits was instituted, at a starting rate of 6d per gallon.[65] In the United Kingdom, the duty on spirits at this time was some 11s per gallon.[66] Low though the *impôt* might have been, this innovation led inevitably to an increasing dependence of States' revenue

---

60 *Comet*, 31.3.1828.
61 Himmelfarb, *Idea of Poverty*, p. 385.
62 25.9.1764, IA, AQ 0988/01; IA, AQ 0942/03.
63 Intoxicants were thought to impart physical stamina (B. Harrison, *Drink and the Victorians: The Temperance Question in England, 1815–1872* (London, 1971), p. 39).
64 21.2.1780, IA, AQ 0964/01.
65 R.P. Hocart, *An Island Assembly: The Development of the States of Guernsey, 1700–1949* (Guernsey, 1988), p. 25.
66 J. Burnett, *Liquid Pleasures: A Social History of Drinks in Modern Britain* (London, 1999), p. 166.

on alcohol consumption. Conflict was thus intensified between the recognition of alcohol as a problem and reluctance to endanger fiscal and commercial interests by discouraging its use.

Around 1840, a branch of the British temperance movement was established in Guernsey.[67] Local temperance advocates seem to have been energetic, but their success was always circumscribed. Nevertheless, they appear to have influenced a St Peter Port committee investigating poor law problems in 1848. This committee set out an urgent plea for vigorous action on drink, suggesting that three-quarters of Guernsey's public houses might beneficially be closed.[68] The law-makers' response was, however, lukewarm, and came in the form of a provisional ordinance exper-imenting with Sunday closing for three months.[69] The issue was revisited several times over the next decade, and Sunday closing was definitively instituted in 1859.[70]

Notwithstanding this restriction, the number of liquor outlets continued to grow through the second half of the century.[71] In 1903, an article in the *Star* claimed that Guernsey and Glasgow had 'recently been qualified as the two most drunken places in the British Isles'.[72] In the United Kingdom, spirit consumption was just over a gallon per head in 1904.[73] In Guernsey that same year imports equated to nearly two and a half gallons per head.[74] According to the 1904 States' Committee on Inju-rious Beverages, half of Guernsey's alcohol imports consisted of the noxious Berlin Spirit – cheap ethyl alcohol distilled in northern Europe from agricultural discards.[75] Spirits were, furthermore, retailed at a minimum of 80 degrees proof in Guernsey's public bars, and in larger measures than in England.[76] The States were again called upon for action. However, they continued to equivocate. Their only response was to reduce the maximum retail strength to 70 degrees proof, with an exemption for spirits sold in sealed bottles.[77]

For much of the eighteenth, nineteenth and twentieth centuries, alcohol was thus consistently cheap and abundant in Guernsey. A study of poor law records indicates that excessive consumption yielded its share of misery, not least in the form

---

[67] Anon., *A Short History of the Temperance Movement in Guernsey, 1566–1900* (Guernsey, 1900), p. 22. The temperance movement had begun in Scotland and northern Ireland in the 1820s (Harrison, *Drink and the Victorians*, pp. 95, 103–6).

[68] *Rapport du Comité nommé par les Chefs de Famille de la Ville et Paroisse de Saint Pierre-Port le 5 Avril 1848* (Guernsey, 1849), p. 8.

[69] Ord, 22.1.1849. An ordinance of 15.4.1611 had decreed that public houses should close on a Sunday, but this had long lapsed.

[70] Ord, 5.10.1859. For a useful summary of Guernsey's licensing legislation, see Anon., *Temper-ance Movement in Guernsey*, pp. 8–18.

[71] In the late 1860s, a newspaper numbered outlets at 165 (*Star*, 15.6.1867).

[72] *Star*, 7.11.1903.

[73] Burnett, *Liquid Pleasures*, p. 182.

[74] *Star*, 6.10.1904. Some would have been re-exported, but this still indicates a high consumption.

[75] *Star*, 6.10.1904.

[76] *Star*, 6.10.1904; 80 degrees proof is equivalent to 45.6% AbV.

[77] *Star*, 6.10.1904.

of neglected and abused families, and lives ruined or truncated through alcoholism. Such phenomena are, however, impossible to quantify.[78]

Whether this was in any way the 'fault' of the poor themselves is also doubtful. The insular establishment was at least partly complicit, and blaming the poor conferred a convenient absolution as well as perhaps justifying a harsh relief regime. Life for many working people was a relentless grind towards an unappealing culmination. It is not hard to understand why some might seek a few hours' escape in drink. In reality, as Charles Dickens observed, problem drinking was not so much the cause of poverty as a particularly pernicious consequence of it.[79]

Housing

Just as with alcohol, conditions peculiar to Guernsey also generated a distinctive set of housing problems. St Peter Port suffered in particular from these. Its small area and large population exerted constant pressure on housing supply, which in turn put pressure on rents. By the mid-nineteenth century, with a population of over 17,000, the parish contained 2,662 houses, a third of which were occupied by their owners.[80] This left a mass of poorer parishioners disproportionately concentrated in houses under multiple occupation. Gregory Stevens Cox has described slum accommodation clustered near the harbour in the 1820s.[81] A few decades later, Cornet Street and Rosemary Lane, to the south of the town centre, became veritable ghettoes for the poor, their medieval houses greatly sub-divided.[82]

In 1833, a basic room in St Peter Port might cost around 2s a week.[83] This was already on a par with the cost of such accommodation in London, which at this time was between 1s 6d and 2s.[84] By 1896, the typical rent for an unfurnished room in St Peter Port had risen to between 3s and 4s.[85] This again was on a par with London, where single rooms in working-class areas cost on average 3s 11d in the 1890s.[86] In provincial English towns, rents were substantially lower: the average paid for a single room in York in 1900 was 1s 7d.[87] In parts of rural England, a whole cottage might be had for 2s a week in 1904.[88]

---

78 Alcohol is no longer cheap in Guernsey, but it has left a cultural legacy: a recent study found that alcoholism has persisted as a significant social problem into the twenty-first century (J. Wolfe, 'Guernsey: social work on a small island', in M. Payne and S.M. Shardlow (eds), *Social Work in the British Isles* (London, 2002), p. 210).

79 In a letter of 1844, Dickens castigated 'that monstrous doctrine which sets down as the consequences of Drunkenness, fifty thousand miseries which are, as all reflective persons know, and daily see, the wretched causes of it' (M. House, G. Storey and K. Tillotson (eds), *The Letters of Charles Dickens*, 12 vols (Oxford, 1965–2002), 4, pp. 30–31).

80 IA, AQ 0974/01.

81 Steven Cox, *St Peter Port*, p. 91.

82 A local newspaper renamed the latter 'Pestilence Alley' (*Star*, 20.6.1905). For an early-twentieth-century photograph, see Plate 2.

83 *Comet*, 14.10.1833.

84 Burnett, *History of Housing*, p. 69.

85 *Le Baillage*, 16.5.1896.

86 Burnett, *History of Housing*, pp. 146, 148.

87 Burnett, *History of Housing*, p. 147.

88 E.H. Hunt, *Regional Wage Variations in Britain, 1850–1914* (Oxford, 1973), p. 80.

In the absence of effective public health legislation, rooms and tenements occupied by Guernsey's poor were often insanitary as well as expensive.[89] In 1852, parish surgeons issued a damning report on Charles Lethbridge's property, 'George House' at the Longstore (on the northern edge of town). The house contained 'one hundred and fifty inmates huddled together in rooms, some of which are affirmed to be like rabbit-hutches, and to which light and air are admitted by the doors alone'.[90] Half a century later, little had changed: the 1901 census showed 11.4 per cent of St Peter Port's population to be living in just one or two rooms.[91] The corresponding figure for England and Wales as a whole was 8.2 per cent, with figures of 4.4 per cent, 4.8 per cent and 9.9 per cent in industrial towns such as Sheffield, Manchester and Leeds.[92] By World War I, the problems of overcrowding and insanitary conditions were acknowledged to have reached acute proportions.[93] The States responded by initiating a modest social housing programme in the early 1920s, after which the situation marginally improved.[94] Nevertheless, even in 1951, while 52 per cent of England's population had exclusive access to the five domestic necessities identified in the census of that year, the figure for Guernsey was only 36 per cent.[95] Moreover, as late as the 1960s, there remained substantial numbers of poor town parishioners living in one or two rooms and having to climb stairs or cross yards to draw water or visit the toilet.[96]

Prices and wages

The high demand and restricted supply that pushed up rents also had their effect on food prices. Town parishioners who lived in rented rooms without gardens were particularly exposed. In mid-eighteenth-century St Peter Port, the price of local butter was 1s per pound and meat 6d per pound, when in parts of England they might be had for 5d and 3½d respectively.[97] At this period, it was local farmers who pushed up prices, but, with increasing reliance on imported foods in the nineteenth century, town-dwellers became more vulnerable to informal price-fixing by importers and wholesalers. An outsider commented that, because Guernsey had a known advantage on dutiable goods, a visitor might arrive expecting to find everything 'dirt-cheap':

[89] It was 1936 before a Guernsey law equivalent to the 1875 Public Health Act of England and Wales was implemented (D.A. Jeffs, 'Through the eyes of the MoH', in D.A. Jeffs (ed.), *One Hundred Years of Health: The Changing Health of Guernsey, 1899–1999* (Guernsey, 1999), p. 12).

[90] *Comet*, 14.10.1852.

[91] 1901 census enumerators' books (microfilm, PL).

[92] Burnett, *History of Housing*, p. 153.

[93] *Billet*, 20.12.1919.

[94] *Billet*, 6.12.1922.

[95] These were an internal piped water supply, a kitchen sink, a fixed bath, a toilet, and a cooking stove or range (*British Medical Journal*, 2.2.1957).

[96] *Billet*, 8.11.1961.

[97] *Case of the Town Parish versus the Nine Country Parishes*, p. 27; Burnett, *Cost of Living*, p. 137. Note that the Guernsey pound weighed marginally more than the pound avoirdupois.

but a day's marketing will speedily undeceive him. The fact is, that the real necessaries of life are decidedly dearer there than in many of the rural districts in England and Ireland, and not materially cheaper than in London or Dublin. For example, good beef and mutton fetch from 7d to 9d the pound; bacon, from 9d to 11d; bread from 2d to 2½d; potatoes, from 1s 6d to 2s the bushel … All articles of English produce or manufacture, such as cheese, cloth, hosiery, etc., are the same price as at home, with the addition of freight … The only articles materially affected by the commercial privileges enjoyed by the island are grocery and wines … the extreme facility, in so small a place, to keep the supply always a little below the demand [has] a constant tendency to raise prices to an artificial level.[98]

The small number of importers controlling Guernsey's narrow supply gateway also precluded islanders from benefiting to any great extent from price falls experienced in the United Kingdom after the mid-1870s, when developments in transport and food-chilling technology facilitated mass imports from the New World, and wheat and meat prices dropped by over 50 per cent and 25 per cent respectively in twenty years.[99] In 1888, a local newspaper observed that people in England paid 10 per cent less for their meat than in Guernsey, where 'the butchers exercise a monopoly prejudicial to consumers'.[100] In 1924, a States' report found the cost of food and food preparation to be about 9 per cent higher in Guernsey than in England.[101]

Had wages, too, been higher than in England, islanders would have been no worse off than contemporaries across the Channel. However, for much of the period, Guernsey's working families were pinched on both sides, since wages were in fact lower than in many parts of England. During the Napoleonic period, when both prices and wages were inflated, an unskilled labourer in St Peter Port earned from 15s to 18s per week. This dropped to between 9s and 12s thereafter, and remained at approximately this level throughout the 1840s and 1850s.[102] This was a period in which builders' labourers in southern England were paid on average 16s per week.[103] According to the *Comet*, 16s per week is what skilled craftsmen, not labourers, were earning in Guernsey's building trade as late as 1861.[104] The disparity between insular and English wage rates persisted throughout the nineteenth and well into the twentieth century. Reflecting on the period immediately before World War II, an islander observed that Guernsey workmen's pay remained obstinately 'lower than English standards, with a longer working week'.[105]

---

[98] Anon., 'Guernsey – its present state and future prospects, part 1', *The Dublin University Magazine*, 28 (1846), pp. 626–7.
[99] W.H. Fraser, *The Coming of the Mass Market, 1850–1914* (London, 1981), p. 16.
[100] *Le Baillage*, 11.2.1888.
[101] *Billet*, 11.6.1924.
[102] *The Guernsey and Jersey Magazine*, 4 (1837), p. 361; TNA, HO 98/88.
[103] H. Phelps Brown and S.V. Hopkins, *A Perspective of Wages and Prices* (London, 1981), p. 11.
[104] *Comet*, 25.4.1861.
[105] Anon., *Nos Iles: A Symposium on the Channel Islands* (Teddington, 1944), p. 82.

Peaks and troughs of distress

Life was thus not always easy for wage-dependent families in Guernsey, even when work was plentiful. In the eighteenth century, St Peter Port was the only parish which had a preponderance of such families, but, as an entrepôt vulnerable to weather, war and trade cycles, it experienced full employment only intermittently.[106] Oscillations between times of stagnation and boom could, moreover, be very pronounced. In the 1720s, a petition to the Privy Council complained that half the town's poor were out of work.[107] In the 1780s and 1790s, by contrast, employment abounded, with 'only Cripples and old people' in the workhouse.[108]

This late eighteenth-century boom was, however, the entrepôt's last. The opening decade of the new century saw the imposition of anti-smuggling legislation and the merchants' withdrawal from trade. Large numbers of entrepôt workers found themselves redundant. Emigration was for the first time resorted to on a large scale. Those who could joined parties bound for North America, establishing colonies in what came to be known as 'Guernsey County' in Ohio and 'Guernsey Cove' in Prince Edward Island.[109] The many who remained in the island suffered badly in the food shortages and high grain prices which affected much of northern Europe in 1812 and 1816.[110] In 1818, a letter to a local newspaper contrasted the turn-of-the-century bustle with the present empty warehouses, artisans in 'squalid wretchedness' and their children 'half naked and half starved'.[111] In 1817, 1818 and 1819, there was further mass emigration to Baltimore, Philadelphia, Gaspé and Quebec.[112] Paradoxically, however, this coincided with the beginnings of large-scale immigration from parts of south-west England that were even more distressed. These new arrivals only added to the pool of underpaid workers competing for scarce jobs. Begging remained a live issue, and ordinances repressing it were enacted as late as 1826.[113] To add to the misery, exceptionally harsh winters in the late 1820s and early 1830s brought outdoor work to a standstill for weeks at a stretch, while soaring coal prices hampered the poorest in heating their homes and cooking their food.[114] Such difficult conditions resulted in excess deaths.[115] These were augmented by further fatalities in the cholera outbreak of 1832.[116]

The seventeen years which intervened between the 1832 cholera epidemic and the second cholera outbreak of 1849 saw scant improvement – perhaps even a deterioration. Indeed, the 1840s seem to have been a decade of the rawest hardship

---

[106] T. Dicey, *An Historical Account of Guernsey* (London, 1751), p. 33; Stevens Cox, *St Peter Port*, p. 54.
[107] 19.7.1722, Watkins MS, vol. II (PL, LL940).
[108] TNA, T 64/153.
[109] Jamieson, 'Channel Islands and overseas settlement', pp. 281, 286.
[110] 26.4.1812, IA, AQ 0964/02; various entries for 1816, IA AQ 0965/01.
[111] *Mercure*, 19.12.1818.
[112] Crossan, *Guernsey, 1814–1914*, p. 41.
[113] Ord, 12.12.1826.
[114] *Comet*, 15.2.1829; 17.11.1831, IA, AQ 0965/02.
[115] *Comet*, 15.2.1829 observed: 'during this winter many persons have died from want of proper sustenance'.
[116] S.K. Kellett-Smith, 'The Guernsey cholera epidemic of 1832', *TSG*, 20 (1980), pp. 643–55.

for the poor of Guernsey, and of St Peter Port in particular, their number greatly swollen by English economic migrants. In the mid-1840s, the island experienced what a Guernsey newspaper called 'a famine period'.[117] The potato blight and disastrous harvest which affected all of western Europe in 1846/7 inflated food prices, bringing many wage-dependent families to the brink. In March 1847, the *Comet* publicised the plight of one St Peter Port household earning only 12s a week which was forced to spend two-thirds of its income on food alone.[118] Matters came to a head in May, when sixty women staged a protest in front of the Royal Court.[119] The Court responded by organising the emergency import of wheat and maize flour, and special loaves were sold at reduced cost to the poor of both town and country.[120] A further major wave of emigration, this time to Australia, ensued during the 1850s.[121]

These traumatic events marked the peak of nineteenth-century distress and heralded something of a turning point. The United Kingdom's own economy picked up in the 1850s, and this improvement had local repercussions. The abatement of distress-related immigration from south-west England reduced pressure on insular resources. Urban improvement projects instigated by English municipal authorities stimulated demand for Guernsey's stone. The British middle classes' increasing ability to travel made Guernsey more of a tourist destination. For all these reasons and many others, hunger ceased to be a collective phenomenon in Guernsey during the second half of the nineteenth century, and became instead a matter of individual calamity.

Of course, life for Guernsey's poor continued to have its ups and downs. The late 1860s and early 1870s in particular saw a temporary resurgence of hardship when the discharge of workers from harbour construction projects in Guernsey and Alderney coincided with a slump in the stone trade and rising prices for French food imports occasioned by the Franco-Prussian War.[122] In the 1880s, conditions seem to have stabilised under the beneficent influence of the developing horticultural industry. The end of the century was thus a period of relative prosperity, disturbed only by the swings of the British trade cycle, when demand for stone and horticultural exports slackened off.

Between 1900 and World War I, however, British trade slumps became sharper and more frequent.[123] Stone-workers and greenhouse hands were periodically laid off, and emigration again set in on a significant scale.[124] Worse was nevertheless yet to come. The major depressions affecting Britain in the 1920s and 1930s hit Guernsey's exports hard, causing serious local unemployment for prolonged periods.

---

[117] *Star*, 3.4.1848.

[118] *Comet*, 15.3.1847.

[119] *Comet*, 10.5.1847.

[120] Ord, 11.5.1847; *Star*, 14.5.1847.

[121] Crossan, *Guernsey, 1814–1914*, pp. 55–6.

[122] Crossan, *Guernsey, 1814–1914*, pp. 113–18, *Star*, 30.1.1868, 4.2.1868, 14.11.1868, 7.1.1869, 27.8.1870; 17.2.1870, 20.2.1871, IA, AQ 40/04.

[123] P. Wardley, 'Edwardian Britain: empire, income and political discontent', in P. Johnson (ed.), *Twentieth-Century Britain: Economic, Social and Cultural Change* (London, 1994), pp. 57–78.

[124] Crossan, *Guernsey, 1814–1914*, pp. 56–7.

Worklessness reached a peak in the winter of 1931/2, when 711 men were officially registered as unemployed.[125] These 711 men equated to about 6 per cent of Bailiwick males aged 18 to 64 enumerated in the 1931 census, but did not include the jobless in the smaller islands.[126] Adjusting the figure accordingly and adding a margin for youngsters and others who did not register yields a conjectural male unemployment total for Guernsey in the region of 9 or 10 per cent. This was nowhere near the rate of unemployment experienced in Britain, which peaked at 17 per cent in 1932.[127] However, it has not been exceeded since and was enough to make a lasting imprint on a small community.

Comparisons with elsewhere
Quantification of poverty is difficult in our own times, and more difficult still for far-off periods whose standards of living and perceptions of poverty were very different from our own. This, of course, has not prevented historians from attempting the exercise. Many have likened early modern society to a squat pyramid, with vast wealth at the top resting upon a broad base of poverty – poverty of the most basic kind, where people's needs for food, shelter and warmth might not be satisfied. Robert Jütte has estimated that people suffering this kind of poverty comprised at least two-thirds of most early modern European populations.[128] Such evidence as exists for early modern Guernsey suggests that there was an insular base of poverty commensurate with this generalisation. However, at this point in Guernsey's history, before fortunes had been made in privateering and trade, there was no vast wealth at the top. One scholar has described even patricians, with their diminutive estates, as 'poor' in comparison with English compeers.[129] In the eighteenth century, this situation changed, but it also introduced a more pronounced dichotomy between town and country. Because poverty manifested itself differently in urban and rural parishes, these require separate analysis, so we shall begin with the countryside.

Olwen Hufton's work on eighteenth-century France affords a useful standard against which to measure Guernsey's rural experience, not only because the mid-1700s marked the nadir of modern Guernsey rural poverty, but because it was also up to this time that the insular countryside had most in common with France's *pays de petite culture*. Professor Hufton estimated that the poor might have comprised 'speculatively, perhaps as much as a half' of the pre-Revolutionary French population, with 'something approaching a third' compelled to beg at some time in their lives.[130] In her study, Hufton demonstrated the chronic reduction of French peasants and smallholders to rags, starvation, mendicancy and even infanticide, on a truly

[125] *Billet*, 2.12.1932.
[126] *Census 1931: Jersey, Guernsey and Adjacent Islands* (London, 1933), p. 34.
[127] B. Harris, 'Unemployment and the dole in interwar Britain', in Johnson (ed.), *Twentieth-Century Britain*, p. 205.
[128] Jütte, *Poverty and Deviance*, p. 50.
[129] A.J. Eagleston, *The Channel Islands under Tudor Government, 1485–1642: A Study in Administrative History* (Cambridge, 1949), p. 158.
[130] O. Hufton, *The Poor of Eighteenth-Century France, 1750–1789* (Oxford, 1974), pp. 24, 126.

mass scale.[131] This certainly puts Guernsey into perspective, for, although hunger did exist in Guernsey's rural parishes, it was intermittent, and nowhere can we find evidence to suggest that, even at its height, it either reached the pitch described by Professor Hufton or affected the proportion of the population she identified in France.

It is harder to draw comparisons with the rural poor of England, because, by and large, these were not land-holding peasants but landless agricultural labourers. An extensive Victorian literature made much of the anti-indigence virtues of Guernsey's 'peasant proprietorship', contrasting the island's frugal and self-reliant smallholders with improvident, relief-habituated English farmhands.[132] But, for all that, standards of living for the poorest Guernsey rurals may well have been lower than for many English landless labourers, who, through precocious advances in English agriculture, had long benefited from material conditions superior to those experienced by peasants in much of continental Europe.[133] In 1834, Henry Inglis observed that insular rurals of all ranks still ate barley bread, when, in England, even the poorest labourers had long forsaken it for better-quality wheaten bread.[134] These contrasts deepened as England entered the mid-century era of 'high farming' and the lot of English agricultural labourers improved.[135] The English MP Edward Denison, visiting in the 1860s, felt that an English landlord would be 'hooted at' by his lowliest cottagers for suggesting they should emulate the lifestyle of a Guernsey farmer, let alone that of a smallholder.[136]

We turn now to St Peter Port, for which contemporary evidence allows us to adopt a more quantitative approach, albeit an unscientific one by modern standards. In 1817, 'a Parishioner' sent a letter to a local newspaper discussing the problem of poverty and analysing the distribution of wealth.[137] According to the Parishioner's analysis, the top 10 per cent of his neighbours lived in affluence, and a further 35 per cent lived in comfort. Beneath them, 35 per cent earned a tolerable living through work, and the bottom 20 per cent were 'poor'. Tentative corroboration for the proportion in the grip of material deprivation comes from an emergency distribution of blankets and clothing made to St Peter Port's poorest families as an anti-cholera precaution in 1832.[138] Those who received hand-outs equated to about 20 per cent of the families enumerated in St Peter Port in the previous year's

---

[131] Hufton, *Poor of Eighteenth-Century France*, p. 355.

[132] See Appendix 1.

[133] R. Floud, R.W. Fogel, B. Harris and S.C. Hong, *The Changing Body: Health, Nutrition, and Human Development in the Western World since 1700* (Cambridge, 2011), pp. 105–24, 151–69, 258–95.

[134] H.D. Inglis, *The Channel Islands*, 2 vols (London, 1834), 2, p. 39; Burnett, *Cost of Living*, pp. 10, 180.

[135] B.A. Holderness, 'The origins of high farming', in B.A. Holderness and M. Turner (eds), *Land, Labour and Agriculture, 1700–1920: Essays for Gordon Mingay* (London, 1991).

[136] B. Leighton (ed.), *Letters and other Writings of the Late Edward Denison* (London, 1872), pp. 141–50.

[137] *Gazette de Guernesey*, 15.3.1817. The discussion, though encompassing the whole island, was clearly based on St Peter Port.

[138] IA, AQ 0991/05.

census.[139] Most of the clothing distributed consisted of shifts and drawers. That families stood in want of such basics is an illustration of what the term 'poor' actually meant.

Evidence suggests that proportions assigned to the various categories in 1817 held good throughout the first half of the nineteenth century, and perhaps until as late as the 1860s, when the fortunes of the wealthiest diminished, those of the middle class increased, and conditions for the poorest began marginally to improve. They also bear broad comparison with nineteenth-century estimates for English towns of similar socio-economic make-up, although, here too, there was no attempt at 'scientific' evaluation of poverty until the eve of the twentieth century.[140]

So much for analyses and comparisons. All contain subjective and discrepant elements, and their value is limited. Olwen Hufton has remarked that 'a study of poverty must predominantly be a qualitative not a quantitative one'.[141] Thus we must not lose sight of individuals among proportions and percentages. As testimony to the sufferings of real people, it may be apposite to describe the case of Sarah Foy, a young widow with three children who starved to death at her lodgings in Rosemary Lane in 1865. As the *Star* recorded:

> Dr Carey deposed that the deceased was in an emaciated state and that death had been caused by exhaustion. It appeared that the deceased had for a considerable time been in a state of complete destitution, and that she and her family had no means of existence but what was procured by the begging of the children … It did not transpire whether the deceased had received parochial relief, but it was stated that she had some time since been urged by one of the members of the Poor Law Board to go into the hospital [St Peter Port's workhouse], but had refused to do so.[142]

How could a family known to the authorities be allowed to sink into such a condition? What was it about the workhouse that so repelled this woman that she preferred begging and, ultimately, starvation? Whether Guernsey's quota of poor fell below or above that of other places is in some ways immaterial. More pertinent to our present purpose is the extent to which the island's welfare system alleviated their condition or allowed it to oppress them. The following chapters will explore this theme.

---

[139] The 1831 census counted 2,864 families in St Peter Port, and 559 families received hand-outs in 1832 (*Billet*, 6.10.1831; IA, AQ 0991/05).

[140] P. Wood, *Poverty and the Workhouse in Victorian Britain* (Stroud, 1991), pp. 8–9.

[141] Hufton, *Poor of Eighteenth-Century France*, p. 7.

[142] *Star*, 16.5.1865.

II

Welfare

3

Beginnings of Parochial Poor Relief

Pre-Reformation

Parishes

Parishes began to develop in western Europe in the second half of the first millennium.[1] They arose primarily from the setting of territorial boundaries around churches to determine the area from which the tithe (intended to support a priest) would be collected.[2] In Guernsey, evidence points to the establishment of parishes by the early eleventh century.[3]

In the course of time, Rome's imposition of a duty on the inhabitants of all parishes to share in the upkeep of their churches necessitated the establishment of communal church maintenance funds.[4] The earliest such funds were established in twelfth-century France and Germany, and lay office-holders charged with their management appeared soon afterwards. In France, these were known as *fabriciens*, *marguilliers* or *trésoriers*.[5] In England, such officers first appeared in the thirteenth century, and came to be known as churchwardens.[6] Guernsey's records indicate that parishioners were actively contributing to church upkeep and running costs by at least the fourteenth century. There is litigation dating from the 1360s on the division of these costs between the parishioners of the Vale and the Prior of St Michel du Valle, in which the parish was represented by its *thesaurius* (*trésorier*), who was by then annually presenting his accounts in the parish church.[7]

Nowhere in medieval Europe was there a clear distinction between the ecclesiastical and secular activities of parishes. Sunday Mass provided an opportunity to announce news or discuss issues, and, in the absence of other public buildings,

---

[1] L. Genicot, *Rural Communities in the Medieval West* (Baltimore, 1990), p. 26.
[2] N.J.G. Pounds, *A History of the English Parish: The Culture of Religion from Augustine to Victoria* (Cambridge, 2000), pp. 76, 267.
[3] D.M. Ogier, 'The origins of Guernsey's parishes and the ownership and maintenance of their ancient church buildings', *The Jersey Law Review*, 9 (2005), p. 326.
[4] Pounds, *English Parish*, p. 38.
[5] B. Kümin, 'The English parish in a European perspective', in K. French, G. Gibbs and B. Kümin (eds), *The Parish in English Life, 1400–1600* (Manchester, 1997), p. 24.
[6] Pounds, *English Parish*, pp. 182–4.
[7] Ogier, 'Guernsey's parishes', p. 328.

churches served a variety of communal purposes.[8] Aside from their religious function, Guernsey's medieval churches served as storage places for parochial weaponry and as venues for the public passing of contracts and the election of Jurats. Such activities would have created a need for some form of secular parochial organisation. Evidence of such in Guernsey exists from the fifteenth century: there are records of a *Douzaine* appointing a granger of St Peter Port in 1444 and of parish constables from 1481.[9]

Welfare

Under the Roman Catholic regime of pre-Reformation Europe, charity towards the poor was seen as a Christian duty through which salvation could, in part, be earned. Scripture deemed the poor to be closer to heaven than the wealthy, and the latter at risk of damnation if they took pride in their wealth. It was felt that prayers offered by the poor for the rich in return for their charity were particularly effective in securing remission of sins.[10] Charity could be spontaneous and indiscriminate – a coin deposited into the first outstretched hand – but the fact that it was a religious duty meant that it was in practice substantially co-ordinated and dispensed by the various branches of the church. Each parish in Christendom had officially been made responsible for its poor by the sixth-century Synod of Tours.[11] Monasteries and other foundations administered by religious orders were also major centres of charity, as were hospitals, which at this time were ecclesiastical rather than medical foundations.[12]

Medieval Guernsey had many Christian charitable institutions. At least two leper houses are known, in St Sampsons and St Saviours.[13] From the mid-fourteenth century, St Peter Port had a small hospital – the Hospital of St Julian, located at Glategny, on the northern edge of the town.[14] St Julian's Hospital was endowed as an act of personal piety and, in common with all its medieval counterparts, provided shelter to itinerants as well as care for the community's sick, needy, dying and abandoned.[15]

Fraternities, or confraternities, also existed in pre-Reformation Guernsey. Records have been found for at least forty-four in the sixteenth century.[16] These were lay organisations created for the purpose of ensuring the salvation of their

---

8   Kümin, 'English parish in a European perspective', pp. 21–2.
9   Ogier, 'Guernsey's parishes', pp. 339–40.
10 P. Slack, *Poverty and Policy in Tudor and Stuart England* (Harlow, 1988), pp. 18–19; P.A. Fideler, *Social Welfare in Pre-Industrial England: The Old Poor Law Tradition* (Basingstoke, 2006), pp. 14–15.
11 J.E. Olson, *Calvin and Social Welfare: Deacons and the Bourse Française* (London, 1989), p. 18.
12 Pounds, *English Parish*, p. 149.
13 J. McCormack, *Channel Island Churches* (Chichester, 1986), p. 307.
14 McCormack, *Churches*, pp. 308–9.
15 For details of the Hospital's endowment, see TNA, C 143/298/20.
16 D.M. Ogier, *Reformation and Society in Guernsey* (Woodbridge, 1996), pp. 183–5. Dr Ogier's book is authoritative on all aspects of welfare immediately prior to and after the Reformation. Sections of this chapter which deal with this period are substantially derived from his work rather than from primary research of my own.

members' souls. Each was formally associated with a particular parish church or chapel. Their activities ranged from funding Masses for the dead and paying for funerals to assisting in the celebration of religious feasts and supplying charity to the poor. On joining a fraternity in Guernsey, members would usually covenant to make a regular contribution to the fraternity's funds, often in the form of a corn *rente*.[17] Prominent among the activities of Guernsey's fraternities seems to have been the distribution of alms, often in the form of corn or bread, to poor households in their respective parishes.[18]

The poor of Guernsey's pre-Reformation parishes also benefited from funds raised through 'obits', a long-established institution of the medieval church. Obits were anniversary Masses offered for the souls of named deceased persons. They had to be paid for – either by an endowment made in the person's lifetime, by means of a bequest, or by friends and relatives after death. Such payments were gathered into funds, and, in medieval Guernsey, it appears to have been the custom for parish churches to allocate one-third of these funds to the poor. Among other things, obit funds were used to pay for regular doles of bread at the parish church door.[19]

A further portion of Guernsey's obit funds seems to have been reserved for the parish clergy, forming a resource called *clers*. This resource was separate from *le trésor*, which was dedicated to church maintenance.[20] While the latter was the responsibility of parochial *trésoriers* and their co-adjutors the *collecteurs*,[21] those in charge of the funds set aside from obits were known as *procureurs*. Guernsey's fraternities also appointed *procureurs* to manage their funds. *Procureur* was the usual designation of officers entrusted with the management of charitable funds all over francophone Europe, and, in some medieval French parishes, poor funds were managed by a *procureur de charité*.[22] *Procureurs* commonly functioned as agents or proxies as well as trustees. From the early 1500s, parish *procureurs des pauvres et clercs* are mentioned

---

17   *Rentes* will feature elsewhere in this book, so it is worth explaining what they were. They derived essentially from the mode of buying and selling real property in Guernsey, whereby all or part of the purchase price was converted into a perpetual charge of so much *rente* per annum payable to the vendor. As property was valued in terms of the corn it could produce, these *rentes* were originally paid in kind. As Guernsey later developed a money-based economy, *rentes* came to be expressed in monetary terms. As long as the *rentes* continued to be paid annually, the purchasers of real property held it as freehold. On the purchasers' death, the obligation to pay the *rentes* descended to those who inherited the property, and, on the vendors' death, *rentes* originally payable to them became payable to their heirs. Those to whom the *rentes* were payable could also sell them on to third parties, donate them as gifts, or leave them as bequests. Over time, many *rentes* were redeemed by landowners on terms prescribed in the original conveyance. Guernsey abandoned its traditional mode of property purchase during the twentieth century, and, although some *rentes* remain in existence today, no new *rentes* are now created (J. Duncan, *The History of Guernsey* (London, 1841), pp. 285–6; G. Dawes, *Laws of Guernsey* (Oxford, 2003), pp. 622–4).

18   Ogier, *Reformation and Society*, pp. 25–30.

19   Ogier, *Reformation and Society*, pp. 30–31.

20   Ogier, *Reformation and Society*, p. 24.

21   *Collecteurs*, who collected funds for *le trésor*, are known from at least 1515 (pers. comm., Dr D.M. Ogier).

22   A.A. Babeau, *Le Village sous l'Ancien Régime* (Paris, 1879), p. 311.

in Royal Court registers, appearing before the Court as representatives of the funds of the poor and those maintained for the clergy.[23]

This brings us to the eve of the Reformation. By this time, as the above evidence shows, distinct parochial structures had evolved in relation to welfare, and the parish was already well-established as a primary agent of relief.

Reformation

Throughout the medieval period, Channel Island churches were under the jurisdiction of the diocese of Coutances in Normandy, and it is via Normandy that the Reformed religion reached the Islands.[24] The Reformation came early to this part of France, and insular clerics visiting or studying there may have been exposed to heretical teachings as early as the 1520s.[25] In later decades, the repression of Protestants in Normandy brought many of them to the Islands, and among them were evangelists who became active locally.[26] The Protestantism these Normans brought with them was of a Calvinist character, as was usual in France. Calvinism appears to have made a number of local converts in the first half of the sixteenth century. These included members of the elite: the future Bailiff Guillaume De Beauvoir, for example. After the accession of the Catholic Queen Mary to the English throne in 1553, Guernsey's Calvinists felt themselves to be at risk of persecution, and some sought refuge elsewhere. Guillaume De Beauvoir, for one, fled to the Calvinist heartland of Geneva, where he became a deacon of Geneva's 'English' church.[27]

Despite the conversion of such as De Beauvoir, Guernsey's parish churches had continued operating under the traditional Catholic regime throughout the reigns of Henry VIII, Edward VI and Mary.[28] Definitive change came only after the accession of Elizabeth I in 1558. The new queen took action to foster local Protestantism, sending over a succession of Commissions, which *inter alia* redistributed property formerly belonging to the local Catholic churches and fraternities to individuals of a more acceptable religious hue.[29]

In 1559, Guillaume De Beauvoir, safely back from Geneva, wrote to John Calvin requesting his help with Guernsey's fledgling church. Calvin sent him the minister Nicolas Baudoin, who was appointed to the parish of St Peter Port. Guernsey's first Calvinist consistory met there in 1563, and, within a relatively short period of time, the nine other parishes also adopted the new structures.[30]

[23] Pers. comm., Dr D.M. Ogier.
[24] Tim Thornton has characterised the Reformation in the Channel Islands as 'a Norman Reformation' (T. Thornton, *The Channel Islands, 1370–1640: Between England and Normandy* (Woodbridge, 2012), pp. 80, 110).
[25] Thornton, *Channel Islands*, pp. 74, 79–80.
[26] Ogier, *Reformation and Society*, p. 53.
[27] Thornton, *Channel Islands*, p. 88.
[28] Ogier, *Reformation and Society*, p. 49.
[29] Ogier, *Reformation and Society*, pp. 62ff.
[30] Ogier, *Reformation and Society*, pp. 59, 67–8, 95.

Ultimately, the transformation of the island's religious complexion was secured by a wholesale change in the personnel of the Royal Court. In 1565, seven Catholic Jurats were dismissed by the Privy Council, and new Jurats of Protestant affiliation, including Guillaume De Beauvoir, were appointed in their place. From this point, Guernsey's religious revolution was substantially complete, and, on the practical ground that Guernsey needed French-speaking ministers, Calvinism was established as the most viable form of Protestantism. The new Calvinist, or Presbyterian, regime was endorsed by the English Privy Council, and, in 1569, the Council formally confirmed Guernsey's withdrawal from the diocese of Coutances.[31] Presbyterianism was to endure as Guernsey's 'established' religion for approximately a century. It was replaced by Anglicanism (at least nominally) in 1662, when Charles II imposed Anglican forms.[32]

Post-Reformation

The Presbyterian era, 1560s–1660s

The disappearance of Catholicism from Guernsey also saw the disappearance of traditional organised charity. Under a hostile Royal Court, fraternities, Masses, doles and so on were suppressed and eventually died out.[33] However, the new religion swiftly filled the gap. Calvinists regarded the Bible as the infallible word of God containing all the rules of faith and practice God intended for His Church. In Matthew's parable of the sheep and the goats, 'the just' fed the hungry, gave drink to the thirsty, welcomed the stranger, clothed the naked, visited prisoners and the sick.[34] Although, for Calvinists, salvation came from God's grace alone and could not be earned through such activities, their performance was a way of demonstrating election – 'by their fruits, ye shall know them'.[35] Calvin therefore regarded the functions outlined in Matthew's parable as among the essential duties of a Church.[36]

Distinctions between the religious and the secular were blurred in the godly polity which came about after the Calvinists assumed ascendancy in Guernsey's Royal Court. Darryl Ogier has described an 'inter-penetration' of church and Court, forming 'an interlocking executive' in which all were ultimately subject to the word of God.[37] The welfare regime introduced by the Calvinists therefore came to be embodied primarily in an ecclesiastical document and only secondarily in laws. This document was the 'Discipline', first drawn up in 1576 and revised in 1597,

---

[31] Ogier, *Reformation and Society*, pp. 62, 69–73, 81; Thornton, *Channel Islands*, pp. 106–7, 124.

[32] J. Marr, *The History of Guernsey: The Bailiwick's Story* (1982; Guernsey, 2001 edn), p. 37.

[33] Ogier, *Reformation and Society*, p. 83, 117–18.

[34] Matthew, 25:31–9.

[35] Matthew, 7:16.

[36] S. Kahl, 'The religious roots of modern poverty policy: Catholic, Lutheran and Reformed Protestant traditions compared', *European Journal of Sociology*, 45 (2005), p. 119.

[37] Ogier, *Reformation and Society*, pp. 106, 112.

which codified the constitution of the Channel Islands' Presbyterian church.[38] The Channel Islands' Discipline was modelled on Calvin's Ecclesiastical Ordinances of 1541 which set out a constitution for the Reformed church at Geneva.[39] The Ordinances defined four types of ministry – pastors, teachers, elders and deacons. It was to the deacons that Calvin allotted the primary welfare role.[40] The Channel Islands' Discipline stipulated that insular deacons (assisted if need be by elders) should visit the poor, the sick, the impotent and prisoners, to comfort them and assist them. The funds for such assistance were to be raised from parishioners and distributed under the direction of the parish consistory.[41]

These funds came from several sources. Deacons took collections at the church door after sermons, and, if necessary, by calling on parishioners at their homes. Parishioners, for their part, were encouraged to deposit small sums in the church poor box (*le tronc* or *la boëte*), as also to make more substantial donations and bequests as acts of personal piety. Many such donations and bequests came in the form of *rentes*. These were added to the parochial poor *rentes* which had survived the Reformation. In St Peter Port, there was a general *acte de confession* on 1 December 1567 whereby those owing *rentes* to the poor pre-dating the new regime were invited to acknowledge their obligations.[42] Some poor funds also came from fines. Ordinances were passed assigning part of the penalty for certain offences to the poor.[43] Such resources were accumulated into new parochial poor funds henceforth known as *le bien des pauvres*, or *la bourse des pauvres*.

A set of poor relief accounts survive for Presbyterian St Peter Port beginning in 1634.[44] These show that the poor of the parish were relieved by seven deacons, whose accounts were audited regularly by the minister and elders. The deacons made weekly payments to a number of named persons on a 'permanent' list, as well as one-off payments by way of casual relief. Regular payments usually took the form of small cash sums, supplemented by remittances in kind, such as bread, textiles or clothing. Casual hand-outs could also take both forms. In October 1634, there were twenty-nine regular relief recipients on St Peter Port's list. Basing ourselves on F.B. Tupper's population estimate for 1615, this equated to about 1.5 per cent of parishioners.[45] Save five men, they were all women and children, receiving sums equivalent

---

38 The text of the Channel Islands' Discipline is reproduced in English translation in W. Berry, *The History of the Island of Guernsey* (London, 1815), pp. 245–55. In organisational terms, each parish had its own 'consistory', a body comprising minister, elders and deacons. Above the consistories were all-island 'colloquies' which met several times a year, and these in turn sent representatives to the pan-island 'synods', held every year or two years (Ogier, *Reformation and Society*, p. 95).

39 Ogier, *Reformation and Society*, pp. 87, 94–5.

40 R.M. Kingdon, 'Social welfare in Calvin's Geneva', *American Historical Review*, 76 (1971), pp. 59–60; Olson, *Calvin and Social Welfare*, pp. 27–9, 32.

41 Ogier, *Reformation and Society*, pp. 100, 166–7.

42 IA, AQ 1051/01.

43 Ord, 4.10.1630, for instance, specified that five *sols* of the fine levied for illegal hawking in the Town Church porch were to go to the poor (IA, AQ 0988/01).

44 IA, DC/HX 061–05.

45 Tupper reckoned St Peter Port's 1615 population at 1,910 (F.B. Tupper, *The History of Guernsey*

on average to about 6d sterling per week. The regular weekly total disbursed was under £1 sterling, and amounted to no more than £50 a year.[46]

Presbyterian St Peter Port also had two poorhouses: the former St Julian's Hospital at Glategny and another house in Berthelot Street. Both appear to have been small and under-used. That at Glategny was described in the 1630s as containing two living chambers, a kitchen and a cellar, and accommodating only two people. That in Berthelot Street was partly rented out and the income diverted to other poor-related purposes. Neither house seems to have survived beyond the end of the seventeenth century.[47] Residential relief does not, therefore, appear to have played a large part in the Presbyterian welfare strategy, and it is perhaps not surprising that when, in 1627, Jurat Thomas De l'Isle left the States money to endow a new residential institution for the poor, nothing came of it.[48]

The institution De l'Isle had in mind was what he called *une maison de correction*. The term was a direct translation of the English 'house of correction', where the 'idle' or 'immoral' poor were sent to be disciplined and reformed. The first such institution was London's Bridewell, chartered in 1553, with others of a similar nature following in a further fifteen towns before the end of the 1500s. A statute of 1576 coined the generic term 'house of correction' for this kind of establishment, and required Justices of the Peace (JPs) to set them up in their respective counties.[49]

In Guernsey's case, Jurat De l'Isle's bequest coincided with a slump in stocking exports, and the States spent much of it in buying up the stocks of destitute knitters, shelving indefinitely the matter of such an institution.[50] The house of correction proposed by Thomas De l'Isle was never built, and it is a circumstance which, as we shall see in Chapter 6, was to have repercussions in the future.[51]

Paul Fideler has described England in the forty years following the Reformation as dotted with 'welfare experiments pioneered by godly little commonwealths'.[52] In the centrality of ecclesiastical structures to its welfare regime, Presbyterian Guernsey was not radically different from Puritan-run English municipalities in the sixteenth and seventeenth centuries, some of which, such as Dorchester, Southampton, Salisbury and Plymouth, were near enough to be known of in the island.[53] However, Puritan welfare structures in all these English towns ultimately withered away as a

---

and its Bailiwick (Guernsey, 1854), p. 227).

[46] For a detailed analysis of St Peter Port's seventeenth-century poor relief accounts see Ogier, *Reformation and Society*, pp. 169, 191–5.

[47] Ogier, *Reformation and Society*, pp. 167, 170.

[48] Acte, 19.5.1627; Ogier, *Reformation and Society*, p. 168.

[49] J. Innes, 'Prisons for the poor: English bridewells, 1555–1800', in F. Snyder and D. Hay (eds), *Labour, Law and Crime: An Historical Perspective* (London, 1987), pp. 42–122.

[50] Acte, 19.5.1627.

[51] Dr Darryl Ogier has alerted me to a record in St Peter Port's Pier Accounts of repairs to *la maison de correction* in September 1628 (IA, AQ 0645/12). I suspect that this was either the ex-hospital at Glategny or the house at Berthelot Street, which may have been used for similar disciplinary purposes.

[52] Fideler, *Social Welfare*, pp. 80, 92–6.

[53] For more on these municipalities, see P.A. Slack, *From Reformation to Improvement: Public Welfare in Early Modern England* (Oxford, 1999), pp. 29–52.

system elaborated through parliamentary statute took their place country-wide.[54] Before we look at Guernsey's legislation, it is worth recapitulating how England's poor laws evolved.

For some time before the Reformation, the English parliament had, in common with continental (and Guernsey) counterparts, passed laws aimed at suppressing begging and vagrancy.[55] These laws had been primarily concerned with punishment, and contained no positive measures to support the poor and forestall a resort to begging in the first place. This changed in 1536 when an Act passed under Henry VIII introduced the novelties of organised 'voluntary' collections for the impotent poor and compulsory employment for poor children, laying full responsibility for these categories of people on their parishes. A further Act followed in 1547, which, while continuing the provision for 'voluntary' collections, also infamously imposed slavery as a punishment for refusal to work, and allowed the children of beggars to be taken from them and given to anyone willing to teach them some 'honest labour or occupation'. This Act was, however, largely repealed in 1550. The 1552 Act 'for the Provision and Relief of the Poor' sought to place financial matters on a sounder footing by laying down that two collectors of alms for each parish were to be elected annually and parishioners were to be urged to give weekly, with pressure being exerted if necessary. An Act of 1563 took this further by providing for the summons before a JP and possible prison sentence for those who refused to contribute. Ultimately, an Act of 1572 introduced the concept of a compulsory poor rate. JPs were made responsible for assessing and taxing, and officials termed 'overseers' were to supervise distributions. A quarter of a century later, the 1598 Act 'for the Relief of the Poor' added a few refinements: JPs became supervisors and hearers of appeals only; the relief of the poor was made the direct responsibility of four overseers in each parish; 'all inhabitants and all occupiers of land' were to be rated, and begging was forbidden except when licensed. This was complemented by an Act of the same year for 'the Punishment of Rogues, Vagabonds and Sturdy Beggars' which allowed the whipping and sending back of unlicensed beggars and vagrants by parish constables. Last but not least, the Act of 1601 – the famous '43rd Elizabeth' – was the summation and consolidation of all English poor relief legislation as it had developed to date. Parochial overseers (reduced in number from four to two) were to be responsible for the estimation of need, the making of rates, the collection of monies, the distribution of payments and the keeping of accounts – all under the supervision of JPs. In this, the Elizabethan poor law achieved its definitive form.

As we have seen, relief of the poor under Guernsey's Presbyterian regime was primarily an ecclesiastical matter, and the role of legislation only secondary. Surviving ordinances from this period cannot be seen as constituting a progression in the English sense. They were issued as necessary in response to the exigencies of the time. Many were short-lived, reiterating broadly similar, though not identical,

---

[54] Slack, *Poverty and Policy*, p. 156.
[55] The account which follows in based on P.A. Slack, *The English Poor Law, 1531–1782* (1990; Cambridge, 1995 edn), pp. 51–6 of which list the relevant statutes.

measures at intervals of years. Some were composite ordinances, addressing poor relief alongside other matters. The underlying purpose of such legislation seems to have been to identify the limits of ecclesiastical responsibility. Successive ordinances made it clear that those unable to maintain themselves were in the first instance to be supported by their families.[56] Those who had no kin, providing they were elderly, might be allowed to beg rather than receive relief.[57] The poor of working age were, by contrast, expressly banned from begging and were instead to be compulsorily hired out, apprenticed or otherwise put into service by parochial Constables and *Douzeniers*.[58] Each parish was responsible only for its own poor; strangers to the island and incomers from other parishes were ineligible for relief.[59]

The end result of all these legislative strictures was to leave only a small residue of particularly helpless native parishioners eligible for support from their own parishes.[60] The low percentage of St Peter Port parishioners in receipt of relief in 1634 corroborates the residual nature of Guernsey's parochial assistance. We may contrast St Peter Port's figure of 1.5 per cent with an average English urban figure of 5 per cent in the early seventeenth century, rising to as much as 20 per cent in years of crisis.[61]

There is little doubt that Guernsey's early modern ruling class were aware of English legislative developments. Certainly, some of the ordinances passed by the Royal Court in the sixteenth and early seventeenth centuries exhibited features similar to Westminster legislation.[62] Significantly, however, none of the sophisticated administrative structures created by the English parliament had any parallel in Guernsey. This is because these structures related principally to modes of funding, and funding, in Guernsey, remained completely voluntary. While it is true that an option was tentatively opened in 1598 for parishes to levy taxes should alms ever fall short,[63] no evidence exists that any such taxes were raised until well over a century later.

Poor relief in Guernsey was thus first and foremost an ecclesiastical matter throughout the Calvinist period, and, if resemblances are to be found north of the Channel, they lie more with Presbyterian Scotland than with England. John Knox was minister of the English church at Geneva when Guernseyman Guillaume De Beauvoir was serving as a deacon there. Knox and his followers drew up a Book of

---

[56] Ords, 20.1.1589, 25.8.1592, 15.4.1611.

[57] Ords, 20.1.1589, 21.1.1598, 15.4.1611.

[58] Ords, 30.9.1566, 21.1.1598, 15.4.1611.

[59] Ords, 20.1.1589, 21.1.1598, 15.4.1611.

[60] Those denied support to which they felt themselves duly entitled were authorised to apply to the Court for enforcement (Ord, 15.4.1611).

[61] Slack, *Poverty and Policy*, pp. 53, 71–5, 175–9.

[62] From Henry VIII to Charles I, the Privy Council had issued circulars containing instructions for alleviating social distress. In 1631, these were consolidated into a book – *Orders and Directions* – which included detailed guidance on poor relief. Another volume, entitled *Four Statutes*, had been published in 1609, providing details of vagrancy and poor relief legislation to ensure uniformity (Slack, *Poverty and Policy*, pp. 138–40). It is quite possible that Guernsey legislators had sight of these publications.

[63] Ord, 21.1.1598. The provision was restated in Ord, 15.4.1611.

Discipline for the Scottish Presbyterian church in 1577, which, as in Guernsey, gave each parish church the task of providing for its poor, and made deacons responsible for collecting and distributing alms.[64] Scotland made more of a gesture towards English administrative models than Guernsey, in that it passed laws in 1574 and 1579 which were close copies of the English statute of 1572 introducing a compulsory poor rate. Nevertheless, these remained a dead letter, and Scotland's kirk sessions (analogous to Guernsey's consistories) continued notwithstanding to dispense poor relief along Calvinist lines. Ultimately, in a new poor law Act of 1592, the Scots parliament accepted the kirk sessions as official agents of relief. These bodies were to exercise this function for the next 250 years and, until that time, Scotland remained without a statute-based relief apparatus.[65]

The first post-Presbyterian century, 1660s–1760s

On 15 July 1662, Charles II brought Presbyterianism to an end in Guernsey by issuing a decree notifying Guernsey's Governor of his appointment of an Anglican Dean for the island.[66] Troops were sent over to forestall resistance, and recalcitrant clergy were removed from their livings. Parish ministers thenceforward resumed the title of Rector, and church services began to be conducted – more or less – according to the Book of Common Prayer.[67]

As of 21 May 1663, St Peter Port's poor law accounts were no longer kept in the names of deacons, but of *collecteurs*.[68] Other parishes gradually followed suit. According to a Victorian account of the transition, this was merely a terminological change: personnel and function remained largely unaltered.[69] At around this time, the office of parochial *procureur* also re-emerged from the shadows. It is possible that one or more of St Peter Port's former Presbyterian deacons had performed the traditional *procureurs'* work as trustees and agents of the poor. A receipt survives from 1621 issued by an official referring to himself as *procureur des pauvres de la paroesse de Saint piere port* [*sic*]. After the 1660s, this role was formally entrusted to named individuals sworn in by the reconstituted Ecclesiastical Court, such as Jean

---

64 R.L. Greaves, 'The social awareness of John Knox: the problems of poverty and educational reform', *Renaissance and Reformation*, 12 (1976), p. 37.

65 R. Mitchison, 'The making of the Old Scottish Poor Law', *Past & Present*, 63 (1974), pp. 59–60, 62.

66 Ogier, 'Guernsey's parishes', pp. 340–1.

67 Changes other than these were slow to follow, partly because many of Guernsey's clergy in the late seventeenth and eighteenth centuries were Protestant refugees from France who had no experience of Anglicanism. For details of the persistence of Calvinist ways, see Marr, *History of Guernsey*, pp. 37–40.

68 IA, DC/HX 061–05. The title of *collecteur* had not disappeared with the Reformation. Throughout the Presbyterian era, the parish registers of St Saviours and St Martins had recorded the accounts of *collecteurs* and *trésoriers*, though the duties of these officers appeared to concern church maintenance rather than the poor. In 1632, after some confusion in St Peter Port, the Royal Court decreed that those who collected funds for church upkeep should uniformly be known as *collecteurs* throughout the island. (This information, and other data on seventeenth-century *collecteurs* and *procureurs* in this paragraph, originates from a personal communication with Dr D.M. Ogier.)

69 2.1.1863, IA, DC/HX 054–05.

Mogeur, authorised by the Court to act as St Peter Port's *procureur pour les biens du Thesor et des Povres* [*sic*] in February 1669. These *Procureurs*, whom subsequent records show managing poor funds and representing parish interests in poor-related disputes and litigation, were at one remove further from the poor than *Collecteurs*,[70] who continued to do all the day-to-day work of collection and distribution previously performed by the deacons. In the later seventeenth and eighteenth centuries, St Peter Port seems to have had six *Collecteurs*, and each of the country parishes four. No parish appears to have had more than one *Procureur*.

The abandonment of Presbyterian forms did not, however, mean that poor relief was secularised. The fact that post-Restoration relief officers were sworn into office by the Ecclesiastical Court shows that their work was still regarded as belonging to the ecclesiastical sphere. In general terms, the fuzzy boundary between the ecclesiastical and the secular which had been a feature of Presbyterian Guernsey persisted long beyond the Restoration. In England, by contrast, the obligation imposed on parishes to perform secular tasks delegated by central government had by this time led to the development of a discrete set of civil parochial structures.[71] These, moreover, now encompassed welfare, which had explicitly been brought under secular jurisdiction when the English poor relief system was placed under the supervision of JPs.[72]

Throughout the seventeenth century, poor relief funds in all of Guernsey's parishes still seem to have emanated entirely from church collections, donations and bequests, fines and *le bien des pauvres*. While they were not being taxed for the poor, however, Guernsey's seventeenth-century parishioners were being taxed for other parochial purposes. In St Peter Port, records survive of a tax in 1608 for the building of a parochial charnel house, and of taxes in 1674 and 1678 to finance repairs to the parish church.[73] From 1715 onwards, St Peter Port's *Douzaine* began to record all parochial taxes in a series of dedicated 'Tax Books'.[74] These books log increasingly frequent taxes for all sorts of parochial purposes, both ecclesiastical and secular.

It is perhaps not surprising, therefore, that, in 1724, St Peter Port became the first parish in Guernsey to levy a rate for the poor.[75] Rating for the poor had long since become almost universal in English parishes.[76] Its adoption in St Peter Port can be traced to economic factors. The 1720s were years of dearth throughout Europe. In adjacent Lower Normandy, as in most parts of France, the harvest of 1723 had

[70] To match practice adopted for other parochial titles in this book, the names of these officers will henceforth appear with an initial capital.
[71] Slack, *Poverty and Policy*, p. 131.
[72] Slack, *Poverty and Policy*, pp. 114, 131.
[73] Ogier, 'Guernsey's parishes', pp. 340–2; ord, 4.5.1678.
[74] IA, AQ 1002/03.
[75] While 'rate' is the English term for such a levy, Guernsey's records were kept in French and the term *taxe* was used in most pre-twentieth-century parish registers. After English became widely spoken in the nineteenth century, however, the word 'rate' was more generally favoured in everyday contexts. For the purposes of this book, the terms 'rate' and 'tax' will be used interchangeably in respect of parochial levies.
[76] The larger English towns all levied poor rates by 1600, one-third of English parishes levied them by 1660, and, by 1700, the practice was all but general (Slack, *Poverty and Policy*, p. 170).

been particularly bad, and was doubtless also bad in Guernsey.[77] On 29 October 1724, a St Peter Port parish meeting heard that the needs of the poor were becoming urgent and funds from the usual voluntary sources had run out. The *Procureur* had advanced his own cash to fill the deficit and required reimbursement. It was resolved at the meeting that 4,000 *livres tournois* (about £285 sterling) should be raised for the poor by means of a rate, to which a total of 475 parishioners contributed.[78]

Meanwhile, at island-wide level, the States, to which regulation of grain supplies in times of dearth had been specifically reserved in 1607,[79] themselves responded to the food shortage by taking action to procure emergency supplies.[80] Initially, the States had intended to fund these supplies from the harbour dues. Objections seem to have arisen, however, and it was subsequently resolved that each individual parish should pay for its own share of the emergency grain, with authorisation to levy a tax to fund the expense, if required.[81] This opened a further branch of parochial aid to the poor. From this time on, while the States might instigate emergency imports, the costs of such imports were always paid by the parishes. Individual parishes evolved their own ways of covering these costs, but, in St Peter Port at least, they were not charged to the poor rate until 1812.

The advent of poor rates in St Peter Port (of which there were ten in the fifteen years following 1724)[82] seems to have led to a tightening of the town parish's policy towards the poor. In 1730, a parish meeting decided that 'permanent' parochial paupers should be provided with distinctive clothing. Some twenty-eight people were to be supplied with kersey outer garments (blue for the under-40s, grey for the over-40s) and white shirts and shifts.[83] The outfits of the under-40s were to be prominently emblazoned with the words 'St. Pierre Port'. The idea may have been borrowed from England, where a statute of 1697 had required relief recipients to wear a badge bearing a large 'P' (for 'pauper') and the name or initial of their parish. The 1697 Act has been interpreted as designed to 'humiliate and deter' the poor.[84] It is possible that pauper uniforms also had something of this function in St Peter Port. Equally, their introduction may have aimed to set a demarcation between paupers the town acknowledged as its own and the many alms-seekers now arriving from other parishes.

The principle of demarcation had been clearly set by a major ordinance passed on 18 April 1726, shortly after St Peter Port's first poor rate. From that time on, islanders who moved from one parish to another had to acquire a certificate from

---

[77] R.M. Schwartz, *Policing the Poor in Eighteenth-Century France* (Chapel Hill, 1988), p. 69.

[78] 29.10.1724, St Peter Port Délibérations des Chefs de Famille, 1715–79, PL.

[79] R.P. Hocart, *An Island Assembly: The Development of the States of Guernsey, 1700–1949* (Guernsey, 1988), p. 4.

[80] *Acte*, 15.7.1725.

[81] *Acte*, 3.2.1726.

[82] IA, AQ 0988/01.

[83] 4.3.1730, St Peter Port Délibérations des Chefs de Famille, 1715–79, PL. Kersey was a coarse woollen fabric akin to serge.

[84] J. Styles, *The Dress of the People: Everyday Fashion in Eighteenth-Century England* (London, 2007), p. 272.

the authorities of their new parish officially accepting them as parishioners.[85] Such an acceptance would confer *un établissement* and, with it, eligibility to apply for relief in the new parish. In this case, there is no doubt that the term was borrowed from England, where the 1662 Act of Settlement and successor Acts had created an entitlement to relief in one's 'parish of legal settlement' on fulfilment of certain criteria.[86] The 1726 ordinance also applied to strangers who moved to Guernsey parishes from outside the island. However, such strangers could solicit a certificate of parochial acceptance only once they had formally been *reçus habitants* (constituted denizens) of Guernsey. The ordinance thus also set out a procedure by which non-natives could acquire the status of denizens. The procedure was an onerous one requiring the support of the Royal Court and the Governor, so that it effectively erected a barrier against poor strangers ever acquiring an entitlement to relief.

In the mid-1730s, St Peter Port's ratepayers expressed a desire to stop levying poor rates and revert to voluntary contributions for the poor. For a couple of years, they managed to raise the equivalent of about £185 sterling annually by voluntary means. This, however, proved insufficient, and in September 1738, a parish meeting heard that funds for the poor were again completely exhausted. It was at this point that ratepayers decided their interests would best be served by building a workhouse. It was hoped that such an institution would obviate any future need for rates. Admission to the workhouse would become the only form of relief, and, once inside, the product of inmates' labour would pay for their keep. Accordingly, on 5 October 1738, a further parish meeting agreed to levy an annual tax of 4,000 *livres tournois* for the next few years, both to cover ongoing relief costs and to accumulate funds for the construction of a workhouse. The product of the rates was to be complemented by private subscriptions.[87] Some time elapsed before sufficient funds had been built up, but the workhouse was eventually opened in 1743.

Guernsey's country parishes, whose resources were more limited than St Peter Port's, had shown a marked disinclination to follow the town's rate-raising example. Rural parochial records for this period are lacunary, but, taking St Saviours as an example, the earliest surviving record of a tax which could be said, at least indirectly, to have been for the poor came after parishes had been made responsible for their own emergency grain costs: on 11 October 1726, St Saviours levied a tax to make up losses incurred on selling imported grain to poor parishioners at below cost price. St Saviours' first true poor rate (in the sense that it seems to have covered routine poor-related expenditure) came as late as 10 November 1744 and raised 350 *livres tournois* (£25 sterling).[88] It was not repeated for several years. St Saviours appears to have been among the first of the country parishes to have levied such a rate.

---

[85] A direct line can be traced between this and Presbyterian poor-related legislation regarding strangers and natives who moved between parishes (see above, n. 59).

[86] K.D.M. Snell, *Parish and Belonging: Community, Identity and Welfare in England and Wales, 1700–1950* (Cambridge, 2006), pp. 85–6.

[87] 15.6.1737, 21.9.1738, 5.10.1738, St Peter Port Délibérations des Chefs de Famille, 1715–79, PL.

[88] IA, AQ 0116/01.

Having taken their decision to invest substantial sums in a workhouse, St Peter Port began to exert pressure on the country parishes to do more for their own poor, who were still flowing into town. From the late 1730s, the 1726 'settlement' ordinance was more stringently enforced, and, in November 1741, a St Peter Port parish meeting decided to give all natives of other parishes living in town three months to obtain a certificate of parochial acceptance, or otherwise return home.[89] The urban-dominated Royal Court further added to the pressure by ordering parishes to submit lists of their regular relief recipients and accounts of their annual receipts for the poor in what it said was a preliminary to the introduction of more rigorous regulations.[90]

The intention behind such pressure seems to have been to induce the country parishes to follow St Peter Port's lead and establish their own rural workhouse. The rigorous regulations threatened by the Court never materialised. Instead, in January 1748, plans for a country workhouse were laid before a rural audience at a St Martins parish meeting.[91] Having approved in principle the idea of a jointly run rural workhouse, St Martins resolved to begin negotiations with other parishes to see whether such a project could be realised.[92] In due course, another six of the nine rural parishes were persuaded to join the scheme, and the foundation deed of what became known as the 'Country Hospital' was signed on 6 April 1751.[93] Although the Hospital's future running costs were to be met by the seven participating parishes, St Peter Port made a tellingly large contribution to its construction.[94]

Once in operation, the new institution, centrally located in the Castel parish, was chiefly to be funded by twice-yearly payments from each parish set according to the value of the property on which individual parishes were assessed for island-wide general taxes. These payments became known as *les demi-années*. Annual sums payable ranged from a maximum of £35 15s (Castel, St Saviours) to a minimum of £11 (Torteval, St Sampsons).[95] Any shortfall in the Hospital's budget was to be made up by extraordinary levies at a uniform rate in each parish. From the beginning, these levies took place regularly and, as *les demi-années* remained at the same level

---

[89] 18.11.1741, St Peter Port Délibérations des Chefs de Famille, 1715–79, PL.
[90] Ords, 7.4.1746, 27.4.1747, Jugements, Ordonnances et Ordres du Conseil, November 1745–April 1757, Greffe.
[91] St Martins had in the past possessed its own parochial poorhouse, as had also St Peters, whose poorhouse was still in operation in the mid-1700s. These, however, were no more than cottages, with space for only two or three paupers (T.F. Priaulx, 'Les pauvres', *Quarterly Review of the Guernsey Society*, 24 (1968), p. 35; M. Brock, 'La maison des pauvres, St Peters', *Quarterly Review of the Guernsey Society*, 18 (1962), pp. 4–6).
[92] 8.1.1748, IA, AQ 0767/10.
[93] IA, DC/HX 044–01. The original signatories were St Martins, St Saviours, St Andrews, Castel, the Vale, St Sampsons and Torteval. The Forest eventually joined the scheme in 1769 and St Peters in 1798, when it closed its parochial poorhouse (IA, DC/HX 272–06).
[94] Contemporary sources claim that around £1,000 sterling was contributed by the 'Gentlemen of the Town' (T. Dicey, *An Historical Account of Guernsey* (London, 1751), p. 196; *The Case of the Town Parish versus the Nine Country Parishes respecting a Change in the Rates and Representation, appointed to be heard before the Committee of the Privy Council at 11 o'clock, on Thursday April 26, 1759*, p. 18, PL).
[95] IA, AQ 0511/04.

for the entire duration of the Hospital's existence, extraordinary levies eventually yielded far more than set payments.

Building of the Country Hospital began in April 1752 and was completed by November 1753. However, the Hospital remained unoccupied until 1756 (presumably to avoid running costs). At this time the Seven Years War began, and the rural parishes – much to St Peter Port's chagrin – converted the conveniently empty Hospital into barracks to accommodate their quota of soldiers sent over for the war, to finance whose lodgings they would otherwise have had to raise a tax.[96]

The Hospital building was repaired at the end of the war, and St Peter Port finally had the satisfaction of seeing forty paupers from the seven participating parishes admitted in December 1764.[97] From this point onward most of the rural parishes began, at least intermittently, to levy poor rates, pushed to do so by the obligation to contribute to Hospital running costs. In St Saviours, poor rates became annual from 1764.[98] In many of the smaller parishes, however, rating remained sporadic for decades to come. St Andrews levied its first poor rate in 1764, but the next came only in 1774.[99] As late as 1815, Thomas Quayle reported that there were still some Guernsey parishes which did not raise a poor rate every year.[100]

Even so, Guernsey's parochial poor relief system had, by the 1760s, broadly achieved the form it was to retain for the next century and a half – still an ecclesiastical matter, largely unencumbered by legislation, and with facilities for both residential ('indoor') and non-residential ('outdoor') relief. The next chapter will look in detail at how the provision of outdoor relief went on to develop after the foundation of Guernsey's workhouses.

---

[96] *Case of the Town Parish versus the Nine Country Parishes*, p. 19. Until the building of Fort George in the late eighteenth century, islanders were required to provide quarters for soldiers who could not be accommodated at Castle Cornet. Each parish had its quota of soldiers, for whose lodgings at public houses and in the homes of private householders parochial authorities had to pay (Hocart, *Island Assembly*, p. 6.)

[97] J. Jeremie, *Historical Account of the Island of Guernsey* (Guernsey, 1821), pp. 183–4; Duncan, *History of Guernsey*, p. 502.

[98] IA, AQ 0116/02.

[99] IA, AQ 0208/08.

[100] T. Quayle, *A General View of the Agriculture and Present State of the Islands on the Coast of Normandy subject to the Crown of Great Britain* (London, 1815), p. 289.

4

Outdoor Relief, Mid-Eighteenth to Mid-Twentieth Centuries

Insular framework

General considerations

The mid-eighteenth-century founders of the Town and Country Hospitals had hoped that their institutions would obviate any future need for outdoor relief. However, practical considerations ensured that this form of relief did not cease, and indeed continued to be dispensed by Guernsey's parishes for the next 250 years. Since the nature of outdoor relief differed between St Peter Port and the country parishes, the relief regimes of town and country will be analysed separately. There was, nevertheless, an all-island framework under which all parishes nominally operated, so we will begin with an examination of this.

Unlike in England and Wales, the law played a minimal part in Guernsey's poor relief framework. In the former jurisdiction, the relief system had been created by statute, and was subject to legal oversight, so that, by the late 1700s, a compilation of poor law statutes and judicial decisions filled three volumes.[1] In Guernsey, by contrast, most poor-related ordinances passed between the sixteenth and eighteenth centuries were *ad hoc* and temporary, forgotten once the problems which had given rise to them had passed, only for similar ordinances to be issued when new problems arose. As late as the mid-nineteenth century, there was no single reference source for any of Guernsey's ordinances. A Royal Commission investigating the island's criminal law in 1846 observed that ordinances were 'scattered about' in all sorts of registers, and not 'properly collected'.[2] Only after the Royal Commission's visit was an effort made to compile past ordinances, and even then the compilations were far from exhaustive.[3] In the absence of any poor law digests or compendia up to this point, there cannot be said to have been a gradually accumulating body of poor law in the English sense.

---

1   E. Bott (ed. F. Const) *The Laws Relating to the Poor*, 3 vols (1771; London, 1807 edn).
2   *Second Report of the Commissioners appointed to inquire into the State of the Criminal Law of the Channel Islands* (London, 1848), p. 137.
3   Printed selections of ordinances issued from the sixteenth century onwards began to be published in 1852 under the title *Recueils d'Ordonnances*.

Instead, the day-to-day administration of parochial welfare was based on unwritten custom. At our mid-eighteenth-century starting point, each parish had a number of unpaid officers with poor relief responsibilities: *Collecteurs*, six in St Peter Port and four in the country parishes, who took collections and worked directly with the poor; and the *Procureur*, who represented parish interests in dealings with other bodies and exercised general supervision over poor relief matters. These officers, who had periodically to submit their accounts for public audit, were elected for varying terms by parochial *Chefs de Famille*.[4] Their work extended only to the native poor. Constables, because of their public order duties, had special responsibility for needy strangers.

Parochial taxation

Once poor rates (and other rates) had become common in all parishes, the practice for levying them was broadly as follows: in the first instance, *Douzaines* set the amount to be collected and agreed on a list of ratepayers. The proposed rate was then discussed at a parish meeting, and *Chefs de Famille* voted to approve or disapprove. If the rate was approved, an application was made to the Royal Court for a *remède* or permission to levy a tax.[5]

Those whom the *Douzaine* placed on the tax list were assessed on the value of all their capital assets, real and personal.[6] This form of taxation was particularly suited to Guernsey's rural economy, where many owned the property on which they lived, but few had a cash income of any size. Property values were expressed for tax in quarters of wheat – that is, in terms of what the land would yield.[7] The amount to be paid in rates was fixed by individual *Douzaines* at so much per quarter of property. This amount was always higher in St Peter Port than in the country parishes. In 1833, St Peter Port ratepayers paid 8d in rates on every quarter they owned, but rural ratepayers paid only 3d or 4d a quarter.[8] Thus a St Peter Port ratepayer owning property worth twenty-five quarters paid about 17s 6d in rates (25 × 8d). However,

---

4 *Chefs de Famille* were adult male ratepayers, who are estimated have comprised, on average, two-thirds of ratepayers in each parish. Until a law of 1892 extended the parochial vote to ratepaying unmarried women, widows and women legally separated from their husbands, they were the only parishioners entitled to speak and vote at parish meetings (R.P. Hocart, *An Island Assembly: The Development of the States of Guernsey, 1700–1949* (Guernsey, 1988), pp. 34, 71).

5 *Billet*, 18.3.1834 states that the purpose of a *remède* was to 'verify the legality of the deliberations and the observation of due form'.

6 This was different from the way in which poor rates were raised in England and Wales, where from the late seventeenth century, the usual practice was to rate occupiers of real property on the annual rental value of the property they occupied (P.A. Slack, *Poverty and Policy in Tudor and Stuart England* (Harlow, 1988), p. 174). Rating practice in Guernsey was closer to the situation in Scotland before the introduction of the new Scottish poor law in 1845. Here, although poor rates were infrequent, the burden of taxation fell on the 'heritors' (landowners) of a parish who were assessed on the basis of the landed property they owned (R. Mitchison, 'The making of the old Scottish poor law', *Past & Present*, 63 (1974), p. 67).

7 A Guernsey quarter was equivalent to three Winchester bushels (W. Berry, *The History of the Island of Guernsey* (London, 1815), p. 118).

8 28.3.1833, IA, AQ 0965/02.

a country parishioner owning property to the same value paid half that sum or less (25 × 3d or 4d).[9]

Prior to 1868, all parochial rates were levied on this basis. After that date, a new law divided parochial rates into two classes.[10] The first class, destined for the poor, church upkeep and education, was levied, as previously, on real and personal property. The second class, for minor objects such as pumps and street cleaning, was based on the annual rental income, or potential income, arising from real property. It was leviable in the first instance on owners, though occupiers could be required, if the proprietor wished, to reimburse two-thirds of the amount levied.[11]

In England and Wales, the threshold for payment of poor rates was low. Relief to the poor was mainly funded by the marginally less poor.[12] Before the Poor Law Amendment Act of 1834, anyone not in receipt of relief was potentially liable to be rated.[13] After 1834, it became increasingly common to rate even those on relief.[14] This was far from the case in Guernsey. Thresholds for taxation were entirely a matter of custom, and varied between parishes. *Douzaines* also exercised a certain amount of discretion, and, because payment of rates gave adult men a vote in parish affairs (and, later, a theoretical entitlement to poor relief), they were careful whom they taxed. In England and Wales in 1845, about 20 per cent of the total population paid the poor rate.[15] The proportion in Guernsey was 6 per cent in 1836, rising to 10 per cent in 1905.[16]

Settlement and deportation legislation

The ordinance of 18 April 1726 had made eligibility for parochial relief conditional on having what was called a 'settlement' in the parish where relief was sought. Birth in a parish conferred a *de facto* settlement, but islanders could acquire settlement in a parish other than that of their birth on being granted a certificate of acceptance by the authorities of that parish. Strangers, too, could apply for such a certificate, but they had first to be formally constituted denizens (*reçus habitants*). Since the denization process was all but inaccessible to poor strangers, this effectively rendered them permanently ineligible for relief in any of Guernsey's parishes.

---

[9]   In 1833, twenty-five quarters equated to £500. By this point, property was normally valued in money and converted back into quarters at a standard rate of £20 per quarter (F.B. Tupper, *The History of Guernsey and its Bailiwick* (Guernsey, 1854), p. 458).

[10] O in C, 30.7.1868.

[11] We should note, however, that, some twenty years after the 1868 law was passed, second-class rates were only levied in St Peter Port (J.L. Pitts, *Guernsey and its Bailiwick: A Guide and a Gossip* (Guernsey, 1890), p. 54).

[12] J. Innes, 'The state and the poor: eighteenth-century England in historical perspective', in J. Brewer and E. Hellmuth (eds), *Rethinking Leviathan: The Eighteenth-Century State in Britain and Germany* (Oxford, 1999), pp. 260–61.

[13] S.A. King, *Poverty and Welfare in England, 1700–1850: A Regional Perspective* (Manchester, 2000), p. 114.

[14] K.D.M. Snell, *Annals of the Labouring Poor: Social Change and Agrarian England, 1660–1900* (Cambridge, 1985), p. 110.

[15] Anon., *The Local Taxes of the United Kingdom* (London, 1846), pp. 186–7.

[16] *The Guernsey and Jersey Magazine*, 5 (1838), pp. 297–8; *Billet*, 11.10.1905. See also R.-M. Crossan, *Guernsey, 1814–1914: Migration and Modernisation* (Woodbridge, 2007), p. 153.

The concept of settlement was gradually developed through a series of laws passed in 1770, 1778, 1821 and 1867. These will be analysed first, and then we shall turn to the deportation laws, which were the principal means by which Guernsey dealt with strangers ineligible for help.

Increasing non-observance of the cumbersome 1726 parochial certification law led in 1770 to an attempt to replace it with an ordinance granting native incomers to a parish 'settled' status on completion of seven consecutive years' residence, after which the parish would be obliged to relieve them, as also their children.[17] Alarmed at the mention of children at a time when large numbers of them were being born to in-migrants to St Peter Port, the town *Douzaine* objected.[18] The ordinance was swiftly withdrawn and replaced with another reinstating certification and explicitly ruling that children would henceforth be deemed settled not in their birthplaces, but in the parishes where their fathers were legally settled.[19]

Dissatisfaction with the certification system continued, however, and in 1778 it was abolished. A new settlement ordinance was issued which replaced certification with a procedure whereby natives and strangers *reçus habitants* could 'earn' settlement in a new parish by fulfilling one or more of a set of practical conditions.[20] These conditions were essentially an adaptation of similar provisions established by Westminster's 1662 Act of Settlement and subsequent settlement statutes.[21] Under the 1778 ordinance, any native or *habitant* moving to a new parish and buying a house there worth at least 500 *livres tournois* (about £40 sterling), or building a house of similar value on land he had bought in the parish, acquired a settlement in that parish on having lived in the house for a year and a day. For those moving to new parishes who purchased neither houses nor land, settled status would be acquired after fourteen consecutive years' residence. Apprentices serving their terms in new parishes would acquire settlement after seven consecutive years' with their master, likewise servants, who acquired settlement after seven years with a single employer, or fourteen years if they worked for more than one. Finally, the ordinance restated the provision that all legitimate children, wherever born, would take their fathers' settlement, adding that illegitimate children would take their mothers'. The ordinance was silent on married women, presumably on the assumption that, once married, a woman's identity was subsumed under her husband's and she simply acquired his settlement. The net effect of the 1778 ordinance was to make the acquisition of new settlements time-consuming for all natives save those able to buy

---

[17] Ord, 22.1.1770.

[18] 21.1.1770, IA, DC/HX 079–01.

[19] Ord, 23.4.1770.

[20] Ord, 5.10.1778.

[21] By this time, the principal ways in which one could earn a settlement in a new parish in England and Wales were as follows: by owning real property within the parish; by renting property in the parish with a minimum annual rental value of £10; by paying parish rates; by serving a public annual office in the parish; by service in the parish for a full year while married, and by serving a legal indentured apprenticeship and residing in the parish for forty days during one's term (K.D.M. Snell, *Parish and Belonging: Community, Identity and Welfare in England and Wales, 1700–1950* (Cambridge, 2006), pp. 85–6).

property, and to leave all strangers who had not been *reçus habitants* ineligible for relief.

In 1821, with post-Napoleonic immigration in full spate, the matter of settlement was addressed once more. A fresh ordinance was issued which again restricted the acquisition of new settlements to natives and those *reçus habitants*, while making the 1778 provisions more stringent by abolishing the acquisition of settlement through buying or building a house and increasing the time it took apprentices and servants to earn settlements in new parishes.[22] The one provision which appeared slightly to improve matters was an entirely new one conferring settlement on the payment of parish rates. In theory, this provision applied to strangers as well as natives. In practice, any gains to the former were negated by the spur given *Douzaines* to exclude them from their tax lists.

The 1821 ordinance remained in force for forty-six years. It was replaced in 1867 with Guernsey's fifth and final settlement law.[23] This law differed from preceding ones in a number of ways. It was the first to take the form of an Order in Council, and the first to deal with settlement in the whole Bailiwick, rather than Guernsey alone.[24] It also addressed for the first time the status of married women.[25] More importantly, while retaining paternal inheritance as the basis for settlement, the 1867 law finally rescinded the principle first set in 1726 by offering not just natives and *habitants* the chance to acquire settlements in the various prescribed ways, but extended this facility to all British subjects. Thus, as of 1867, any native or any incomer from the United Kingdom could earn a settlement as follows: by paying tax in a new parish; by occupying as sole tenant for ten years a house or houses in the parish with a minimum annual rental of £12; by buying real estate worth a minimum of seven quarters (c. £140) in the parish and residing in it for three years; by serving a five-year apprenticeship in the parish and residing in it for a further five years before reaching the age of thirty; or by working as a domestic or farm servant in the parish for ten years after the age of twenty, but only if unmarried.

As is obvious, however, these conditions were quite onerous and still left many migrants (and their children) unable to gain a settlement in Guernsey. Much the most significant of all the changes embodied in the 1867 law was therefore the entirely new provision which allowed any stranger who had lived in the Bailiwick for twenty consecutive years after coming of age to acquire settlement in the parish where they had resided longest.[26] A similar provision also applied to the Bailiwick-born children of migrants, who were to be deemed settled in the parish where

---

[22] Ord, 30.4.1821.

[23] O in C, 26.6.1867.

[24] For the purposes of the 1867 law, all provisions which applied to Guernsey's ten parishes also applied to Sark and Alderney (which were component parishes of the Guernsey Deanery on an equal ecclesiastical footing with the others). For more on poor relief in these islands, see Appendix 3.

[25] Under the new law, a woman would assume her husband's settlement on marriage, and, in the event of his death or desertion, she would be deemed to belong to the parish in which her spouse was settled at the time of this event.

[26] So long as no public relief had been received, save in case of illness or accident.

they had accrued most residence after having lived for twenty years in the Baili-wick from the date of their birth. For the next forty years, Guernsey's parochial authorities maintained (by analogy with the other criteria) that only subjects of Her Majesty could acquire settlement through residence, notwithstanding that this was not explicit in the wording of the law. This situation was ultimately reversed in 1909, when a legal challenge was mounted against the deportation of an Italian who had lived in Guernsey for forty-seven years.[27] From this point onwards, migrants from anywhere in the world could, in theory, gain a settlement through twenty years' unbroken residence on the same terms as the British.[28]

After 1867, there were no further changes to the criteria for acquisition of settle-ment. The only slight modification of the law came in 1925, when settlement was made insular rather than parochial after the States took over the funding of poor relief from the parishes.[29]

What, then, became of all the strangers in need of relief who were for so long denied a settlement in Guernsey?

Before the mid-1700s, when large-scale immigration first began, poor strangers were only intermittently a problem. Those targeted by poor-related ordinances were mainly destitute refugees from famines, wars or religious upheavals in France. They were unwelcome, and the remedy prescribed by the ordinances was simple: expul-sion and/or punishment.[30] From the 1760s, with numbers of sojourning entrepôt workers on the rise, experiments were made with more sophisticated measures. An ordinance of 1767 stipulated that anyone importing non-local workers should deposit surety with the Crown Officers against their requiring relief.[31] Another of 1772 insisted that workmen arriving in Guernsey should produce a letter from their parishes of settlement accepting liability in case of need, or, failing this, identify their settlements on oath.[32] Later ordinances repeated these measures in different permutations, and an ordinance of 1786 reiterated provisions for all three.[33] This, however, was the last such law. The fast-growing migrant contingent made such measures unworkable, and, by the close of the century, all experiments had been abandoned.

At this point, the older type of stranger ordinance was resurrected. With the French Wars at their height in the late 1700s and early 1800s, the Royal Court passed several ordinances aimed chiefly at intercepting undesirables from France. One of 1801 was typical in authorising Constables summarily to expel any newly

[27] *Guernsey Evening Press*, 18.5.1909. See also Crossan, *Guernsey, 1814–1914*, pp. 180–1.
[28] In England and Wales the principle had been established as early as 1803 that any foreigner could gain a settlement on the same terms as a native, and, since 1876, a mere three years in one parish had conferred settlement (A.F. Vulliamy, *The Law of Settlement and Removal of Paupers* (1895; London, 1906 edn), p. 81; Snell, *Parish and Belonging*, p. 116).
[29] O in C, 24.7.1925.
[30] See, for instance, ords, 1.10.1537, 21.1.1589, 15.4.1611, 26.1.1685.
[31] Ord, 30.5.1767.
[32] Ord, 27.4.1772.
[33] Ord, 23.5.1786.

arrived stranger they might deem potentially troublesome.[34] Within a short space of time, these simple and expeditious powers became the standard way to deal with all unwanted strangers.

With numbers of poor English migrants escalating at the end of the Wars, the settlement ordinance of 1821 restated and refined Constables' powers of expulsion. This ordinance charged Constables actively to prevent the long-term settling of strangers whose presence might prove vexatious. It recommended particularly vigorous exercise of the power to expel on or around a stranger's arrival, but set no time limit beyond which expulsion should not be used. Within two decades, as visiting Royal Commissioners learned in 1846, summary powers enshrined in the 1821 ordinance were being widely exercised in respect of any non-local who 'applies for relief, or who is in such a situation that the Constable thinks it necessary to relieve him'.[35] Moreover, while the ordinance nominally gave deportees a right of appeal to the Court, they were seldom informed of this, and, if the Court intervened, it was usually to approve 'an application by the Constables to compel the departure of those who refuse obedience to their orders'. The Commissioners found this situation objectionable, concluding that 'being a stranger and in want comes to be considered in the nature of an offence to be treated with more or less rigour at the discretion of the Constables'.[36]

In this the Commissioners were correct, since the 1821 law and its predecessors were broadly analogous to English vagrancy laws which made it a crime for a person to wander from place to place without visible means of support. In England, however, the 1662 Act of Settlement had instituted a formal separation between criminal vagrancy and work-related mobility by providing a procedure whereby migrants who fell into pecuniary distress could be removed to their home parishes and then compulsorily relieved in them.[37] By the time the Royal Commissioners made their comments, English settlement and vagrancy law had branched into two quite distinct paths, and migrants could be removed to their settlements only after a judicial hearing and the issue of a removal order by one or more JPs. Such orders doubled as orders of maintenance on the receiving parishes.[38]

Despite criticism by the Royal Commission, Guernsey never introduced any

---

34 Ord, 19.1.1801.

35 *Second Report of the Commissioners*, p. xxviii.

36 *Second Report of the Commissioners*, p. xxviii.

37 Slack, *Poverty and Policy*, p. 31; A.L. Beier, *Masterless Men: The Vagrancy Problem in England, 1560–1640* (London, 1985), pp. 171, 173.

38 This process was so expensive and time-consuming that poor law authorities often hesitated to use it, with the result that, by the 1840s, fewer than 4 per cent of relief applicants were removed. The proportion further decreased after a statute of 1846 introduced the concept of 'irremovability' under which a fixed period of residence in a parish gave non-settled relief applicants immunity from removal. The Irremovability Act of 1846 set this period at five years; an Act of 1861 reduced it to three years, and, by 1865, any pauper could apply for relief in a new parish without risking removal if they could prove continuous residence (by now in any parish within one union rather than a single parish) for just twelve months (M.E. Rose, 'Settlement, removal and the New Poor Law', in D. Fraser (ed.), *The New Poor Law in the Nineteenth Century* (London, 1976), p. 27; Snell, *Parish and Belonging*, pp. 116–17).

laws regulating the modalities of pauper deportation. Indeed, the sole effect of the Commissioners' comments seems to have been to prompt parochial authorities increasingly to arm themselves with Court orders in potentially contentious cases, such as those involving the disabled, sick, very old and very young, particularly where admission to an institution was envisaged. In spite of this development, fewer than 700 individuals were removed by Act of Court in the period between 1814 and 1914, while the number summarily deported exceeded 10,000.[39]

In the late nineteenth century, the time limit for summary deportation was reduced to a year and a day of a stranger's arrival.[40] In 1925, the authority to deport was removed from the Constables, and transferred to the newly constituted States' Central Poor Law Board.[41] In 1937, it passed to the Stranger Poor Assistance Committee of the States' Public Assistance Authority, which was expressly directed by article 12 of the new Public Assistance Law to 'consider the advisability of repatriation' in each stranger case.[42] After World War II, developments in social security rendered pauper deportations rare. Nevertheless, at the time of writing (2015), the 1937 law still stands in amended form. In an anodyne throwback to a less beneficent age, it is used to repatriate stranded non-locals who lack the funds to go home.[43]

States' involvement in poor relief

The role of the States in funding and co-ordinating poor relief is another aspect of the all-island framework which requires examination. At the beginning of the period covered by this chapter, the States played no part in welfare matters and exhibited no desire to increase their involvement.[44]

The first modern departure from this *status quo* came in the 1780s. The change was initiated by St Peter Port's resentment at having to fund the temporary relief and repatriation of sick or stranded garrison dependants. St Peter Port hosted the bulk of the garrison and, in the 1760s and 1770s, it had repeatedly petitioned the States for the burden to be shared. Initially, the States had ordered the country parishes to take a set quota of destitute military wives and children.[45] However, this arrangement proved a source of contention and, in 1788, the States finally decided to assume the burden themselves. The rationale on which they reconciled themselves to accepting this charge was that it was an appropriate all-island *quid pro quo* for Westminster's commitment to insular defence. The agreement was enshrined in an Act of the States.[46] In 1828, it was reworked in an ordinance, whereby the States undertook to

---

[39] Acts of Court are recorded in the *Livres en Crime* and registers of ordinances at the Greffe. Deportations are listed in IA, AQ 0999/01. For detailed analysis of both of these sources, see Crossan, *Guernsey, 1814–1914*, pp. 161–8.
[40] Ord, 25.4.1892.
[41] O in C, 13.9.1925.
[42] O in C, 22.10.1937.
[43] *Billet*, 6.3.2012.
[44] There had been some States' welfare activity in Presbyterian times (see n. 212, below), but by the mid-1700s, welfare had long been strictly parochial.
[45] Acts of Court, 7.3.1767, 16.10.1770, 13.3.1787, IA, DC/HX 180–14.
[46] *Acte*, 19.4.1788.

refund parochial expenses incurred in respect of discharged soldiers and their families; dependants of soldiers dying in garrison; destitute naval and military pensioners
and their families; and shipwrecked seamen and sailors.[47]

After 1828, there was no expansion in the States' poor relief role for over sixty
years. The next change to the *status quo* came only in 1892 and concerned non-mil-
itary strangers. St Peter Port, whose population was about 30 per cent composed of
such strangers, had since the 1840s lobbied the States to help with stranger costs
generally. This had been resisted by rural States members, whose parishes hosted few
non-natives. When French immigration to the country parishes increased in the late
nineteenth century their attitude changed and, in 1892, the States passed a majority
vote to reimburse relief and repatriation expenses in respect not just of the military
but of all non-settled strangers.[48]

Given the short shrift meted out to such strangers, this was hardly a major drain
on States' finances. By 1900, stranger relief in all its forms was costing the States no
more than £600 annually. By contrast, the parishes were collectively spending about
£5,000 per year on the relief of native parishioners.[49] St Peter Port, whose spending
accounted for over half of this total, led a campaign over the first two decades of
the twentieth century to persuade the States to assume co-ordination of the whole
of insular poor relief and take over part of its funding.[50] For many years their efforts
were stymied both by the rural parishes' unwillingness to co-operate and by the fact
that States' revenues, still drawn chiefly from the *impôt*, were felt to be unequal to
the burden. Ultimately, the *impasse* was broken by the introduction of a new States'
income tax and the collapse of the parochial welfare funding system.

States' income tax was introduced in 1919,[51] and the collapse of parish welfare
funding was precipitated by an unsuccessful bid a few years later to institute a
parallel parochial income tax. A new parochial income tax law came into force at
the beginning of 1924.[52] However, the law was so badly formulated that the tax
proved impossible to levy.[53] No parochial rates were collected that year, and, without
a source of income, St Peter Port's poor law authorities had by June accumulated
debts of nearly £6,000.[54] By August, the proposed parochial income tax had been
abandoned and a States' committee had been tasked with devising an alternative
solution, this time 'on the basis of the assumption by the States of the whole cost of
the poor'.[55]

The committee's proposals were accepted in the spring of 1925, and this in turn
led to the passage of an entirely new insular poor law.[56] The new law transferred all

---

[47] Ord, 26.3.1828.
[48] Ord, 25.4.1892. For detail, see Crossan, *Guernsey, 1814–1914*, pp. 157–8.
[49] *Billets*, 30.10.1901, 5.7.1905.
[50] *Billets,* 30.12.1903, 5.7.1905, 10.7.1907, 5.6.1908.
[51] O in C, 20.12.1919.
[52] O in C, 11.10.1923.
[53] *Billets*, 16.7.1924, 30.7.1924; Hocart, *Island Assembly*, pp. 101–2.
[54] 30.6.1924, IA, DC/HX 051–01.
[55] *Billet*, 8.10.1924.
[56] *Billet*, 18.3.1925.

poor relief costs, indoor and outdoor, to the States, to whom an ordinance of the following year also transferred ownership of the Town and Country Hospitals.[57] While the law left distribution of relief to parochial authorities, these were henceforth to be supervised by an over-arching States' committee with the power to set maximum rates. This committee took the form of a thirty-nine-member Central Poor Law Board comprising a States-elected President, twenty-four States members and fourteen parochial office-holders. Parochial poor rates, not collected since 1923, were never again levied.

The arrangements of 1925 were to stand for thirteen years. As time went on, the States grew increasingly frustrated at the inability of the Central Poor Law Board, as constituted, to exert sufficient control over the parishes. 'Although we pay the piper, we cannot call the tune', a report observed.[58] A committee was charged with investigating the matter, and further reports followed.[59] The process finally culminated in the 1937 Public Assistance Law, which created a further tier of supervision in the guise of the States' Public Assistance Authority.[60] Under the Authority were several subordinate boards controlling specific branches of relief: the Hospital Board (in charge of both Hospitals), the Children Board, the Stranger Poor Assistance Committee and the Central Outdoor Assistance Board. This last fulfilled the same functions in relation to outdoor relief as had been performed by the 1925 Central Poor Law Board, now abolished. No change was made in funding arrangements, and parochial poor law authorities remained in existence (with increased States representation), retaining responsibility for day-to-day administration of outdoor relief under the new title of 'Parochial Outdoor Assistance Boards'. The States' Public Assistance Authority survived until 2004, and Parochial Outdoor Assistance Boards until 2005.[61]

Such were the all-island structures under which outdoor relief was dispensed from the mid-eighteenth century onwards. It now remains to examine the practical operation of the system at parish level, and we shall begin with the country parishes.

Welfare in practice: the country parishes

Before entering into detail, we should note for the purposes of context that, though small in area, all of Guernsey's country parishes were comparatively large in terms

---

[57] O in C, 24.7.1925; ord, 1.5.1926.
[58] *Billet*, 3.7.1936.
[59] *Billets*, 8.7.1936, 7.10.1936, 30.6.1937.
[60] O in C, 22.10.1937. The term was borrowed from the Public Assistance Committees of county and borough councils to which the 1929 Local Government Act transferred the powers of English and Welsh Poor Law Guardians and Scottish Parochial Boards when they were abolished in 1930, turning poor relief into 'public assistance' and abolishing the term 'pauper'. The same terminological changes were prescribed by the new Guernsey law. For more on the 1929 Act see M.A. Crowther, *The Workhouse System, 1834–1929: The History of an English Social Institution* (1981; London, 1983 edn), p. 109.
[61] *Billet*, 24.4.2005.

of population. Whereas nearly half of English and Welsh parishes had fewer than 300 inhabitants in 1831,[62] none of Guernsey's rural parishes was in this category, and seven out of the nine already contained populations in excess of 1,000. Torteval and the Forest were the smallest parishes, with 378 and 695 inhabitants respectively; Castel and St Martins were the largest, with 1,937 and 1,652.[63]

Taxation and spending

Regular rates began to be levied in the country parishes from the 1760s and, by the early 1800s, most country parishes seem to have levied rates most years. From fairly early on, it became the practice of each parish to levy just one parochial rate each year.[64] This rate covered all parochial purposes, although the bulk was spent on poor relief.[65]

As we saw in Chapter 2, there was an enormous disparity between the collective value of rural and urban assets as assessed for tax. In 1814, the assets of the nine country parishes were collectively valued at approximately £765,440, while those of St Peter Port were valued at £1,834,400, which meant that just 29 per cent of Guernsey's taxable wealth was in rural hands.[66] In later decades, the success of commercial horticulture increased the rural share, but, even as the twentieth century began, residents of the country parishes still held less than half of the island's taxable assets.[67]

For most of the late eighteenth and nineteenth centuries, individual rural ratepayers were also much less wealthy than their urban counterparts. In 1796, the average Vale ratepayer paid tax on 20 quarters' worth of property (equating to about £400); the figure for the average St Peter Port ratepayer the previous year had been 127 quarters (about £2,540).[68] Again, this gulf narrowed as the countryside grew wealthier, but, even in 1899, the average rural ratepayer paid tax on property worth only £1,250, while the average urban ratepayer paid tax on £2,150.[69]

While individual rural ratepayers might pay less, however, a greater proportion of country-dwellers paid tax than did townsfolk. In the mid-1830s, approximately 31 per cent of men aged over 20 paid rates in the country parishes, while the equivalent figure for St Peter Port was around 19 per cent.[70] The greater rural proportion reflected both the wider rural participation in landownership and the lower property thresholds at which country-dwellers were required to pay rates.

[62] N. Longmate, *The Workhouse: A Social History* (London, 1974), p. 25.
[63] *Billet,* 6.10.1831.
[64] *Billet,* 30.10.1901.
[65] Of the £365 raised in the Castel parish in 1860, £10 went on the church and churchyard, £10 on the parish school, £10 on road maintenance, and £335 on welfare (F.F. Dally, *Agriculture of the Channel Islands* (Guernsey, 1860), p. 52).
[66] Berry, *Island of Guernsey*, pp. 126–44, 161.
[67] In the early 1900s, St Peter Port's assets were valued at about £3,143,725 and those of the country parishes at £3,019,400 (*Billet*, 5.7.1905).
[68] 9.5.1795, IA, AQ 1003/04; 30.3.1796, IA, AQ 1132/045.
[69] *Billet*, 30.10.1901.
[70] Estimates based on *Billet*, 6.10.1831 and *The Guernsey and Jersey Magazine*, 5 (1836), pp. 297–8.

Despite the more even spread of burdens, the countryside's lower collective wealth inevitably translated into lower sums raised in poor rates than in St Peter Port, and hence into lower poor relief spending. While St Peter Port raised £4,950 in poor rates in 1879, the nine country parishes raised only £1,709 between them – an average of £189 per parish.[71] As a result, the total amount spent on poor relief in Guernsey's country parishes that year equated to about 2s per parishioner, as compared with 5s in St Peter Port.[72] Both these figures were lower than the 6s 3d per head of population spent in England and Wales that year, and the figure for the countryside strikingly so.[73]

Administration of relief – personnel

From at least the late 1700s, the *Procureur* was the most prestigious of the rural welfare personnel. As well as representing his parish in negotiations with other bodies, he was in overall charge of poor law funds and, as an *ex-officio* member of the Country Hospital Board, arranged admissions, remitted payments and participated in the institution's governance. Rural *Procureurs* sometimes also dispensed relief on a face-to-face basis, usually in emergencies. The role of rural *Collecteurs* was less prestigious but perhaps more onerous. They looked after the day-to-day needs of the local poor, and, in a conflation of the ecclesiastical and secular, gathered in the rates as well as taking church collections.

There was little change in these arrangements until the 1870s, when the States attempted to rationalise rural practice along lines already established in St Peter Port. By a law of 1876, each parish was to have a ten-member 'Poor Law Board' comprising the senior of the two Constables, the *Procureur*, the four *Collecteurs*, one *Douzenier*, the two Churchwardens and the parish Rector, who was to preside over meetings.[74] The inclusion of the last three on country Poor Law Boards demonstrates the enduring ecclesiastical complexion of rural poor relief. These new Boards were to take over management of the *bien des pauvres* and determine the sums to be raised by rate for the poor. *Collecteurs* were to continue visiting the native poor in their own homes, providing them with the relief the Boards had determined. *Procureurs* could provide emergency assistance at their own discretion, but this was subject to subsequent approval by the Board. Henceforth *Procureurs* and *Collecteurs* were to serve no longer than three years before calling for elections. Constables remained responsible for relieving strangers, for which they were answerable to their *Douzaine*.

Matters remained on this footing until 1925, when the Order in Council transferring poor relief funding to the States modified the constitution of the country Poor Law Boards to remove *Collecteurs*, Churchwardens and Rectors, while retaining *Procureurs* as treasurers and secretaries.[75] The removal of *Collecteurs*, Churchwardens

71 *Comet*, 10.3.1880. See also Crossan, *Guernsey, 1814–1914*, p. 154.
72 Guernsey sums have here been converted into sterling for comparative purposes.
73 K. Williams, *From Pauperism to Poverty* (London, 1981), p. 170.
74 O in C, 27.6.1876.
75 O in C, 24.7.1925.

and Rectors from Poor Law Boards marked a historic milestone in that it implicitly drew a line under ecclesiastical participation in Guernsey's parochial poor relief. A further law the next year officially made insular poor relief a secular matter.[76] Another important change resulting from the 1925 law was the withdrawal from Constables of stranger relief responsibilities and the transfer of such responsibilities to the parochial Boards.[77]

With the parishes' rate-raising powers also removed by the 1925 law, the new country Poor Law Boards were effectively only the administrators of relief. Nevertheless, despite the fact that maximum relief rates were now centrally set, they retained extensive discretion over the nature, extent and recipients of relief within their own parishes.

After the removal of *Collecteurs* from parochial Poor Law Boards, this office shrank into obscurity and *Procureurs* assumed the front-line welfare role on their own. To cope with the additional duties, some parishes now began to appoint a second *Procureur*. The Public Assistance Law of 1937 made this arrangement mandatory for the four largest country parishes.[78] In 1950, the States resolved that the five remaining country parishes should also have two *Procureurs*.[79]

In 1937, the Central Poor Law Board was replaced in its outdoor supervisory role by the Central Outdoor Assistance Board acting under the Public Assistance Authority, and the old parish Poor Law Boards were restyled Parochial Outdoor Assistance Boards.[80] These were to be composed of four States members who were also parish residents, the senior Constable and the two *Procureurs* – or the sole *Procureur* plus a ratepayer-elected parishioner. One member from each of the Parochial Boards was to represent their parish on the Central Outdoor Assistance Board. As we have seen, all of these structures, central and parochial, were to endure until the twenty-first century.

Administration of relief – practice

The change of the rural poor law authorities' title to Parochial *Outdoor* Assistance Boards in 1937 partly reflected the fact that, in this year, the country parishes lost direct control of their Hospital, which was removed from the jurisdiction of its original Board and brought under that of a new central Hospital Board, which also managed the Town Hospital and operated under the States' Public Assistance Authority.

Although the country parishes had been disinclined to use the Hospital when it was first built in the 1750s, this institution soon came to play a central role in rural welfare. By 1783, it already accommodated 100 rural parishioners. By 1818, inmate numbers had risen to 180 – a figure which equated to 2 per cent of the country

76 O in C, 30.4.1926.
77 This was one of the first resolutions of the new Central Poor Law Board and also applied to St Peter Port (IA, DC/HX 272–11).
78 St Sampsons, the Vale, Castel and St Martins.
79 *Billet*, 15.2.1950.
80 O in C, 22.10.1937.

population.[81] For later nineteenth-century inmate numbers, we are obliged to rely on census returns, since few of the Hospital's records have survived. Enumerators' books for the six decades between 1841 and 1901 show an average complement of about 150, drawn from all nine parishes roughly in proportion to their size.[82]

As matters turned out, a strong rural predilection for indoor relief was created by the 1752 Hospital funding formula. Parishes paid according to fixed rates and not per inmate, so that the expense was the same whether they admitted one or twenty. Hence the country parishes consigned virtually all of their long-term poor to the Hospital: the chronically sick, the mentally and physically handicapped, the elderly who could no longer live alone, and orphans, widows, abandoned wives and unmarried mothers who were admitted for shorter spells.

Then as now, residential relief was more expensive than domiciliary assistance, but rural indoor expenses were pared to the bone and subsidised in part by the Hospital farm. It consistently cost less to keep an inmate in the Country Hospital than in the Town Hospital: 5¾d per head per day in 1847, as compared with 7d in town; 3s as compared with 3s 5¼d in 1919.[83] By keeping Hospital costs within strict limits, the country parishes effectively kept a check on the rates, since, from the time the parishes began to levy them, the lion's share had gone to the Hospital. As late as 1904, the institution still absorbed almost three-quarters of all rural poor rates.[84]

One consequence of the Hospital's monopoly of poor rates was that outdoor relief, in most rural parishes, was for many decades almost entirely funded from non-rate sources. Each country parish was strongly independent and had its own way of dealing with its outdoor poor. Nevertheless, a pattern emerges which seems to have been common to many. Rural outdoor relief took two main forms: ongoing weekly disbursements to a small number of recipients and more extensive distributions normally coinciding with such festivals as Easter and Christmas. The former were chiefly funded from church-door and poor-box collections, the latter from bequests and donations collected together in *le bien des pauvres*. Typical of Easter and yuletide distributions were the hand-outs of bed linen, clothing, footwear, meat and groceries customarily made to thirty or forty needy families in the Vale.[85] Mass distributions could also take the form of grain, flour, bread or potatoes made available to all the poor of a parish during food shortages.[86]

As for weekly disbursements, with all 'chronic' paupers by and large consigned to the Country Hospital, this went chiefly to what were known as *les pauvres honteux*.[87] Insufficiently helpless to be sent to the workhouse, these *pauvres* limped along

[81] Inmate numbers from J. Jeremie, *An Historical Account of the Island of Guernsey* (Guernsey, 1821), pp. 183–4; country population from *Billet*, 15.9.1821.
[82] Census enumerators' books, 1841–1901 (microfilm), PL.
[83] *Comet*, 13.5.1847; IA, DC/HX 253–02.
[84] *Billet*, 5.7.1906.
[85] IA, AQ 0397/11; IA, AQ 0397/05.
[86] For examples, see 23.3.1757, IA, AQ 0452/02; 20.10.1768, IA, AQ 0208/08; 26.1.1773, IA, AQ 0452/02; 18.12.1816, IA, AQ 0511/04; *Star*, 24.5.1847.
[87] This term, which roughly translates as the 'shame-faced poor', was used all over francophone Europe. Some parishes, such as St Martins, refrained from identifying their *pauvres honteux* by name.

through their own efforts, supplemented by help from kin and sundry other assistance. A country parish's *pauvres honteux* typically fell into two categories. In the first were the elderly folk who received a regular dole – a loaf of bread or a small cash sum every week. In the second were the impoverished families of working age assisted more intermittently with food, fuel, cash or clothing in times of stress or sickness. Typically, a parish would keep a separate list of each.

The number of names on the rural parishes' outdoor lists was low. In the mid-1870s, St Peters, with a population of about 1,150, gave seven or eight named individuals a weekly dole of 6lb of bread and provided another dozen or so with occasional help in the form of small cash sums, meat, bread or flour. They also sent 9d per week to an out-parishioner in St Peter Port.[88]

The country parishes additionally paid for medical services. By the 1840s, all rural parishes appear to have retained their own doctor who treated the poor either on a stipendiary basis or for a set fee per visit.[89] When these doctors' efforts were unsuccessful, parishes would also pay for pauper burials.

Total sums spent on rural outdoor relief were minimal. St Martins was fairly typical of the larger country parishes in spending just £68 on outdoor relief – about 8d for each of its 1,825 parishioners – in the whole of 1846.[90] Expenditure on poor strangers (funded exclusively from the rates) was particularly light, rising from an average yearly total per country parish of about £4 in the 1840s to about £12 in the 1890s.[91]

The poor law practices of country parishes remained largely unaltered for the duration of the nineteenth century. In later decades, slightly fewer rural parishioners were permanently consigned to the Hospital, slightly more parishioners were regularly assisted at home, slightly more help was given in cash form, and ecclesiastical sources of funding were increasingly supplemented by the rates. Nevertheless, an official audit carried out in 1925 showed how little rural habits had essentially changed.[92] In that year, the country parishes collectively spent £6,000 on the Country Hospital, and £6,384 on outdoor relief. Of outdoor spending, 41 per cent went on relief in kind (meat, groceries, bread, milk, boots, clothing, coal, doctors' services and burials). St Saviours and St Peters provided virtually all of their outdoor relief in kind, and only four parishes provided less than half of relief in this form (the Vale, St Sampsons, St Martins and St Andrews). At £12,384, total rural relief expenditure stood at about 6s per head of population over the course of 1925. In St Peter Port, total poor law spending that year amounted to £16,655, or just over £1 per head of population.[93]

---

88   IA, AQ 0115/01.

89   1.2.1841, IA, DC/HX 075–01.

90   By contrast, this parish spent £160 on the Country Hospital that year (IA, AQ 0517/24).

91   *Rapport du Comité nommé par les Chefs de Famille de la Ville et Paroisse de Saint Pierre-Port le 5 Avril 1848* (Guernsey, 1849), PL; *Billet*, 4.4.1892.

92   *Billet*, 21.7.1926.

93   Based on an estimated population mid-way between the 1921 and 1931 figures in *Census 1921: Jersey, Guernsey and Adjacent Islands* (London, 1924) and *Census 1931: Jersey, Guernsey and Adjacent Islands* (London, 1933).

How far, we may legitimately ask, did such a low level of rural expenditure actually reflect a low level of rural need? Victorian writers insisted that rural 'cases of distress' were 'neither so numerous nor so aggravating' as in St Peter Port.[94] Certainly, more country-dwellers possessed land to provide or supplement subsistence than did townsfolk, and extensive rural kin networks would have functioned as a safety net. If any proof of rural poverty were needed, however, we need look no further than the periodic emergency distributions of grain. Sufficient numbers remained at risk of hunger in the countryside to warrant their continuation until as late as the mid-nineteenth century.[95] As late as 1915, the inhabitants of St Peters, whose farmland was reckoned among the best in the island, were described by the island's Medical Officer of Health as Guernsey's 'poorest' and 'least advanced in modern ways'.[96] The country farmers who paid the rates were renowned for their 'peasant parsimony'.[97] The sums they raised and spent on poor relief were thus perhaps as much a function of culture as of objective need or available resources. In an environment where no-one was opulent and everyone was expected to be self-reliant, poor relief was regarded as the most basic of all backstops, and it was not this, but twentieth-century social security which finally improved the lot of Guernsey's rural poor.[98]

Welfare in practice: St Peter Port

In 1800, St Peter Port accommodated a population of more than 11,000.[99] It was similar in size to Southampton, and unusual among eighteenth- and nineteenth-century European towns in comprising only one parish.[100] St Peter Port never developed municipal institutions, but as it steadily increased in wealth and importance over the eighteenth century its authorities developed a strong sense of their own status. From the mid-eighteenth century, St Peter Port's Constables began calling themselves 'High Constables' (ostensibly to distinguish themselves from their newly instituted assistants, but with English connotations flattering to their self-image).[101]

---

[94] P. Jeremie, *On Parochial and States Taxation in Guernsey* (Guernsey, 1856), p. 84.

[95] Ord, 11.5.1847; *Star*, 14.5.1847.

[96] *Billet*, 8.9.1915.

[97] Berry, *Island of Guernsey*, p. 299.

[98] See Chapter 10.

[99] Parishioners were estimated at 8,450 and non-settled strangers at up to 3,000 (15.12.1800, Royal Court Letter Book 1, Greffe). This excluded the 5000-strong garrison (Chapter 1, n. 52).

[100] In 1801, Southampton and its immediate suburbs accommodated 11,089 in ten parishes (J. Marshall, *An Analysis and Compendium of all the Returns made to Parliament relating to the Increase of Population in the United Kingdom of Great Britain and Ireland* (London, 1835), p. 171).

[101] In England, High Constables were county officers of elite social standing. Their tasks included supervising the collection of county rates and oversight of parish constables within the hundred for which they were responsible (C. Emsley, *Crime and Society in England, 1750–1900* (1987; Harlow, 1996 edn), p. 217).

In mid-nineteenth-century correspondence with English authorities, the parish's *Douzaine* regularly referred to themselves as 'the Corporation of this Town', 'the municipality of this town', or even 'the municipal corporation of the town of St Peter Port'.[102] Such pretensions were perhaps not entirely misplaced, since, with 16,658 inhabitants in 1881, St Peter Port contained a population similar in size to that of many English provincial urban poor law unions.[103]

We shall begin our analysis of St Peter Port by looking at the general character of the parochial welfare regime, since this provides an opportunity to put the parish into comparative context. Firstly, we shall examine St Peter Port's changing administrative structures; next we shall deal with the modalities of taxation, and thirdly we shall investigate the total amounts raised and spent on all forms of relief. In the second half of our analysis, we shall revert more narrowly to outdoor relief.

Evolving welfare structures
Prior to the foundation of the Town Hospital in the 1740s, St Peter Port is reported to have spent the equivalent of £500 sterling a year on welfare payments to some 200 paupers.[104] Once the Hospital was open, regular recipients were given the choice of either entering the institution or ceasing to receive payments, but few chose the former, at least to begin with. There were just fifty-three admissions in the year the Hospital opened.[105]

The new Hospital's Board of Directors was given control of all St Peter Port's poor funds: *rentes* and other investments, proceeds of church-door collections, contents of poor-boxes.[106] It had been the intention of the original founders that their institution would eliminate any further need for rates, since inmates' labour would make the Hospital self-supporting. For eight years following 1743 there were indeed no more rates, but, in 1751, a parish meeting authorised the raising of some £285 to meet the Hospital's needs, which had become 'pressing'.[107] After this, poor rates were levied intermittently for a few years, and then restored to their annual footing from 1765.[108]

Between 1751 and 1812, St Peter Port's poor rates were essentially for indoor use, levied on the application of the Hospital Treasurer who also set the amount to be raised. Outdoor relief (which, contrary to initial hopes, had continued in existence) was funded specifically from church-door collections, which, in 1766, yielded

---

102 See entries for 18.9.1841, 20.6.1844, 27.11.1847, 21.3.1863, IA, AQ 0965/02.

103 For instance, those of Reading or Canterbury which in 1881 contained 13,491and 17,060 inhabitants respectively (*A Statement of the Names of the Several Unions and Poor Law Parishes in England and Wales; and of the Population, Area, and Rateable Value thereof in 1881* (Cmd 5191), pp. 77, 300); PP 1883 LXXX. For more on poor law unions, see below, n. 115.

104 T. Dicey, *An Historical Account of Guernsey* (London, 1751), p. 186.

105 IA, DC/HX 079–01; IA, DC/HX 117–01.

106 IA, DC/HX 117–01.

107 22.8.1751, St Peter Port Délibérations des Chefs de Famille, 1715–79, PL; 24.8.1751, IA, AQ 1003/01.

108 Rates were raised in 1753, 1755, 1756, 1757, 1762 and 1763 (IA, AQ 1003/01). The only gaps after 1765 were one or two in the mid-1780s (IA, AQ 1003/02).

over £80.[109] As in the country parishes, outdoor recipients were distinguished from Hospital inmates by the designation *pauvres honteux*. Also as in the country parishes, outdoor relief was disbursed by the *Collecteurs*, each of whom was responsible for one of six districts and ultimately answerable to the Hospital Board.

This situation changed in the winter of 1811/12, which saw a pan-European grain shortage, very high food prices and unusually harsh weather. In response to the exceptional hardship suffered by St Peter Port's poorer parishioners, *Chefs de Famille* resolved in January 1812 that a portion of the Hospital rate should henceforth be set aside for outdoor relief (initially £300).[110] This marked a turning point and, from 1812 onwards, outdoor relief in St Peter Port came chiefly to be funded by tax. As of this date, parochial tax books began to record the precise sums levied for both indoor and outdoor relief, and a new register of regular outdoor recipients was opened, noting their names and the allowances each received.[111] This was centrally held at the Hospital.

Amounts spent on outdoor relief rose relentlessly in the two difficult decades following 1812. By 1832, after several hard winters and a cholera and smallpox epidemic, it was discovered that outdoor expenditure had almost quadrupled in twenty years.[112] This provoked an immediate tightening-up of outdoor relief policy. Henceforward no-one was to be admitted to the outdoor list without the collective sanction of the Hospital Board and, once a month, the six *Collecteurs* were to be accompanied by six Hospital Directors on review visits to all paupers in their districts.[113]

These measures signally failed to curtail expenditure, however, and outdoor costs continued to rise throughout the next decade. The root of the problem lay in adverse economic conditions, which did not improve over the 1830s and distinctly worsened in the 1840s. Matters once more came to a head when St Peter Port ratepayers were asked to provide £1,650 for outdoor relief alone in the wake of the 1847 food shortage. This request coincided with the revolution of February 1848 in France, which caused a drop in the value of the French government securities now favoured by St Peter Port's fund-holding ratepayers. They refused to approve the rate, and insisted instead that 'the pruning knife must be applied'.[114]

The 'pruning knife' ultimately took the form of a committee under Advocate Robert MacCulloch with a brief to investigate the establishment in St Peter Port of a body 'in the nature of a Board of Guardians'.[115] MacCulloch's committee published

[109] IA, DC/HX 165–01.
[110] 6.2.1812, St Peter Port Délibérations des Chefs de Famille, 1780–1817, PL; 22.2.1812, IA, AQ 0964/02.
[111] IA, AQ 1004/03; IA, DC/HX 018–02.
[112] *Star*, 10.12.1832; for figures see, 29.3.1848, St Peter Port Délibérations des Chefs de Famille, 1844–66, PL.
[113] 19.12.1832, IA, DC/HX 135–03; 9.1.1833, St Peter Port Délibérations des Chefs de Famille, 1818–43, PL; *Star*, 7.1.1833; IA, DC/HX 017–01.
[114] *Star*, 17.3.1848, 19.3.1848.
[115] *Star*, 5.4.1848; 5.4.1848, St Peter Port Délibérations des Chefs de Famille, 1844–66, PL. Following the 1834 Poor Law Amendment Act, England and Wales were divided into 644 Poor Law Unions each containing on average twenty-five parishes, whose elected Boards of

its recommendations in August 1849, and they were adopted at a parish meeting the following October.[116] Legislation was drawn up, and approved by the Privy Council at the end of 1852. The resulting Order in Council was Guernsey's first true poor law.[117]

From January 1853, oversight and management of all St Peter Port's poor law activities were to be exercised by the new St Peter Port Poor Law Board.[118] The Board was to have twenty members, headed by a President and Vice-President elected for terms of up to three years by St Peter Port *Chefs de Famille*. The parish Rector and one of the Churchwardens had *ex-officio* seats, as did the *Procureur* and parish Constables. A Hospital sub-committee chaired by the Poor Law Board Vice-President, who doubled as Hospital Treasurer, was to have management of the workhouse. The six *Collecteurs* were abolished and replaced by ten *Surveillants*, or Overseers, elected for terms of two years. These also had seats on the Board and performed much the same work as *Collecteurs* had done previously, only now over five districts instead of six. Overseers were to visit their districts in pairs every four months and submit lists of relief recipients to the Poor Law Board, which the latter would review twice-yearly. No-one was to be relieved for more than one month without Poor Law Board approval. Constables retained their special responsibility for strangers, but their disbursements were now subject to the approval of the Board. It remained the *Procureur*'s duty to manage the permanent poor fund and represent St Peter Port in official dealings with the States, Royal Court and other parishes. Oaths of office sworn by the Poor Law Board President, Vice-President and Overseers were to be administered by the Royal Court, rather than the Ecclesiastical Court. From this point onwards, therefore, the administration of poor relief in St Peter Port was largely a secular matter.

The St Peter Port Poor Law Board remained in existence for over eighty years. It survived the States' assumption of poor relief funding in 1925 with a slight modification of its constitution, whereby the Rector and Churchwarden were finally removed and nine States members resident in the parish were given seats in their stead.[119] Its essential functions were, however, left unaltered, and it continued in operation for a further twelve years. The Board's final abolition came only in the late 1930s. It was dissolved when the Public Assistance Law came into force in January 1938, and the administration of indoor and outdoor relief in St Peter Port was formally divided into two. The former was made the responsibility of an entirely

---

Guardians controlled both indoor and outdoor relief. They were supervised at government level by a central Poor Law Commission (Williams, *From Pauperism to Poverty*, p. 79).

[116] *Rapport du Comité nommé par les Chefs de Famille de la Ville et Paroisse de Saint Pierre-Port le 5 Avril 1848*; *Star*, 25.10.1849. For a photograph of Robert MacCulloch, who went on to become H.M. *Procureur*, see plate 7.

[117] O in C, 28.12.1852.

[118] The title (rendered in French as *Conseil d'Administration pour les Pauvres de la Ville et Paroisse de Saint Pierre-Port*) was borrowed from England and Wales, where, in 1847, the Poor Law Board had taken over from the Poor Law Commission as the national supervisory body for poor relief (A. Brundage, *The English Poor Laws, 1700–1930* (Basingstoke, 2002), p. 69).

[119] O in C, 24.7.1925.

new all-island Hospital Board, and the latter the responsibility of an equally new St Peter Port Outdoor Assistance Board, both of which were under the oversight of the States' Public Assistance Authority. The St Peter Port Outdoor Assistance Board consisted of the *Procureur*, the ten Overseers and twelve States members resident in the parish.[120] This body was to persist in much the same form until the early twenty-first century.

Taxation

When St Peter Port first introduced poor rates in 1724, 'all masters of professions, such as carpenters, masters of ships, shop keepers, publicans and retailers of liquors' were rated alongside wealthier merchants and gentlemen.[121] At this date, any parishioner estimated to be worth at least five quarters (about £100) was liable to be taxed.[122] In a reflection of greater urban dependence on cash-earning, Guernsey's traditional property tax was combined at this time in St Peter Port with elements of a simple income tax, and the earnings of tradesmen and retailers were taken into account alongside their capital assets.[123]

In subsequent decades, tradesmen and retailers were progressively dropped from the tax list as the increasingly wealthy upper bands of ratepayers began to appreciate the advantages of restricting the rate burden to themselves. Adult males who paid rates became *Chefs de Famille* with a voice and a vote at parish meetings, and, by limiting their numbers, a degree of control was preserved over parish affairs. From the 1760s, no-one was rated on fewer than ten quarters.[124] The rate-paying proportion of St Peter Port's population fell from 10.9 per cent to 5.8 per cent between 1724 and 1821, while the collective value of taxable assets rose sixfold.[125] As ratepayers became an increasingly elite band, it was no longer found necessary or desirable to include income in assessments, and, by the early nineteenth century, parochial taxation in St Peter Port was confined to real and personal property located in Guernsey.[126]

Throughout the nineteenth century and beyond, St Peter Port's *Douzaine*

---

[120] O in C, 22.10.1937.

[121] *The Case of the Town Parish versus the Nine Country Parishes respecting a Change in the Rates and Representation, appointed to be heard before the Committee of the Privy Council at 11 o'clock, on Thursday April 26, 1759* (Guernsey, 1843), p. 40, PL.

[122] G. Stevens Cox, *St Peter Port, 1680–1830: The History of an International Entrepôt* (Woodbridge, 1999), p. 97.

[123] R.P. Hocart, 'Review of *St Peter Port, 1680–1830* by Gregory Stevens Cox', *TSG*, 24 (1999), p. 741.

[124] IA, AQ 1003/01.

[125] IA, AQ 1002/03; IA, AQ 1004/03; Stevens Cox, *St Peter Port, 1680–1830*, p. 164; *Billet*, 15.9.1821.

[126] Professional and business incomes, salaries, pensions, annuities and military half-pay were all exempt from assessment (Dally, *Agriculture*, p. 53). Real estate situated in England was exempt from 1736, and real estate situated in other Channel Islands from 1821 (J. Duncan, *The History of Guernsey* (London, 1841), pp. 201–2; Jeremie, *On Parochial and States Taxation*, p. 6). Government securities, in which St Peter Port's wealthiest parishioners had invested heavily after their withdrawal from trade, were, from the 1820s onwards, assessed according to a formula which converted holdings into taxable quarters (13.3.1822, IA, AQ 0965/01).

continued to follow a restrictive policy in admitting people to the tax list. Early nineteenth-century ordinances making it possible to rate strangers after twelve months' residence were ignored, and very few urban strangers were taxed.[127] Many potential native ratepayers were also passed over. In 1854, of St Peter Port's 1,500 house-owners (most of them natives and *prima facie* candidates for taxation) only 650 were required to pay rates.[128]

In 1906, the Guernsey Reform Association initiated a test case against the St Peter Port authorities to establish the right of their secretary, Francis Wilson, to be taxed with property worth only two quarters (£50).[129] This formed part of a campaign aimed at securing greater popular participation not only in parochial government but also in States' elections, in which only ratepayers were allowed a vote.[130] The Court found in Wilson's favour, prompting outrage from *Douzaines* from all over the island and the submission of a formal petition to the States to the effect that eight quarters (£200) should henceforth be established as the legal threshold for tax.[131] The States had no difficulty in agreeing to this measure, but when the resulting *projet de loi* was submitted to the Privy Council the Council withheld their sanction on the ground that this threshold was too high.[132] As a result, no specific threshold for taxation was ever enshrined in law, and *Douzaines* retained their right to exercise discretion. As late as 1911, the proportion of St Peter Port's population assessed for tax – just 9 per cent – remained lower than it had originally been in 1724.[133]

Sums raised in rates: overall relief spending
Poor rates were levied on the parishioners of St Peter Port for two centuries.[134] Records show that, although the parish never called on its full complement of potential ratepayers, this did not translate into higher rate bills for those who did contribute. One of the advantages of exercising tight control over the number and complexion of ratepayers was that similarly tight control could be exercised over rates and spending. Funds raised for the poor never exceeded 1 per cent of collective taxable wealth in any year between the 1720s and 1920s, increasing from a mere 0.1 per cent in 1724 to 0.3 per cent in 1922.[135] This meant that, while the average late nineteenth-century urban ratepayer in England and Wales was paying about £10 per

[127] Ords, 22.5.1810, 30.4.1821. See also Crossan, *Guernsey, 1814–1914*, p. 95.
[128] 8.3.1854, IA, AQ 0966/01.
[129] *Star*, 30.1.1906. Note that, by the later nineteenth century, one quarter had come to be valued at £25 (Pitts, *Guernsey and its Bailiwick*, p. 54).
[130] Home Office records contain a letter from Reform Association President Frederick Luff dated 18 May 1906, in which Luff complained that, out of an insular population of 43,000, there were only 4,000 ratepayers (TNA, HO 45/10344/140975).
[131] *Star*, 13.11.1906.
[132] *Billet*, 20.3.1907. See also Hocart, *Island Assembly*, pp. 73–4.
[133] *Census 1911: Islands in the British Seas* (London, 1913); IA, AQ 1009/01.
[134] All rates levied between 1724 and 1923 are recorded in St Peter Port's Tax Books (listed in bibliography).
[135] IA, AQ 1002/03; IA, DC/HX 272–02.

year in poor rates, a contemporary St Peter Port ratepayer typically paid less than half that sum.[136]

As the economy grew and the population rose, the general trend in absolute amounts raised and spent was upwards.[137] By and large, St Peter Port's poor law spending increased at points of economic crisis, never to return to previous levels. By 1800, at around £1,000, total annual expenditure was three times higher than it had been in 1724. By the 1820s, after two decades of stress, expenditure had reached £4,000. From the 1820s until the end of the century, it plateaued at between £4,500 and £5,500, rising slightly as the twentieth century began. This slight increase was followed by a sudden and dramatic doubling in the second decade of the twentieth century: from £7,909 in 1913, St Peter Port's poor law expenditure rose to £14,628 in 1919.[138] This precipitous increase was due partly to the inflationary impact of World War I and partly to social hardships engendered by the conflict.

In comparative terms, figures for the century between 1821 and 1921 show that poor law expenditure per head of population in St Peter Port was on average nearly 20 per cent lower than the global English and Welsh average.[139] At the turn of the twentieth century, St Peter Port's per capita spending was just 4s 6d, compared with 7s 2d over the whole of England and Wales.[140] Of course, the English and Welsh average masked significant regional disparities. London was at the top of the scale at 15s 10d per head, and Northumberland towards the bottom at 4s 2d.[141] In spending terms, we might thus broadly liken St Peter Port to localities at the lower end of the English and Welsh spectrum.

Figures for outdoor relief expenditure in St Peter Port, as distinct from other poor law expenditure, exist only from 1812. The amount spent outdoors increased fairly rapidly over the first thirty years, from an annual average of £495 in the decade 1812–21 to £1,150 by the 1840s.[142] Having reached this level, it stabilised over the sixty years from 1850 to 1910, averaging about £1,900 per year.[143] Finally, in parallel with general poor law spending, it rose precipitously in the First World War, doubling to an annual average of £4,069 in 1913–24.[144] By 1937, it had climbed further to £5,750.[145] Again, outdoor spending per head of population tended to be

---

[136] Sir R.H. Rew, 'Local taxation in rural districts', *Journal of the Royal Agricultural Society of England*, 7 (1896), p. 654; Crossan, *Guernsey, 1814–1914*, p. 155.

[137] See Appendix 2 for rates raised at approximately decennial intervals between the 1720s and 1920s. This appendix also contains ten-yearly figures for indoor and outdoor relief expenditure, where available.

[138] IA, DC/HX 272–02.

[139] IA, DC/HX 045–01; IA, DC/HX 178–01; IA, DC/HX 168–01; IA, DC/HX 020–01; IA, DC/HX 272–02; Williams, *Pauperism to Poverty*, pp. 148, 169–72.

[140] IA, DC/HX 272–02; Williams, *Pauperism to Poverty*, p. 171.

[141] D. Fraser, 'The English poor law and the origins of the British welfare state', in W.J. Mommsen and W. Mock (eds), *The Emergence of the Welfare State in Britain and Germany, 1850–1950* (London, 1981), p. 23.

[142] 28.3.1848, St Peter Port Délibérations des Chefs de Famille, 1844–66, PL.

[143] With shallow peaks in the 1870s and 1880s, and troughs in the 1860s and 1890s.

[144] IA, DC/HX 272–02.

[145] IA, DC/HX 266–03.

lower than the global average spent outdoors in England and Wales. In 1841, St Peter Port's outdoor spending stood at about 1s 2d per capita, as compared with an average of 3s 8d in England and Wales.[146]

As in the country parishes, outdoor spending was not the main focus of St Peter Port's poor law budget. The bulk of expenditure went to the Hospital. Over the sixty-seven years for which detailed Poor Law Board accounts survive (1858–1924), the overall total spent indoors was 47 per cent higher than the total spent outdoors.[147] In England and Wales generally, the reverse situation pertained, with about 40 per cent more spent on outdoor than on indoor relief during the same period.[148] The main reason for this difference seems to have been that St Peter Port kept a much stricter curb on outdoor relief than did poor law unions across the Channel. In England and Wales, there were never less than four times more outdoor than indoor paupers in any year between 1840 and 1930, notwithstanding repeated bids by the central authorities to clamp down on outdoor relief.[149] In St Peter Port, by contrast, numbers admitted to the Hospital appear consistently to have exceeded those on outdoor relief until the late nineteenth century, with a small drop to just below outdoor levels in the first quarter of the twentieth century.[150]

One factor which greatly facilitated St Peter Port's containment of outdoor expenditure was the ineligibility of most strangers for relief. Non-natives accounted for over a third of St Peter Port's population from the 1820s to the end of the century and, although Constables did relieve strangers on a casual basis, it was rare for them to do more.[151] On the infrequent occasions when a Constable wished to provide a stranger with longer-term relief, he was obliged to submit particulars of the case to the *Douzaine* and gain their formal approval (after 1853, the Poor Law Board's approval).[152] With non-natives peaking at around 38 per cent of St Peter Port's civilian population in 1848, strangers comprised only 6 per cent of regular outdoor recipients, numbering a mere nineteen individuals, whose stays in Guernsey averaged forty-two years.[153] By contrast, over 600 strangers were deported from St Peter Port in that same year, about 10 per cent of whom had lived in the parish for five years or more.[154]

After 1853, St Peter Port's Constables were formally bound by the Poor Law Board constitution 'to send all Stranger Poor from the island when they become

---

[146] IA, DC/HX 020–01; IA, DC/HX 272–02; Williams, *Pauperism to Poverty*, p. 169.

[147] IA, DC/HX 272–02.

[148] Williams, *Pauperism to Poverty*, pp. 169–72.

[149] Snell, *Parish and Belonging*, p. 218. See also below, nn. 239, 242.

[150] Admissions to the Hospital and outdoor pauper numbers stood at 308 and 170 respectively in 1832; 317 and 221 in 1848; 235 and 230 in 1901; 222 and 244 in 1925 (Hospital statistics from IA, DC/HX 053–02; IA, DC/HX 057–02; IA, DC/HX 272–02; IA, DC/HX 051–01; outdoor statistics as in nn. 159–63, below).

[151] For migrant numbers, see Crossan, *Guernsey, 1814–1914*, pp. 60, 70.

[152] When such approval was granted, the stranger in question was no longer relieved from the Constable's funds but from the general poor rate.

[153] Crossan, *Guernsey, 1814–1914*, p. 71; *Rapport du Comité nommé par les Chefs de Famille de la Ville et Paroisse de Saint Pierre-Port le 5 avril 1848*.

[154] IA, AQ 0999/01.

chargeable; excepting that the said Constables may consult, if they think fit, the said Board, whose advice they shall follow'.[155] Poor Law Board accounts show that, in the thirty-four years between 1858 and 1891, stranger costs accounted for an annual average of just 4.7 per cent of St Peter Port's total relief spending. Significantly, a substantial proportion of this went on passes purchased by the parish for deportees' sea crossings. In the three decades over which deportation costs were separately itemised in St Peter Port's poor law accounts (1860s, 1870s and 1880s), they absorbed an average of a quarter to a third of annual stranger spending.[156]

The constant inflow of migrant labour coupled with strangers' ineligibility for relief and the facility for expeditious deportation exerted a downward pressure on rate bills as well as wage bills. St Peter Port's rate-paying employers enjoyed flexibility of hiring and firing without having to support large numbers of redundant workers in times of slack, or strangers who became sick or disabled after years of work. In many instances, relief costs were simply transferred to English poor law unions.[157] St Peter Port's ratepayers would not have conceived themselves as beholden to the ratepayers of south-west England, but it was, in part, this *de facto* subsidy that kept parochial bills so low.

Having established the general parameters within which St Peter Port's welfare regime operated from the mid-eighteenth to the mid-twentieth century, we shall now revert in more detail to outdoor relief.

Number and profile of outdoor relief recipients

It is impossible to establish a complete series of outdoor pauper statistics for St Peter Port since records are incomplete and inconsistent. The most that is feasible in numerical terms are periodic snapshots from a miscellany of sources. A letter from a *Collecteur* published in a newspaper of 1832 put the total number of outdoor recipients at 170.[158] In 1848, the MacCulloch committee investigating reforms to St Peter Port's poor relief system numbered them at 221.[159] In 1901, *Collecteurs'* records numbered them at 230.[160] In 1925, Poor Law Board minutes put them at 244 and, in 1930, outdoor relief returns numbered them at 194.[161] Unhelpfully, most of these sources simply enumerated all individuals receiving relief at a given time, conflating long-term with temporary recipients and not including their dependants. What is striking, however, is the narrow range between the lowest and highest figures, and the consistency of the proportion of the population these figures represent. As

---

[155] IA, DC/HX 272–11.

[156] IA, DC/HX 272–02. For detailed analysis, see Crossan, *Guernsey, 1814–1914*, pp. 158–60.

[157] As in the case of my great-great-grandfather Robert Taylor, who was removed to Yeovil workhouse in 1876 when he went blind after thirty years in the island (28.9.1876, *Livre en Crime*, vol. 42, Greffe; 13.10.1876, D/G/Y 60/14, Somerset Record Office).

[158] *Star*, 13.2.1832.

[159] *Rapport du Comité nommé par les Chefs de Famille de la Ville et Paroisse de Saint Pierre-Port le 5 avril 1848.*

[160] IA, DC/HX 185–01; IA, DC/HX 192–03; IA, DC/HX 193–01; IA, DC/HX 194–01; IA, DC/HX 197–01; IA, DC/HX 198–01.

[161] 7.12.1925, IA, DC/HX 051–01; IA, DC/HX 257–02.

against the population of St Peter Port at the nearest census, this proportion stood at 1.2 per cent in 1832, 1.3 per cent in 1848 and 1901, 1.5 per cent in 1925, and 1.2 per cent in 1930.[162]

As regards profile, a register of long-term recipients surviving for the period 1862–1901 enables us to ascertain the make-up of the cohort granted ongoing help.[163] Of the approximately 500 individuals recorded over the forty years, 80 per cent were women (mostly widows), and 90 per cent were over 60 when they were admitted to the register. They clearly equated to the core of elderly folk assisted on a regular basis by Guernsey's country parishes. About half of St Peter Port's long-term recipients received outdoor relief for periods in excess of five years. Their periods on outdoor relief usually terminated with their death or transfer to Hospital.

On temporary or occasional outdoor recipients there is much less information. However, what evidence there is suggests that they tended to be younger and to include more men with families. Of the temporary recipients listed in the report of the 1848 MacCulloch committee, half were male and nearly 90 per cent had dependent children.[164] These were the urban equivalent of the impoverished rural families assisted by the country parishes on a semi-regular basis. In the countryside, occasional recipients tended to outnumber long-term ones. In St Peter Port, this situation was reversed. MacCulloch's report numbered the latter at 163 and the former at 58, making a mid-century ratio of four long-termers to every occasional recipient. This may indicate that elderly rurals were more able to rely on kin for support, or perhaps it simply reflects the strong rural preference for institutional care.

The vast majority of St Peter Port's outdoor recipients naturally lived within the parish boundary. However, parochial authorities also sent relief payments to a small number of parishioners residing elsewhere. There were eight regular non-resident recipients in 1836 and thirty-one in 1880.[165] Most were living in Guernsey's country parishes, but, more rarely, St Peter Port might also send money to recipients resident in Jersey, the south of England or further afield. In 1932, it was sending a weekly remittance to a Mrs Thom in Basel.[166]

Nature and amount of relief

Outdoor relief given in St Peter Port was not intended to provide full maintenance. The parish explicitly expected recipients to eke out their allowances with earnings of their own or with help from families, charities and other sources.[167] Thus, in 1833, the 30-year-old widow of Charles Norton supplemented the parish's weekly 1s 6d

---

[162] Census figures from *Billet*, 6.10.1831; PP 1852–3 LXXXVIII; PP 1903 LXXXIV; *Census 1921: Jersey, Guernsey and Adjacent Islands* (London, 1924); *Census 1931: Jersey, Guernsey and Adjacent Islands* (London, 1933).

[163] IA, DC/HX 021–03.

[164] *Rapport du Comité nommé par les Chefs de Famille de la Ville et Paroisse de Saint Pierre-Port le 5 avril 1848.*

[165] 23.12.1836, IA, DC/HX 017–01; 5.11.1880, IA, DC/HX 072–02.

[166] 8.2.1932, IA, DC/HX 051–01.

[167] 29.3.1848, St Peter Port Délibérations des Chefs de Famille, 1844–66, PL.

with another 2s earned by working 'at what she can'.[168] In 1868, Joshua Ahier, a former St Peter Port Constable, *Douzenier*, *Procureur*, Town Hospital Director and Churchwarden who had fallen on hard times, supplemented his weekly allowance of 3s 6d by working as a librarian at the Mechanics' Institution.[169] Maria Blondel, described as 'crippled', and on the register of permanent recipients for its entire forty-year duration, received only 1s a week between the ages of 30 and 60, and made up the gap by taking in sewing at home.[170]

Between 1814 and 1914, the minimum an unskilled workman in St Peter Port might earn when in full employment ranged from 12s to 17s a week. During this period, the majority of weekly relief payments fell somewhere between 1s and 3s 6d. The small number of parochial allowances in excess of 3s 6d went either to parents of large families relieved for short periods or to very old couples on the permanent pensioner register.[171] Slightly more allowances at the upper end of the scale were granted as the century progressed, but payments rose substantially only mid-way through the Great War, when inflation forced the Poor Law Board to increase the sum usually granted to families to about 7s 6d a week and raise pensions to elderly couples to about 4s 6d.[172] Thereafter, allowances never reverted to their earlier level, but neither did they rise to English inter-war levels. In 1925, a *Times* enquiry found that a couple with four children would receive 39s per week in relief in Bethnal Green, 30s in Birkenhead and 41s in Walsall.[173] In December 1930, irrespective of dependants, three-quarters of St Peter Port's outdoor claimants were receiving only between 5s and 10s per week; 6 per cent were on less than 5s, and just 5 per cent received more than 20s.[174]

Cash payments were, however, only part of the story, for a large proportion of St Peter Port's relief was not in the form of cash at all. Much assistance was given partly or wholly in kind. *Collecteurs'* accounts from the 1820s and 1830s show sundry recipients being provided with clothing, bed linen and food.[175] Poor Law Board records from the 1920s and 1930s show boots and grocery vouchers dispensed in much the same way.[176] As in the country parishes, help was also given with burials and medical attendance, and recipients included beneficiaries not on the parish's regular lists. The various forms of assistance in kind dispensed by St Peter Port are examined in the following section. Such is their scope that, for most of the eighteenth and nineteenth centuries, they almost certainly accounted for a larger share of outdoor spending than cash payments.

[168] 25.4.1833, IA, DC/HX 017–01.
[169] 7.12.1868, IA, DC/HX 054–05. Ahier had been a soap and candle maker before the collapse of his business. His obituary is in the *Monthly Illustrated Journal* for May 1885.
[170] IA, DC/HX 021–03.
[171] IA, DC/HX 018–02; IA, DC/HX 175–01; IA, DC/HX 175–02; IA, DC/HX 021–03.
[172] IA, DC/HX 052–01.
[173] S. Fowler, *Workhouse: The People, the Places, the Life Behind Doors* (Richmond, 2007), p. 252.
[174] IA, DC/HX 257–02.
[175] IA, DC/HX 179–01.
[176] IA, DC/HX 051–01; 19.8.1936, IA, AS/MB 011–05.

Mass distributions in kind

One-off help in kind at its most extensive took the form of subsidised food or fuel offered to the public in times of shortage and/or high prices. On several occasions in the eighteenth century, special taxes distinct from the poor rate were raised to cover losses sustained when selling imported grain to poor parishioners at below cost price.[177] Buyers came from the lower ranks generally and were not limited to those on poor relief. The last separate tax for such a purpose was levied in 1801, to finance the purchase of wheat and coal for sale to parishioners unable to afford the high prices then current.[178]

From 1812, the cost of commodities destined for mass parochial sale or distribution was met from the poor rate funds now set aside for outdoor relief. These funds were also occasionally supplemented by charitable subscriptions. In the difficult decade between 1810 and 1820, a charitable 'Committee for the Relief of the Poor' made large-scale distributions of bread, coal, clothing, footwear and blankets in full-blown collaboration with parochial authorities.[179] After this Committee had faded away, the many pinch-points of the next thirty years saw the subsidised sale or (more rarely) the free distribution by the parish of bread, flour, potatoes and coal, as well as soup, which was dispensed from a regular winter soup kitchen.[180] In 1848, Robert MacCulloch's poor law reform committee expressed a wish to abolish this form of mass assistance, which its members discountenanced as 'the first step on the road to pauperism'.[181] Parochial authorities attempted to implement this proposal, but a reversion to previous practice was eventually forced by the widespread distress accompanying the severe winter of 1851/2.[182]

In the improving conditions of the second half of the century, large-scale emergency aid became less frequent in St Peter Port, although the parochial soup kitchen remained a fixture through the decades. Interestingly, one of St Peter Port's last mass distributions came as late as 1895, when, again faced with a harsh winter, the Poor Law Board handed out free food and fuel to a large number of poor parishioners, whether these were in receipt of relief or not.[183] In a low-wage environment, it was

---

[177] Such taxes are recorded in 1757, 1768, 1775, 1795 and 1796 (IA, AQ 1003/01; IA, AQ 1003/02; IA, AQ 1003/04).

[178] 16.4.1801, IA, AQ 0942/03.

[179] This *Comité pour le Soulagement des Pauvres* seems first to have come into existence in 1812, and to have lasted until at least 1820. See *L'Indépendance*, 15.11.1817, 3.1.1818, 1.12.1818; also 8.12.1816 and 27.12.1820, IA, AQ 096/01, and entries for 1816, 1817 and 1818 in IA, AQ 1004/03.

[180] See the following IA records: 26.4.1812, AQ 0964/02; 10.12.1816, AQ 0965/01; 17.11.1831, DC/HX 135–03; 17.12.1838, DC/HX 075–01; 2.8.1843, AQ 0965/02; 11.6.1847, DC/HX 166–01; 22.12.1852, AQ 0966/01; 29.12.1853, DC/HX 054–05.

[181] *Rapport du Comité nommé par les Chefs de Famille de la Ville et Paroisse de Saint Pierre-Port le 5 avril 1848.*

[182] 22.12.1852, IA, AQ 0966/01.

[183] 14.2.1895, IA, DC/HX 054–07.

impossible also to keep relief levels low without periodic hardship intervention.[184] Regular distributions of coal to those not otherwise on relief continued until at least World War II.[185]

Burials

Another benefit in kind provided as 'outdoor relief' was burials. The first evidence of parish burials in the modern period comes from 1736, although, on sanitary grounds, the parish must long before this have buried corpses whose disposal was unprovided for. The 1736 reference relates to a resolution by *Chefs de Famille* to cut costs by ceasing to pay the parish gravediggers for digging pauper graves and the sexton for ringing the bell at pauper funerals.[186]

Once the Town Hospital was in operation in 1743, all parish burials were conducted from there. Constables or *Collecteurs* would apply to the Hospital for the burial of deceased paupers in their charge and were billed by the Hospital for the service.[187] Inmates would collect the corpses, transfer them to cheap unornamented deal boxes made in the Hospital's carpenter's shop and carry them to St Peter Port's various cemeteries.[188] Following a brief graveside service, interment took place in unmarked pauper vaults. The vaults, once full, were left for two or three decades, and then reused after decomposition had taken place. In the eighteenth century, paupers were buried at the Cimetière des Soeurs and the Cimetière des Frères; in the nineteenth century, at the Strangers' Cemetery and Candie Cemetery, and finally, from 1932, at the Foulon Cemetery.[189]

The most frequent candidates for parish burial were Hospital inmates or regulars on outdoor relief, such as Mary Ann Gilbert in 1821.[190] However, the parish also buried parishioners not in receipt of relief whose families could not afford a private funeral. Jean Heaume, who accidentally drowned in 1765, was one such parishioner, as was the child of Thomas Power, who died unexpectedly in 1769.[191] Many other non-paupers were also buried by the parish: strangers without known relatives, such as the negro who died of smallpox in 1796 or the three Irish navvies killed at

---

[184] On the relationship between mass intervention and low personal relief, see K.G. Persson, 'The seven lean years, elasticity traps, and intervention in grain markets in pre-industrial Europe', *The Economic History Review*, 49 (1996), p. 712.

[185] The new Central Poor Law Board decided in 1925 that there should be three coal deliveries yearly, 'one hundredweight being given to needy applicants, Islanders or Strangers, whether in receipt of relief or not' (IA, DC/HX 272–06).

[186] 13.3.1736, St Peter Port Délibérations des Chefs de Famille, 1715–79, PL.

[187] IA, DC/HX 076–07.

[188] After 1853, the Hospital bought in cheap coffins from the lowest outside bidder (27.6.1853, IA, DC/HX 130–04).

[189] See loose sheet in IA, DC/HX 060–02, and 14.12.1932, IA, DC/HX 051–01.

[190] 27.11.1821, IA, DC/HX 124–02. Appended to the record of Mrs Gilbert's burial is a note to the effect that she had received a small pension from the British government, and claimed on her deathbed to be the natural daughter of Louis XVI.

[191] 17.6.1765, 6.4.1769, IA, DC/HX 119–01.

the harbour works in 1858.[192] The parish also buried shipwrecked mariners washed ashore,[193] and executed criminals.[194]

As all over the British Isles, St Peter Port's nineteenth-century parishioners considered it a profound mark of shame to be buried by the parish, and they took steps – in the form of burial clubs and other savings schemes – to avoid this fate if at all possible.[195] 'I have often been impressed with the sadness of funerals from the hospital', the Rector of St Peter Port remarked in 1902, 'and I should be glad if I could do anything to make them more seemly.'[196] He donated a bier and a pall to the Hospital, and two years later St Peter Port's ultra-cheap coffins were replaced by better-quality varnished ones.[197] Parish burials, however, continued to be conducted from the Hospital for nearly half a century more. Only in 1948 were they entrusted to a professional undertaker, and the workhouse connection which so many found distasteful was finally severed.[198]

Emigration

During the eighteenth century, small parties of Town Hospital inmates were from time to time dispatched to North America. These were usually children and young people, sent to start new lives across the Atlantic with departing sea captains.[199] At this time, however, there was no pauper emigration from the wider parish. Large-scale emigration from Guernsey began only in the early 1800s, when anti-smuggling legislation prompted collective departures to Ohio and Prince Edward Island.[200] Nevertheless, once this precedent had been set, the emigration of the poor came increasingly to be seen both as a solution to individual paupers' problems and as a relief to the remaining community. Thus, in 1818, following a number of mass departures amid post-Napoleonic distress, St Peter Port *Chefs de Famille* sanctioned a special tax to assist struggling parishioners to leave Guernsey, and appointed a committee to assess applicants and arrange transport to North America.[201] No further taxes were raised exclusively to fund emigration after 1818, but throughout the 1820s and 1830s parochial authorities continued to assist aspiring emigrants by means of discretionary grants from outdoor funds.

---

192 28.12.1796, IA, DC/HX 121–02; 25.2.1858, IA, DC/HX 130–04.
193 13.1.1799, IA, DC/HX 121–02.
194 7.4.1780, IA, DC/HX 119–04.
195 On English attitudes, see T.W. Laqueur, 'Bodies, death and pauper funerals', *Representations*, 1 (1983), pp. 109–31.
196 Rev. G.E. Lee to Town Hospital House Committee, 31.10.1902, IA, DC/HX 249–02. For a photograph of the Reverend Lee, see Plate 3.
197 3.11.1902, IA, DC/HX 056–04; 4.7.1904, IA, DC/HX 135–06.
198 22.11.1948, IA, AS/MB 065–02.
199 See 3.3.1750 and various entries for 1752, IA, DC/HX 117–02; entries for 1765, IA, DC/HX 119–01; 21.4.1767, IA, DC/HX 079–01; 6.4.1768, IA, DC/HX 119–01.
200 A.G. Jamieson, 'Channel Islands and overseas settlement, 1600–1900', in A.G. Jamieson (ed.), *A People of the Sea: The Maritime History of the Channel Islands* (London, 1986), pp. 281, 286.
201 6.3.1818, IA, AQ 0965/01; *L'Indépendance*, 7.3.1818.

After another period of acute distress in the 1840s, St Peter Port began in 1849 to ring-fence a portion of the poor rate specifically for pauper emigration.[202] In 1853, the new Poor Law Board authorised its President, along with any two Board members, to make summary grants to emigrants (who did not have to be currently in receipt of relief).[203] The formal hypothecation of part of the poor rate for emigration continued until the late 1870s, fell into abeyance in the 1880s and 1890s, then resumed for a few years after 1907.[204] The years of peak demand for assisted emigration were the early 1850s and early 1870s, when spending for this purpose reached as much as £300 or £400 annually.[205] In these years, emigration-related spending equated to about 7 per cent of St Peter Port's total welfare budget.[206]

The number of emigrants assisted by the parish is hard to assess, but evidence suggests that perhaps fifty poor people were helped to leave the island in each of the peak years.[207] Most assisted emigration was voluntary, but, since it was essentially a way of curtailing future relief costs, there were a number of unwilling departures. Coercion was particularly in evidence among the more inveterate paupers at the Town Hospital, and this, in due course, produced a number of unwelcome returns.[208]

Throughout the early nineteenth century, the commonest destinations of parish-assisted emigrants were the United States and Canada. From the 1850s, a small amount of pauper emigration also took place to Australia (and later New Zealand), for which the parish was successful on several occasions in obtaining free passages from colonial governments.[209] After World War I, parish-assisted emigration ceased. However, in 1923, the States set up a committee of their own to help with emigration, and this persisted until after World War II.[210]

Medical relief

Perhaps the most important non-cash benefit offered by St Peter Port was medical relief, for no charitable or voluntary medical provision existed in Guernsey until the Victoria Cottage Hospital was established in the 1880s.[211] In the seventeenth century, the States had for a time attempted to organise some form of all-island

---

[202] IA, DC/HX 020–01.

[203] 11.2.1853, IA, DC/HX 054–05.

[204] IA, DC/HX 272–02.

[205] IA, DC/HX 020–01; IA, DC/HX 272–02.

[206] In England and Wales, guardians were empowered by the 1834 Poor Law Amendment Act to assist paupers wishing to emigrate. Demand was strong during the 1830s and 1840s, but, in contrast to St Peter Port, had diminished considerably by the 1850s. In 1870, existing arrangements for pauper emigration were dismantled as it was no longer deemed useful in reducing relief spending (G. Howells, '"For I was tired of England Sir": English pauper emigrant strategies, 1834–60', *Social History*, 23 (1998), pp. 181–94; A. Digby, *Pauper Palaces* (London, 1978), p. 102).

[207] See entries for 1870–73 in IA, DC/HX 272–02.

[208] See section on 'Policy and regime', Chapter 6.

[209] 8.6.1874, 20.6.1874, IA, DC/HX 059–01.

[210] *Billets*, 29.6.1923, 9.4.1947.

[211] See section on 'Charity', Chapter 4.

medical provision, to which the parishes were required to contribute. In 1611, 1623 and 1632 respectively, they engaged the services of surgeons Guillaume Charnasse, James House and Samuel De La Place. Each parish was ordered to pay a share of their stipends.[212]

By the eighteenth century, however, individual parishes were making their own medical arrangements. Records for St Peter Port in the 1730s show *Collecteurs* paying practitioners for treating the poor on an *ad hoc* basis, as on 15 May 1734, when *Collecteurs* paid a Dr Carré 58 *livres tournois*.[213] From its opening in 1743, the Town Hospital also provided medical treatment and, from 1752, the institution retained its own stipendiary surgeon. There is, however, no record of the Hospital surgeon treating outdoor paupers, whose needs appear to have been met *ad hoc* until at least the 1780s. Non-inmates admitted to the Hospital in an emergency were attended by other doctors summoned as the occasion arose.[214]

At some time in the later eighteenth century, St Peter Port's *Douzaine* appear to have appointed an outdoor stipendiary practitioner distinct from the Hospital's surgeon. Since this doctor's stipend was paid out of the Constables' rate, as distinct from the poor rate, his chief purpose, at least initially, seems to have been to attend strangers, in particular those associated with the garrison. This is corroborated by the fact that, from 1788, the States undertook to pay one-third of his salary as part of their funding of military stranger relief.[215]

Somewhat confusingly, the roles of this outdoor poor law doctor and the Hospital surgeon seem to have coalesced over the next decades, for, in 1820, they were being performed by a single individual now simply known as the 'parish surgeon'.[216] At this point, other St Peter Port doctors became dissatisfied at the parish surgeon's monopoly of public medicine and launched an orchestrated protest.[217] The parish responded in 1821 by reinstituting two distinct posts – a stipendiary Hospital surgeon and a stipendiary outdoor surgeon – to which different incumbents would henceforth be appointed annually: the former by the Hospital's Directors, and the latter by the Constables and *Douzeniers*.[218] Parish poor law doctors appointed on this basis were obliged to pay for their own medical supplies, and seem to have delegated much of their work with the poor to apprentices.[219]

The 1821 arrangement remained in place until 1842, when the rapidly increasing urban population brought about an important change. In this year, the parish was divided into a northern and a southern district, and the single outdoor surgeon was replaced by two outdoor surgeons appointed one to each district at £40 a year. They

[212] *Actes*, 5.11.1611, 29.9.1623, 7.12.1632.

[213] IA, DC/HX 178–03.

[214] January 1780, St Peter Port Délibérations des Chefs de Famille, 1780–1817, PL.

[215] *Acte*, 19.4.1788.

[216] 13.12.1820, IA, AQ 0965/01.

[217] *Star*, 19.12.1820.

[218] 4.1.1821, St Peter Port Délibérations des Chefs de Famille, 1818–43, P.L; 4.1.1821, IA, AQ 0965/01; 25.2.1821, IA, AQ 0964/02; *Star*, 9.1.1821.

[219] 6.2.1826, IA, DC/HX 135–02; 12.3.1834, IA, AQ 0965/02.

were henceforth to be assisted by two parish midwives on £5 a year.[220] The Hospital retained its own dedicated surgeon.

This system lasted until 1853, when the newly established Poor Law Board restructured medical services as part of its general reforms. Under the 1853 reorganisation the two districts and two midwives were retained, but the post of Hospital surgeon was abolished and the two remaining parish doctors were given shared responsibility for both indoor and outdoor work.[221] These doctors were to be paid £50 annually on condition that they performed their duties in person. The parish also undertook to provide all medical supplies.[222]

Perhaps the most significant innovation introduced by the new Poor Law Board was the poor law dispensary established at the Town Hospital in 1853. The dispensary was open for three hours from Monday to Saturday and one hour on Sunday, when one or other of the parish doctors was in attendance. Anyone in possession of a medical order (which could be issued by any Poor Law Board member) could be seen by a doctor and obtain free medicines on prescription.[223] Charitable dispensaries had existed in the United Kingdom since the late eighteenth century, and were also beginning to be built from union rates at this time.[224] The St Peter Port dispensary operated for over a century. In the inter-war period, it was redesignated the Town Hospital's 'outpatient department', and continued to treat patients until the 1960s.[225]

In the late 1820s, St Peter Port's single outdoor practitioner had complained of being overworked, with 120 patients actively receiving treatment.[226] Numbers seeking poor law medical care seem to have risen considerably as the century progressed, since doctors' registers from the 1860s and 1870s suggest that at least 1,000 medical orders were issued per year.[227] Recipients evidently included many people not otherwise on relief. The registers show that they were suffering from all the ailments commonly associated with the nineteenth-century poor: strains, sprains and hernias, fevers, bronchitis, rheumatism, pneumonia, consumption, skin conditions, syphilis and eye infections.[228] Most of these people were initially seen in their own homes, usually two or three times, and this was followed up, as necessary, by admission to the Hospital or outpatient visits to the dispensary.

St Peter Port's medical expenditure stood at an average of about £350 a year between the 1850s and World War I, accounting for some 6 per cent of its total

[220] 16.11.1842, IA, AQ 0965/02; 5.12.1842, IA, DC/HX 130–01.
[221] This was the opposite of the trend in England and Wales, where the consolidation of duties of the district and workhouse medical officer was abandoned from the late 1840s (P. Wood, *Poverty and the Workhouse in Victorian Britain* (Stroud, 1991), p. 111).
[222] 24.1.1853, 31.1.1853, IA, DC/HX 054–05; 31.1.1853, 5.12.1853, IA, DC/HX 130–04.
[223] 24.1.1853, 31.1.1853, IA, DC/HX 054–05. From 1884, a prescription charge of 2d was introduced (7.4.1884, IA, DC/HX 054–06).
[224] F.B. Smith, *The People's Health, 1830–1910* (1979; London, 1990 edn), pp. 31, 205.
[225] 1.4.1938, IA, AS/MB 011–05; 24.6.1964, IA, AS/MB 065–02.
[226] 1.12.1829, IA, AQ 0965/02.
[227] IA, DC/HX 063/02; IA, DC/HX 138–11; IA, DC/HX 049–02; IA, DC/HX 049–03.
[228] IA, DC/HX 063–02.

welfare budget.[229] This was higher than the average budgetary proportion spent on medical services by poor law unions in England and Wales, which was closer to 4 per cent.[230] The higher proportion was not so much a sign of St Peter Port's generosity as of its comparatively lower spending on other aspects of relief. For many, medical attendance was the only form of poor law assistance they ever received.

Tenor of parish welfare

We have so far discussed St Peter Port's low ratepayer numbers, its low level of rates, its low level of allowances and its low level of expenditure. All this points to a signally small-scale welfare regime. It now remains to investigate what mentality underpinned this regime, and what strategies were used to keep it small-scale. First and foremost, there was a universal understanding that welfare was a concession and not a right. This was insisted on by ratepayers and accepted as the *status quo* by lower social strata. As Advocate Henry Tupper is quoted as saying, 'no-one must be suffered to die from hunger, but the rich have also a right to demand that the poor should labour for their living'.[231] The first line of defence was the simple refusal of claims. Mere settlement in St Peter Port was no guarantee that a relief claim would be entertained, since eligibility did not equate straightforwardly to entitlement. Rather, the success of a claim often hinged on subjective criteria such as 'decency' or 'moral rectitude'. In 1835, Mrs Marquis, described as 'industrious, striving against poverty', was granted 3s 4d per week for herself and four children.[232] In 1833, Elizabeth Jamouneau was refused relief on the basis that her child was illegitimate.[233]

Applicants sometimes disputed refusals with Town Hospital Directors or the Poor Law Board, but they virtually never appealed to the Royal Court.[234] In England and Wales, it was relatively common for poor persons denied relief to plead their case before magistrates, who in some instances manifested greater sympathy with claimants than with local officials.[235] In Guernsey, more recourse was had to the Court by parochial authorities than by aggrieved claimants, and this body tended to function as the enforcement arm of the former rather than as a neutral arbiter.[236] Indeed, judicial impartiality was for a long time technically impossible in poor law-related proceedings concerning St Peter Port, since the Court and St Peter Port's poor law administration shared many of the same personnel. From the foundation of the Town Hospital, Jurats residing in town had *ex-officio* seats on the Hospital Board.

229 IA, DC/HX 272–02.

230 M.W. Flinn, 'Medical services under the New Poor Law', in D. Fraser (ed.), *The New Poor Law in the Nineteenth Century* (London, 1976), p. 52.

231 *Star*, 5.4.1848.

232 23.2.1835, IA, DC/HX 017–01.

233 7.10.1833, IA, DC/HX 130–02.

234 By this time, the ordinance of 15.4.1611 allowing those denied support to apply to the Court for enforcement had been long forgotten (see Chapter 3, n. 60).

235 D.R. Green, 'Pauper protests: power and resistance in early nineteenth-century London workhouses', *Social History*, 31 (2006), p. 139.

236 This was recognised by the Royal Commissioners of 1846 (*Second Report of the Commissioners*, p. xxviii).

Thus in 1848, as at many other points, all twelve serving Jurats were also Board members and directly involved in relief decisions.[237]

From the inception of St Peter Port's new Poor Law Board in 1853, Jurats no longer served *ex-officio*, though they could still be elected as members. However, the advent of the Poor Law Board only served to tighten relief policy. The *Star* newspaper described St Peter Port's mid-century reorganisation of poor relief as 'a measure strictly analogous' to England's 1834 Poor Law Amendment Act.[238] It had been one of the long-term aims of the English Act to deter all but the truly destitute from applying for relief. The Act's originators had envisaged that outdoor assistance would eventually be abolished altogether, so that applicants would have no choice but to enter a workhouse if they wished to be relieved. Since conditions in these workhouses would be made 'less eligible' (i.e., less desirable) than those endured by the most poorly paid outside, ultimately only the desperate would apply for relief.[239] Despite the *Star*'s comment, St Peter Port's new Poor Law Board had no explicitly stated 'less eligibility' policy. Nevertheless, there was a marked tendency after 1853 to use six-monthly relief reviews to screen out outdoor recipients by offering them a choice between entering the Hospital or losing their allowance altogether.[240] Indeed, a set of negative criteria began to be established in St Peter Port, which were more designed to legitimise exclusion than determine eligibility. Among other things, the new Board laid down that any parents who failed to send their children to school or have them vaccinated, would be automatically excluded from relief.[241]

In 1877, perhaps influenced by the 1870s English 'crusade' against outdoor relief, the Poor Law Board drew up a set of outdoor relief rules of which 1,000 copies were distributed to the parish poor.[242] In many ways, these were simply a formalisation of what had already become policy. The rules stated that all outdoor relief was to be denied to able-bodied people without children. It was also to be denied to women with illegitimate children, as to persons of 'immoral character' generally. Caution was additionally to be exercised in granting relief to the elderly whose grown-up children were 'evidently in a position to maintain them'. To all in the above categories, 'the House' would be 'opened in case of necessity'.[243]

---

[237] *Rapport du Comité nommé par les Chefs de Famille de la Ville et Paroisse de Saint Pierre-Port le 5 avril 1848.*

[238] *Star*, 23.10.1849.

[239] P. Murray, *Poverty and Welfare, 1830–1914* (London, 1999), p. 25.

[240] As John Brimage, Mrs Rogers and Samuel Dawson on 2 February 1857 (IA, DC/HX 054–05).

[241] *Constitution et Règlement du Conseil d'Administration pour les Pauvres de la Ville et Paroisse de Saint Pierre-Port* (Guernsey, 1861), pp. 28–9. In England and Wales, relief was not made dependent on school attendance until 1873 (Fraser, 'English poor law and the origins of the British welfare state', p. 15).

[242] The English 'crusade' was sparked off by a surge in outdoor relief spending during the 1860s depression and was vigorously promoted by the Charity Organization Society. In November 1869, Poor Law Board President George Goschen, later Vice-President of the COS, issued his famous 'Goschen Minute', which conceptualised the state as provider of last resort and apportioned responsibility for all those not actually destitute to charity. The crusade was popular among ratepayers and guardians, and resulted in significant cut-backs in outdoor relief during the 1870s (Brundage, *English Poor Laws*, pp. 107–8, 114).

[243] 9.4.1877, IA, DC/HX 054–06.

In those cases where relief applicants had overcome these hurdles and had their claims granted, continuity was never guaranteed and summary withdrawals of relief were common, both before and after 1877. In many cases they were instituted as a direct reprisal for behaviour of which the authorities disapproved. In 1837, Elizabeth Bott, a widow, was peremptorily struck off the relief list when she gave birth to an illegitimate child.[244] In 1879, John Chant's relief was stopped after he was discovered in an adulterous relationship.[245] In 1921, the allowance paid to Mr Brown, father of a large family, was halved when he was seen entering a pub.[246]

Assistance was, moreover, never given unconditionally. Able-bodied recipients who were otherwise unemployed were usually obliged to do odd jobs at the Town Hospital. Females were required to help with the laundry or cleaning; males to perform maintenance work or crack stone in the Hospital stone-yard.[247] In the 1850s, a register was opened to record their names and allotted tasks.[248] Nor did the obligation to work apply exclusively to the able-bodied. When teenager Henry Russell was given a wooden leg after the amputation of his club foot in the 1870s, he was obliged to pay for it by working in the Hospital's shoemaker's shop.[249]

In all cases where there was the slightest possibility of monetary restitution, parochial authorities pursued it scrupulously. Adolphe Monnier's parish burial in 1862 was paid for by selling his box of tools.[250] Treatment costs for Charles Bennett, run over by a tram in 1886, were recovered by actioning the Tramway Company.[251] Relief recipients who inherited money or were later discovered to have funds of their own were required to make restitution.[252] Claimants with life insurance policies were asked to assign their policies to the parish.[253] English poor law authorities were prevailed upon to fund the relief of strangers unsuited to deportation.[254] Fathers of bastards and the adult children of elderly recipients were compelled, through moral pressure or Court action, to reimburse advances and/or assume support themselves.[255]

The result of such judgmental and begrudging policies was to stigmatise the very action of claiming relief and to deter the self-respecting from ever voluntarily seeking help. Parochial administrators happily acquiesced in this. In the early 1900s, the Poor Law Board President personally solicited a discretionary States' pension for

[244] 18.6.1837, IA, DC/HX 130–02.

[245] 7.7.1879, IA, DC/HX 054–07.

[246] 6.6.1921, IA, DC/HX 052–01.

[247] 8.11.1866, IA, DC/HX 054–05.

[248] IA, DC/HX 178–04.

[249] 17.3.1875, IA, DC/HX 069–01; 8.4.1878, IA, DC/HX 054–06.

[250] 13.8.1862, IA, DC/HX 136–07.

[251] 7.2.1887, IA, DC/HX 054–06.

[252] 5.1.1876, IA, DC/HX 054–06; 6.9.1909, IA, DC/HX 046–01.

[253] 2.9.1912, IA, DC/HX 046–01.

[254] 12.4.1822, IA, AQ 0965/01; 12.6.1926, IA, DC/HX 051–01.

[255] Procedures for claiming maintenance in respect of illegitimate children were regularised by O in C, 29.2.1868. The reciprocal maintenance obligations of children, parents and grandparents were formalised in O in C, 25.7.1924.

a former States worker in order to spare him the 'dishonour' of poor law help.[256] As late as the mid-1950s, a leading islander observed that many of Guernsey's poor would rather endure 'an existence which words could not describe' than apply for parish relief.[257]

Conclusion

In town and country alike, parochial *Douzaines*' control over tax lists concentrated decision-making in the hands of like-minded groups whose interests lay in keeping calls on their purses to a minimum. They conceived their core duties as limited not only to their own communities but to the truly helpless within those communities. For such helpless parishioners they ran their Hospitals, and these Hospitals absorbed the bulk of parochial funds. This relegated outdoor relief to the status of an optional extra – occasional, partial and, above all, discretionary.

Such an approach acted as a brake on overall relief expenditure. In England and Wales, Karel Williams has estimated that people in receipt of poor relief in all its forms comprised 10.8 per cent of the total population in 1848 and 2.4 per cent in 1901.[258] Guernsey's figures are lacunary, but surviving evidence suggests an insular proportion no higher than 2.6 per cent in the former year and 1.6 per cent in the latter.[259]

Opinions differ as to the balance between public welfare and voluntary charity in nineteenth-century Britain. Robert Humphreys has asserted that 'a greater amount of assistance to the poor was provided statutorily than was available voluntarily', and that 'there is no justification for believing that Victorian charity outweighed the Poor Law in relieving poverty'.[260] Steven King and John Stewart have argued the reverse, contending that 'selectivity and insufficiency' were the pre-eminent characteristics of public welfare wherever delivered, putting 'charity rather than state welfare' at the core of poor people's 'economy of makeshifts'.[261]

What of Guernsey? In 1840, Jonathan Duncan found that funds raised by 'the religious and benevolent institutions of Guernsey' for the 'combined objects of religion and humanity' amounted to £4,058.[262] The total sum raised in poor rates by St Peter Port that year was £2,800, and the collective sum raised by the country

[256] IA, DC/HX 239–05.
[257] Sir John Leale, quoted in *Star*, 4.3.1954.
[258] Williams, *Pauperism to Poverty*, pp. 158, 161.
[259] Pauper figures for St Peter Port as given in n. 150, above; rural figures based on Country Hospital inmate totals in census enumerators' books (microfilm, PL) and an estimate of outdoor numbers; population figures from PP 1852–3 LXXXVIII and PP 1903 LXXXIV.
[260] R. Humphreys, 'Bygone charity – myths and realities', *LSE Working Papers in Economic History*, 23 (1994), pp. 10, 29 (this paper is based on studies of Bristol and Aberdeen in the1880s).
[261] S.A. King and J. Stewart, 'Welfare peripheries in modern Europe', in S.A. King and J. Stewart (eds), *Welfare Peripheries: The Development of Welfare States in Nineteenth and Twentieth Century Europe* (Bern, 2007), pp. 12–13.
[262] Duncan, *History of Guernsey*, pp. 368–9.

parishes around £900.[263] While not all funds raised for 'religion and humanity' were spent locally, Duncan's figure did not include informal personal giving. Moreover, 1840 saw no dearths or epidemics requiring exceptional fund-raising. Taking all sources together, the conclusion thus seems inescapable that, in the 1840s at least, more relief was provided to the poor by Guernsey's voluntary sector than by its parishes.

It has been shown that the low number of islanders in receipt of parochial assistance was not a function of absence of need.[264] Reluctant to claim, and without guaranteed help when they did, the poor were forced by necessity to adopt other expedients. The next chapter will investigate the range of alternative resources which might have been available to them – self-help, familial help, community help as well as charitable help – and it will explore the varied ways in which islanders combined these resources in their own 'economy of makeshifts'.

[263] IA, DC/HX 020–01.
[264] See Chapter 2.

5

Self-Help and Voluntary Charity

The historian Olwen Hufton coined the term 'economy of makeshifts', using it to describe the way in which the poor of eighteenth-century France assembled a living from a variety of disparate sources.[1] For Guernsey's poor, rural and urban alike, such a 'composite' living was always a necessity. Many of the rural poor had some scrap of land, but this seldom met a family's needs, and other expedients – fishing, labouring, working at a trade or craft – were indispensable. All household members played their part, with wives hawking produce, younger children sent weeding or bird-scaring, older girls put into service and boys sent out to labour on farms or in quarries. For poor urban families – who owned no land – the family economy was even more vital. If the household head worked at an unskilled occupation such as carting, portering, stone-cracking or general labouring, continuous employment could not be guaranteed and wives might have to help by charring, laundering or doing sewing or shoebinding at home. Urban children, much as their country cousins, would also have to supplement the family income in whatever ways they could. Such an existence was precarious and, without other resources to eke out the 'income package', or to act as stop-gaps when income failed, life would have been impossible for many such people. There was, however, a range of additional resources on which both the rural and urban poor could draw to complement their other activities, and it is with these that this chapter will be concerned. We might broadly divide such resources into three categories: first, prerogatives granted the poor as a matter of customary right; second, opportunities for self-help afforded by the commercial and mutual sectors, and third, the various forms of charity on offer. We will examine each of these in turn.

Customary rights

Modern historians of England have recognised the importance to the rural poor of certain rights vouchsafed even the humblest members of communities by simple virtue of their membership. These ranged from the right to gather brushwood and cut turf to that of taking fish or grazing animals. Such rights were largely exercised

---

[1] O.H. Hufton, *The Poor of Eighteenth Century France, 1750–1789* (Oxford, 1974), pp. 69–127.

on common land. The poor of pre-industrial England regarded these rights as part of their 'property' – assets of real value in eking out an existence under marginal conditions.[2]

While Guernsey's poor enjoyed a number of such customary rights, their scope (with one exception) was limited and in marked decline from the sixteenth century. In the medieval and early modern periods, islanders had benefited from rights to graze livestock and cut furze on fairly extensive common lands belonging to the Crown. These were located the length and breadth of the island and occupied marginal areas such as marshland at the King's Mills and heathland at Les Landes du Marché, Grandes Mielles and L'Ancresse.[3] Most of these areas were, however, sold to private individuals under Elizabeth I, following which the inhabitants of the neighbouring districts lost their access to them.[4] By the eighteenth century, all that remained of Guernsey's common land were small tracts of cliff in St Martins and the Forest.[5] Similarly, medieval landholders all over the island had enjoyed the right of *banon*, or unrestricted winter grazing over open fields, but many of these fields had been enclosed by the sixteenth century and, in 1718, *banon* was officially abolished.[6]

The one common right of profound and enduring importance concerned not the land but the foreshore. This was the right to harvest seaweed (*vraic*) for use as fertiliser and fuel. The significance of this commodity to the rural economy should not be underestimated. As late as the mid-1800s, the equivalent of some fifteen cartloads of seaweed were collected by every rural household each year.[7] Access to seaweed was closely regulated by the Royal Court, whose earliest surviving ordinance on the subject dates from 1536.[8] Loose seaweed washed up on the beach could be taken all year round, but cutting of the more prized crop attached to rocks was permitted only twice yearly, in the months of February and March, and again in June, July and August. In a concession to the poor, cutting in the first month of the summer harvest was restricted to households owning no livestock, on condition that the harvesters carried their seaweed manually from the sea to the high tide mark. Poor families made full use of this concession to gather as much as they could of this

2   For a discussion of this subject, see E.P. Thompson, *Customs in Common* (London, 1991) and J.M. Neeson, *Commoners: Common Rights, Enclosure and Social Change in England, 1700–1820* (Cambridge, 1993).

3   R.P. Hocart, *Guernsey's Countryside: An Introduction to the History of the Rural Landscape* (Guernsey, 2010), pp. 47–8.

4   Vale parishioners were exceptional in retaining rights to graze livestock at L'Ancresse despite sale of the land (R.A. Henry, *The History of L'Ancresse Common* (Guernsey, 2008), pp. 9–10, 66).

5   Hocart, *Guernsey's Countryside*, pp. 48–9.

6   In Guernsey, enclosure took place consensually, as landowners exchanged strips and erected earth banks around consolidated holdings; this was often done to protect land from the beasts of those with unenclosed strips (Hocart, *Guernsey's Countryside*, p. 44).

7   J.M. Neeson, 'Gathering the humid harvest of the deep: the midsummer cut vraic harvest in nineteenth-century Guernsey', *TSG*, 26 (2009), p. 521.

8   Hocart, *Guernsey's Countryside*, p. 49.

valuable commodity to manure their own holdings, burn on their hearths, or hawk to their neighbours in return for cash or goods.[9]

On a different tack, but no less important, Guernsey's customary law also protected widows' property rights. Before a deceased man's children could inherit, his widow was entitled to one-third of his personal property and life enjoyment of one-third of his real property.[10] As a consequence of the law, many eldest sons found themselves obliged to build wings on to family farmhouses or, at the very least, to set aside rooms in their cottages.[11] Widows were traditionally among the most vulnerable members of society, and this provided them with a practical safeguard.

Most of these rights, such as they were, had evolved at a time when a majority of islanders lived off the land. In eighteenth- and nineteenth-century St Peter Port, where only a few owned houses, kept livestock or tilled fields, such rights had minimal value. The urban poor therefore focused on a rather different range of resources (which of course were also open to countryfolk). The first of these resources we shall consider are those which individuals might access independently – through everyday commercial channels, or through membership of associations or groups.

Resources for self-help

In St Peter Port, as in other towns, pawnbroking was much used by the poor as a means of securing short-term credit when other funds ran dry. In England, it had begun as a sideline for bankers and goldsmiths after 1650, and by 1750 there were 250 large pawnshops in London alone.[12] Prior to the 1850s, pawnshops *per se* are hard to find in Guernsey, but St Peter Port had many 'marine stores' and second-hand shops which, in other localities, were well known to accept low-value pledges in return for small advances.[13] From 1851, Guernsey's census enumerators' books always identified a clutch of pawnbrokers in town, often non-local, often based in poorer districts: Hirsch Fink, a 'clothier and pawnbroker' from Prussia who operated from Church Square in 1851; Englishmen Sydney Potter and William Gould, trading from the Pollet and Tower Hill respectively in 1861; the Smythson family in Cornet Street and Anna Green in the Canichers in 1871; the Polish 'jeweller and pawnbroker' Lazarus Harris in Cliff Street in 1881; and many others. An early twentieth-century register from a Cornet Street pawnbroking establishment shows parishioners regularly pledging their Sunday-best on a Monday and redeeming it for use the following weekend.[14] In her study of the pawnshop economy of York,

---

[9] Neeson, 'Humid harvest', pp. 529, 531; D.T. Ansted and M.A. Latham, *The Channel Islands* (London, 1862), p. 515.

[10] P. Jeremie, *On Real Property and Taxation in Guernsey* (Guernsey, 1841), p. 147.

[11] Hocart, *Guernsey's Countryside*, p. 86.

[12] A. Tomkins, *The Experience of Urban Poverty, 1723–82: Parish, Charity and Credit* (Manchester, 2006), p. 204.

[13] Tomkins, *Urban Poverty*, pp. 208, 213.

[14] IA, AQ 0685/01.

Alannah Tomkins has analysed the way in which pawning was adroitly used by the poor not only to cover routine expenses but to regain their footing after a crisis and to stave off recourse to the parish for so long as they possessed some pledgeable property.[15] The shops owned by Fink, Potter, Harris and others doubtless served St Peter Port's poor in similar ways.

Box clubs (also known as slate clubs) were another institution in evidence locally. These were semi-formal unions of wage-earners whose weekly subscriptions were pooled into funds paying out sickness benefits, funeral costs or widows' pensions. Smaller clubs might be quite *ad hoc*, often based in public houses, and of no long duration. In England, they came into existence from the mid-1660s.[16] Paul Slack has seen in them 'something of the character of fraternities'.[17] A number of such clubs existed in both St Peter Port and the country parishes from the 1760s.[18] They tended to be run by self-limiting groups with a common interest. In the countryside, farmers' mutuals were popular. These were often organised on a parish basis. St Martins set up such a society in 1821 to insure against the death and disease of livestock; farmers from the Castel parish established a similar society in 1840.[19] In St Peter Port, early nineteenth-century migrants ran a 'British Tradesmen's Club' from the Lyme Packet Inn near the Town Church, offering assistance to 'members, who, through unavoidable misfortune, or want of employ, may be under the necessity of returning to their native country'.[20] Military pensioners, too, had their own local benefit club.[21] Tailors had a Provident Burial Society through which members might save for their own funerals.[22] Quarrymen in St Sampsons and the Vale established a Granite Benefit Club in 1850 to provide financial support in the event of death or serious injury.[23] In 1864, Dr Auguste Constantin founded *la Société de Secours Mutuels*, which catered for people of French origin.[24] Canon William Foran presided over the Guernsey Mutual Medical and Benefit Association, which served English-speaking Roman Catholics.[25] There was even a Guernsey Total Abstinence Benefit Society providing services to those who had signed the pledge.[26]

15 Tomkins, *Urban Poverty*, p. 229.
16 J. Innes, 'The "mixed economy of welfare" in early modern England: assessments of the options from Hale to Malthus (c.1683–1803)', in M. Daunton (ed.), *Charity, Self-Interest and Welfare in the English Past* (London, 1996), p. 144.
17 P.A. Slack, *The English Poor Law, 1531–1782* (1990; Cambridge, 1995 edn), p. 43.
18 M.A. Ward, 'Guernsey's insurance history: an initial essay', *TSG*, 22 (1989), p. 665; G. Stevens Cox, *St Peter Port, 1680–1830: The History of an International Entrepôt* (Woodbridge, 1999), p. 123.
19 Ward, 'Guernsey's insurance history', pp. 667, 669.
20 *Star*, 5.11.1822. Steven King observes that migrants were particularly drawn to such clubs, which acted as a substitute for absent kith and kin (S.A. King, *Poverty and Welfare in England, 1700–1850: A Regional Perspective* (Manchester, 2000), p. 174).
21 21.3.1826, IA, DC/HX 083–01.
22 *Guerin's Almanac* (Guernsey, 1894).
23 *Comet*, 24.10.1850.
24 Ward, 'Guernsey's insurance history', p. 670.
25 *Press Directory and Almanac* (Guernsey, 1913).
26 TNA, FS 1/937.

From the mid-nineteenth century onwards, these small home-grown associations were joined by the major United Kingdom mutuals. The Independent Order of Rechabites seems to have been first to come to Guernsey in 1840, but within the next three decades the Oddfellows, Foresters, Royal Liver Friendly Society, Hearts of Oak Benefit Society, National Deposit Friendly Society, Rational Sick and Burial Association and many others all had a local presence.[27] In response to a petition from the Guernsey branch of the Oddfellows in the 1860s, a number of United Kingdom statutes relating to Friendly Societies were registered locally in 1868.[28] By 1912, Guernsey's Chamber of Commerce estimated that some 5,000 local people belonged to friendly societies or slate clubs of some kind. This equated to about half the working-age male population.[29]

Despite these numbers, it is important to note that the slate clubs and friendly societies of Victorian and Edwardian times had significant limitations. To begin with, any benefits they offered (other than widows' benefits) were usually paid only to the named subscriber; thus the medical expenses, burial costs, etc. of other family members were not covered. Further, until the twentieth century, most societies accepted male subscribers only (among the major societies, only the Rechabites accepted women until the Foresters began admitting them in 1892). New male members were, moreover, accepted only up to a set age limit, which could be as low as 40, and a joining fee was payable which went up with age. *La Société Fraternelle de l'Île de Sarnia*, for instance, required an entrance payment of 24s for a man aged 35 in 1883, and this was to be followed by regular weekly payments of sixpence.[30] For a family man on a low wage of, say, 15s a week, this would have been hard to afford. Thus, in Guernsey as in England, membership of box clubs and friendly societies was primarily the preserve of better-paid workers, and those most exposed to poverty – lone women, the elderly, the intermittently employed – were by and large excluded.[31]

Among other options available to working people – although again chiefly the better-paid – was commercial insurance. Life insurance policies were commonly seen as a means of saving for old age, as well as providing for dependants in case of illness or death. As many as thirty-nine companies offering such insurance, including the Accidental Death Insurance Company and the Medical Invalids' Insurance Company, were listed in a local almanac in 1862.[32]

Trade unions also had an insurance function. One historian has characterised

[27] Anon., *A Short History of the Temperance Movement in Guernsey, 1566–1900* (Guernsey, 1900), p. 26; *J.W. Hill & Company's Historical Directory of the Channel Islands* (Guernsey, 1874); *Almanach de la Gazette de Guernesey* (Guernsey, 1874); *Press Directory and Almanac* (Guernsey, 1913).

[28] O in C, 19.6.1868. See also *Billet*, 30.10.1867.

[29] 20.5.1912, IA, AQ 40/06.

[30] Ward, 'Guernsey's insurance history', p. 671.

[31] P. Johnson, 'Risk, redistribution and social welfare in Britain from the poor law to Beveridge', in Daunton (ed.), *Charity, Self-Interest and Welfare*, p. 233.

[32] *Almanach Journalier* (Guernsey, 1862).

them as 'non-profit insurance groups organised by risk groups themselves'.[33] By the late nineteenth century, several home-grown trade unions existed in Guernsey. One such was the 'Guernsey Society of Stoneworkers', which organised a strike for higher wages in 1889.[34] By the early twentieth century, these local bodies had been joined (or replaced) by branches of major United Kingdom unions, among which were the Dock, Wharf, Riverside and General Workers Union and the National Union of Quarrymen. The latter was described by the *Star* in 1913 as working 'quietly and unobtrusively for the benefit of the men'.[35]

Membership of a Masonic lodge might similarly confer collective protection. Masonry flourished in Guernsey from the mid-eighteenth century and, by the 1860s, the island had five lodges.[36] Membership was by no means restricted to the privileged classes, and lodges performed a distinct welfare role. In the difficult year of 1812, Guernsey's masons actively raised funds for 'the relief of the distressed part of that fraternity'.[37] Later in the century, the Royal Masonic Benevolent Institution paid regular stipends to a number of local pensioners.[38]

Among the most significant of all collective bodies serving members' welfare interests were the churches. In 1841, Jonathan Duncan enumerated no less than twenty-one places of worship in St Peter Port alone.[39] Nonconformists were the best-represented, including Baptists, Congregationalists, Plymouth Brethren, Unitarians, Quakers and Methodists of the Wesleyan, Primitive, Bible Christian and New Connexions.[40] Most of these denominations also had churches and chapels in the countryside, where the spirit of Calvinism remained strong.[41] In an English context, Joanna Innes has noted that Nonconformists made a point of maintaining their own poor because of the residual connection between parochial relief and the Anglican church.[42] This was even more the case in Guernsey, where poor law office-holders were sworn in by the Anglican Ecclesiastical Court until as late as the 1920s. Guernsey's English and French Wesleyan circuits appointed officers from among their number to supervise collections and manage poor funds.[43] Baptist, Congregationalist and Brethren chapels deployed their elders and deacons in much the same way. The Salvation Army, present in Guernsey from 1881, provided support to poorer adherents, and Roman Catholics also assisted less well-off

[33] M. van Leeuwen, 'Histories of risk and welfare in Europe during the 18th and 19th centuries', in O.P. Grell, A. Cunningham and R. Jütte (eds), *Health Care and Poor Relief in 18th and 19th Century Northern Europe* (Aldershot, 2002), p. 43.

[34] *Comet*, 10.7.1889, 23.8.1890, 27.8.1890, 20.9.1890.

[35] *Star*, 13.2.1912, 23.9.1913.

[36] Stevens Cox, *St Peter Port*, pp. 121–2; *The Freemasons' Magazine*, 8 (1868), pp. 325–6.

[37] *Gazette de Guernesey*, 25.1.1812.

[38] *Star*, 22.5.1879.

[39] J. Duncan, *The History of Guernsey* (London, 1841), p. 366.

[40] L.L. Clarke, *Redstone's Guernsey Guide* (Guernsey, 1841), pp. 124–7.

[41] W.R. Chapman, *His Praise in the Islands* (1984; Guernsey, 1995 edn).

[42] Innes, '"Mixed economy of welfare"', p. 145.

[43] See records of the poor fund belonging to Victoria Road French Methodist chapel in IA, AQ 0824/01.

co-religionists.[44] Even Guernsey's non-parochial Anglican churches (five in number by the end of the nineteenth century) collected and dispensed funds to struggling members of their own congregations.[45]

For believers of all ranks, religious belonging was chiefly a matter of family inheritance or personal conversion. However, the poor were as aware of the policies of churches and chapels as they were of box clubs or pawnbrokers, and some will have exercised a degree of agency in choosing an affiliation. In the next section of this chapter, which deals specifically with charity, agency on the part of the poor was minimised, for – in disposing of their own money – philanthropists reserved the selection of recipients to themselves.

Charity

Historians have observed that neighbourly charity – performing sundry services for struggling friends, relatives or workmates – was pervasive within working-class communities.[46] While such everyday kindnesses must have been as common in Guernsey as anywhere else, they have by their nature left little trace. The good deeds of the better-off have, on the other hand, made a greater impact on the records. Such records show that many among Guernsey's well-to-do quietly and discreetly provided help to their poorer neighbours. For eleven years in the late nineteenth century, a group of St Peter Port ladies collectively supplied retired Irish shopkeeper Hugh McCoubrey with 7s a week, out of concern that an application for parish help would see him deported.[47] Businessman Anthony de Saint-Dalmas maintained the elderly widow Hannah Windsor from his own purse for years, again to avert her deportation.[48] Retired army officer Charles Le Mesurier Carey similarly supported the widowed Mrs Burke, and the Reverend Penfold the octogenarian Mrs Macfarlane.[49] The discretion of such people may perhaps be contrasted with the more ostentatious charities of others, such as celebrity resident Victor Hugo, whose treats and dinners for poor children were often reported by the press.[50]

Many people from the middling and upper ranks also left money to the poor in their wills. In 1811, Elizabeth Henry left £200 worth of 3 per cent Consols to the

---

[44] Much poor relief work was performed by the Roman Catholic nuns present from 1868 (J. Marr, *The History of Guernsey: The Bailiwick's Story* (1982; Guernsey, 2001 edn), p. 57; 1.2.1884, IA, DC/HX 136–01; 22.9.1910, IA, DC/HX 046–01).

[45] For papers relating to the 'Pauvres Honteux Fund' and 'Sick and Poor Fund' of Holy Trinity Anglican church, see IA, AQ 0670/02.

[46] D. Weinbren, 'Supporting self-help: charity, mutuality and reciprocity in nineteenth-century Britain', in P. Brigden and B. Harris (eds), *Charity and Mutual Aid in Europe and North America since 1800* (Abingdon, 2007), p. 2.

[47] 16.1.1906, IA, DC/HX 249–01.

[48] 6.11.1865, IA, DC/HX 054–05; 11.9.1871, IA, DC/HX 059–01.

[49] 6.11.1865, IA, DC/HX 054–05; 3.6.1901, IA, DC/HX 056–04.

[50] *Star*, 23.12.1869.

pauvres honteux of St Peter Port.[51] In 1832, Jurat Eléazar Le Marchant left £100 to the poor of the town.[52] Admiral Sir James Saumarez, well-known for philanthropic activities of all kinds, left £1,000 to be divided between all ten of Guernsey's parishes when he died in 1836.[53]

The public-spirited might also organise *ad hoc* subscriptions in response to accidents or crises. Newspapers regularly published appeals on behalf of victims of everyday misfortunes, such as the widow and children of Samuel Du Plain, who drowned in 1837 while bathing.[54] In emergencies affecting the whole community, larger-scale subscription campaigns were mounted, often headed by leading citizens. During the many hard winters and food shortages between 1812 and 1820, Admiral Saumarez himself presided over the *Comité pour le Soulagement des Pauvres*, which distributed coal, boots, food, clothing and blankets to the poor of St Peter Port.[55] The cholera epidemics of 1832 and 1849 were further triggers for major subscription funds, as was the food shortage of 1847, when 'British residents', among others, appealed for donations to their own 'Guernsey Poor Relief Fund'.[56] The First World War saw a particular proliferation of charitable funds for relief activities of all sorts.[57]

Some private individuals and groups developed ongoing relationships with parochial welfare authorities as outlets for their benevolence. The St Peter Port Soup Kitchen was one such public–private venture. The parish had begun distributing soup to the poor around 1812.[58] After this was deemed an inappropriate use of parish funds in the early 1850s, the work was partly privatised. While the parish continued to provide both subsidies and workhouse inmates to dole out the soup, co-ordination was delegated to a charitable committee and donations were solicited from the public.[59] From the 1850s to the 1940s, the St Peter Port Soup Kitchen became a regular annual fixture, with an appeal launched for donations each autumn and pints of subsidised soup dispensed to poor parishioners over the winter.[60] Another notable public–private venture was that entered into with the States by the Reverend Peter Mignot in the 1930s. During this hard-pressed decade, the retired clergyman made a series of extremely substantial donations from his private fortune to part-finance States' relief work to the unemployed.[61]

Female involvement in charity, though not necessarily in collaboration with public bodies, was widespread. In Guernsey as elsewhere, it was part of the general

[51] 30.6.1811, St Peter Port Délibérations des Chefs de Famille, 1780–1817, PL.
[52] 8.3.1832, IA, AQ 0965/02.
[53] For this, and the Admiral's many charitable interests, see his obituary in *The Guernsey and Jersey Magazine*, 2 (1836), p. 320.
[54] *Comet*, 25.9.1837.
[55] Chapter 4, n. 179.
[56] For the 1832 cholera fund, see IA, AQ 0402/06 and AQ 0402/04–01 *et seq*. For the 1849 fund, see *Star*, 15.11.1849. For the British Residents' fund, see *Star*, 12.5,1847, 21.6.1847.
[57] 17.9.1914, IA, DC/HX 046–01; *Billet*, 18.5.1917.
[58] 26.4.1812, IA, AQ 0964/02.
[59] 8.1.1855, IA, DC/HX 054–05.
[60] Anon., 'The soup kitchen', *Quarterly Review of the Guernsey Society*, 23 (1967), pp. 92–3.
[61] *Billet*, 2.12.1932; A. Mignot, *Mignot Manoeuvres: An Alderney Genealogy* (Alderney, 2013), pp. 51–3.

culture of the female middle and upper classes, who were precluded from work or public office until well into the twentieth century.[62] Many St Peter Port ladies sponsored their own small-scale charities. Dorcas circles, which repaired old clothes and made new clothes for the poor, were particularly popular.[63] Among others, Miss Jacob ran her own Dorcas group from Queen's Road in the 1870s; Miss Collings from Clifton in the 1880s.[64]

Another British innovation which took hold among Guernsey's charitable sister-hood was that of Ragged Schools. The first had been founded in the 1830s and by 1855 there were more than 300 in Britain.[65] From 1853 until 1899, a Ragged School, superintended initially by Miss Lidstone and later by Mrs Roberts, operated from Berthelot Street, St Peter Port. As well as giving scores of the poorest urban children a basic education, the school also provided them with hot meals.[66] By 1899, both ladies had retired, but their place was in part taken by Mrs Maude Vessey, who ran a 'Children's Mission' from the Fosse André. Mrs Vessey gave sewing lessons to girls and supplied poor children with books, clothing and footwear.[67]

Miss Louisa Thurstan, the sister of a clergyman who had once served as Town Hospital chaplain, was particularly energetic among female philanthropists. As well as using her own home as a half-way house for discharged inmates (such as the ex-prostitute Mrs Bailey in 1890 and the disabled youth George Smith in 1892),[68] Miss Thurstan also ran her own 'Men's Mutual Improvement Institute', based in Fountain Street.[69]

In addition to these enterprises, many dozens of small female-run blanket-lending societies and clothing societies came and went over the years.[70] There was also at least one private charity for the relief of indigent lying-in women, *L'Amie des Pauvres*, organised by a Miss Grace and a Miss Chant.[71]

As well as these private endeavours, many women also gave their time to ventures organised and structured by the church. As in the United Kingdom, all of Guern-sey's denominations ran their own range of charitable enterprises.[72] In the nineteenth century, church 'visiting societies' were particularly in vogue. The concept had been

---

[62] Not until 1919 were women permitted to serve in parochial public office, and even then this was restricted to *femmes non couvertes*, i.e. single women, widows and the judicially separated (O in C, 9.2.1919).

[63] These societies, which had originated in Britain after Waterloo, were named after the biblical woman of Joppa who made garments for the poor (J. Styles, *The Dress of the People: Everyday Fashion in Eighteenth-Century England* (London, 2007), p. 251–2).

[64] *Almanach de la Gazette de Guernesey* (Guernsey, 1874); *Le Lievre's Almanack* (Guernsey, 1886).

[65] G. Himmelfarb, *The Idea of Poverty: England in the Early Industrial Age* (London, 1984), pp. 372–3.

[66] I.C. Salazar Gourley, 'A survey of the history and development of education in the Bailiwick of Guernsey, Channel Islands, pre-Reformation–1976' (unpub. MA dissertation, University of British Columbia, 1976), pp. 16–17, 111; *Billet*, 29.12.1897.

[67] *Star*, 13.2.1897.

[68] 11.8.1890, IA, DC/HX 136–02;1.2.1892, IA, DC/HX 057–01.

[69] *Star*, 5.1.1888.

[70] See, for example, 18.9.1839, IA, AQ 0965/02 and *Star*, 26.11.1849.

[71] *Guerin's Almanack* (Guernsey, 1894).

[72] F.K. Prochaska, *The Voluntary Impulse: Philanthropy in Modern Britain* (London, 1988), p. 23.

inaugurated by English Methodists with their 'Benevolent or Strangers' Friend Society' founded in London in 1785, following which the idea had spread geographically and over other denominations. These visiting societies focused primarily on working people not in receipt of parochial relief, and offered food, coal, clothing, blankets and advice on housekeeping and childcare, as well as religious tracts and Bibles.[73]

St Peter Port's own 'Benevolent and Strangers' Friend Society' was founded in 1813 in association with Ebenezer Methodist chapel. By 1840, it employed sixteen volunteer visitors assigned to eight St Peter Port districts, who dispensed small cash allowances and other useful items to some fifty named recipients.[74] Another such society was the *Société Charitable de l'Ile de Guernesey*, founded in 1819 and run by an eighteen-strong all-female committee. In 1837, its volunteers made 350 domiciliary visits, disbursing £30 in cash and £65 worth of bedclothes, babies' 'changes', underwear, aprons and shawls.[75]

Another major player in St Peter Port was the Anglican-run 'Provident and District Society', which aimed to encourage working people 'to maintain their families without parochial assistance' through 'forethought and frugality'. In the winter of 1849/50, it lent out 450 blankets and relieved eighty-five cases of distress. It also acted as a savings bank, taking £1,279 in deposits over the course of 1849.[76]

These Protestant associations had their Roman Catholic counterpart in the Society of St Vincent de Paul, founded in Paris in 1833. A Guernsey branch seems to have been active among St Peter Port's Catholic community from at least the 1860s.[77] The Salvation Army, which by the 1890s had outposts in St Martins, St Sampsons, the Vale and St Peter Port, also ran a wide variety of enterprises for and among the poor, again including a savings bank.[78]

Aside from such private and church ventures, Guernsey also had a number of more formal charitable foundations. These usually had the distinction of being established and run by men. Among them were a number of funds administered by the Royal Court, the oldest and most important of which was the De La Court Fund, first endowed by a bequest from Jurat Jean De La Court in 1588 but subsequently augmented with bequests from other testators.[79] By the nineteenth century, the De La Court Fund was chiefly used to relieve maritime casualties, such as shipwreck victims, seamen's widows and fishermen who had lost boats or tackle. In the 1870s, it was disbursing about £350 annually to sixty or so recipients.[80] In addition to this, the Royal Court administered three smaller funds, all set up in the

---

73 F.K. Prochaska, *Women and Philanthropy in Nineteenth-Century England* (Oxford, 1980), pp. 98–100.
74 Relief Book of the Guernsey Benevolent and Strangers' Friend Society, 1839–61, PL.
75 IA, AQ 0299/16–2.
76 *Star*, 24.7.1850.
77 *Star*, 14.11.1868.
78 For the Salvation Army Savings Bank, see correspondence from 1884 in IA, DC/HX 062–03.
79 For the history of this Fund, see *The Guernsey and Jersey Magazine*, 3 (1837), pp. 46–8.
80 Annual details of the Fund's disbursements are given in local almanacs, such as *Le Lievre's Almanac* and *Press Directory and Almanac*.

nineteenth century: Jean Priaulx's Fund, founded in 1829 to provide the poor with trusses and extended to all surgical appliances in 1881; Sir William Collings' Fund, established in 1849 to give general assistance to 'natives or strangers resident seven years', and the Victoria Fund, set up in 1897 to help those ineligible for assistance from the other funds.[81]

Guernsey also had its own formal public Savings Banks. The first, known simply as the Guernsey Savings Bank, was founded by a group of leading islanders in 1822, some twelve years after Henry Duncan had opened the earliest such institution in Scotland.[82] The Bank's opening prospectus stated explicitly that its rules were modelled on those of an English County Savings Bank, and expressed its founders' hope that, by 'forming a secure place of deposit for the superfluous earnings of the humble but industrious classes' it would 'efficiently prevent distress'.[83] The formula proved popular and successful, and the Guernsey Savings Bank was joined in 1859 by a second such institution, which called itself the Penny Savings Bank.[84]

Another British idea replicated in Guernsey was that of the reformatory school. Energetically promoted by social reformer Mary Carpenter, private and charitable reformatories had become numerous in England after the passage of the 1854 Youthful Offenders Act.[85] In the 1840s and 1850s, bands of unruly urchins 'loose on the streets' had become a major irritation to St Peter Port's better-off and, under the aegis of Bailiff Peter Stafford Carey (who had served as a judge in England), a group of influential parishioners founded their own private reformatory in 1856.[86] The institution was at first financed entirely voluntarily, and took boys (only) from a variety of sources. However, in 1859, the Royal Court agreed to use the reformatory for male offenders aged 16 and under who would otherwise be sentenced to prison, and HM Receiver General was authorised to fund their maintenance from Crown revenues.[87] The maximum number of boys accommodated in the institution at any one time was twenty. They came from the most disadvantaged sections of the local community. A newspaper reported in 1861 that, of the thirty youngsters admitted that year, only seven could read and write, and twenty had lost at least one parent.[88] The experiment was, however, short-lived. The institution closed in 1862 owing to lack of funds. Subscriptions had dried up, and the Receiver General's contributions did not cover actual costs. For several years thereafter Guernsey's juvenile offenders were once more consigned to adult prison. Finally, a law was passed in 1880 which permitted young offenders to serve their sentences in Certified Reformatory Schools in England.[89]

---

[81] On all the Royal Court Funds, see T.F. Priaulx, 'The De La Court Fund', *Quarterly Review of the Guernsey Society*, 25 (1969), pp. 67–71.
[82] R.A. Cage, *The Scottish Poor Law, 1745–1845* (Edinburgh, 1981), p. 71.
[83] *Star*, 5.2.1822; 16.2.1822, IA, AQ 0965/01.
[84] *Star*, 17.11.1859.
[85] Prochaska, *Voluntary Impulse*, p. 67; Himmelfarb, *Idea of Poverty*, p. 378. See also M. Carpenter, *Reformatory Schools, for the Children of the Perishing and Dangerous Classes, and for Juvenile Offenders* (London, 1851).
[86] *Billet*, 16.7.1862.
[87] *Star*, 15.12.1859.
[88] *Star*, 8.8.1861.
[89] *Billet*, 2.4.1879; ord., 6.9.1880.

Aside from the short-lived reformatory, charitable provision of any sort for local children was conspicuous by its absence. For a time in the 1860s, Guernsey had had a private 'Refuge for Destitute Children', but it closed in 1864 when its founder, the Reverend Osmond Dobrée, left the island.[90] Perhaps to remedy this loss, a major initiative was launched in 1869 to establish a charitable home for girls. The object of this enterprise, which again involved Sir Peter Stafford Carey,[91] was primarily to provide an alternative to the Town Hospital, where girls were thought to be exposed to corrupting influences. An inaugural meeting in March 1869 was attended by many leading islanders, including, as well the Bailiff, most of the Anglican clergy, St Peter Port Poor Law Board President Abraham Bishop, and figures well known for charitable activities, such as Major Charles Le Mesurier Carey and Captain Oswald Borland.[92]

Despite its high-powered launch, the project never seems to have materialised on the ambitious scale originally envisaged. Instead, a modest establishment was opened the following year by St John's vicar Thomas Brock and his wife in the house next to their vicarage.[93] They called it the 'St John's Industrial Training Home'. According to a local newspaper, it was intended for girls in 'destitute or dangerous positions', who would be trained for domestic service. 'Compassionate people' were called upon to sponsor suitable children at a cost of 4s 6d per week.[94] In 1878, the Industrial Home moved from St John's to a more westerly site at Amherst, at which time the Reverend and Mrs Brock also transferred its running to a ten-strong 'management committee'.[95] The Home continued in existence for a further two decades, and closed in the spring of 1897.[96]

The precise connection between the Industrial Home and the meeting attended by the Bailiff and others in March 1869 is unclear. However, this gathering may well have led indirectly to the establishment of Guernsey's own version of the 'Charity Organization Society' (or COS). This Society, which exerted considerable influence on late nineteenth-century British philanthropic thinking, had started in London in 1868 as the 'Society for Organizing Charitable Relief and Repressing Mendicity'.[97] Its aim was to co-ordinate the work of charitable bodies, encourage co-operation between charity and the poor law and provide trained investigators to scrutinise relief claims.[98] The inaugural meeting of the Guernsey Society for Organizing Charitable Relief, held in November 1870, was attended by most of the dignitaries who

---

90   *Star*, 15.9.1864.
91   Still Bailiff and knighted in 1863.
92   *Star*, 25.3.1869.
93   St John's church was an Anglican district church built in 1838 to serve the northern suburb of St Peter Port, which was predominantly inhabited by the working class.
94   *Star*, 19.2.1870, 1.3.1870.
95   *Star*, 20.7.1878.
96   21.1.1897, IA, DC/HX 179–04.
97   M.E. Rose, 'Introduction: the poor and the city, 1834–1914', in M.E. Rose (ed.), *The Poor and the City: The English Poor Law in its Urban Context, 1834–1914* (Leicester, 1985), p. 11.
98   According to David Englander, the COS's investigative fervour caused poor people to reconstrue the meaning of the acronym as 'Cringe or Starve' (D. Englander, *Poverty and Poor Law Reform in Nineteenth-Century Britain, 1834–1914* (Harlow, 1998), p. 29).

had participated in the girls' home gathering the previous year.[99] Again, in spite of the fanfare attending its launch, this body does not appear to have distinguished itself. No evidence has been found of any formal relationship with the poor law, nor any co-ordinating role among charities in general. By the late 1870s, the Guernsey Society for Organizing Charitable Relief had become just another of the island's visiting societies, distributing bread, meat and coal fortnightly to selected families.[100] The date of its demise is unknown.

A more enduring institution was Guernsey's cottage hospital. Cottage hospitals, the first of which had been founded in Surrey in 1859, were small-scale local alternatives to the voluntary hospitals or workhouse infirmaries located in major English towns. Patients, usually drawn from the skilled working classes and lower middle classes, could be treated by their own general practitioner in return for a small fee. The fee was based on patients' ability to pay and subsidised by the hospitals' charitable revenues, which came from regular subscribers, donations and fund-raising activities.[101] Guernsey had never had a voluntary hospital, and the only alternative to home-nursing or a commercial nursing home were the sick wards of the Town and Country Hospitals. As a newspaper observed, however, most islanders found these so 'repulsive' they 'would rather do anything than go into them'.[102] The initiative behind the opening of the Victoria Cottage Hospital in 1888 came from Dr Ernest Laurie Robinson, who had established a local branch of the St John Ambulance Association in 1886 and a Voluntary Nursing Corps in 1887.[103] The hospital initially offered four beds at a fee of between 3s and 4s per week, and was staffed by volunteer nurses under a trained superintendent.[104] In 1897, it moved to the Amherst site vacated by the defunct Industrial Home.[105] Patient numbers grew from an annual total of around eighty-five in the first five years to 560 in the course of 1935.[106] In 1936, the Victoria Hospital 'Corporation' was created by an Order in Council which gave a corporate existence to the hospital's Association of Subscribers while vesting in them all the assets and responsibilities of its former trustees.[107] Just four years later, however, the hospital was commandeered by occupying German troops. When the war came to an end it did not reopen, and its buildings were sold to the States in 1947.[108] Notwithstanding the lack of a physical presence, the Victoria Hospital Corporation nevertheless remained in existence (and continues to exist to this day). As of 1950, the Corporation was authorised to use its funds to finance medical training and provide assistance with living costs and medical

[99] *Star*, 26.11.1870, 17.12.1872.
[100] *Star*, 7.4.1877.
[101] M.E. Roberts, *The Cottage Hospitals, 1859–1990* (London, 1991).
[102] *Star*, 21.1.1888.
[103] Victoria Cottage Hospital Minutes, 1888–1946, PL.
[104] *Star*, 21.1.1888.
[105] W. Gallienne, 'The Victoria Cottage Hospital (Amherst)', in D.A. Jeffs (ed.), *One Hundred Years of Health: The Changing Health of Guernsey, 1899–1999* (Guernsey, 1999), p. 51.
[106] *Star*, 1.2.1894; Gallienne, 'Victoria Cottage Hospital', p. 53.
[107] O in C, 3.7.1936.
[108] *Billet*, 30.11.1983.

expenses to individuals suffering chronic disease or disability.[109]

A decade or so after the Cottage Hospital was founded, Guernsey also acquired its first charitable residential provision for the elderly. In England, most towns possessed at least one endowed almshouse for the aged poor, some dating back to the Middle Ages.[110] However, such institutions had never existed in Guernsey, and the pioneering initiative came in the form of the 'Victoria Cottage Homes'. These Cottage Homes, financed by contributions from over 500 subscribers, were part of a project to commemorate Queen Victoria's Diamond Jubilee, and were modelled on the London Cottage Homes, run under COS auspices, where able-bodied old people were accommodated in small independent units. The promoters of the Victoria Homes project explicitly intended their facility to preserve the 'respectable elderly' from ending their days in the Town or Country Hospital.[111] By 1901, the Homes offered independent accommodation to a total of sixteen residents.[112] Growth in the sector was, however, slow, and, fifty years on, the Victoria Homes had been joined by just three other voluntary facilities for the aged: Le Platon and Les Côtils Homes, run by Roman Catholic nuns, and the Hostel of St John, an offshoot of the St John Ambulance Association. In the 1950s, these four facilities together accommodated approximately a hundred elderly people.[113]

The last formal charity we shall examine here are Guernsey's District Nursing Associations. By the First World War, the island hosted three separate Associations, respectively serving St Sampsons and the Vale, the southern country parishes, and St Peter Port. These were funded by donations, treatment fees, fund-raising events and, from time to time, parish contributions.[114] They formed a valuable adjunct to (and substitute for) the poor law medical service. In 1920, St Peter Port's three nurses collectively made 3,485 visits, and their midwife dealt with 153 maternity cases.[115] In 1922, the town Association established a maternity home – the Lady Ozanne Home – which they opened to poor women from all Guernsey's parishes.[116] Like its cottage hospital counterpart, however, the Lady Ozanne Home ceased functioning during the Occupation, and it was eventually sold to the States in 1954.[117] Proceeds from the sale of the Home were shared between all three insular District Nursing Associations, which continued to serve the island on a voluntary basis until 1977, when, by mutual agreement, their functions were assumed by community nurses paid and organised by the States.[118]

This account of charitable provision is far from exhaustive but gives some idea of the range of support which existed alongside parochial welfare in Guernsey. In

[109] O in C, 21.7.1950.
[110] Tomkins, *Urban Poverty*, pp. 86–99.
[111] *Billet*, 3.11.1897; *Star*, 11.5.1897, 13.5.1897.
[112] *Star*, 24.12.1901.
[113] See Chapter 10.
[114] A. Jones, 'The community nursing service', in Jeffs (ed.), *One Hundred Years of Health*, p. 81.
[115] *Guernsey Weekly Press*, 5.11.1921.
[116] *Guernsey Weekly Press*, 5.11.1921, 23.9.1922.
[117] *Billet*, 7.4.1954.
[118] Jones, 'Community nursing', p. 85.

some respects, provision was surprisingly extensive, particularly that offered by the churches, both for their own members and for the wider community. In other respects, there were serious gaps. This was notably the case with residential provision of all kinds – for the sick, the young and, particularly, the old.

In Guernsey, as elsewhere, there was significant overlap between the parochial and charitable spheres.[119] Figures mentioned above, such as Charles Le Mesurier Carey and Anthony de Saint-Dalmas, held parochial poor law offices at the same time as engaging in private philanthropy.[120] So too did Henry Ollivier, who perhaps provides the best illustration of all.[121] Ollivier's parochial poor law career began in 1899, with his election as St Peter Port Overseer, and ended in 1941 with his death, aged 81, while serving as President of the Public Assistance Authority.[122] Throughout this time and before, Ollivier had also worked in a charitable capacity, for which he was awarded an OBE.[123] Among other things, he had served as fund-raiser for the Guernsey Society for Organizing Charitable Relief, president of the United Friendly Society and a vice-dean in the French Methodist Circuit.[124] All too aware of the stigma attaching to parish relief, Ollivier, Carey, Saint-Dalmas and most of their colleagues conceived of the voluntary sector as the first line of defence against indigence, and the parish simply as a back-stop for the residue for whom nothing else could be done.

For those who had indeed exhausted all alternatives (including outdoor relief), the Town or Country Hospital was usually the final destination. Despite the philanthropists' best efforts, Guernsey's voluntary safety net clearly had many holes, since the number admitted to the Hospitals in their two centuries of existence ran into scores of thousands. It is now time to focus in depth on the nature of this institution. The third section of this book will take the form of a detailed study of the Town Hospital in its classic phase as a workhouse, between 1743 and World War I.

---

[119] N. McCord, 'Poor law and philanthropy', in D. Fraser (ed.), *The New Poor Law in the Nineteenth Century* (London, 1976), p. 100.

[120] Both served in various capacities on St Peter Port's Poor Law Board (see accounts for 1860 and 1875 in IA, DC/HX 272–02).

[121] For a photograph of Ollivier, see Plate 8.

[122] *Guernsey Evening Press*, 13.11.1941; *Star*, 19.11.1941.

[123] *Star*, 4.1.1939.

[124] *Star*, 26.11.1870; IA, DC/HX 015–04.

III

Town Hospital

6

Overview

Foundation

St Peter Port first decided to raise a tax to fund poor relief in 1724. In the mid-1730s, parishioners tired of this, and an attempt was made to revert to voluntary contributions. These proved insufficient and, on 21 September 1738, a parish meeting heard that poor relief funds had run out, necessitating an immediate levy of 4,000 *livres tournois* (about £285 sterling). A fortnight later, *Chefs de Famille* took the decision to build a workhouse.[1] Where did parishioners get this idea? What wider knowledge and experience might have suggested such a course?

St Peter Port had had a small medieval hospital which, although used for the poor in the Calvinist era, had not survived beyond the seventeenth century.[2] Many of Europe's 10,000 or so medieval hospitals had met a similar fate. During a wave of welfare reform in the sixteenth and seventeenth centuries they had been superseded by larger institutions.[3] Typical of these in an English context were the major London hospitals – St Bartholomew's, St Thomas's, Christ's, Bridewell, Bethlem – most refounded or remodelled in the sixteenth century.[4] Of these, Bridewell is of particular interest to the workhouse historian. Whereas the others were intended for the sick, disabled and infirm, Bridewell was conceived as a 'house of labour and occupations' where the 'idle' poor were to be set to work.[5] As well as being the ancestor of the house of correction, it was also the ancestor of the modern workhouse. Bridewell had no parallel elsewhere and it was soon imitated all across northern Europe. Amsterdam, Bremen, Lübeck, Hamburg and Danzig all had Bridewell-type workhouses by the early 1600s.[6] The French version came in the form of the *hôpital général*, designed to reform the 'idle' poor through work and religious instruction. The first such *hôpital* was opened in Lyon in 1622, and several

---

[1] 29.10.1724, 15.6.1737, 21.9.1738, 5.10.1738, St Peter Port Délibérations des Chefs de Famille, 1715–79, PL.
[2] See Chapter 3, n. 47.
[3] R. Jütte, *Poverty and Deviance in Early Modern Europe* (Cambridge, 1994), pp. 127–8.
[4] P.A. Slack, *Poverty and Policy in Tudor and Stuart England* (Harlow, 1988), p. 119.
[5] P.A. Slack, *From Reformation to Improvement: Public Welfare in Early Modern England* (Oxford, 1999), pp. 20–1.
[6] Jütte, *Poverty and Deviance*, pp. 171, 174; C. Lis and H. Soly (trans. J. Coonan), *Poverty and Capitalism in Pre-Industrial Europe* (1979; Brighton, 1982 edn), pp. 119–20.

were founded in Normandy and Brittany in the second half of the seventeenth century.[7] As well as *hôpitaux généraux*, eighteenth-century France had a network of state-sponsored *dépôts de mendicité*, punitive institutions aimed at clearing beggars from the streets, which were more akin to houses of correction.[8] By the 1730s, St Peter Port's merchants, trading widely with French, Dutch and Baltic ports, would have been well acquainted with European institutions of this kind. Through their contacts with fellow francophone merchants in London's Huguenot community, they would also have had knowledge of the French Protestant Hospital in Finsbury. This was founded in 1718 as an asylum for indigent émigrés, and Guernsey names appear among its eighteenth-century Directors.[9]

Guernsey merchants would also have been aware of other developments in England and Wales. In the seventeenth century, the Bridewell concept had been extended in the form of 'Corporations of the Poor'. These were all-in welfare systems centred on a workhouse but also administering outdoor relief across the several parishes of one city. The first was the London Corporation of the Poor, founded in the 1640s.[10] This was followed by twelve other Corporations established by Act of Parliament between 1696 and 1712, some of them in towns such as Plymouth and Bristol, with which Guernsey had trading links. These Corporations were conceived of as public–private ventures and were to a large extent financed by charitable subscriptions.[11]

In a reaction against the excesses of Charles II's reign, several campaigning societies were also established in the late seventeenth century to advance Britain's 'moral regeneration', one of which was the SPCK (Society for Promoting Christian Knowledge).[12] Among the SPCK's original aims had been to establish a network of charity schools, but, by the 1710s, workhouses had eclipsed schools as the focus of its regenerative efforts. The SPCK adopted many ideas from the Corporations of the Poor and is thought to have sponsored the landmark 'Workhouse Test Act' passed by the Westminster parliament in 1723.[13] This Act, which was permissive rather

[7]   Royal edicts of 1662 and 1673 required all major cities to establish *hôpitaux généraux* (D. Hickey, *Local Hospitals in Ancien Régime France: Rationalization, Resistance, Renewal, 1530–1789* (Montreal, 1997), pp. xvi, 54–8).

[8]   The French state had created these *dépôts* in the mid-1700s owing to a lack of co-operation by *hôpitaux généraux* in carrying out a royal edict ordering beggars and vagabonds to be confined in designated *hôpitaux* (Hickey, *Local Hospitals in Ancien Régime France*, pp. xv, 177–83).

[9]   One such was Paul Le Mesurier who served as Lord Mayor of London (Anon., *French Protestant Hospital Charter and By-Laws* (1723; Rochester, 2000 edn), pp. 44–53). For the Hospital's history, see T. Murdoch and R. Vigne, *The French Hospital in England: Its Huguenot History and Collections* (Cambridge, 2009).

[10] Slack, *Poverty and Policy*, pp. 154–5.

[11] P.A. Fideler, *Social Welfare in Pre-Industrial England* (Basingstoke, 2006), p. 153.

[12] C. Rose, 'The origins and ideals of the SPCK, 1699–1716', in J. Walsh, C. Haydon and J. Taylor (eds), *The Church of England, c.1689–c.1833* (Cambridge, 1993); W. Allen and E. McClure, *Two Hundred Years: The History of the SPCK* (London, 1898).

[13] T.V. Hitchcock, 'Paupers and preachers: the SPCK and the parochial workhouse movement', in L. Davison, T.V. Hitchcock, T. Keirn and R.B. Shoemaker (eds), *Stilling the Grumbling Hive: The Response to Social and Economic Problems in England, 1689–1750* (Stroud, 1992), pp. 146–58.

than mandatory, empowered parishes to build workhouses and deny sustenance to relief applicants refusing to enter them, thus functioning as a 'test' of need.[14] The Workhouse Test Act provided national recognition for the SPCK workhouse movement and promoted a mushrooming of new foundations. By 1777, there were 1,916 workhouses in England, housing over 90,000 paupers.[15] Scotland, too, was influenced by the movement, with institutions such as Glasgow's 'Town's Hospital' established on SPCK guidelines in 1731.[16]

The SPCK had a country-wide network of subscribing members who were expected to spread the Society's ideas throughout the regions.[17] These members were kept supplied with all its published material, including the influential 1725 handbook, *An Account of Several Work-Houses for Employing and Maintaining the Poor*, which provided practical models for the running of a workhouse. Although the SPCK had no Guernsey-based members, Peter Dobrée, a London merchant and nephew of the leading St Peter Port shipowner Nicolas Dobrée, is known to have been an early sympathiser. He joined the Society as a full subscribing member in 1746.[18]

Nicolas Dobrée, a descendant of the Huguenot Jean Daubraye who fled to Guernsey from Brittany in the 1560s, was born in St Peter Port in 1678. When parishioners were first taxed for the poor in 1724, he was assessed as St Peter Port's wealthiest parishioner jointly with two others.[19] Dobrée's main commercial interests lay in the import of wine and brandy from France. He also served as Admiralty Agent in Guernsey.[20] A vigorous and energetic man, he saw through the construction of the harbour's north pier and published navigation charts of Bailiwick waters based on his own survey. In the view of Gregory Stevens Cox, 'if any one person may be seen as the founder of St Peter Port as a successful entrepôt, that person is Nicolas Dobrée'.[21]

Dobrée also took a full part in parish life. He had become a *Douzenier* by 1715, and he served intermittently as a *Collecteur* between the 1720s and 1740s, voluntarily assuming a co-ordinating role in poor relief.[22] Dobrée's will shows that he owned

[14] A. Brundage, *The English Poor Laws, 1700–1930* (Basingstoke, 2002), p. 12.
[15] T.V. Hitchcock, 'The English workhouse: a study in institutional poor relief in selected counties, 1696–1750' (unpub. DPhil thesis, Oxford University, 1985), pp. 101, 119; Hitchcock, 'Paupers and Preachers', p. 145.
[16] R.A. Cage, *The Scottish Poor Law, 1745–1845* (Edinburgh, 1981), p. 46; Anon., *An Account of Several Work-Houses for Employing and Maintaining the Poor* (1725; London, 1732 edn), p. 181.
[17] Hitchcock, 'Paupers and Preachers', pp. 151–61.
[18] Peter Dobrée, born in St Peter Port in 1714, was the son of Nicolas Dobrée's brother Peter. He died in London in 1753. For his membership, see SPCK Subscription Book, 1698–1768, C1/1, Cambridge University Library.
[19] R.P. Hocart, 'A Guernsey merchant and his family in the reign of George II', *TSG*, 21 (1983), p. 362. For a contemporary portrait of Nicolas Dobrée, see Plate 6.
[20] As such, it was his duty to take possession of all prizes brought in by privateers (Hocart, 'Guernsey merchant', pp. 363, 368).
[21] G. Stevens Cox, *The Guernsey Merchants and their World in the Georgian Era* (Guernsey, 2009), pp. 4, 188.
[22] A parish register records that Dobrée took personal responsibility for organising the collection

property in the Isle of Wight: several farms in the western parishes of Calbourne, Shalfleet and Northwood which he visited fairly frequently.[23] It is interesting to note that Northwood had a workhouse from 1727, and that there were others close by, at Newport and Brighstone, from 1729.[24]

It is unclear whether the original proposal for a workhouse emanated from Nicolas Dobrée himself. However, from the moment St Peter Port decided to build one, he took the closest possible interest. On several occasions, he sought his London-based nephew Peter's advice on practical issues relating to workhouses.[25] Many of his early concerns centred on the legal status of such an institution. In the late 1730s, Dobrée and his St Peter Port colleagues attempted to secure an Order in Council enshrining the legal identity of their proposed workhouse.[26] However, their approaches to the Privy Council proved unavailing. As Peter Dobrée pointed out, such approaches might have yielded more fruit if they had been made under States' rather than parochial auspices.[27] As it was, in January 1742, the parish resolved to start building without further ado, and the Hospital's identity was never embodied in any legal document.[28]

In the spring of 1742, St Peter Port appointed a committee to seek out an appropriate site for the projected workhouse, report back on likely costs and generally oversee the undertaking. A call for additional subscriptions was also launched, and Nicolas Dobrée was appointed Treasurer of the funds.[29] Altogether, 105 individuals subscribed cash or *rentes* for the establishment of the new workhouse.[30] On the inside back cover of the Town Hospital's second daybook is a *tableau d'honneur* recording the names and contributions of the principal donors.[31] The *tableau* is a roll-call of leading parishioners – merchants, shipowners, advocates, clergymen – who in total gave the equivalent of nearly £4,500 sterling. Nicolas Dobrée himself contributed £150 and his brother William Dobrée of London £100. But by far the largest sum – £1,000 – was given by James Perchard of Geneva.[32]

On Christmas Eve 1742, the site on which the new workhouse was to be built

of the whole of the fourth poor tax in 1728 (IA, DC/HX 178–03).

[23] JER/BAR/3/4/16, Isle of Wight Record Office. See also Dobrée's correspondence in IA, AQ 804/77, IA, AQ 804/79, IA, AQ 807/20, IA, AQ 807/40.
[24] *Account of Several Work-Houses*, pp. 122–3.
[25] IA, AQ 807/32; IA, AQ 807/53.
[26] 6.11.1738, 28.11.1739, St Peter Port Délibérations des Chefs de Famille, 1715–79, PL.
[27] IA, AQ 807/32. In 1750, Jersey's States encountered no difficulty in securing a founding Order in Council for their workhouse, which was not parochial but intended for the whole island (see Appendix 3).
[28] 12.1.1742, St Peter Port Délibérations des Chefs de Famille, 1715–79, PL.
[29] 4.3.1742 and 6.4.1742, St Peter Port Délibérations des Chefs de Famille, 1715–79, PL. The first call for subscriptions had been made when the decision to establish a workhouse was taken in 1738.
[30] Watkins MS, vol. III, LL 940 WAT, PL.
[31] IA, DC/HX 117–01.
[32] Perchard, a wealthy Guernsey merchant who had retired to Geneva in 1722 for religious reasons, also donated £1,000 each to the French Hospital in London and *La Soupe*, a Huguenot charity soup kitchen in Spitalfields. He died in Geneva in the 1760s (February 1749, IA, AQ 0452/02).

was purchased by the parish of St Peter Port from Peter Carey and his wife.[33] It comprised about one English acre in an area known as *le Truchot*, a few hundred yards from the shore, to the north of the town centre. A few weeks later, the Town Hospital's first daybook was opened.[34] To begin with, it contained only building accounts. Some dozen leading citizens paid for the ongoing work out of their own pockets, to be reimbursed later from subscription funds. The last batch of building accounts is dated 1745, but parts of the building were in a suitable state for occupation within eight months. On 22 August 1743, the new Hospital received its first inmates.[35] A total of fifty-three people entered the institution over the next three months, followed by a further seventy-eight in 1744.[36]

At the back of the Hospital's fourth daybook, opened in 1758, is an undated founding statement.[37] The text states that, prior to the opening of the workhouse, St Peter Port had been paying relief to nearly 200 people, many of whom squandered their allowances in drink, leaving their children to fall into bad ways rather than learn trades and become useful citizens. It was the founders' aim to remedy these evils by establishing a house where paupers would be taught religion and made to work diligently. This text was a stock formula which could almost have been lifted from the SPCK's *Account of Several Work-Houses*.[38] In his *Historical Account of Guernsey*, published in 1751, Thomas Dicey wrote a supplement on the Town Hospital in which he replicated essentially the same words.[39] Dicey further observed that, 'not above 70' of those originally on relief entered the new workhouse, adding that one of the benefits of having such an establishment was that 'strong bodied People … naturally prone to Idleness … chuse rather to work in their own Cottages or Dwellings than in a Publick Work-house'. Given that fewer people would apply for relief, and that those who did would earn their own keep by working inside the Hospital, better-off parishioners, Dicey asserted, would eventually be relieved 'from paying any Tax at all to the Poor'.[40] This, too, was an intrinsic part of the SPCK message.[41] Thomas Dicey had never visited Guernsey, but received much of his information from 'a very worthy Merchant in London, a Native of the Island'.[42] F.B. Tupper stated a century later that this was 'Mr Dobrée', likely to have been Nicolas Dobrée's nephew Peter, who, as we have seen, was an SPCK member.[43] The evidence is circumstantial rather than direct, but all this certainly suggests that SPCK influence was crucial in inspiring the foundation of the Town Hospital.

[33] The contract was signed on behalf of the parish by St Peter Port's Rector, its two Church-wardens and two of its *Collecteurs*. For more details, see *Billet*, 18.3.1925.
[34] 13.3.1743, IA, DC/HX 117–01.
[35] 22.8.1743, IA, AQ 1051/01.
[36] 7.10.1743, IA, DC/HX 079–01; IA, DC/HX 117–01.
[37] IA, DC/HX 118–02.
[38] See, for instance, *Account of Several Work-Houses*, pp. 87–8.
[39] T. Dicey, *An Historical Account of Guernsey* (London, 1751), p. 187.
[40] Dicey, *Historical Account*, pp. 192, 193, 195.
[41] *Account of Several Work-Houses*, pp. 101, 106, 128, 169. See also Hitchcock, 'Paupers and Preachers', p. 156.
[42] Dicey, *Historical Account*, p. xxii.
[43] F.B. Tupper, *The History of Guernsey and its Bailiwick* (Guernsey, 1854), p. 340.

Finally, the use of the title 'Hospital' for St Peter Port's institution should not mislead us as to its purpose. In England and Wales, the term 'workhouse' began to be used to the exclusion of others only with the creation of what became known as the 'workhouse system' under the 1834 Poor Law Amendment Act.[44] In the eighteenth century, the SPCK and its collaborators were not fastidious about terminology. The designations 'Hospital', 'Working-Hospital', 'Charity House', 'House of Maintenance', 'House of Industry' and 'Charity Hall' all featured alongside that of 'workhouse' in their literature.[45] For St Peter Port's francophone ratepayers, the choice of 'Hospital' was the most obvious, since *'hôpital'* was the term by which workhouses were known in France.

Governance

On 28 September 1743, the Town Hospital's Board of Directors sat for the first time in full session. Chairman of the Board and foremost in authority was the Hospital's Treasurer, a post already occupied by the 65-year-old Nicolas Dobrée. St Peter Port's Rector, Churchwardens, *Procureur*, *Collecteurs* and all Jurats resident in the parish had been granted *ex-officio* seats, and it had been decided to complement these with four elected Directors chosen annually from among the *Chefs de Famille*.[46] The Board was to meet every Friday at 2.00 p.m. on Hospital premises. Day-to-day running was delegated to a team of paid employees (initially a mistress, a master and two under-mistresses), but executive decisions concerning admissions, discharges, discipline, expenditure and all aspects of general policy were the preserve of the Board, who also had control of such relief as continued to be dispensed outside.[47]

Nicolas Dobrée served as Treasurer until 1746, when Thomas De Lisle was elected to succeed him.[48] Dobrée, however, stayed on as 'Supervisor' or 'Inspector' of the Hospital until his death at the age of 73 in 1751. According to Thomas Dicey, his role was 'to examine often the Conduct of the Poor in the Hospital', and to call extraordinary Board meetings when necessary.[49] The post of Supervisor was not retained after Dobrée's death, but it was decided to grant ex-Treasurers permanent *ex-officio* seats on the Board.

On the inside back cover of the first daybook is a list of all Treasurers between 1743 and the early nineteenth century.[50] Until 1769, fresh incumbents were elected almost yearly. After this date, spells in office became increasingly protracted, with

[44] J.S. Taylor, 'The unreformed workhouse, 1776–1834', in E.W. Martin (ed.), *Comparative Development in Social Welfare* (London, 1972), p. 61; M.A. Crowther, *The Workhouse System, 1834–1929: The History of an English Social Institution* (1981; London, 1983 edn), p. 24.

[45] *Account of Several Work-Houses*, pp. 61, 62, 118, 144, 150, 161, 171, 181.

[46] 28.9.1743, IA, DC/HX 079–01. The number of annually elected Directors was later increased to six.

[47] IA, DC/HX 117–01.

[48] 22.11.1746, IA, DC/HX 079–01.

[49] Dicey, *Historical Account*, p. 189.

[50] IA, DC/HX 117–01.

just five Treasurers serving in the four decades to 1809. The longest-serving Treasurer was Jean Condamine, in office for fifteen years between 1795 and 1809. It is unclear why tenures lengthened in this way. Possibly, leading parishioners lost interest when the founding generation passed away, and the post was left to whomsoever was willing to fill it. Whatever the case, elite attention seems to have been refocused on the Hospital by the economic crisis of the early 1800s. In 1809, the long-serving Condamine was forcibly ousted by a group of influential parishioners, and a ruling was passed to the effect that no future Treasurer should stay in post more than a year without submitting himself for re-election.[51] To share the growing burden of responsibility, the post of Vice-Treasurer was created four years later, also on a yearly tenure.[52]

Over the next few years, the increased frequency of elections and consequent proliferation of ex-Treasurers caused the Board to grow to an unwieldy size. By 1822, Board members numbered more than thirty.[53] By 1848, they exceeded forty.[54] Ultimately, this tendency to growth was checked by the Order in Council of 28 December 1852 which reorganised the administration of poor relief in St Peter Port and instituted the new Poor Law Board. Membership of the Board was statutorily limited to twenty. Members were headed by a President and Vice-President who had to serve a minimum of one year, but could serve up to three years before calling for elections. Jurats lost their *ex-officio* seats, and the place of the six annually elected Directors and unlimited number of ex-Treasurers was taken by just three biennially elected members chosen from ex-Treasurers or ex-Presidents.[55] The Board had overall control over both indoor and outdoor relief, but the House Committee, a permanent seven-member sub-committee chaired by the Poor Law Board's Vice-President, was henceforth to administer the Hospital.

The House Committee continued in existence until 1925. Changes to its mode of operation were relatively few, save that women were admitted to serve as members in 1920.[56] Five years later, the House Committee was replaced by an eight-member 'Executive Committee' when the States assumed responsibility for poor relief funding.[57] Notwithstanding that ownership of the Hospital was transferred to the States, control of the establishment remained with the St Peter Port Poor Law Board, of which the Executive Committee was a sub-committee performing almost exactly the same functions as the old House Committee.

---

[51] 2.3.1809, IA, DC/HX 079–02.
[52] 1.2.1813, IA, DC/HX 079–02.
[53] 3.6.1822, IA, DC/HX 135–02.
[54] These included nine ex-Treasurers as well as all twelve Jurats of the Royal Court (*Rapport du Comité nommé par les Chefs de Famille de la Ville et Paroisse de Saint Pierre-Port le 5 Avril 1848* (Guernsey, 1849), PL).
[55] This was extended to include former Vice-Presidents and *Procureurs* by O in C, 10.5.1860.
[56] Mrs L. d'A. B. Collings joined the House Committee in 1920 after her election as Overseer following O in C, 9.10.1919, which enabled *femmes non couvertes* to serve in public parochial office (6.1.1920, IA, DC/HX 052–01). In England and Wales, women had been serving as guardians since the 1870s (S. Fowler, *Workhouse: The People, the Places, the Life Behind Doors* (Richmond, 2007), p. 33).
[57] O in C, 24.7.1925.

The Executive Committee survived for only twelve years. It was abolished by the 1937 Public Assistance Law.[58] This law officially restyled both the Town and Country Hospitals 'public assistance institutions', and created a unitary 'Hospital Board' to supervise both, which was chaired by the President of the Public Assistance Authority. The sixteen-strong Board was directly answerable to the States, and ten of its members were to be elected by the States from among States members. From this point onwards, the workhouse was no longer in the control of its founding parish.

Physical Structures

As might be expected of a building substantially completed within eight months, the original Hospital was of modest proportions. Thomas Dicey described it as a two-storey rectangular block 110ft long by 40ft wide, surmounted by garrets and underlain by two vaults and three cellars. The building faced east towards the shore, between which and the Hospital there were at this time few buildings, giving inmates 'a fine Prospect of the Sea'. Behind the Hospital against the western boundary wall were lean-tos accommodating a bake-house, a wash-house, a provision store, a tailor's shop, a shoemaker's shop, lock-ups for lunatics and a shed for cordage. On a terrace immediately in front of the Hospital was a ropewalk and, in the front yard, an outhouse used for casting lead. By 1750, the whole one-acre site, which encompassed open ground to the east and north-west, was enclosed by a wall.[59]

In 1762, it was decided to build a whole new block containing a cellar, two storeys and a garret floor in the garden in front of the Hospital.[60] This building, separate from the main block and screened off from it by a wall, was initially used to accommodate soldiers stationed in St Peter Port during Seven Years War.[61] The new block again served this purpose during the War of American Independence.[62] After this time, no more soldiers were quartered at the Hospital, and, in 1810, the detached block became the permanent home of the Town Hospital's girls.[63] A porter's lodge was also built at this period, the garrets were ceiled, and the ancillary buildings along the back wall were connected to the main block.[64]

In 1817, with the post-Napoleonic slump exerting major pressure on Hospital accommodation, the original block was extended 60ft southwards to house the sick.[65] In 1824, a whole new wing measuring 100ft by 20ft was built on the north

---

58 O in C, 22.10.1937.

59 Dicey, *Historical Account*, pp. 187–8.

60 20.1.1762, St Peter Port Délibérations des Chefs de Famille, 1715–79, PL.

61 They had earlier been lodged elsewhere in the building (29.6.1756, IA, DC/HX 079–01).

62 16.9.1779, IA, DC/HX 119–04.

63 At various subsequent stages, the block also accommodated women and infants, and, in the twentieth century, boys.

64 7.1.1811, IA, DC/HX 079–02; T. Quayle, *A General View of the Agriculture and Present State of the Islands on the Coast of Normandy subject to the Crown of Great Britain* (London, 1815), pp. 290–4.

65 5.5.1817, IA, DC/HX 079–02; 15.7.1817, St Peter Port Délibérations des Chefs de Famille, 1780–1817, PL.

side of the front yard at right angles to the original block.[66] In 1825, the Hospital's principal entrance was repositioned so that it directly faced the main door of the new wing.[67] The entrance was adorned with a substantial double archway originating from a property situated at L'Hyvreuse (now Cambridge Park) which had come into the possession of the parish during the eighteenth century.[68] In 1826, a mortuary was built in the Hospital yard.[69]

By the early 1830s, the Hospital had by and large reached its definitive form. Entering by the new main gate, in the original building to the left were the infirmary, boys' quarters, refectory and master's room. In the 1824 wing facing the entrance were the men's quarters and the boardroom. The detached building on the eastern side of the yard housed the women, girls and infants.[70] The only further changes to the main site were the building of washrooms and lavatories in 1850,[71] a chapel in 1896[72] and a two-storey annexe behind the original block in 1904.[73] The ground-floor layout of the Hospital's main buildings as at 1885 is shown below.

Figure 1. Ground floor plan of Town Hospital, 1885 (source: IA, 6287)

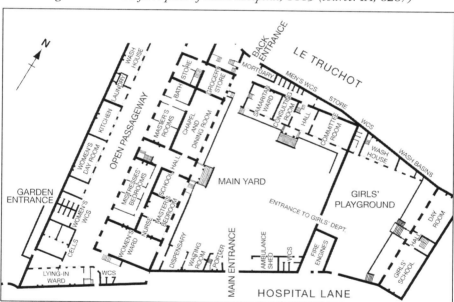

[66] 1.3.1824, IA, DC/HX 135–02.
[67] 31.10.1825, IA, DC/HX 135–02.
[68] The structure was removed stone by stone and re-erected at the Hospital. The idea had first been suggested in 1817 as a relief scheme for unemployed men (25.11.1817, IA, AQ 0965/01).
[69] 6.3.1826, IA, DC/HX 135–02.
[70] L.L. Clarke, *Redstone's Guernsey Guide* (Guernsey, 1841). p. 15.
[71] 29.8.1849, 9.1.1850, St Peter Port Délibérations des Chefs de Famille, 1844–66, PL; *Star*, 10.1.1850.
[72] 27.12.1895, 18.11.1896, IA, DC/HX 057–01.
[73] 3.8.1903, DC/HX 056–04.

Away from the principal site, the Hospital's main buildings were complemented by a substantial daughter building erected in 1832 on Hospital land several hundred yards to the north-west.[74] Originally built as a 'house of separation' for refractory inmates, it served as the Hospital's lunatic asylum from the 1840s to the 1930s. It was severed from the rest of the Hospital in the early 1870s, when a major new road cut through the site to take traffic from the seafront to the west of the island.[75] Both this and the main buildings still exist, although the 1762 block in front of the Hospital was demolished in the 1960s and replaced by a modern structure.

Patterns of occupation

At the opening of the Hospital, it was agreed that any pauper could be admitted short-term on the basis of a ticket signed by the Treasurer and two *Collecteurs*, but that the Board would collectively decide which of these would be received as long-term residents.[76] As time went on, the right to admit was also claimed by Constables and *Procureurs*, so that, by the mid-nineteenth century, it had become a matter of uncertainty and contention.[77] The position was definitively clarified at the inauguration of the St Peter Port Poor Law Board in 1853. Under the new regime, it was determined that the President, Vice-President, Constables and *Procureur* might all admit paupers provisionally, but that the House Committee would have final jurisdiction over long-term stays.[78] The discharge of inmates was, from the outset, the exclusive prerogative of the Hospital authorities and remained so well into the twentieth century.[79]

Numbers
Evidence suggests that, in the 200 years between the Town Hospital's foundation and World War II, some 30,000 to 35,000 individuals passed through the institution.[80]

---

74 IA, DC/HX 178–01.
75 15.4.1872, IA, DC/HX 054–05; Anon., 'St Julian's Avenue – a centenary', *The Review of the Guernsey Society*, 28 (1972), p. 3.
76 14.3.1765, IA, DC/HX 079–01.
77 6.4.1840, IA, DC/HX 075–01.
78 19.1.1853, IA, DC/HX 054–05.
79 This received its last iteration as rule 2(3) of the 1925 Central Poor Law Board Handbook: 'when an inmate of the workhouse claims to be discharged, the Executive Committee may withold granting of such discharge until such time as it is satisfied that such inmate on such discharge will be in a position to support him or herself and dependants' (IA, DC/HX 272–10).
80 For the eighteenth and early nineteenth centuries, the most useful information on workhouse occupancy is to be found in the daybooks, many of which provide year-end head-counts broken down by age and sex (IA, DC/HX 117–01, 117–02, 118–01, 118–02, 119–01, 119–02, 119–03, 119–04, 120–01, 121–01, 121–02, 121–03, 121–04, 122–01, 123–01, 123–02, 124–02). An early series of abstracts of accounts beginning in 1811 gives more detailed analysis, including admission and discharge figures (IA, DC/HX 045–01, 178–01), but the period from 1859 to 1924 is best provided for. Detailed statistics in a consistent format are to be found in annual abstracts of accounts published in an unbroken series between these dates (IA,

Figure 2. Average annual admissions and year-end totals, Town Hospital, 1752–1943

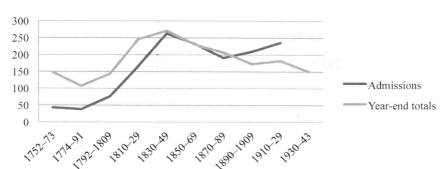

Figure 2 shows the trend in Hospital occupancy between the mid-eighteenth and mid-twentieth centuries.[81]

The Hospital's core long-term population was composed, as Thomas Dicey put it, of 'Mad, Naturals, Lame, Sick, Bed-ridden [and] infirm old People'.[82] Over and above this, there was a temporary population of more or less able-bodied paupers which ebbed and flowed according to economic conditions. Between the 1740s and 1760s, the average year-end population was about 150. This made the Town Hospital, by contemporary standards, a large workhouse. Parliamentary returns of 1776 indicated that just 9 per cent of England's 2,100 workhouses had a capacity of over 100.[83]

A period of prosperity between the end of the American War of Independence in 1783 and the beginning of the French Revolutionary Wars in 1793 saw a drop in year-end totals. These reached a low point in the mid-1780s, when only eighty or so individuals were in residence at the end of each year. Visiting Customs Commissioner William Stiles remarked that at this time 'the Hospitals … had in them only Cripples and old people'.[84] However, these exceptional conditions did not last for long. Inmate numbers gradually built up again in the late 1790s, and averaged about 125 at each year's end as the eighteenth century came to a close.

In the first decade of the nineteenth century, following the passage of the anti-smuggling Acts, a much steeper rise set in, and numbers reached the unprecedented level of 173 in December 1807. Thereafter, year-end totals continued to

---

DC/HX 272–02). After 1924, year-end head-counts continue in Poor Law Board Minutes (IA, DC/HX 051–01) and Hospital Board Minutes (IA, DC/HX 015–04, AS/MB 065–02, 065–05, 068–01). Figures used in this section are synthesised from all of these sources, unless an alternative source is specified.

81 For actual figures, see Appendix 4.
82 Dicey, *Historical Account*, p. 190.
83 S.A. King, *Poverty and Welfare in England, 1700–1850: A Regional Perspective* (Manchester, 2000), p. 38.
84 W. Stiles to H.M. Treasury, 23.8.1800 (TNA, T 64/153).

climb with each successive year, and exceeded 200 for the first time in the dearth year of 1811. This marked the beginning of a protracted period of hardship for St Peter Port's poorest parishioners. Between the end of the Napoleonic Wars and the late 1850s, Hospital inmates averaged over 250 at each year's end. Taking inmates as a proportion of parish population, the worst decade was the 1820s. In 1821, Hospital inmates equated to 2.3 per cent of St Peter Port's population, or one inmate for every forty-four inhabitants.[85] In terms of absolute numbers, however, it was the 1830s and 1840s which saw the highest year-end totals. In 1838 and 1844, the December head-count exceeded 300. Nevertheless, because St Peter Port's population had also increased, the 1841 ratio of inmates to parishioners was one for every fifty-nine.[86]

From the late 1860s onwards, economic conditions in St Peter Port grew relatively more benign, and year-end head-counts gradually sank. From 226 in 1861 the head-count fell to 213 in 1881. In the 1890s, there was a sharper fall, and the average year-end number finally dropped back below 200 – a level not seen since 1811. From this point until the 1920s, year-end totals stabilised at around 175, even during World War I. Numbers then rose by about 5 per cent during the mid-1920s, but quickly fell again as the 1930s began. By 1931, the year-end head-count was 125, and Hospital inmates equated to just 0.7 per cent of St Peter Port's parishioners, or one inmate for every 134 inhabitants.[87]

Year-end head-counts are a useful guide to the overall trajectory of the workhouse population, but they are merely a snapshot of inmates on one day. A more dynamic picture is provided by admissions figures, which are also shown in Figure 2. For the eighteenth century we have admission and discharge data for only nine years, scattered between 1754 and 1799.[88] In these years, numbers of new admissions were relatively small – an average of about forty-six annually, with roughly the same number of discharges. This enables us to assess turnover. The forty-six annual admissions and discharges equated to some 37 per cent of an average year-end total of 124. That is to say, the number of entrances and exits in the course of a year amounted to only just over a third of the number in the institution at year's end. Thus turnover was comparatively low.

For the nineteenth century, we have admission and discharge data for all but seven years, and hence a more complete picture is available.[89] In the first decade of the century, admission numbers began to climb sharply as economic conditions deteriorated and distress levels rose. From seventy in 1805, they shot up to 251 in 1811 and thence to 347 in 1829. This was accompanied by an increase in discharge numbers and hence in turnover.[90] By the 1830s, the number of arrivals and departures in the course of each year stood at 100 per cent of the year-end total. This

---

[85] Population figure from *Billet*, 15.9.1821.

[86] PP 1841 XXVII; 1841 census enumerators' books (microfilm), PL.

[87] *Census 1931: Jersey, Guernsey and Adjacent Islands* (London, 1933).

[88] The years are 1754, 1760, 1767, 1769, 1770, 1777, 1783, 1790 and 1799.

[89] These data are derived from annual abstracts of accounts. Dedicated admission and discharge registers were kept between 1809 and 1898, but, since these took the form of a rolling tally, they are less easy to use than the annual summaries.

[90] For figures, see Appendix 4.

represented an almost threefold rise in turnover from eighteenth-century levels.

We have seen that year-end head-counts slowly declined over the later nineteenth century, reverting to pre-1811 levels after 1890. However, admission and discharge numbers did not revert to earlier levels, and turnover remained high, with annual numbers of arrivals and departures persistently broadly commensurate with year-end head-counts. Further, admission and discharge numbers began to rise again in the 1890s, even as year-end totals continued to diminish. The net result of this conjunction of trends was that, by the first decade of the twentieth century, annual numbers of entrances and exits actually exceeded year-end totals by an average of 42 per cent. This level of turnover was unprecedented in the Hospital's history.[91]

In the opening decades of the nineteenth century, rising turnover was clearly linked to rising levels of distress. The question is why, with falling year-end head-counts as well as external evidence indicating an easing of distress after 1860, did turnover remain high, and why did it rise still further from 1890? The reason, as Figure 3 shows, lay in the growing propensity of St Peter Port's parishioners to resort to the Hospital for medical treatment.

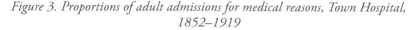

Figure 3. Proportions of adult admissions for medical reasons, Town Hospital, 1852–1919

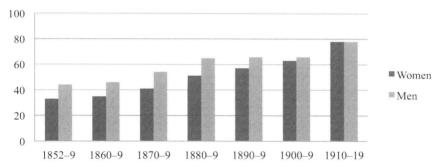

Cause of admission statistics were kept only from 1852. These, however, show that some 39 per cent of all adult admissions were already due to medical reasons by the 1850s.[92] By the 1870s, this proportion had risen to 52 per cent, and, by 1910–19, only a fifth of new entrants were being admitted for non-medical reasons. Since statistics exist only from mid-century, it is not possible to identify precisely when the rising trend in medical admissions was first initiated. However, we may tentatively speculate that it may have been triggered by improvements in medical

---

[91] High though this was by Town Hospital standards, it was lower than that of most English workhouses. This was due in no small part to the fact that admissions and discharges were strictly under the control of the Board, and inmates were not free to leave and readmit themselves, as they did – often for just a few hours – in England and Wales (Crowther, *Workhouse System*, pp. 44, 208–9).

[92] For figures, which include admissions for mental illness as well as physical illness and injuries, see Appendix 5.

facilities around the second decade of the nineteenth century. As we saw earlier in this chapter, an extension was built on to the main block in 1817 specifically to accommodate the sick. In addition to this, St Peter Port's indoor and outdoor medical provision was reorganised in 1821.[93]

Composition of the inmate cohort

We have seen that the size and turnover of the Town Hospital's population were in a constant state of evolution. This is also true of its composition. Figures 4 and 5 show the distribution of inmates by age and sex in 1756 and 1911.[94] In the former year, the Hospital's population was predominantly female and predominantly young: women and girls comprised 64 per cent of all inmates, and under-15s comprised 38 per cent. In the latter year, the Hospital's population was predominantly male and predominantly old. At 56 per cent of inmates, men and boys now outnumbered women and girls; the proportion of under-15s had declined to just 8 per cent, and the proportion of over-60s had increased to 44 per cent.

Figure 4. Inmate distribution by age and sex, Town Hospital, 1756

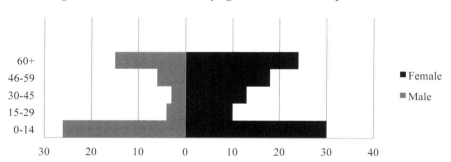

Figure 5. Inmate distribution by age and sex, Town Hospital, 1911

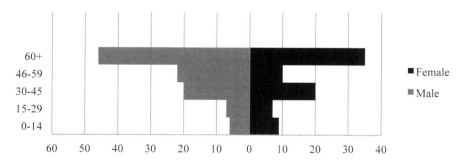

[93] See section on 'Medical relief', Chapter 4.
[94] Figures are based on data from 1.1.1756, IA, DC/HX 117–0 and http://www.1911census. co.uk.

The female preponderance among inmates was strongly marked throughout the eighteenth century. Year-end head-counts reveal the presence, on average, of seven women for every three men.[95] Few data survive for admissions during the eighteenth century, but those that do survive suggest that more women were also admitted than men. In the first batch of adults to enter the Hospital in 1743, there were, for instance, twenty-one women and eight men.[96] However, as Figure 6 shows, the sex balance among admissions appears to have altered decisively in the third decade of the nineteenth century. Whereas men accounted for only 37 per cent of all adult admissions in 1811–19, they accounted for 52 per cent in 1820–9 and, from this point until well into the twentieth century, the number of adult male admissions to the Hospital consistently exceeded the number of adult female admissions by some 10 to 15 per cent.[97]

Figure 6. Average annual adult admissions by sex, Town Hospital, 1811–1919

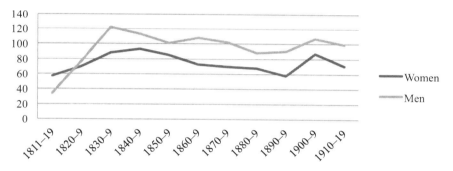

Although the initial steep rise in men's admissions was partly due to economic distress, it is likely that, even as early as the 1820s, it was also partly due to the greater propensity of men to be admitted for medical treatment than women. At all events, statistics kept from mid-century show that, by the 1850s, some 44 per cent of all adult male admissions were ascribed to medical reasons, while only 33 per cent of women's admissions fell into this class. A greater proportion of men's than women's admissions continued to be ascribed to medical reasons until the second decade of the twentieth century.[98]

There were practical reasons why more men than women entered the Hospital for medical care. Not only were men at an intrinsically higher risk of injury because of their working environments, they were also a net drain on family finances when out of action and at home. Treating them in Hospital both relieved the burden on their families and hastened their reinstatement as breadwinners.

Although more men than women were admitted to the Hospital in all decades

---

[95] See Appendix 6 and Figure 7, below.
[96] 22.8.1743, 7.10.1743, IA, DC/HX 079–01.
[97] Appendix 6.
[98] See Appendix 5 and Figure 3, above.

after 1820, women continued to outnumber men in year-end head-counts until as late as the 1870s. Figure 7 graphically depicts this phenomenon.

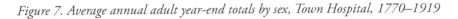

Figure 7. Average annual adult year-end totals by sex, Town Hospital, 1770–1919

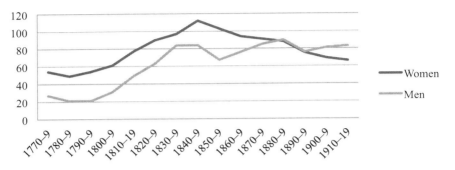

The reason for this apparent anomaly is that, up to the 1870s, more women were admitted to the Hospital on grounds of poverty than on grounds of ill-health, and, since the former was less susceptible to treatment than the latter, their stays tended to be longer than men's, and they were therefore more likely to be present at year's end.[99] The reason why this situation changed in the 1880s was that, in this particular decade, illness and injury finally superseded poverty as the main reason for women's admissions. Their average stay-length accordingly declined and, with it, their presence at year's end. From this point until at least the 1930s, men outnumbered women in both admissions and year-end head-counts, and the Hospital was transformed from a predominantly female to a predominantly male institution.[100]

The change in women's reasons for admission had many causes, not least the general improvement in Guernsey's economy triggered by the rise of commercial horticulture. However, perhaps the most important one was the demise of seafaring as a male occupation, since this left fewer women struggling to earn a living alone. It was also partly this factor which transformed the Hospital from a predominantly young into a predominantly old institution, for the demise of seafaring also affected children, who were less liable than previously to find themselves orphaned or otherwise fatherless. Figure 8 (below) illustrates changes in the Hospital's child population between 1790 and 1919.[101]

During the eighteenth century, when wartime influxes of military and naval personnel compounded the effects of seafaring, an average of 53 children were present in the Hospital at each year's end, accounting for 39 per cent of the institution's population. As soldiers and sailors departed *en masse* at the end of the Napoleonic Wars, child numbers rose still further, reaching a mid-winter average of 114 in 1810–19 (48 per cent of Hospital population). The highest ever number

---

[99] Appendix 5.
[100] Appendix 6.
[101] For numerical data, see Appendix 7.

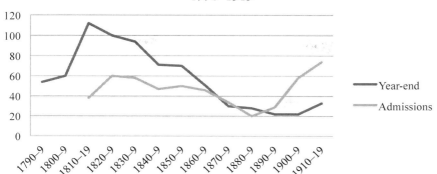

Figure 8. Average annual child admissions and year-end totals, Town Hospital, 1770–1919

of children resident at year's end – 144 – was recorded in 1819. This marked the peak of the child presence in the Hospital. By the 1840s and 1850s, the average number of children in mid-winter head-counts had dropped to seventy-one, and it continued to fall until a low point of twenty-three was reached in 1890–99, which equated to just 13 per cent of the Hospital's population.

The mid-century opening of alternative children's residential institutions, such as the Reformatory and the Industrial School, played a role in the decline in child numbers.[102] However, the primary reason for the fall seems to have been an improvement in children's economic circumstances, which occurred in tandem with that of their mothers. This is borne out by cause of admission statistics, which show a reduction in the proportion of children admitted on poverty-related grounds to just 32 per cent in 1910–19, by which time the remaining 78 per cent of child admissions were ascribed to medical reasons. It is to this increase in medical admissions that the steep late nineteenth-century climb in child admissions is chiefly due (see Figure 8).

The decline of child numbers on Hospital rolls was not, however, the only factor responsible for the 'ageing' of the institution's population. As Figures 4 and 5 show, there was also a rise in the number and proportion of over-60s. In 1756, there were thirty-nine over-60s in the Hospital, comprising 26 per cent of inmates. In 1911, there were eighty-one over-60s, comprising 44 per cent.[103] Until the late nineteenth century, female over-60s consistently outnumbered male over-60s in the Hospital (which partly accounted for the female year-end predominance).[104] This phenomenon was strongest in the 1700s, when women on average comprised 66 per cent of

---

[102] For more on these institutions, see section on 'Charity', Chapter 5.

[103] For figures over intervening years, see Appendix 8.

[104] Note that, although most eighteenth-century head-counts supplied age data, those taken in the nineteenth and twentieth centuries did not. For this period, we are therefore reliant on census enumerators' books.

over-60s in mid-winter head-counts. By 1861, however, the female proportion had declined to 55 per cent and, from the 1880s, the elderly sex balance appears to have reversed itself, with men comprising 52 per cent of over-60s in 1881 and 57 per cent by 1911 (partly accounting for the defeminisation of the year-end cohort).

It is interesting to note that, in the majority of English workhouses, men outnumbered women among the over-60s from at least the beginning of the nineteenth century, even though women lived longer and exceeded men in the general population. Reasons scholars have advanced for this situation include old men's greater inability to care for themselves and their inferior usefulness to grown-up children.[105] The fact that the reverse situation so long prevailed in the Town Hospital was almost certainly a reflection of the highly distorted sex ratio in the wider parish: the relative deficit of old men in the Town Hospital reflected their still stronger deficit in St Peter Port at large. However, this merely disguised a tendency which existed in the Town Hospital as much as it did in English workhouses – namely that, in proportion to their numbers outside, male St Peter Port parishioners aged 60 and over were more likely to find themselves in the workhouse than female parishioners of the same age. The 1851 census shows that there were only sixty-one male over-60s for every 100 female over-60s in St Peter Port at large, but that there were seventy-four male over-60s for every 100 female over-60s inside the Hospital.[106] With the demise of seafaring as a significant occupation for Guernseymen, the cohort of male St Peter Port parishioners aged over 60 gradually increased. By 1911, the absolute number of male over-60s in the parish had risen by 41 per cent relative to 1851. This growth in numbers sufficed to produce a Hospital ratio in that year of 131 male over-60s for every 100 female over-60s.[107] In this, the Town Hospital now fully conformed to the pattern in workhouses elsewhere.

By the early twentieth century, the Town Hospital had evolved in ways unanticipated at its opening. It had begun in 1743 essentially as a repository for the destitute poor and, since poverty afflicted women and children worse than men, these had dominated its population throughout the eighteenth century. The following century saw changes in both the Hospital's function and its population. There were two major watersheds. The first came in the 1820s, when the Hospital's medical department began to expand. Meeting a particular male need for medical care, this caused a masculinisation of admissions, but not, at first, of the long-stay population, since women (and children) continued to be admitted predominantly on grounds of long-term poverty. The second watershed occurred in the 1870s, when the demise of seafaring and economic upturn caused female and juvenile poverty to recede in St Peter Port. This impacted on the Hospital in three ways. Firstly, it led to a further major expansion of the Hospital's medical role, as health became the primary ground for the admission of both sexes. Secondly, it led to the masculinisation of the long-stay population, as men filled up the gap left by the women who no longer

105 D. Thomson, 'Workhouse to nursing home: residential care of elderly people in England since 1840', *Aging and Society*, 3 (1983), pp. 52, 64; Crowther, *Workhouse System*, p. 234.
106 1851 enumerators' books (microfilm), PL.
107 1851 enumerators' books (microfilm, PL); http://www.1911census.co.uk.

required poverty-related care. Thirdly and lastly, it also led to the ageing of the long-stay population, as old folk filled up the gap left by the children, who now, like their mothers, required less long-term care.

As a result of these concurrent developments, the Town Hospital had, by the early twentieth century, evolved two quite distinct specialisms: medical care and elderly care. At this stage, it was possible that the Hospital might have followed Jersey's General Hospital (and many English, Welsh and Scottish poor law institutions) in evolving into a conventional medical and surgical hospital.[108] However, as the institution developed further in ensuing twentieth-century decades, it was in the care of the elderly that it ultimately came to specialise. Its final years as a geriatric hospital will be covered in Chapter 9.

Finances

Expenditure

In its first decade of existence, the Town Hospital's annual expenditure was in the region of £360 sterling, and each inmate cost about 1¾d per day to keep.[109] These costs encompassed food, clothing, bedding, heating, lighting, maintenance, staff salaries, medical costs and expenses associated with the provision of work. Capital projects, such as new buildings and improvements to facilities, were funded by special taxes, and as much construction work as possible was done by inmates.

By the 1760s, rising occupancy had increased annual expenditure to about £650.[110] By the 1810s, Napoleonic inflation had compounded a further sharp rise in occupancy to push annual spending above £3,000.[111] An easing of inflation saw a slight drop from this level in the 1820s, but average yearly expenditure again exceeded £3,000 in the three hard-pressed decades between 1830 and 1859.[112] Outgoings then fell back below £3,000 in the 1860s and 1870s, but, from 1880, they embarked on a rise from which there were no further falls, ultimately exceeding £4,000 in 1901. By this stage, each inmate cost 1s 2¾d per day to keep. The main contributors to the late nineteenth-century increase were staff salaries and medical expenditure, which had collectively risen by 64 per cent between 1880 and 1901 and now accounted for one-third of the Hospital's budget.

World War I saw another milestone, as a new bout of wartime inflation pushed annual spending above £5,000 for the first time in 1916. With prices of essential commodities continuing to climb for the rest of the decade, expenditure more than doubled in the next four years, reaching £11,743 in 1920. Each inmate now cost 3s 11¾d per day to keep. In subsequent decades, spending never returned to

---

108 For Jersey's General Hospital, which had also begun as a workhouse, see Appendix 3.
109 1754 accounts, IA, DC/HX 079–01; Dicey, *Historical Account*, p. 191.
110 IA, DC/HX 165–01.
111 IA, DC/HX 079–01; IA, DC/HX 045–01.
112 For annual accounts between 1811 and 1857, see IA, DC/HX 045–01; IA, DC/HX 178–01; IA, DC/HX 020–01. For 1858–1924, see IA, DC/HX 272–02. See also Appendix 2.

pre-World War I levels, and the remainder of the twentieth century saw a sustained upward trajectory in Hospital expenditure.[113]

Income

It had been the original aim of the Hospital's founders to create a self-financing institution. Nevertheless, by 1751, the Hospital found itself so short of revenue that the parish had no alternative but to raise a rate to cover costs.[114] Rates were levied intermittently for the next fourteen years, and then annually from 1765.[115] From this point onwards, parochial taxation became the Town Hospital's single most important source of revenue.[116] Nevertheless, income from the rates continued for many decades to be supplemented by Hospital's original sources of funding, and indeed by income from other quarters. It is these supplementary sources that we shall now examine.

Donations from founding subscribers had come in two main forms – cash and *rentes*. In 1750, James Perchard's cash gift of £1,000 and other cash donations were invested in British government stock.[117] This formed the kernel of the Hospital's holdings in the British Funds, which by 1910 were valued at £3,549 and produced an annual income of about £85.[118] In addition to the *rentes* donated by founding subscribers, the Hospital was also granted all *rentes* formerly belonging to the poor of St Peter Port. These were recorded in a volume entitled *Rentail des Pauvres*.[119] Initially, these *rentes* were paid wholly in kind, supplying much of the grain from which the Hospital made its bread and beer. From 1769, payments in cash were permitted, and from 1861 they were made mandatory.[120]

In 1811, income from the Hospital's *rentes* and Consols supplied some 13 per cent of its revenue, with *rentes* yielding four and a half times more than Consols.[121] Revenue from this source, however, dropped steadily as the *rentes*, in particular, came to be redeemed. By 1925, *rente* income had dropped to the point where it was excluded from the general budget, and set aside to form a fund for inmates' treats.[122] Income from government stock was also negligible by this stage, the original Consols

---

[113] By the Hospital's final decade (the 1980s), annual spending had reached £1,260,843, with a daily per capita cost of £33 18p (*Billet*, 30.11.1983).

[114] 22.8.1751, St Peter Port Délibérations des Chefs de Famille, 1715–79, PL; 24.8.1751, IA, AQ 1003/01.

[115] IA, AQ 1003/01; IA, AQ 1003/02.

[116] At various times in the 1830s, 1840s, 1850s, 1870s and again in World War I, the Hospital was in deficit by the end of the financial year and resorted to bank loans in waiting for a new infusion of rate funds (IA, DC/HX 178–01; IA, DC/HX 020–01; IA, DC/HX 075–02; IA, DC/HX 054–06; IA, DC/HX 272–02).

[117] 18.4.1750, IA, DC/HX 079–01. After the various government stocks and annuities were consolidated into one fund in 1752, holdings became known as Consols.

[118] IA, DC/HX 274–011.

[119] IA, AQ 1051/01.

[120] 21.11.1769, St Peter Port Délibérations des Chefs de Famille, 1715–79, PL; 11.11.1861, IA, DC/HX 054–05.

[121] IA, DC/HX 045–01.

[122] 7.12.1925, IA, DC/HX 051–01.

having been sold in 1919 and the proceeds reinvested in the singularly unremuner-
ative War Loan.[123]

Aside from donations in the form of cash and *rentes*, the Hospital was given the
plates for Nicolas Dobrée's navigation charts, of which it had sold 1,189 copies by
1778.[124] It also benefited from an annual charity sermon and, from 1765, an annual
Crown grant, initially direct from the pocket of HM Governor but, as of 1835, paid
from Crown revenues.[125]

Such revenue sources increased the Hospital's prestige but did not greatly swell its
coffers. A far more important source were the inmates themselves, since the Hospital's
founders had not intended that care should be provided free of charge. Conditions
of entry stipulated that new entrants must cede all their real and personal property
to the Board.[126] The Hospital kept inventories of incoming residents' goods. These
were often pathetically scant, such as the ancient bed, chest, bolster and counterpane
surrendered by 84-year-old Jeanne Chevalier in 1754.[127] Scant as it was, however,
such property was usually sold off for the Hospital's benefit. Pensions, insurance
pay-outs and friendly society benefits were another form of property appropriated
by the Hospital. Sometimes, a small portion might be reserved for the inmate as
pocket money or, as in the case of Thomas Queripel, who in 1839 received 10s
a week from the Harmony Friendly Society, the inmate's keep was deducted and
the remainder sent to dependants outside.[128] Appropriation of inmates' worldly
goods continued well into the twentieth century, by which time St Peter Port's Poor
Law Board routinely took out bonds on any real property inmates might own as a
pre-condition of long-term residence.

Where there was no property to annex in advance, the Hospital sought, if possible,
to recoup inmates' costs retrospectively. Repayments were required from the fortunate few who came into money while inside. Elizabeth Thoume, for instance,
arranged to settle at a rate of 4½d per day on receiving a legacy after two years and
four months of residence in 1846.[129] Recoveries were made from relatives of dead
inmates in respect of past care. In 1871, Poor Law Board accounts recorded recoveries of £81 from such relatives.[130] Relatives of the living, notably putative fathers
of illegitimate children, were pursued for financial contributions, as Abraham Allez
and Isaac Le Geyt, sued in Court for the care costs of illegitimate offspring in 1838,
or Francis Garrio and Peter Robilliard, similarly sued in 1867.[131] The Hospital also

---

[123] 7.7.1919, IA, DC/HX 052–01; IA, DC/HX 272–02.

[124] 6.10.1778, IA, DC/HX 119–04.

[125] 6.7.1835, IA, DC/HX 130–02. The grant never exceeded £10.

[126] IA, DC/HX 079–01.

[127] 8.5.1754, IA, DC/HX 118–01. The requisitioning of property on entrance was ubiquitous
   in continental institutions, and customary in all home nations of the United Kingdom. In
   England and Wales, it was officially sanctioned by the Poor Law Commission set up by the
   Poor Law Amendment Act of 1834 (Crowther, *Workhouse System*, p. 194).

[128] 31.12.1839, IA, DC/HX 075–01. A similar requisitioning of pensions and benefits was also
   practised in England and Wales (Crowther, *Workhouse System*, p. 213).

[129] 20.7.1846, IA, DC/HX 130–01.

[130] IA, DC/HX 272–02.

[131] 7.5.1838, IA, DC/HX 075–01; 20.5.1867, IA, DC/HX 136–07. Recoveries from relatives

made personal injury claims in respect of inmates, as in 1867 against Mr Le Patourel for leaving a pit uncovered in front of his brewery, into which Susan De Carteret fell and injured herself.[132]

The Hospital actively generated income by taking paying boarders. The most profitable fee-payers were non-pauper lunatics, but there were also middle-class alcoholics sent for treatment in the Hospital, unruly adolescents admitted by parents as shock therapy, and many non-destitute elderly or disabled people whose families could not or would not care for them at home. Between 1858 and 1924, takings from fee-paying boarders of all kinds averaged nearly £500 a year, which was more than the income from *rentes* and Consols combined. In some years, such as 1874 when they yielded £1,027, boarders' payments could account for as much as 30 per cent of the Hospital's income.[133]

The Hospital also derived revenue from hiring out its facilities and selling its by-products. When the entrepôt was at its height, the institution's cellars and vaults were in some demand for the storage of wines and spirits.[134] At this time, it also sold pigs and pig-dung, bran as a by-product from milling grain and yeast from brewing beer.[135] In the 1830s, it charged for the use of such equipment as its winnowing machine and 'ventilating warm air stove' (for drying laundry).[136] Until 1853, the Hospital's carpenter made coffins for public sale as well as for parish burials.[137] As late as 1915, the institution allowed the public to use its telephone for a fee, hired out its water bed and sold its food waste to the highest bidder.[138]

The Town Hospital's most symbolically significant source of income was inmates' labour. In their bid to have the institution pay for itself, the Hospital's founders had energetically launched a wide variety of semi-industrial ventures, many of which fed into their own business interests. Women and girls spun wool and knitted it into stockings for export, local sale or Hospital use. Men and boys laid cordage for local shipping, picked oakum for caulking, processed tobacco and cast scrap lead into pigs.[139]

In 1752, Directors added weaving to the workhouse repertoire as a way to

---

were also routinely made under the English regime. For policies followed by Cheltenham union, see C.V. Seal, 'Poor relief and welfare: a comparative study of the Belper and Cheltenham poor law unions, 1780 to 1914' (unpub. PhD thesis, Leicester University, 2009), p. 145.

[132] 1.4.1867, IA, DC/HX 136–07.

[133] IA, DC/HX 272–02.

[134] They were probably built with this intention. In 1754, the Hospital made 5 per cent of its total receipts from leasing them out (IA, DC/HX 079–01).

[135] 1754 accounts, IA, DC/HX 079–01.

[136] 3.1.1830, IA, DC/HX 135–03. See also 1838 accounts in IA, DC/HX 020–01.

[137] 27.6.1853, IA, DC/HX 130–04.

[138] IA, DC/HX 272–02.

[139] Dicey, *Historical Account*, pp. 191–2; IA, DC/HX 117–01. The probable destination for the lead was French smugglers, to whom Guernsey merchants had a sideline in selling metals at this time (Stevens Cox, *Guernsey Merchants*, p. xviii). Lead-casting was discontinued in 1780; tobacco-processing and cordage-laying ceased in the early 1800s, and oakum-picking in the 1860s.

improve revenue after the previous year's resort to taxation. Looms were bought and a master weaver engaged.[140] Large amounts of coarse linen-based cloth were produced – cheesecloth, sateen, drugget, but mostly grogram, which was always referred to by its French name, *beslinge*. Attempts were made to sell it to parishioners, and a stall was set up in the Town Church porch.[141] Its poor quality deterred potential customers, however, and Directors eventually resolved to use it to make as much inmate clothing as possible.[142] Cloth production stopped in the 1770s when the master weaver left, restarted in the 1780s when a new weaver was engaged, faltered again in the 1790s and was restarted once more in 1812.[143] In this third and final phase, sailcloth and canvas were offered for sale, and linen-based fabrics were made for internal use.[144]

In 1817, an enterprising new Treasurer, William Collings, established two entirely new ventures: a straw hat manufactory, which he staffed with the Hospital's boys, and an inmate-operated sedan-chair taxi service.[145] In the 1820s, the Hospital opened its own stone-yard, in which able-bodied male inmates broke up granite for export or local use.[146] Throughout the first half of the nineteenth century, fishing nets, coal sacks, mattresses and cushions were also manufactured for public sale.[147] From the 1870s, home-made floor mats were added to the list and, from the early 1900s, the Hospital sold wheelbarrows and chopped firewood.[148]

In addition to all this, the Hospital also hired out its inmates to perform various tasks around the parish, and inmate labour was used throughout the Hospital.[149] Until the early twentieth century, inmates performed virtually all the work of the house: brewing, baking and general cooking; sweeping, scrubbing and cleaning; childcare and nursing; laundry-work; sewing and mending; teaching; repairs and maintenance; painting and decorating; carpentry; gardening; porterage; hairdressing; shoe-making; tailoring; and much more.

Although absent from the balance sheet, inmates' domestic work had a far greater impact on finances than the Hospital's manufacturing ventures, which, despite their imaginative diversity, ultimately proved unprofitable. Provision of work entailed costs, and the able-bodied component of the workhouse population was too transient (and the non-able-bodied too frail) to generate a greater level of income than was required to cover these costs. Thus, while the Hospital made about £92

[140] 7.6.1752, IA, DC/HX 079–01; 22.8.1752, IA, DC/HX 118–01.
[141] 30.6.1754, IA, DC/HX 079–01.
[142] 19.6.1757, IA, DC/HX 079–01.
[143] 22.7.1788, IA, DC/HX 120–01; 1.2.1813, IA, DC/HX 079–02; Quayle, *General View*, p. 294.
[144] IA, DC/HX 139–10; IA, DC/HX 135–02. Textile production continued until the late 1830s.
[145] Both of these ventures lasted until around 1830 (3.3.1817, IA, DC/HX 079–02; 20.12.1830, IA, DC/HX 135–03).
[146] Stone-breaking continued until 1913 (IA, DC/HX 083–01; IA, DC/HX 272–02).
[147] See advertisement in *Gazette de Guernesey*, 6.2.1819.
[148] 9.10.1871, IA, DC/HX 054–05; 2.1.1872, IA, DC/HX 059–01; 14.12.1903, IA, DC/HX 080–03; IA, DC/HX 135–06.
[149] Tasks for which inmates were hired out are explored in detail in the section on 'Routines and rhythms' in Chapter 9.

sterling from its enterprises in 1770, its expenses in providing equipment, materials, training and supervision amounted to £90 10s.[150] Long before the eighteenth century was out, Directors had perforce to resign themselves to the fact that manufacturing would never have more than therapeutic, educational, or punitive value. Even so, ratepayers would not have countenanced a situation where the poor were kept 'for nothing'. In default of financial profit, William Collings provided a moral justification for his ventures: 'in destroying idleness', he asserted, 'we may expect an improvement in morals, good order, and a gradual benefit to the parish'.[151] It was perhaps just a *post hoc* rationalisation, but one to which most ratepayers heartily subscribed.

Policy and regime

The inability of the Town Hospital's founders to secure an Order in Council embodying its regulations and constitution was in many ways an advantage to its subsequent Directors, since it gave them exceptional freedom to improvise policy and alter rules at will. By the same token, it put inmates at a disadvantage, since entrance to the institution meant submission to an internal system of authority undefined by law and unchecked by external supervision. This was not the case in Jersey, where the constitution and regulations of the General Hospital were passed in the form of a law, and Jurats paid supervisory visits from the outset.[152] Neither was it the case in England and Wales, where most pre-1834 workhouses of similar size had formal charters or articles of incorporation, and those belonging to the post-1834 'workhouse system' were controlled by a central directorate which employed inspectors to monitor compliance and offered inmates a right of appeal against treatment contravening its directives.[153]

From the time the Town Hospital first opened its doors, there was a tension between 'deserving' inmates – orphans, widows, old folk, the sick and disabled – and those whom society viewed as 'undeserving' – drunkards, prostitutes, vagrants and wasters. As well as providing care to the first group, the Hospital had also to preserve order among the second group. Lock-ups were built for this purpose, and there were facilities for corporal and other types of punishment.[154]

On the whole, the early regime was relatively liberal. Nicolas Dobrée knew most of his inmates personally and his correspondence shows that he took a quasi-paternal interest in them.[155] Misdemeanours were punished and the refractory were

[150] 31.12.1770, IA, DC/HX 119–02.

[151] 18.3.1818, IA, DC/HX 079–02.

[152] M. Phillips, *Poor People* (Jersey, 2001), pp. 52–3.

[153] A. Digby, *Pauper Palaces* (London, 1978), p. 34; Hitchcock, 'English workhouse', p. 122; F. Driver, *Power and Pauperism: The Workhouse System, 1834–1884* (Cambridge, 1993), pp. 42–4.

[154] See section on 'Discipline', Chapter 9.

[155] See letters to Pierre Dobrée concerning the escapades of inmate Daniel Bott in the 1740s (IA, AQ 807/52).

disciplined, but the compliant majority were not treated unkindly. 'Deserving' inmates were allowed to smoke in the grounds, and tobacco and snuff were bought for their use.[156] They were also given occasional treats, such as wine on Christmas Day. Dobrée himself shared out thirty-three bottles among inmates to celebrate Christmas 1748.[157]

However, with the passage of time and the demise of the founding generation, personal interest and paternalism faded. As St Peter Port's commercial patriciate grew richer, they moved out to salubrious suburbs, leaving the 'filth, noise and crowds' of central districts to their poorer neighbours.[158] No longer in daily proximity, the poor became an increasingly unknown quantity to the rich, and their growing numbers imparted a vague sense of menace.[159] Insensibly, the Town Hospital began to move from policies which merely disciplined the refractory to policies which embodied a measure of hostility towards paupers in general. The beginnings of this attitudinal change can be detected in a tightening of Hospital burial policy in the early 1770s. Previously, friends or relatives of deceased inmates had been free to remove and bury bodies privately. From 1772, however, pauper burials became mandatory for all those who died in the Hospital, and relatives were prohibited from any involvement.[160]

It was, however, the early nineteenth-century ousting of Treasurer Jean Condamine which finally sealed the transition from the old order to the new. Condamine, who had served in the post since 1795, was perceived by a group of concerned parishioners to have become lax and complacent, and, after a campaign of some duration, was forced out of office in 1809.[161] Condamine's removal opened the way to an intensification of severity which characterised the first half of the nineteenth century. With a new Treasurer and Board in place from the spring of 1809, Hospital rules were overhauled and a raft of disciplinary innovations introduced.[162] Perhaps most

---

[156] IA, DC/HX 117–01.

[157] 26.12.1748, IA, DC/HX 117–02.

[158] G. Stevens Cox, *St Peter Port, 1680–1830: The History of an International Entrepôt* (Woodbridge, 1999), pp. 135, 138.

[159] For similar developments in England, see D. Valenze, 'Custom and humanity: changing attitudes towards the poor in eighteenth-century England', in J. Garnett and C. Matthew (eds), *Revival and Religion since 1700* (London, 1993), p. 76.

[160] 7.7.1772, IA, DC/HX 079–01. This policy remained in force until 1913, when rules were finally changed to allow the unconditional removal of inmates' bodies by friends or kin (IA, DC/HX 272–04). Under the post-1834 regime in England and Wales, the remains of those dying in workhouses could freely be claimed by anyone who undertook to bear burial costs (J.-M. Strange, *Death, Grief and Poverty in Britain, 1870–1914* (Cambridge, 2005), pp. 134, 148).

[161] An initial attempt to dislodge Condamine in 1805 failed, but efforts to oust him resumed in January 1809, when the *Douzaine* held an election for the post of Treasurer against his wishes, at which *Chefs de Famille* voted overwhelmingly for Daniel De Lisle. After Condamine lodged a protest, the Royal Court issued an ordinance giving him one month to submit his accounts and call another election. At the expiry of this month, Condamine resigned, taking with him most of the Hospital Board, and De Lisle entered into office with a new team of Directors (20.3.1805, 4.9.1805, IA, DC/HX 079–02; 26.1.1809, 2.3.1809, 5.4.1809, IA, DC/HX 079–02; *Gazette de Guernesey*, 21.1.1809, 4.2.1809, 11.2.1809).

[162] For a summary of these, see Quayle, *General View*, pp. 292–3.

significantly, the Hospital also took on a stronger carceral function. The institution had from its opening been used for the preventive detention of social undesirables, who were usually brought in informally by the Constables, without Court involvement. In the early 1800s, however, the Royal Court itself took to issuing orders of confinement in the Hospital for offenders against public order. The legal basis for this was unclear, but, with a perceived upsurge in disorder amid post-Napoleonic distress, St Peter Port's well-to-do felt the lack of a house of correction, and were to some extent co-opting the Hospital to supply its place.[163] In August 1817, the Hospital's Board was convened to discuss a proposal of Sir James Saumarez and others that the Hospital should equip itself with a separate building for those undergoing 'correction'.[164] The Board declined, not least because ratepayers had begun to object to bearing costs which, if offenders had been detained in prison, would have been paid from Crown Revenues.

In due course, ratepayers' objections led to a clarification of the basis upon which the Royal Court founded its orders of confinement. In October 1824, the Court ordered the confinement in the Hospital of Sally Guard, who had been removed from a disorderly house, and the Board made a formal protest to the Bailiff.[165] The following month, the Court responded by issuing an Act setting out its position.[166] This Act asserted that the Royal Court was entitled by law to order parochial officers to provide for destitute paupers, and, since Sally Guard lacked the means to maintain herself, the parish must keep her.[167] From this date onwards, all Court orders seeking a person's confinement in Hospital specifically consigned that person to the care of the *Procureur des Pauvres*, and this became the standard formula for ordering detention within the workhouse.

Throughout the 1820s, pressure mounted on the States to provide a house of correction. However, after several debates on the subject, Bailiff Daniel De Lisle Brock drew a line under the matter in 1831 by convincing members that, if the States agreed to finance such a house, they would probably soon be asked to fund the workhouses and the prison as well.[168] Meanwhile, the growing number of miscreants sent to the Hospital were causing disciplinary problems, and this, together with the States' categorical refusal to provide a house of correction, resurrected the idea of a separate house on Hospital premises. Early in 1832, an outbreak of disorder among young female inmates seems finally to have spurred the Board

---

[163] For more on houses of correction and Guernsey's lack of such an institution, see Chapter 3, p. 51.
[164] 11.8.1817, IA, DC/HX 079–02.
[165] 14.10.1824, IA, DC/HX 135–02. The Board's protest contained the following phrase: '*l'Hôpital a été bâti dans le dessein de fournir un asile à la vieillesse et l'indigence, mais jamais dans l'intention d'en faire une maison de correction*' (tr. 'the Hospital was built to shelter the aged and the indigent, and never to serve as a house of correction'. It is interesting to note that, in 1876, the St Peter Port Poor Law Board began using this phrase to preface its annual abstracts of accounts with no hint of the original context (IA, DC/HX 272–02).
[166] 11.11.1824, IA, DC/HX 135–02.
[167] Ostensibly, this was based on the ordinance of 15.4.1611 (Chapter 3, n. 60), though the Act did not refer to it.
[168] *Billets*, 26.3.1828, 10.2.1831; *Comet*, 31.3.1828, 26.3.1829, 14.2.1831.

to take action.[169] A parish meeting was called to authorise a special tax to fund the construction of a facility in a far corner of the workhouse garden in which to segregate disruptive elements under a punitive regime.[170] On the Treasurer's insistence that this 'was absolutely necessary to maintaining order', the measure was approved by a two-thirds majority of voters.[171]

By the autumn of 1832, the Hospital's new 'house of separation', designed to accommodate about twenty-five, had received its first inmates.[172] Its regulations specified a diet of barley bread and vegetable soup (though inmates showing 'contrition' might have meat once a week). Clothing was to consist of striped cotton or linen shirts and outerwear of 'variegated' colours. Male inmates were to pass their days breaking stone and grinding corn on a multi-handled corn-mill.[173] In 1833, 45-year-old Charles McBride, a retired NCO from Londonderry, was appointed to supervise the facility under the ultimate authority of the Hospital master.[174]

To use English analogies, the 'house of separation' served as a combination of casual ward, refractory ward and house of correction. 'Filthy vagabonds', such as 34-year-old Jean Liez, and 'drunken layabouts', such as 50-year-old Sampson Toy, were relegated here, as were unruly inmates such as Julie Diggins, sent as punishment for insulting the workhouse mistress.[175] Petty offenders consigned by the Court to spells under the care of the *Procureur des Pauvres* also served their terms here.[176]

In 1846, Royal Commissioners sent to investigate the island's criminal law expressed doubts as to the legitimacy of the Court's policy. 'Whence do you derive the power to put a person there?' they asked. 'We choose our own prison', replied Jurat Hilary Carré. Advocate Robert MacCulloch elaborated: 'the party concerned must be a pauper, and incapable of maintaining himself without parochial assistance'. 'This is apparently a punishment for crime', the Commissioners concluded. 'It appears, therefore, that you inflict one specific punishment on a man if he is a pauper, and another if he is not.' The Commissioners advised establishing a proper house of correction and/or introducing hard labour to the prison.[177]

Dissatisfaction with Court use of the Hospital continued to rankle with sections of the ratepaying public. The Commissioners' visit reopened agitation

---

[169] See section on 'Women', Chapter 8.

[170] 7.2.1832, 5.3.1832, IA, DC/HX 135–02.

[171] *Star*, 16.3.1832.

[172] 16.11.1832, IA, DC/HX 135–02.

[173] 4.2.1833, IA, DC/HX 135–02. See also Anon., *The Strangers' Guide to the Islands of Guernsey and Jersey* (Guernsey, 1833), p. 82.

[174] 29.4.1833, 5.8.1833, IA, DC/HX 135–02; IA, DC/HX 130–02. During the cholera outbreak of 1832, McBride had been in charge of an improvised cholera ward in the girls' section of the workhouse.

[175] 15.4.1833, IA, DC/HX 130–02; 20.11.1838, 14.11.1839, IA, DC/HX 075–01.

[176] These usually followed on from short prison sentences, and were typically for periods of two, four or six months. For examples, see 16.1.1839, 4.2.1839, IA, DC/HX 075–01.

[177] *Second Report of the Commissioners appointed to enquire into the State of the Criminal Law of the Channel Islands* (London, 1848), pp. xvii, 203. By this time, Jersey had already had a house of correction for nearly a decade (P. Ahier, 'The house of correction in Jersey', *Bulletin of la Société Jersiaise*, 20 (1971), pp. 284–8).

for a States-funded house of correction and, in 1847, the parish appointed a committee to discuss this with the States.[178] Also on the agenda was the issue of a States-funded lunatic asylum, for which some ratepayers had been lobbying since the social reformer Elizabeth Fry had criticised lunatics' quarters at the Hospital in 1833.[179] However, the States remained unwilling to provide funding for either sort of institution, and talks came to nothing. Frustrated by such obduracy, St Peter Port ratepayers decided in 1848 to extend their house of separation to combine the correctional and asylum functions under one roof.[180] Building work began in 1849, but, before it was complete, a further ratepayers' meeting resolved to rid the parish of the house of separation altogether and turn the entire facility over to lunatics.[181] By the summer of 1851, the Hospital's new 'lunatic asylum' had opened, and the house of separation had ceased to exist.[182]

It may partly have been this which finally prompted the States to act on the Royal Commissioners' advice. In 1856, measures were enacted to equip Guernsey's prison with facilities for hard labour.[183] At the same time an Order in Council was issued which defined and classified a wide range of minor offences, from petty theft to animal cruelty, prescribing a scale of penalties from gaol terms with hard labour to fines and birching.[184] Thus, although the Court continued to issue orders consigning drunkards and prostitutes to the Hospital, most of the criminal cases formerly sent to the house of separation were henceforth dealt with by alternative means.[185]

Throughout the period over which the house of separation saga was unfolding, the Hospital had continued progressively to tighten its regime with a variety of other stringent measures. Such measures included the institution in 1822 of a six-fold scheme of classification and separation which prevented contact between married inmates both inside and outside the Hospital.[186] This was followed in 1826 by a scheme for the detention of unmarried mothers, whereby women illegitimately giving birth in the Hospital were to be confined in it for the following five years in order to 'correct their morals'.[187] From the 1830s, forced emigration was increasingly resorted to, leading to many unscheduled returns. In 1838, of four 'ill-behaved' inmates despatched to Nova Scotia, one absconded while changing ship in Jersey

---

[178] 14.7.1847, IA, DC/HX 130–01.

[179] 7.10.1833, IA, DC/HX 130–02.

[180] 26.1.1848, IA, DC/HX 130–01.

[181] 13.7.1850, IA, DC/HX 075–02.

[182] 16.7.1851, IA, DC/HX 075–02.

[183] Ord, 6.12.1856.

[184] O in C, 24.6.1856.

[185] The Court continued to consign drunkards, prostitutes and other social misfits to the Hospital by placing them under the care of the *Procureur* until 1937, when a new formula was introduced placing them instead under the care of the Public Assistance Authority (28.4.1937, IA, AS/MB 011–05). The latest case I have found of individuals confined in the Town Hospital by means of such orders dates from 1958 (24.9.1958, IA, AS/MB 065–02).

[186] 1.7.1822, IA, DC/HX 135–02; 20.6.1831, IA, DC/HX 135–05; 10.2.1834, IA, DC/HX 130–02.

[187] 9.5.1826, IA, DC/HX 135–02. In 1842, the term was reduced to three years, and in 1846 to 'such time as the child required its mother's care' (1.8.1842, 4.5.1846, IA, DC/HX 130–01).

and a second made his way back from Canada a few months later.[188] Attempts were also made at this time forcibly to enlist male inmates for naval service. Charles McBride, of the house of separation, escorted many parties to Plymouth and Portsmouth in the 1830s and 1840s. Of the thirteen inmates he took to Plymouth in September 1840 (which included a 52-year-old), most were rejected by the navy, some escaped and six were readmitted to the workhouse in short order.[189]

On the inauguration of St Peter Port's new Poor Law Board in 1853, all the harshness of the previous half-century was recapitulated in a fresh set of rules.[190] There was no easing of draconian strictures and, as a further refinement to an already bleak regime, the new House Committee both reduced inmates' rations and banned smoking from the premises altogether.[191]

Nevertheless, in 1853, the Hospital was poised on the cusp of a significant change. Over the next two or three decades, raw poverty receded in St Peter Port, and the institution's able-bodied cohort began to shrink. As a result, the 'deserving' contingent of old folk and the sick came to dominate the Hospital's population, and this engendered a gradual softening of policy. From 1867, for instance, the institution opened its doors to charitable outsiders wishing to provide comforts and entertainment to children and the elderly, and, also from around this time, the young and the old were more frequently allowed out for treats and excursions.[192]

In many ways, this paralleled changes in the population and regime of English workhouses over a similar timeframe.[193] Guernsey people at all levels would have been aware of these changes via the English newspapers which circulated in the island. By the end of the century, English mass dailies such as the *Express* and the *Mail* had espoused workhouse reform as a popular cause and were subjecting the remnants of the 'less eligibility' regime to a barrage of criticism.[194] This appears to have encouraged the adoption of a similar stance by both the public and the press in Guernsey: 1901 in particular saw a sustained campaign against Hospital conditions in local newspapers.[195] Ultimately, such publicity seems to have pushed the Royal Court to intervene, and this in turn set in motion the most thorough-going reform of Guernsey's Hospitals since their foundation. Crucially, the Court finally arrogated a supervisory role to itself. In December 1901, it passed an ordinance which instituted quarterly inspections of the Town and Country Hospitals by Jurats and stipulated that all Hospital regulations must henceforth be approved by the Court.[196] In January 1902, it embarked on a systematic review and revision of all

---

[188] 3.3.1838, 27.8.1838 and 16.8.1840, IA, DC/HX 075–01. Hospital authorities took pains to have emigrating inmates sign declarations of 'voluntary departure'. However, the subsequent return of many belies their free will in the matter.

[189] 16.8.1840, 18.9.1840, IA, DC/HX 075–01.

[190] 21.2.1853, IA, DC/HX 054–05.

[191] 21.2.1853, IA, DC/HX 054–05; 19.2.1853, 5.12.1853, IA, DC/HX 130–04.

[192] 4.1.1867, IA, DC/HX 127–01. See also sections on 'Children' and 'The Elderly' in Chapter 8.

[193] Crowther, *Workhouse System*, p. 82.

[194] Wood, *Poverty and the Workhouse*, p. 168.

[195] See, for instance, *Star*, 26.10.1901, 5.11.1901.

[196] Ord, 21.12.1901. See also *Star*, 26.12.1901.

existing workhouse rules, finally approving a new set of regulations for the Town Hospital a year later.[197] From this point onwards, conditions in the Hospital underwent a transformation. A new dietary based on the regulations of the English Local Government Board introduced more varied food.[198] The smoking ban was lifted.[199] Married inmates were given freedom to associate.[200] By this time, however, the institution's workhouse department had effectively become severed from its other departments, and a dual regime was therefore instituted, offering 'house people' less attractive food, more frugal living conditions and the continuation of compulsory work and strict discipline. The separation of 'house' and 'hospital' departments was formalised in 1915, when a new sister-in-charge was given sole control of the institution's infirmary, leaving the master and mistress in charge of the workhouse department only.[201]

By the 1960s, the number of house people in the Town Hospital had dwindled to about a dozen, but the dual regime persisted.[202] While conditions for other inmates were by now comparatively comfortable, the dormitories in which house people slept remained unheated and subject to vermin infestation.[203] House people made do with coarse grey blankets, while other inmates were issued with softer white ones.[204] Ultimately, in 1967, the States saw fit to close the workhouse department altogether, and its last ten occupants were relocated.[205] With the departure of the house people, all vestiges of previous harshness came to an end, and the Hospital was left free to focus entirely on its caring avocation. It is on this aspect of the institution's history that the next chapter will focus, as the role of the Hospital's infirmary and lunatic asylum are examined in depth.

[197] 14.3.1903, IA, DC/HX 056–04. The Greffe register *Ordonnances, 16 Jan 1899–6 Dec 1902* records the review process.

[198] 3.11.1902, IA, DC/HX 056–04.

[199] 16.10.1903, IA, DC/HX 080–03.

[200] 5.4.1909, IA, DC/HX 080–01.

[201] 29.9.1915, IA, DC/HX 080–05.

[202] IA, AS/MB 068–01.

[203] 21.5.1959, 21.10.1959, 22.6.1960, IA, AS/MB 065–02.

[204] 7.10.1963, IA, AS/MB 065–02.

[205] Ironically, this was to the former house of separation, re-designated a 'welfare hostel' under the name 'St Julian's House' (25.9.1967, IA, AS/MB 068–01).

Plate 1: Poor children at Rocquaine, St Peters, c.1870
© *The Priaulx Library, Guernsey*

Plate 2: Poor children in Rosemary Lane, St Peter Port, early twentieth century
© The Priaulx Library, Guernsey

Plate 3: St Peter Port Poor Law Board at the laying of Wells Chapel foundation stone, 1895
Island Archives Service

Plate 4: Town Hospital staff, House Committee members and associates, early twentieth century

Courtesy of ... ... & Galleries (States of Guernsey) 2015

Plate 5: Town Hospital medical and nursing staff, c.1930
Island Archives Service

Plate 6 (above): Nicolas Dobrée (1687–1751), first Town Hospital Treasurer and Supervisor

Guernsey Museums & Galleries (States of Guernsey) 2015

Plate 7 (right): Robert MacCulloch (1804–65), architect of the St Peter Port Poor Law Board

Guernsey Museums & Galleries (States of Guernsey) 2015

Plate 8 (above): Henry Daniel Ollivier (1861–1941), first States' Public Assistance Authority President
Island Archives Service

Plate 9 (left): William Reid McGlashan (1888–1950), first States' Mental Officer
Island Archives Service

Plate 10 (above): Ambrose Collas Robin
(1886–1969), first States' Insurance
Authority Administrator
Guernsey Museums & Galleries (States of
Guernsey) 2015

Plate 11 (right): Edward Thomas
Wheadon (1875–1969), first States'
Insurance Authority President
courtesy of Michael Deane,
deanephotos.com

7

Infirmary and Lunatic Asylum

Infirmary

Doctors

From the Town Hospital's earliest days, there were always some among its inmates who were sick or infirm. Certain areas within the institution were set aside for them, and they were tended by other inmates, usually women, deployed as 'nurses'. At first, the Hospital did not employ a doctor of its own, but called in practitioners as the need arose. Among these were Jean La Serre, a Huguenot refugee from the Languedoc, and his Guernsey-born son William.[1] In 1752, the Hospital decided to cease paying for doctors' visits *ad hoc* and instead to pay William La Serre an annual stipend of £10 (sterling) in return for his regular attendance.[2] La Serre then combined periodic calls at the Hospital with his external private practice. On La Serre's death in 1774, the Hospital's Treasurer, Matthew De Saumarez, himself a former naval surgeon, took over the Hospital work, and he was succeeded four years later by his son John.[3]

By 1805, John De Saumarez was receiving an annual stipend of £30 from the Hospital.[4] After the anti-Condamine 'coup' of 1809, De Saumarez resigned along with Treasurer Jean Condamine. He was replaced as Hospital surgeon by his nephew, John Carey, who also happened to be one of the new Directors.[5] Carey held the post until 1820, when he was replaced by his cousin William Brock, who served as Hospital surgeon for only a year.[6] Both Brock and Carey, and perhaps De Saumarez, seem also to have been responsible for St Peter Port's outdoor poor.[7]

William Brock's departure in 1821 heralded the introduction of a new poor law medical system in St Peter Port. The end of the Napoleonic Wars had left many ex-naval and military surgeons in Guernsey, and they had complained at

---

[1] For the La Serre family, see G. Stevens Cox, *The Guernsey Merchants and their World* (Guernsey, 2009), p. 193.

[2] 2.2.1767, IA, DC/HX 079–01.

[3] 5.4.1774, IA, DC/HX 079–01.

[4] 6.5.1805, IA, DC/HX 079–02.

[5] 19.4.1809, IA, DC/HX 079–02.

[6] 10.12.1820, IA, DC/HX 079–02.

[7] 13.12.1820, IA, AQ 0965/01.

the concentration of poor law work in the hands of a single individual with unde-fined tenure.[8] As we saw in Chapter 4, the parish responded to their complaint by instituting two separate medical officers, one for the Hospital and one for the outdoor poor, each with annual tenure. The Hospital doctor was to be appointed by the Board of Directors at the start of each year, and only practitioners who paid rates in St Peter Port were eligible to apply.[9] The post remained non-residential and part-time, with doctors free to continue in private practice. The first doctor to be appointed to the Hospital under this new system was ex-army surgeon John Terence O'Brien, in 1822.[10] The following year, the Hospital Board resolved as a matter of policy that their medical officer should provide all his own drugs and appliances, but they placed no restriction on his use of apprentices to perform the Hospital work.[11]

Under these conditions, the workhouse post was a reasonably profitable side-line for St Peter Port's practitioners and, for the next two decades, it was always warmly contested. Many of the early appointees, such as Hugh Monk and Nicholas Magrath, had, like O'Brien, served under colours. The medical stipend was held at £30 until 1844, when it rose to £40.[12] This was broadly on a par with stipends received at this time by workhouse medical officers in England and Wales.[13]

When the new St Peter Port Poor Law Board came into being in 1853, it restruc-tured medical services. The separate indoor and outdoor posts were abolished, and two practitioners were given shared responsibility for all indoor and outdoor poor law work.[14] These doctors, both of whom were to be appointed annually by the Poor Law Board, were to be paid £50 on condition that they ceased using appren-tices and performed all their duties in person. As a *quid pro quo*, the parish would now provide medical supplies.[15] A dispensary, serving as an outpatient department for the parish poor, was also opened at the Hospital at this time, and required the personal attendance of one or other of the doctors for a set number of hours daily, including Sundays.[16] The post remained part-time, although it must now have required a rather larger proportion of practitioners' working time.

As a result of the 1853 changes, the role of poor law doctor in St Peter Port became less attractive, and the number of applicants diminished. Henceforward, those who applied were either very young and just starting out, or old hands who had made a career of poor law work. The stipend was held at £50 between 1853 and 1895, when it was raised to £75.[17] By this time the average English workhouse doctor's salary stood at about £100, and it was rare for them to be required to

---

8   *Star*, 19.12.1820. In 1826, *L'Almanach Journalier* enumerated thirteen surgeons and two physicians, all based in St Peter Port.

9   4.1.1821, IA, AQ 0965/01.

10   4.2.1822, IA, DC/HX 079–02.

11   3.2.1823, IA, DC/HX 135–02.

12   5.2.1844, IA, DC/HX 130–01.

13   R.G. Hodgkinson, *The Origins of the National Health Service* (London, 1967), pp. 105–6.

14   In 1853, an additional medical officer was appointed to attend the Hospital's lunatics. His role will be considered in the second half of this chapter.

15   24.1.1853, 31.1.1853, IA, DC/HX 054–05; 31.1.1853, 5.12.1853, IA, DC/HX 130–04.

16   24.1.1853, 31.1.1853, IA, DC/HX 054–05.

17   4.11.1895, IA, DC/HX 054–07. The Hospital doctors' salary eventually rose to £100 in 1919,

perform outdoor as well as indoor work.[18] Also in England and Wales, the Poor Law Commission had set out a schedule of qualifications in its General Medical Order of 1842, without which no doctor could be employed as a workhouse medical officer.[19] Guernsey, by contrast, never specified any minimum qualifications for its workhouse practitioners.[20]

Typical of practitioners who served a short spell at the Town Hospital early in their careers were Dr Frederick De Lisle, who was 27 when appointed in 1873, and Dr John Aikman, 26 when appointed in 1876.[21] These young doctors tended to be more progressive and less tractable than the old hands, and often their tenures ended in conflict with the Board. Aikman, a Scotsman who had worked at the Glasgow Royal Infirmary, tendered his resignation after a major confrontation in 1878.[22] In his parting letter, Aikman alleged that Frederick De Lisle had also been forced to quit following a similar dispute two years earlier.[23]

Alongside these short-stayers were a handful of poor law stalwarts who were reappointed year after year. Among them were Dr Francis Carey, associated with the Hospital from 1859 to 1893; Dr Clifford Crewe, who served intermittently between 1869 and 1900, and Dr Benjamin Collenette, who was first appointed at the age of 40 in 1854 and retired aged 67 in 1881.[24] Poor law dynasties developed over time, with sons following fathers in the medical post. Brothers Basil and Conrad Carey both trod the same path as their father Francis, and Frank Collenette followed in the footsteps of his father Benjamin.[25] Anne Crowther has observed of English doctors that only those who had 'failed to establish a sufficient practice' would seek poor law work, 'knowing that it would rather diminish than increase their prestige'.[26]

Benjamin Collenette, the quintessential long-stayer, seems to have fashioned an entire career among people at the lower end of Guernsey's social spectrum. A staunch Methodist and temperance advocate, he combined his service at the Town

---

and thence to £125 in 1926 and £175 in 1934 (20.10.1919, IA, DC/HX 052–01; 6.12.1926, 8.10.1934, IA, DC/HX 051–01).

[18] S. Fowler, *Workhouse: The People, the Places, the Life Behind Doors* (Richmond, 2007), p. 181.

[19] Hodgkinson, *Origins of the Health Service*, p. 70.

[20] Until 1907, there were no mandatory qualifications for medical practice in the island at all. An ordinance of 7.6.1777 had required non-natives to obtain permission from the Royal Court before entering practice, but made no mention of qualifications, and any natives who so desired were free to set up as doctors without permission or diplomas of any sort. This only changed with the ordinance of 2.2.1907, which required doctors new to the island both to be licensed by the Royal Court and listed in the United Kingdom's Medical Register.

[21] 4.2.1873, 7.8.1876, IA, DC/HX 054–06.

[22] This confrontation will be described in detail later in this chapter (see section on 'Infirmary regime', below).

[23] 1.3.1878, IA, DC/HX 281–25. In 1876, De Lisle left Guernsey for New Zealand, where he served the remainder of his career (C.J. Durand, K. Brock and E.C. Ozanne (eds), *Elizabeth College Register, 1824–1873* (Guernsey, 1898), p. 185).

[24] 6.2.1854, 7.2.1859, 8.2.1869, IA, DC/HX 054–04; 5.12.1881, IA, DC/HX 054–05; 4.1.1893, IA, DC/HX 054–07; 3.12.1900, IA, DC/HX 056–04.

[25] 15.12.1890, 1.12.1897, IA, DC/HX 054–07; 7.12.1903, IA, DC/HX 056–04.

[26] M.A. Crowther, *The Workhouse System, 1834–1929: The History of an English Social Institution* (1981; London, 1983 edn), pp. 156, 158.

Hospital with work as doctor to the Vale Granite Club, St Andrews' Oddfellows, the Loyal Guernsey Oddfellows and the Rechabites. He also served intermittently as medical officer to the Country Hospital – all while running a private practice from La Plaiderie.[27] Tractability, of which Collenette seems to have had a large stock, no doubt recommended him to his poor law employers. Records suggest that he was on occasion prepared to set Poor Law Board wishes above his patients' interests. In 1871, for instance, the Poor Law Board wished to deport the seriously ill John Brennan in order to avoid care costs, and Collenette certified him fit for deportation when he was clearly dying.[28] The 54-year-old's death the day after his deck crossing to Alderney provoked a public scandal, causing the Reverend Thomas Brock to label it an 'act of cruelty' and call for an enquiry.[29] Collenette's loyalty did not, however, go unreciprocated. The Board saw fit to retain his services even when his faults might have offered grounds for dismissal. When, in 1879, Collenette's failure to attend an urgent case resulted in the death of a small girl, the Board merely issued him with a reprimand, reappointing him to the post for three more years in succession.[30]

The closing years of Victoria's reign marked a period of instability in St Peter Port's poor law medical service as many of the nineteenth-century regulars retired. Unprecedentedly, the Poor Law Board was forced to advertise the post in the *Lancet* and *British Medical Journal*.[31] By this point, the stipend was deeply uncompetitive with English workhouse medical officers' salaries and, although the Board's advertisements did attract some English recruits (such as Haydn Brown and Henry Ramsden), few of them stayed long.[32] One exception was Eustace Bostock, a Staffordshire man first engaged in 1904 at the age of 33.[33] Seemingly content with the poor law regime, he reapplied for the post and was reappointed each year between 1905 and 1910. In the latter year he was joined by 29-year-old Guernseyman Albert Bisson, who appears to have been equally at home with the poor law.[34] Anxious to achieve stability, the Poor Law Board then ceased offering the post annually, and the Bostock and Bisson families provided the Hospital with its medical officers for the next sixty years. Eustace Bostock remained continuously in post until 1935, when his nephew Oliver Bostock replaced him. The latter then served until 1963 (with a break during World War II).[35] Albert Bisson served until his death in 1954 (with a break during World War I).[36] Bisson's son Eric then joined Oliver Bostock at the

27 See obituary, *Star*, 25.11.1884.
28 17.3.1871, IA, DC/HX 059–01; 2.5.1871, 20.5.1871, IA, DC/HX 054–05.
29 *Star*, 22.4.1871.
30 3.4.1879, IA, DC/HX 054–06.
31 28.10.1893, IA, DC/HX 054–07.
32 4.1.1893, 4.12.1893, IA, DC/HX 054–07. Ramsden left after a year on discovering that the House Committee chairman had been countermanding his dietary orders (3.12.1895, IA, DC/HX 249–01).
33 5.12.1904, IA, DC/HX 056–04.
34 26.11.1909, IA, DC/HX 255–06. Bisson had trained at the London Hospital and Plaistow Fever Hospital. He subsequently also served as medical officer to Guernsey's Victoria Cottage Hospital and *la Société de Secours Mutuels de Guernesey* (*Star*, 17.11.1954).
35 8.4.1935, IA, DC/HX 051–01; 20.11.1963, IA, AS/MB 065–02.
36 17.12.1954, IA, AS/MB 065–02.

Hospital, remaining in his turn until 1962, when John Strickland, who had been in private practice with both Bissons, succeeded him in the post.[37] Oliver Bostock was himself replaced by Brian Webber in 1963.[38] In 1970, jurisdiction over the Hospital was transferred to the Board of Health. The appointment of doctors by the Public Assistance Authority ceased, and, the following year, Dr Kenneth Wade was appointed the first States' geriatrician, with responsibilities including the Hospital.[39]

Patients

Very little is known about the number and composition of the Hospital's sick and infirm contingent during the eighteenth century. The first figures date from 1811, when fifteen inmates (among a total of 207) were identified as being 'in the infirmary'. These consisted partly of consumptives and partly of the elderly bedridden.[40]

As we saw earlier, the main Hospital building was extended by 60ft in 1817 specifically to house the sick and, in 1820, St Peter Port's poor law medical service was reorganised.[41] From this point onwards, the Hospital seems to have admitted a much larger number of medical and surgical cases. According to a food supply log which incidentally recorded patient numbers, the infirmary contained on average forty patients between 1818 and 1823.[42] By this time, the Hospital's infirmary department was divided into six small wards, three for each sex. These accommodated, respectively, those recovering from operations, those suffering from infectious illness, and chronic invalids. The wards all had Biblical or saints' names. The male wards were known as the Lazarus, Jacob and Samaritan wards; the female wards as the Catherine, Rebecca and Sarah wards.[43] It is not clear whether these wards also accommodated children.

There are no patient numbers for several decades after the 1820s. From 1852, however, statistics on cause of admission began to appear in annual abstracts of accounts, which enables us to chart the steady growth of the Hospital's medical function after that date. The proportion of adults admitted for the treatment of illness or injury rose from 39 per cent in the 1850s to 78 per cent in 1910–19. By this time, 68 per cent of child admissions were also ascribed to medical reasons, so that an average of three-quarters of all early twentieth-century admissions to the Town Hospital were due to illness or injury, and the Hospital's medical function had become predominant.[44]

In the nineteenth and early twentieth centuries, the better-off, in Guernsey as

---

[37] 19.9.1962, IA, AS/MB 065–02. Strickland had been intermittently covering for his partners at the Hospital since 1947 (23.4.1947, IA, AS/MB 065–02).

[38] 20.11.1963, IA, AS/MB 065–02.

[39] 5.1.1971, IA, AS/MB 067–09.

[40] IA, DC/HX 045–01.

[41] 15.7.1817, St Peter Port Délibérations des Chefs de Famille, 1780–1817, PL; 4.1.1821, IA, AQ 0965/01.

[42] IA, DC/HX 101–02.

[43] December 1822, IA, DC/HX 139–10; 6.1.1823, IA, DC/HX 135–02; 15.9.1830, 5.8.1831, IA, DC/HX 135–03; 8.10.1839, IA, DC/HX 075–01.

[44] For detailed statistics, see section on 'Patterns of occupation', Chapter 6.

elsewhere, were treated either at home or in private nursing homes. Public provision in voluntary and workhouse hospitals was aimed at the poor and shunned by those who considered themselves respectable. In the United Kingdom, the working and lower middle classes were from 1859 offered an alternative to such institutions in the form of cottage hospitals. Guernsey's own cottage hospital did not open until 1888, however, leaving the Town and Country Hospitals the sole providers of non-private in-patient care.[45]

People might find themselves admitted to the Town Hospital's infirmary wards for a wide range of reasons. Those who had least choice in the matter were the chance victims of accidents. Such accidents were frequent in an era of scant concern for safety, whether at home, in the workplace or in public spaces. In the four months between November 1862 and March 1863, no fewer than five unconnected individuals were admitted to the Hospital for falls into St Peter Port harbour, which was deficient in railings and lighting.[46] Guerin's mill in the Charroterie was the cause of many industrial accidents, such as the severing of John Dark's thumb in 1849, which resulted in an infection and, ultimately, Dark's death.[47] After the expansion of the stone trade in the 1840s, quarry accidents became common. Stephen Daley's loss of both hands in an explosion at Hamley's quarry in 1883 was typical of the devastating injuries which could result.[48] Domestic accidents were also frequent, particularly those involving children. In 1829, 6-year-old Caroline Le Geyt survived the burns she sustained when her dress caught fire, but many were not so fortunate.[49]

The task of conveyance to the Hospital was normally performed by inmates. Critical cases were carried by up to ten men in a multi-handled basket. Less serious cases were transported in the Hospital's two sedan chairs, in use until the mid-1890s.[50] In 1906, the Hospital acquired an ambulance handcart.[51] In 1908, it was given a horse-drawn ambulance by the Royal Court.[52] This was converted into a motor ambulance in 1927, and remained stationed at the Hospital until 1940, when the St John Ambulance Association stepped in to provide Guernsey with a more comprehensive ambulance service.[53]

There were also many non-emergency admissions to the Hospital infirmary. Individuals with long-term health problems might be brought in when families could no longer care for them. In 1829, Philip Lidstone was admitted after his parents had died. Notwithstanding that he was suffering from severe hydrocephalus and multiple disabilities, they had looked after him at home until he reached the age of

---

[45] See section on 'Charity', Chapter 5.
[46] Pierre Brehaut, Thomas Harding, Robert Lethbridge, Thomas Hamley and Nicolas Le Cheminant (IA, DC/HX 127–01).
[47] 14.8.1849, IA, DC/HX 075–02.
[48] 6.12.1883, IA, DC/HX 130–03.
[49] 7.9.1829, IA, DC/HX 135–03.
[50] 31.12.1894, IA, DC/HX 136–04.
[51] 1.10.1906, IA, DC/HX 056–04.
[52] 23.11.1908, IA, DC/HX 056–04.
[53] 9.5.1927, IA, DC/HX 051–01; 24.1.1940, IA, DC/HX 015–04. The St John Ambulance Association have remained responsible for ambulance provision in Guernsey to the present day.

20.[54] In 1840, George Webber, described as 'a sort of deformed dwarf', was brought in for similar reasons. Bedridden since the age of 2, he had been tended by his parents until the age of 16.[55]

Consumptives were also often admitted to the Town Hospital, usually in the final stages of their disease. Tuberculosis was endemic in Guernsey until World War II, with one in every six insular deaths attributed to it as late as 1903.[56] The illness usually culminated in a lengthy 'decline' which precluded work and, in order to relieve poor families, male sufferers in particular were admitted for the terminal phase.

Others entered the Hospital to be cured of their social maladies. Over the years, the institution became a specialist treatment centre for alcoholism and sexually transmitted diseases. As Dr Collenette wrote in the *British Medical Journal*, 'with the facilities for drinking and getting drunk cheaply in Guernsey, you will not be surprised to hear that we have large numbers of delirium tremens cases'.[57] Such cases were not limited to the poor. Henry MacCulloch, son of former HM *Procureur* Robert MacCulloch, underwent treatment for delirium tremens in 1899.[58] A few years later, Lady Catherine Lawson, the estranged wife of newspaper proprietor Sir Charles Lawson, was admitted for the same reason.[59] In 1900, the Hospital started offering its alcoholic patients the 'Dixon Cure'.[60]

The earliest record of treatment being provided for a sexually transmitted disease was that given by Dr La Serre to Marie Lenfestey and Anne Allez in 1754.[61] At this time, treatment consisted of the application of mercury, nitric acid or copper iodide salts to visible lesions in order to dry them up. Sufferers remained infected, however, since there was no actual cure for syphilis or gonorrhoea until the twentieth century.[62]

The Hospital authorities came to resent the identification of their institution with sexually transmitted diseases. However, the Constables, Court and States saw the management of this social evil as part of the Hospital's role. By the early twentieth century, the States were reimbursing the Hospital in full for the expenses it incurred

[54] After Lidstone's death in 1853, the Hospital's doctors sent his brain to London for examination. The case was written up in 'Congenital absence of the middle portions and left hemisphere of the cerebellum, in a case of chronic hydrocephalus', *Transactions of the Pathological Society of London*, 4 (1853), pp. 31–4.

[55] 20.6.1840, DC/HX 075–01.

[56] D.A. Jeffs, 'Through the eyes of the MoH', in D.A. Jeffs (ed.), *One Hundred Years of Health: The Changing Health of Guernsey, 1899–1999* (Guernsey, 1999), p. 16.

[57] B. Collenette, 'Treatment of disease without alcohol', *British Medical Journal*, 2.12.1871.

[58] 24.10.1899, IA, DC/HX 127–02.

[59] 15.10.1906, 22.10.1906, IA, DC/HX 080–01. Lady Lawson, separated from her husband in 1903 on grounds of her 'habitual drunkenness', was staying at a hotel in St Peter Port (*Victoria Daily Colonist*, 4.1.1903).

[60] 1.10.1900, IA, DC/HX 136–05. On the nature of this cure, see *British Medical Journal*, 14.9.1901.

[61] 23.1.1754, St Peter Port Délibérations des Chefs de Famille, 1715–79, PL.

[62] F.B. Smith, *The People's Health, 1830–1910* (1979; London, 1990 edn), p. 294.

in treating disease arising from prostitution.[63] By 1937, the States had established a free VD clinic at the Hospital, along the lines of the local authority clinics opened in the United Kingdom after the Venereal Diseases Act of 1917.[64] Notwithstanding that the Town Hospital came to specialise in geriatrics, the VD clinic remained on the Hospital site until the 1980s.

In addition to the above, the Hospital played a central role in the management of epidemics of infectious disease in St Peter Port. The most serious epidemics it had to deal with were of smallpox in the eighteenth and nineteenth centuries and cholera in the mid-nineteenth century. We shall consider the latter first. The United Kingdom suffered cholera epidemics in 1831–2, 1849, 1853–4 and 1866.[65] Fortunately, Guernsey was affected only in 1832 and 1849. Both outbreaks were centred on St Peter Port, the first striking in the autumn of 1832. However, parochial authorities had made advance preparations, including the appointment of a parochial cholera committee, which engaged doctors to oversee each of four specially designated districts, and organised street cleaning, fumigation, the provision of medicines, and burials.[66] The committee also arranged for a public cholera ward to be opened at the Town Hospital to which victims of the disease could be transferred from their homes and treated by the cholera doctors in isolation.[67] The facility was installed in the detached building occupied by the girls, who were moved to quarters outside.[68] Notwithstanding these precautions, a total of 103 parishioners, including eight Hospital inmates, died from the disease.[69]

During the outbreak of August 1849, the Hospital itself appears to have become an active centre of infection.[70] One of the first fatalities was Fanny Gray, formerly the mistress of the Town Hospital but now an inmate, and, within a few days, thirty-four other inmates had succumbed.[71] This led to the evacuation of all inmates: men and boys to the Vale Castle; women and girls to Jerbourg Barracks.[72] A cholera ward was again installed in the girls' building, and the rest of the premises were thoroughly fumigated.[73] The cholera ward was eventually closed in November, but the last group of inmates did not return until December.[74] In total, some 128 parishioners perished in the 1849 outbreak, though some of the fatalities were due to the

63 9.1.1911, IA, DC/HX 046–01.
64 *Billet*, 23.4.1937. On United Kingdom clinics, see Crowther, *Workhouse System*, p. 96.
65 Smith, *People's Health*, pp. 230, 233.
66 Ords, 8.11.1831, 20.10.1832.
67 14.12.1831, IA, AQ 0965/02.
68 23.8.1832, 19.10.1832, 5.11.1832, IA, DC/HX 135–03.
69 19.10.1832, 5.11.1832, IA, DC/HX 135–03; S. Kellett-Smith, 'The Guernsey cholera epidemic of 1832', *TSG*, 20 (1980), p. 652–5.
70 A contemporary identified defective drainage as a possible cause of transmission, with the contents of one of the Hospital's cesspits discharging into a drinking water tank (S.E. Hoskins, 'The origin and progress of cholera and small-pox in Guernsey', *The London Medical Gazette*, 12 (1851), p. 384). See also 6.8.1849, IA, DC/HX 075–02.
71 1.8.1849, 20.8.1849, IA, DC/HX 075–02.
72 14.8.1849, 18.8.1849, IA, DC/HX 075–02.
73 18.8.1849, IA, DC/HX 075–02.
74 1.11.1849, 6.12.1849, IA, DC/HX 075–02.

smallpox epidemic then running concurrently.[75]

Smallpox was a perennial problem in St Peter Port, owing to the repeated reintroduction of the disease via the port. Town Hospital registers record outbreaks in almost every eighteenth-century decade from 1743, during which Directors usually arranged for the inoculation of inmates and other poor parishioners.[76] There was something of a lull in the first half of the nineteenth century, but the outbreak of 1849 was followed by a series of further outbreaks in 1855, 1867–8, 1878 and 1894–5.[77] In theory, smallpox vaccination was made compulsory in Guernsey in 1862, but the legislation was poorly enforced.[78] A more stringent law followed the 1894–5 outbreak.[79] The last case of smallpox documented at the Town Hospital occurred in 1911.[80]

The 1894–5 smallpox outbreak coincided with a late nineteenth-century island-wide upsurge in infectious diseases of all sorts, including scarlet fever, typhoid fever and diphtheria.[81] This was variously blamed on immigration from France and the insanitary conditions which continued to prevail in both town and country.[82] Following precedents lately set in England and Wales, the States adopted a proactive stance in combating these diseases. In 1895, they passed legislation which compelled the notification of infectious diseases and permitted the isolation of victims.[83] Four years later, they instituted a States' Board of Health and a permanent Medical Officer of Health.[84]

In 1895, the States had designated the girls' building at the Town Hospital as the most appropriate location in which to isolate victims of infectious disease. In the first years following the 1895 law, infectious cases were few and not unduly disruptive of Hospital routine. However, in 1901 there was a large-scale scarlet fever epidemic during which the entire girls' building was effectively commandeered by the Medical

---

[75] P. Johnston, 'The cholera and smallpox epidemic of 1849', *The Review of the Guernsey Society*, 54 (1998), p. 85.

[76] 22.5.1755, St Peter Port Délibérations des Chefs de Famille, 1715–79, PL; spring 1766, IA, DC/HX 119–01; 4.12.1786, IA, DC/HX 079–01; 5.2.1791, IA, DC/HX 121–01; 1.6.1796, IA, DC/HX 121–02. See also G. Stevens Cox, *St Peter Port, 1680–1830: The History of an International Entrepôt* (Woodbridge, 1999), pp. 72–4.

[77] 9.7.1855, IA, DC/HX 054–05; 9.10.1867, IA, DC/HX 054–05; 2.3.1878, IA, DC/HX 069–01; E. Laurie Robinson, 'Small-pox and vaccination in Guernsey, 1894–5', *British Medical Journal*, 2.5.1896.

[78] Ord, 16.5.1862.

[79] O in C, 14.8.1896. In England and Wales, the first Vaccination Act was passed in 1840, but legislation only became effective when an Act of 1871 introduced fines or imprisonment for parents failing to have children vaccinated (Smith, *People's Health*, pp. 160–1).

[80] 9.3.1911, IA, DC/HX 129–02. In 1977, the disease was declared by the World Health Organisation to have been completely eradicated.

[81] 23.8.1894, IA, DC/HX 080–02; 3.12.1901, IA, DC/HX 056–04.

[82] *Billets*, 24.4.1895, 29.3.1899.

[83] Ord, 5.12.1895. Notification of infectious diseases had first been made compulsory in London in 1889 (P. Wood, *Poverty and the Workhouse in Victorian Britain* (Stroud, 1991), p. 31).

[84] Jeffs, 'Through the eyes of the MoH', pp. 6–8. The appointment of such officers had been mandatory throughout England and Wales since 1872 (A. Hardy, *Health and Medicine in Britain since 1860* (Basingstoke, 2001), p. 30).

Officer of Health and his team, generating considerable friction between the latter and the parochial authorities, as well as complaints from better-off sufferers at confinement in the poorhouse.[85] It is this episode which seems ultimately to have triggered a decision on the part of the States to build an isolation hospital of their own. The opening of the new King Edward VII Hospital in 1903 was attended with some fanfare.[86] In itself, it was a modest institution; however, it marked an important watershed. As the first public medical facility for which the States had taken any responsibility, it was the wellspring of further action which would later culminate in the wholesale transfer of health and welfare provision from parishes to States.

Modes of treatment

Prior to the twentieth century, medicine was concerned more with managing symptoms than with curing disease. With few diagnostic tools, the root causes of many disorders remained obscure, and quinine and opium were the only truly effective drugs. These deficiencies aside, a trained medical practitioner could offer his patients many useful services. He could dress wounds, set simple fractures, manipulate dislocations, manage fevers, soothe skin conditions, lance boils, deliver malpresented babies and palliate disorders such as dropsy and gout.[87] All these activities are documented in the records of Town Hospital medical officers. So too are the 'heroic' methods also favoured in the eighteenth and nineteenth centuries – bleeding, leeching, cupping, purging – which were probably less useful.[88] Leeches were the largest single item in the infirmary budget until the mid-nineteenth century.[89] Venesection, cupping and purgatives were the treatments Hospital doctors prescribed for a stroke in 1847.[90]

A sidelight on the activities of medical officers can also be gleaned from the equipment the Hospital possessed. It owned, at various times, a stomach pump; fracture splints; trusses; enema syringes; an 'electrifying machine'; a hydrostatic bed; a set of 'transfusion instruments'; hydraulic cushions; a fracture bedstead; a case of instruments for reviving the drowned and the hanged and, from 1853, thermometers.[91]

Until 1894, what the Hospital does not appear to have possessed is a set of surgical instruments.[92] Nevertheless, operations were performed at the Town Hospital from the time of its foundation, so doctors must have used their own. Opportunities to undertake major surgery were rare outside Guernsey's two workhouses until the opening of the cottage hospital, so this was an acknowledged perquisite of the

85 3.12.1901, 3.2.1902, IA, DC/HX 056–04.
86 *Guernsey Weekly Press*, 3.1.1903.
87 R. Porter, *Disease, Medicine and Society in England, 1550–1860* (1987; Cambridge, 1995 edn), pp. 8, 62.
88 IA, DC/HX 063–02.
89 See Treasurer's accounts in IA, DC/HX 168–01.
90 J. Ozanne, 'On the treatment of apoplexy', *The British Journal of Homoeopathy*, 5 (1847), p. 65.
91 7.12.1825, IA, DC/HX 082–01; 4.3.1831, IA, DC/HX 135–03; 1832 accounts, IA, DC/HX 178–01; 4.3.1833, IA, DC/HX 135–03; 23.3.1857, IA, DC/HX 130–04; 27.8.1833, IA, DC/HX 130–02; 26.8.1850, IA, DC/HX 075–02; 23.12.1861, IA, DC/HX 130–04; 18.8.1853, IA, DC/HX 130–04.
92 *Star*, 23.1.1894; 5.2.1894, IA, DC/HX 054–07.

medical officer's post. Prior to the invention of anaesthetics, artery clamps and the antiseptic system in the second half of the nineteenth century, surgery everywhere was normally resorted to only in absolute emergencies.[93] In the Town Hospital, early surgical interventions most commonly took the form of amputation for compound fractures and lithotomy for the removal of bladder stones. Many operations of this sort are recorded from the eighteenth century onwards. Often they were performed in front of an audience of apprentices and other practitioners (the Hospital had a dedicated 'operating room' as early as 1831). The removal of 20-year-old William Mills' leg in February 1840 was explicitly recorded as having been performed 'in the presence of a great number of surgeons'.[94] Mills fortunately survived, but death rates from such interventions were relatively high owing to blood loss and sepsis. With improvements in equipment and techniques in the second half of the nineteenth century, the Hospital's doctors attempted a growing range of non-emergency proce-dures. In 1862, for example, an operation was performed to correct five-year-old Emma Ricketts' hare lip.[95] Operations continued to be performed at the Hospital for many decades. In 1930, its theatre was still sufficiently in use to warrant the purchase of a new operating table.[96] Not until 1964 was the decision finally taken to close the theatre down.[97]

Deaths within the Hospital, whether or not they resulted from surgical proce-dures, afforded doctors a useful opportunity for anatomical studies. Westminster's 1832 Anatomy Act, under which unclaimed pauper bodies could be used for medical dissection, did not apply in Guernsey, but this did not prevent the Hospital's doctors from opening cadavers. The Hospital's burial policy was such that no-one could claim a pauper's body, and the building of a mortuary in 1826 was partly moti-vated by a wish to facilitate dissection.[98] When it came to light in 1875 that the asylum supervisor was privately offering lunatics' cadavers to external practitioners, the House Committee ruled that no future dissections should take place without the Chairman's express authorisation.[99]

Infirmary regime
Surgery might provide an occasional highlight for doctors, but the infirmary's day-to-day regime was unglamorously founded on bed-rest and enhanced nutri-tion, with food and drink the single most important component. Until the late nineteenth century, alcohol was routinely prescribed to patients as a stimulant and fortifier. At first, relatively large amounts were used: in one month during 1826, the infirmary consumed six gallons of gin, three gallons of brandy and three bottles of sherry.[100] This declined somewhat during the mid-century tenure of teetotaller

93 Hardy, *Health and Medicine*, p. 28.
94 18.2.1840, IA, DC/HX 075–01.
95 19.8.1862, IA, DC/HX 127–01.
96 12.5.1930, IA, DC/HX 051–01.
97 22.9.1964, IA, AS/MB 065–02.
98 6.3.1826, IA, DC/HX 135–02.
99 20.9.1875, IA, DC/HX 136–09.
100 31.7.1826, IA, DC/HX 083–01.

Dr Collenette and, from the 1880s onwards, alcohol was progressively replaced by alternative fortifiers such as beef tea.[101] Food, however, always remained a vital part of therapy. From the Hospital's earliest days, infirmary patients enjoyed a range of comestibles unavailable to other inmates: eggs, cheese, fresh fish, veal, mutton and poultry, all prescribed in differing amounts according to patients' condition.[102] Interestingly, while gruel was little used in English workhouse infirmaries (being the usual fare of ordinary inmates), the reverse was true in the Town Hospital, and gruel was served only in the infirmary.[103]

Whether or not patients actually received the rations prescribed by the doctors depended on the honesty of those who tended them. In the mid-1840s, medical officers were particularly vociferous in their complaints that the Hospital's nurses and orderlies, who were recruited 'from the cripples, drunkards and prostitutes already inmates of the house', were making 'improper use of those necessary luxuries which belong alone to the patients'.[104] In response to these complaints, the Board decided to take the novel step of engaging two paid infirmary attendants: one male from 1846, and one female from 1849.[105] However, if the Board had hoped that these attendants would improve standards of care, they were to be disappointed. The low pay and unappealing conditions on offer meant that the posts usually only attracted former inmates, or people in receipt of parish relief (at this time, male attendants received about 8s per week, and females 6s, including board and lodging; they ate and slept on the wards with their patients).[106] Such attendants proved scarcely more trustworthy than their unpaid colleagues. Hospital daybooks abound with records of reprimands issued to successive incumbents. Typical of these were admonitions to James MacAllister for molesting female patients in 1854, to Elizabeth Hill for stealing meat in 1870, and to Caroline Whitford for drunkenness on duty in the same year.[107]

Aside from the introduction of paid attendants, conditions changed little over mid-century. In 1878, an unfortunate incident cast a spotlight on the infirmary's continuing unsatisfactory state. In the spring of that year, the 63-year-old master of the Hospital, Thomas Mauger, contracted smallpox from an infirmary patient and died.[108] It transpired that, in an effort to save money, Mauger had refused to comply with an instruction from medical officer John Aikman to burn the dead man's infectious bedclothes, and had instead deposited them in the laundry basket

[101] 1885 accounts in IA, DC/HX 272–02.
[102] See, for instance, 1766 and 1827 infirmary accounts in IA, DC/HX 165–01 and IA, DC/HX 168–01.
[103] V.J. Johnston, *Diet in Workhouses and Prisons, 1835–1895* (London, 1985), p. 124; IA, DC/HX 088–02; IA, DC/HX 100–02; IA, DC/HX 101–01; IA, DC/HX 101–02; IA, DC/HX 109–05; IA, DC/HX 109–09.
[104] See letters to the Board dated 7.10.1844 and 27.1.1846 from Drs M.A.B. Corbin and E.F. Carey (IA, DC/HX 130–01).
[105] 11.3.1846, IA, DC/HX 130–01; 5.11.1849, IA, DC/HX 075–02.
[106] IA, DC/HX 272–02.
[107] 16.6.1854, 18.10.1854, IA, DC/HX 130–04; 21.2.1870, 7.3.1870, 3.10.1870, IA, DC/HX 136–08.
[108] 2.3.1878, IA, DC/HX 136–09.

himself.[109] This episode was publicised in the local press, notably through letters from Dr Marc Corbin, one of the doctors who had complained about pauper nurses in the 1840s.[110] Dr Aikman did not contact the press himself, but submitted a detailed report on the infirmary's deficiencies to the House Committee. His report paints a picture of dirt and neglect: bedding infested with lice; spittoon contents left to fester till they stank; pauper nurses and attendants too obtuse or decrepit to carry out medical instructions. Most strikingly, Aikman identified a culture of 'gross and flagrant' bullying, where the master and mistress 'terrorised' everyone on the wards, depriving patients of special rations in order to save money, and meeting any complaint with 'outrageous and unjustifiable fury'.[111]

Further letters to the press in response to Dr Corbin's, most of them supportive of Aikman, provoked a parish meeting. This meeting resulted in an official letter from Poor Law Board President Francis Shortt to Bailiff Sir Peter Stafford Carey.[112] In his letter, Shortt set out proposals for the separation of the infirmary from the rest of the workhouse and its removal to the detached quarters now occupied by lunatics (the former house of separation). Shortt was doubtless aware that large workhouses in England and Wales had progressively been moving their infirmaries to separate quarters since the passage of the Metropolitan Asylums Act in 1867 (amid similar public outcry over standards).[113] For this plan to be feasible, however, Shortt pointed out that the States would themselves have to assume responsibility for lunatics and build an all-island asylum. He urgently solicited the Bailiff's support in furthering this project. However, no response from Carey was recorded in Hospital registers and, in time, the matter fell by the wayside. Aside from Shortt's unimplemented proposals, the only result of the Aikman affair was the passage of a few feeble resolutions to improve the infirmary, a change of paid attendants and, the following year, the replacement of the Hospital's mistress.[114] The public furore died down, the episode was forgotten and business as usual resumed.[115]

Progress towards a modern hospital

In changing the paid attendants following the Aikman affair, the House Committee briefly flirted with the idea of trained nurses, sourcing a Mrs Buckley from the Institution for Trained Nurses in London.[116] Unfortunately, she proved as unsatisfactory as her untrained colleagues and was dismissed for drunkenness within a few months.[117] At this time, the whole concept of trained nurses was relatively new, not

---

[109] *Star*, 9.2.1878.

[110] *Star*, 12.1.1878, 19.2.1878, 26.2.1878.

[111] IA, DC/HX 281–25.

[112] *Star*, 11.4.1878; 4.6.1878, IA, DC/HX 054–06.

[113] M.W. Flinn, 'Medical services under the New Poor Law', in D. Fraser (ed.), *The New Poor Law in the Nineteenth Century* (London, 1976), pp. 64–5.

[114] 18.3.1878, 20.3.1878, 5.8.1878, 2.12.1878, 20.5.1879, IA, DC/HX 054–06.

[115] Following his resignation from the Hospital, Dr Aikman himself went on to enjoy a long and successful career in private practice. For his obituary, see *Guernsey Weekly Press*, 2.2.1918.

[116] 4.11.1879, IA, DC/HX 179–06.

[117] 9.2.1881, IA, DC/HX 136–09.

just to Guernsey but to the entire British Isles. In England, formal nurse training had begun only in 1860, with the establishment of Florence Nightingale's Training School for Nurses, and it was not until the mid-1870s that English poor law authorities actively began to promote the use of trained nurses in their own workhouses.[118]

In Guernsey, the professionalisation of poor law nursing was beset with false starts. In the two decades following Mrs Buckley's dismissal, trained nurses were again tried on several occasions, but none stayed for long,[119] and the century expired with nursing entirely in untrained hands. This situation changed when the Royal Court assumed oversight over the Hospitals in 1901, and Miss Frances Laws, a certificated nurse from the Poplar Institute, was appointed to superintend the infirmary.[120] Miss Laws made several major improvements and, following a precedent set in English workhouses in 1897, persuaded the Poor Law Board to pass a resolution abolishing the use of inmate nurses in 1903.[121] Unfortunately, Miss Laws resigned her post in 1904 and many of her improvements were lost.[122] By 1910, all seven of the Town Hospital's nurses, including the superintendent nurse, Mrs Ada Collenette, were once more untrained.[123] Progress, however, restarted with World War I, and this time with lasting results. When the conflict began, the Hospital authorities offered thirty-six beds to the military in case of need. However, qualms soon arose about the infirmary's ability to cope with a major influx, and, as a first step towards improvement, Drs Bostock and Bisson recommended replacing Mrs Collenette with a certificated professional.[124] A few months later, 36-year-old London-trained Laura West was appointed as superintendent under the entirely new title of 'sister-in-charge'.[125] Adopting a measure instituted in England in 1913, Sister West began by insisting that the Hospital's infirmary functions be formally severed from its workhouse role.[126] The Poor Law Board acquiesced and, from this point onward, the responsibility of master and mistress was limited to the workhouse department only and the sister-in-charge was given full control of the infirmary. By clarifying lines of command and minimising non-medical interference, this measure considerably boosted the infirmary's professionalism.

Together with Drs Bostock and Bisson, Sister West then proceeded to draft a syllabus for a basic nursing course qualifying local girls to work in Guernsey

[118] Fowler, *Life behind Doors*, pp. 185, 187; Crowther, *Workhouse System*, pp. 176–8.

[119] See, for instance, 9.4.1894 and 7.1.1895, IA, DC/HX 054–07.

[120] 7.7.1902, 1.12.1902, IA, DC/HX 056–04; 24.11.1902, IA, DC/HX 080–03.

[121] 5.1.1903, IA, DC/HX 056–04. For England and Wales, see N. Longmate, *The Workhouse: A Social History* (London, 1974), p. 207.

[122] 8.4.1904, IA, DC/HX 056–04.

[123] 24.10.1910, IA, DC/HX 046–01; IA, DC/HX 272–02.

[124] 31.8.1914, IA, DC/HX 080–05.

[125] 17.9.1914, 2.11.1914, IA, DC/HX 046–01.

[126] 29.9.1915, IA, DC/HX 080–05. On the 1913 separation of workhouse and infirmary functions in England and Wales, see M.A. Crowther, 'The later years of the workhouse, 1890–1929', in P. Thane (ed.), *The Origins of British Social Policy* (London, 1978), p. 50.

hospitals as certificated nurses.[127] While this scheme was slow to yield results, by the mid-1920s three of the Hospital's ten nurses were fully certificated.[128]

An unforeseen change of course

In England and Wales, the Local Government Act of 1929 transferred the infirmary responsibilities of poor law guardians to local councils, so that, by the late 1930s, only a quarter of occupied hospital beds in England and Wales remained under poor law jurisdiction.[129] In Guernsey, the reverse was true: only a quarter of hospital beds were non-poor law.[130] British medical opinion was much preoccupied at this time with the need to co-ordinate the United Kingdom's patchwork of council and voluntary hospitals into a coherent public medical service. In 1929, the British Medical Association had published a pamphlet entitled *A General Medical Service for the Nation* recommending government co-ordination and financial assistance. In 1937, the Voluntary Hospitals Commission issued an influential report – the 'Sankey Report' – which made similar proposals.[131] The Guernsey branch of the British Medical Association was fully abreast of this debate, and in 1937 it submitted its own plans to the States for a modern States' general hospital to replace both Town and Country Hospitals, whose poor law taint members considered ineradicable.[132] In response, the States extended the mandate of their existing Poor Law Enquiry Committee to examine the possibility of building of such a hospital.[133] The preliminary indications were favourable, and, eschewing poor law connections, the States renamed the Committee the 'Island Hospital Committee' in November 1938, at the same time authorising it to find a site, investigate a compulsory health insurance scheme and launch negotiations with the Victoria Cottage Hospital and Lady Ozanne Maternity Home for their eventual absorption into the new facility.[134]

Nevertheless, war was looming at this time, and an unforeseen development abruptly stymied plans for the new general hospital. Early in 1938, the United Kingdom government had set up an Emergency Medical Service in anticipation of war. This service included an Emergency Hospital Scheme, in which all existing hospitals were to be brought under the management of the regional civil defence

---

[127] 3.8.1915, IA, DC/HX 052–01; 15.11.1915, IA, DC/HX 080–05. A similar internal training scheme had operated in larger English workhouses since the 1870s (Crowther, *Workhouse System*, p. 176).

[128] 1924 accounts in IA, DC/HX 272–02. For a photograph of the Hospital's nursing and medical staff at around this time (including Drs Bostock and Bisson), see Plate 5.

[129] M.A. Crowther, 'From workhouse to NHS hospital in Britain, 1929–1948', in C. Hillam and J.M. Bone (eds), *The Poor Law and After: Workhouse Hospitals and Public Welfare* (Liverpool, 1999), pp. 41–2.

[130] The island had a total of 168 hospital beds in 1937, 120 of which belonged to the poor law authorities (24.5.1937, IA, AS/MB 011–05).

[131] J. Lane, *A Social History of Medicine: Health, Healing and Disease in England, 1750–1950* (London, 2001), p. 188.

[132] 19.2.1937, 5.3.1937, IA, AS/MB 011–05; *British Medical Journal*, 14.8.1937.

[133] 30.6.1937, IA, AS/MB 011–05.

[134] 18.2.1938, 13.5.1938, 30.11.1938, IA, AS/MB 011–05; *Billets*, 7.10.1938, 30.11.1938.

administration.[135] The chief purpose of the new Emergency Hospitals was to deal with air raid casualties, which military strategists had predicted would be heavy in the coming war. Following the British government's lead, the States instituted their own 'Emergency Hospital Committee' late in 1938 to prepare for the establishment of an Emergency Hospital in Guernsey. This Committee was entirely separate from the Island Hospital Committee, over which it immediately took precedence.

Lacking the time to build a fresh facility, the Emergency Hospital Committee decided that their best plan would be to adapt the Country Hospital (which, like its urban counterpart, had assumed an increasingly medical role). Work was quickly put in hand to extend and modernise the facility and, over a period of months, the Country Hospital's inmates were either rehomed in the community or transferred to the Town Hospital.[136] On 5 September 1939, the Country Hospital officially reopened as Guernsey's Emergency Hospital.[137]

The anticipated air campaign never materialised, and ten months later Guernsey was occupied by German forces with relatively little loss of life.[138] Nevertheless, the newly adapted Country Hospital proved an asset to islanders under German occupation. Remaining under the (non-poor law) jurisdiction of the Emergency Hospital Committee, it functioned as a regular civilian medical and surgical hospital for the duration of the war.[139]

Ironically, at the time these developments supervened, the Town Hospital was fulfilling more of a medical role than it had ever done previously. In 1938, it was caring for seventy-five medical and surgical patients in its infirmary, while treating an average of forty patients a day in its outpatients' department.[140] Nevertheless, the fact that it was not chosen to fill the emergency hospital role marked the end of its chances of evolving into a general hospital. For the duration of World War II, it became the sole public repository for Guernsey's workhouse inmates, cared-for elderly and long-term sick and disabled. This was a role which it continued to perform well into the post-war period. The subsequent evolution of the infirmary, as of the Hospital in general, is addressed on pages 236–8 below.

Lunatic Asylum

Before embarking on an account of the Town Hospital's facilities for the mentally ill, a short history of institutional provision for lunatics in England and Wales may be apposite, since this provides the context against which knowledgeable

[135] Hardy, *Health and Medicine*, pp. 126–7.

[136] 20.9.1939, IA, DC/HX 015–04.

[137] Although its lunatics, who were housed separately in an annexe, remained on site (4.9.1939, IA, DC/HX 015–04).

[138] A single German air raid in June 1940 killed twenty-nine people (J. Marr, *The History of Guernsey: The Bailiwick's Story* (1982; Guernsey, 2001 edn), p. 291).

[139] 1.12.1940, IA, DC/HX 015–04. See also K. Tough, 'Health in the Occupation', in Jeffs (ed.), *One Hundred Years of Health*, pp. 87–92.

[140] 1.4.1938, IA, AS/MB 011–05.

contemporaries compared themselves.[141] Until the nineteenth century, there was little specialist provision for lunatics in England and Wales aside from the well-known Bethlem Hospital and a limited number of private madhouses and charitable asylums in London and the provinces. Most paupers with a mental illness or mental handicap simply lived out their lives in the community, sometimes supported on outdoor relief. Those unable to do so might be boarded out by their parishes in host families willing to care for them for a fee; they might be lodged in private madhouses at a special pauper rate, or they might simply be consigned to the nearest workhouse.

Acknowledging the shortage of accommodation for pauper lunatics, a statute of 1808 attempted to increase provision by authorising local Justices of the Peace to arrange for the erection of a public asylum in each county at ratepayers' expense. These county asylums were envisaged as a form of poor law institution. Inmates' fees were to be funded by the ratepayers of their home parishes. Applications for committal were to be instigated by parish overseers, supported, from 1811, by a doctor's certificate. JPs were to have final jurisdiction over admissions and discharges.

The 1808 Act was not, however, mandatory. Ratepayers proved reluctant to provide funding and, by 1844, only ten county asylums had been built. To remedy this, a further Act of 1845 made the erection of county and borough lunatic asylums compulsory. This initiated an unprecedented explosion in asylum-building and, within two decades, the number of such asylums in England and Wales had risen to fifty. The 1845 Act also refined committal procedures. If a pauper lunatic required confinement in an asylum, it was now the responsibility of the relieving officers of the poor law unions created by the 1834 Poor Law Amendment Act to initiate proceedings: the officers had first to obtain certificates from two doctors confirming the pauper's insanity, and then to bring the individual concerned before a JP.[142] If all the formalities had been satisfactorily completed, the JP would issue an order committing the pauper to an asylum. This process was applicable only to the pauper insane. Better-off patients admitted to private institutions required only an application from their next-of-kin supported by medical certificates until 1890, when their confinement had also to be sanctioned by a JP.

The post-1845 increase in numbers of county and borough asylums did not, however, mean that all pauper lunatics were henceforth accommodated in these institutions. Throughout the nineteenth century, it remained permissible to accommodate lunatics in workhouses and, until 1874, when government granted parishes a subsidy of 4s weekly for each pauper in a county or borough asylum, the workhouse was often a cheaper preferred option.[143] After the 1870s, however, the workhouse option declined in popularity and, by 1909, all but 15 per cent of pauper lunatics in

---

[141] The following account is derived from A. Scull, *The Most Solitary of Afflictions: Madness and Society in Britain, 1700–1900* (New Haven, 1993); P. Bartlett, *The Poor Law of Lunacy: The Administration of Pauper Lunatics in Mid-Nineteenth-Century England* (London, 1999); K. Jones, *A History of the Mental Health Services* (London, 1972).

[142] Relieving officers had taken over from overseers as instigators of pauper committals since the passage of the 1834 Act.

[143] No-one could be committed to a workhouse, although, from 1867, workhouse medical officers

England and Wales were accommodated in county and borough asylums.

In Guernsey, until the eve of World War II, the only provision for the mentally ill was in the two insular workhouses. The island never hosted any private madhouses, charitable mental institutions or, indeed, any establishments equivalent to English county and borough asylums.

A further English development of relevance to this account is the establishment of the Metropolitan Commissioners in Lunacy. This body was first set up in 1828 to license and inspect private madhouses in the London area. Its powers of inspection were temporarily extended to private madhouses and county asylums countrywide in 1842. From 1845, its members were redesignated simply the Commissioners in Lunacy and given permanent powers of inspection over every private, charitable and poor law facility for the insane throughout England and Wales. The Commissioners' function was mainly advisory, although, from 1862, they could order the release of those confined in county and borough asylums on inadequate documentation. In the early twentieth century, the Commissioners' advice was to be sought on matters pertaining to Guernsey.

Reverting to St Peter Port: after the opening of the Town Hospital in 1743, a majority of the parish's mentally ill and mentally handicapped continued to live in the community, as they also did in England and Wales at this time. Admissions to the Hospital consisted mainly of mentally deficient people incapable of survival outside, who were housed side by side with other inmates. In addition, there were also a small number of 'unmanageable' lunatics, who were usually housed separately. In the eighteenth century, the latter were kept in lean-to sheds against the boundary wall behind the main building.[144] In 1815, Thomas Quayle described these sheds as 'unventilated, filthy and damp', adding that some individuals deemed particularly dangerous had been kept chained up in them for periods of up to seventeen years.[145]

In the era of modernisation which followed the early nineteenth-century ousting of Treasurer Jean Condamine, the Hospital Board arranged for the erection of a number of purpose-built lunatic cells.[146] By the 1830s, the institution possessed a total of seven such cells, three measuring 12ft 10in by 6ft 3in, and the other four 10ft by 7ft 8in. They all had stone-flagged floors and some of them lacked windows.[147]

At this stage, there was no attempt to offer any 'treatment' to lunatics in the Hospital, although Directors and other parishioners would have known of the 'humane therapies' first developed for use with lunatics in the 1790s. These had been pioneered by Philippe Pinel in France, and had spread to England via private

---

were authorised to certify that an insane person already within the house was not in a fit state to leave without danger to himself and others.

[144] 4.3.1753, IA, DC/HX 079–01; T. Dicey, *An Historical Account of Guernsey* (London, 1751), p. 188.

[145] T. Quayle, *A General View of the Agriculture and Present State of the Islands on the Coast of Normandy subject to the Crown of Great Britain* (London, 1815), p. 292. Quayle might have been alluding to Jean Mauger or William Caire, first chained up in 1788 and 1798 respectively (24.9.1788, IA, DC/HX 120–01; 8.3.1798, IA, DC/HX 079–01).

[146] 27.9.1813, 6.5.1822, IA, DC/HX 079–02; 3.6.1822, IA, DC/HX 135–02.

[147] 13.3.1839, IA, DC/HX 075–01.

asylums established by the Tuke family at York in 1796 and the Fox family at Bristol in 1804. By the 1830s, such therapies had been adapted for use in county asylums, notably by Robert Gardiner Hill and John Conolly, superintendents of Middlesex and Lincoln asylums respectively.[148] In 1833, the English social reformer Elizabeth Fry visited the Town Hospital, and strongly criticised its facilities for lunatics, which she contrasted with 'those humane plans which have been found so successful of late years'.[149]

Mrs Fry's criticisms met with no immediate response. However, in 1839, the Hospital's seven existing cells were found insufficient for the twelve cases currently requiring confinement, and a parish meeting was held to discuss what could be done. During the meeting, dissatisfaction was expressed from several quarters concerning the handling of lunacy in general, echoing observations first made by Mrs Fry. A committee was appointed, which included three medical practitioners, to review the whole insular situation regarding the insane.[150] Reporting back, the committee put forward the view that care of the insane was a matter best tackled at all-island level, and that it should therefore fall to the States to build and run a public asylum. Acknowledging, however, that States' agreement in this matter was highly unlikely, they recommended as a fall-back strategy that, rather than continue housing lunatics at the Hospital, St Peter Port should build an entirely separate parochial facility of its own.[151] Ratepayers rejected this plan on the grounds of expense, not least because they had already borne the cost of the house of separation seven years earlier. Problems were solved for the time being by improvising a few extra cells at the Hospital and sending the worst cases to private asylums in England.[152]

For the next few years, the parish funded the stays of four or five lunatics annually at James Duck's asylum at Plympton (later run by Richard Langworthy), John Twynam's asylum near Winchester and William Finch's asylum near Salisbury. In a report published in 1844 by the Metropolitan Commissioners in Lunacy, William Finch's asylum was commended as having 'made genuine efforts to secure its inmates' well-being', but those belonging to John Twynam and Richard Langworthy were both censured as 'utterly unfit'.[153] The 1844 report was widely publicised in the British press, adding to the pressure for reform in England and Wales which culminated in the 1845 statute making the establishment of county and borough asylums compulsory.[154] It is probable that Town Hospital surgeon Marc Corbin also read articles on the subject, for, in October 1844, he addressed a letter to the Hospital Board citing John Conolly's innovations at Middlesex county asylum and

---

[148] Lane, *Social History of Medicine*, pp. 105, 109–10; Jones, *Mental Health Services*, pp. 50–2, 119–21.
[149] Elizabeth Fry to Town Hospital Directors, 7.10.1833, IA, DC/HX 130–02. Mrs Fry was holidaying in the Islands.
[150] 13.4.1839, IA, DC/HX 075–01; *Star*, 14.3.1839.
[151] 5.5.1839, 6.5.1839, IA, DC/HX 075–01.
[152] 25.9.1839, 24.10.1839, 29.10.1839, IA, DC/HX 075–01. See also *Star*, 29.9.1839, 30.10.1839.
[153] Scull, *Most Solitary of Afflictions*, pp. 23, 81, 88, 162, 212.
[154] Scull, *Most Solitary of Afflictions*, p. 164.

castigating 'the dens, chains, bolts, fetters, logs, handcuffs and other barbarous contrivances' still used on St Peter Port's lunatics. He condemned the Hospital's facilities for the mentally ill as 'a disgrace to the community' and urged Directors 'to use every endeavour' to improve them.[155] Already under pressure from mounting relief costs and aware of ratepayers' reluctance to spend money on lunatics, the Board responded with a pledge that they would vigorously petition the States for a public asylum.[156] This, however, achieved nothing, and neither did a second attempt to petition the States for an asylum in 1847.[157]

By the late 1840s, the Town Hospital had taken to accommodating some of its lunatics in the house of separation, chiefly because this was conveniently located away from the main building. In January 1848, a parish meeting agreed to fund an extension to the house of separation in order to increase the accommodation available for lunatics.[158] An additional storey, an extra cell-block and new exercise yards were planned, and construction work began in March 1849.[159] Originally, the plan had been to continue accommodating lunatics alongside those detained in the building on disciplinary grounds, but gradually the idea took shape that it might be better to reintegrate the latter within the main Hospital and turn the entire annexe over to the insane. A commitment to do this was finally made at a parish meeting in July 1850. One factor which found favour among ratepayers was that the projected facility was to include separate accommodation for private fee-payers, thereby obviating the need for respectable parishioners to send mentally ill relatives off-island, as well as enabling it to cover some of its own running costs.[160] Further plans were drawn up and building recommenced.[161] Finally, on 16 July 1851, extension work to the old house of separation was completed and the building reopened as a 'lunatic asylum', which a parish meeting formally placed under the administration of the Town Hospital Board.[162]

In one of the few academic studies of lunacy in offshore British islands, sociologist David Hirst has suggested that the opening of this facility in Guernsey represented an advance over Jersey and the Isle of Man in the management of lunacy. 'The response of each to the public asylum movement was very different', Dr Hirst wrote. 'Guernsey had an asylum by 1852, but Jersey and the Isle of Man opened permanent asylums only in 1868.'[163] This is a misreading of the nature of the Town Hospital facility, which was never a proper public asylum in the sense of the institutions eventually opened in Jersey and the Isle of Man, but merely segregated

155 M.A.B. Corbin to Hospital Directors, 7.10.1844, IA, DC/HX 130–01.
156 4.11.1844, IA, DC/HX 130–01.
157 14.7.1847, IA, DC/HX 130–01; 13.10.1847, St Peter Port Délibérations des Chefs de Famille, 1844–66, PL.
158 26.1.1848, IA, DC/HX 130–01.
159 1.3.1849, 28.3.1849, IA, DC/HX 130–01.
160 13.7.1850, 19.7.1850, IA, DC/HX 075–02.
161 *Star*, 3.10.1850; 26.2.1851, IA, DC/HX 075–02.
162 16.7.1851, IA, DC/HX 075–02; 16.7.1851, St Peter Port Délibérations des Chefs de Famille, 1844–66, PL.
163 D. Hirst, 'Lunacy and the "Islands in the British Seas"', *History of Psychiatry*, 18 (2007), p. 411.

quarters for lunatics within an existing workhouse. In this, the Town Hospital was little different from the 104 English and Welsh workhouses which also had separate annexes for lunatics by the mid-nineteenth century, and whose annexes no-one would have characterised as asylums in their own right.[164]

In this context, it is instructive to recapitulate the Jersey situation. In Jersey, just as in Guernsey, most lunatics were kept within the workhouse until the mid-nineteenth century.[165] However, unlike in Guernsey, this deficiency became an issue (along with others) in an acrimonious mid-century conflict between local reformists and conservatives, into which the British government found itself drawn, largely through the efforts of the participants themselves.[166] As a result, throughout the 1850s, Westminster exerted pressure upon Jersey's authorities to remedy the 'lunatic problem' – pressure which, Dr Hirst has suggested, Guernsey was spared because of the action taken in 1851 in St Peter Port.[167] However, while the Town Hospital's new lunatics' quarters certainly represented an advance on those in Jersey's workhouse, the advantage over Jersey was of short duration. Partly as a result of British government pressure, Jersey's States opened their own purpose-built all-island public lunatic asylum in 1868 and, for the next seventy years, the advantage was decidedly on Jersey's side.[168]

Jersey's new States' asylum was superior to the Town Hospital annexe in almost every way. Its administrative arrangements and regulations were enshrined in law and, following the model of county and borough asylums in England and Wales, it was superintended by a full-time resident medical officer.[169] By contrast, the Town Hospital's 'lunatic asylum' remained legally, financially and administratively part of the workhouse until 1939, and at no time during this period did it have a resident medical superintendent. Rather, it was run by untrained amateurs with intermittent assistance from a general practitioner on a small retainer. As a perspicacious correspondent to a local newspaper observed in 1848, 'a new asylum will require a certain number of regular trained keepers of both sexes, a resident medical man, etc. If the parishioners are not prepared to go to the expense of such a staff, their asylum will not be a proper one.'[170] Such funding was never forthcoming, and the Hospital's 'asylum' never became 'a proper one'. The remainder of this section will analyse the functioning of this facility in detail.

---

[164] Bartlett, *Poor Law of Lunacy*, p. 44.
[165] For more on Jersey's workhouse (the 'General Hospital'), see Appendix 3.
[166] J.D. Kelleher, *The Triumph of the Country: The Rural Community in Nineteenth-Century Jersey* (Jersey, 1994), pp. 152–67.
[167] Hirst, 'Lunacy', pp. 412, 422–4. The decision to turn the house of separation entirely over to lunatics may partly have been motivated by a knowledge of government pressure on Jersey, but there is no indication of this in Town Hospital records.
[168] Hirst, 'Lunacy', p. 425.
[169] Hirst, 'Lunacy', p. 425; Scull, *Most Solitary of Afflictions*, p. 230.
[170] *Star*, 26.1.1848.

Staff

Joseph Hume, a radical British MP who took an interest in the Channel Islands, visited the Town Hospital when it was in the process of extending its house of separation in 1849.[171] He was a member of the parliamentary Select Committee on District Asylums and keen to help establish an up-to-date regime in the proposed new facility. As well as providing copies of eight different parliamentary reports on lunacy and asylums, he offered to furnish the 'new superintendent' with an introduction to the Middlesex county asylum 'to learn the course of treatment there'.[172] Notwithstanding that the Town Hospital's Directors were flattered by Joseph Hume's attention, they did not avail themselves of his offer.[173] No new superintendent was appointed, and supervision of lunatics was instead entrusted to the ex-NCO Charles McBride, who had formerly overseen the house of separation.[174] McBride was assisted by his wife Ellen, who assumed the role of housekeeper, and two paid attendants, one of which was McBride's son Michael, a shoemaker by trade.[175] The daily work of the house – cooking, cleaning, laundry, and so on – was performed by the paid attendants with the unpaid assistance of Hospital inmates, including the lunatics themselves wherever possible.[176]

When Charles McBride retired at the age of 73 in 1861, the McBride family's tenure continued in the form of Michael McBride, who took over his father's supervisory duties, assisted by his step-mother Ellen.[177] Michael McBride's own death in 1882 saw the family's thirty-year tenure finally come to an end. The elderly Ellen McBride was retired, and a married couple were engaged to manage the facility: Mr and Mrs Brady, both untrained and unqualified.[178] The next few years saw the transit of several other untrained couples: Mr and Mrs Shaw (1885–6), Mr and Mrs Bath (1886–99) and Mr and Mrs Robert (1899–1921).[179] It was not until 1921 that the facility finally acquired its first professionally qualified management team, Mr and Mrs McCormick, both still in their 20s when appointed, and both holders of the Medico-Psychological Certificate of Great Britain and Ireland.[180]

As mentioned above, the lunatics' medical needs were serviced by a single general practitioner, who, in return for a small stipend, performed regular rounds at the

---

[171] Hume was in transit from Alderney, where he had gone to monitor progress on the government-financed naval harbour construction project.

[172] Joseph Hume to Town Hospital Board, 27.8.1849, IA, DC/HX 075–02.

[173] They did, however, have Hume's reports bound up into two volumes bearing the gold-embossed legend 'Presented to the Town Hospital by Joseph Hume, Esq., M.P., August 1849' (IA, DC/HX 281–22; IA, DC/HX 281–23).

[174] At £40 per year, McBride's salary was half that received by the master of the Town Hospital (6.2.1854, IA, DC/HX 054–05).

[175] IA, DC/HX 062–03.

[176] IA, DC/HX 272–08.

[177] 5.8.1861, IA, DC/HX 054–05.

[178] 18.1.1882, 1.3.1882, IA, DC/HX 054–06.

[179] 14.4.1885, 8.11.1886, IA, DC/HX 054–06; 6.2.1899, IA, DC/HX 054–04.

[180] 4.4.1921, IA, DC/HX 052–01. This was a qualification for mental nurses instituted in 1891 by the Royal Medico-Psychological Association, an independent body which had grown out of the Association of Medical Officers of Asylums and Hospitals for the Insane (Jones, *Mental Health Services*, p. 234).

facility and made himself available to answer calls as they arose. In 1853, the stipend of the asylum doctor was set at £25, while the Town Hospital doctors received £50 each.[181] This sum remained unaltered for more than fifty years, finally rising to £40 in 1907, by which time the Hospital doctors were receiving £75.[182] The asylum stipend rose further to £60 in 1919, while that of the Hospital doctors was increased to £100.[183]

Regulations drawn up by the new St Peter Port Poor Law Board in 1853 decreed that the medical officer to the 'lunatic asylum' would be employed on a biennial contract, with applications solicited from fresh candidates every two years. However, low prestige and low remuneration made the post unattractive to Guernsey's medical practitioners, and very few applications were received. It therefore remained in the same hands for long stretches, and all incumbents but one had already seen service in the main workhouse. Between 1853 and 1868, the post was held, in turn, by Nicholas Magrath and De Beauvoir De Lisle. From 1868 to 1893, it was served by Francis Carey. Early twentieth-century incumbents were Clifford Crewe, Edmund Gibson, William Duncan and Edward Corbin.[184] These doctors were as unqualified in the treatment of mental illness as the asylum's pre-1921 supervisors.[185]

Between 1851 and 1913, the number of paid attendants (or 'keepers') employed at the facility gradually increased from two to eleven.[186] They were paid roughly the same as their counterparts on the infirmary wards, but had extra allowances of strong beer and spirits, notionally to compensate them for working with 'dirty' cases.[187] Male and female keepers were obliged to live with their charges, eating at the same tables and sleeping on the same wards seven days a week. As observed earlier, they scrubbed and swept as well as supervised. In the 1850s, they were allowed out only for Sunday church services and on two afternoons weekly.[188] By 1913, this had been extended to include one night away from the institution per week.[189] The work of attendants could be dangerous as well as onerous: 27-year-old keeper Edward Flynn died after being stabbed by a lunatic in 1870.[190]

If the Hospital authorities found it difficult to recruit doctors for the asylum, they had no choice but to source attendants from the lowest ranks of society. Such was the public perception of the job that no-one considering themselves 'respectable'

---

[181] 24.1.1853, 31.1.1853, IA, DC/HX 054–05.

[182] 3.12.1906, IA, DC/HX 056–04.

[183] 20.10.1919, IA, DC/HX 052–01.

[184] 24.1.1853, 17.9.1860, 27.9.1868, IA, DC/HX 054–05; 4.1.1893, IA, DC/HX 054–07; 3.12.1900, 5.12.1904, 4.6.1906, IA, DC/HX 056–04.

[185] This was to some extent unavoidable. It was not until 1885 that a certificate course in psychological medicine was introduced by the United Kingdom General Medical Council. The first true specialist qualification in the field was the Diploma in Psychological Medicine, which was available to trainee practitioners at Edinburgh, Durham and London Universities from 1911 (Bartlett, *Poor Law of Lunacy*, p. 130; Jones, *Mental Health Services*, p. 230).

[186] IA, DC/HX 272–02.

[187] 13.10.1902, IA, DC/HX 080–03.

[188] 13.5.1853, IA, DC/HX 130–04.

[189] *Billet*, 3.12.1913.

[190] 10.12.1870, IA, DC/HX 127–01; *Star*, 13.12.1870.

would even consider it.[191] Keepers were thus often recruited from former inmates of the workhouse, and even of the asylum itself. Thomas Ogier was originally admitted to the facility as a patient, but engaged as an attendant when discharged in 1893.[192] Ex-prostitutes and ex-prisoners also featured among attendants' ranks. Alice Ozard, who had previously served a spell in the Channel Island Penitentiary, was taken out of the Hospital to work as an attendant in 1885.[193] Andrew Mitchell was sent direct from prison to work in the asylum on finishing a sentence in 1884.[194] A significant number of attendants, attracted by the perquisites of the job, were themselves alcoholics, and the drunkenness of keepers was a frequent cause of trouble at the asylum, often resulting in dismissal. Alfred Le Patourel was far from atypical in being dismissed in 1886 for striking a patient while drunk.[195]

Turnover among asylum attendants was unremittingly high. Only one keeper has been identified with a record of long service: Alice Delaney, who served between 1858 and 1891. It is an indication of her low status, however, that, when she finally retired after thirty-three years the House Committee refused her request for a pension or gratuity, advising her that she should instead apply for poor relief through the usual channels.[196] There is no record over the entire period between 1851 and World War II of any attendant at the Town Hospital's 'lunatic asylum' ever having held a mental health nursing qualification.

Patients

Between 1853 and 1924, the Town Hospital's annual abstracts of accounts recorded numbers of admissions to the institution on grounds of mental disorder or handicap.[197] Until 1901, these statistics related to the Hospital as a whole and not specifically to the asylum. This was because people with mild to moderate learning difficulties were usually admitted to the main part of the Hospital, with the asylum reserved for the more severely ill. These figures show that, between 1853 and 1901, an average of 7 per cent of all admissions to the Hospital were due to mental illness in its widest sense, which equated to about fourteen individual admissions annually. From 1902, abstracts began to provide admission statistics specific to the asylum itself, and hence an indication of the number of severe cases. There were on average about nine of these admissions yearly between 1902 and 1924. At about seven per year, discharges were almost commensurate. Mid-winter head-counts of patients were provided separately for the lunatic asylum in all abstracts of accounts between 1852 and 1924. These show that there were an average of about thirty patients in the facility at each year's end.

---

[191] As late as 1915, the young Miss Edith Crocker was obliged to withdraw her application for a post she had seen advertised when her parents found out and raised objections (23.3.1915, IA, DC/HX 080–05).

[192] 13.2.1893, IA, DC/HX 136–03.

[193] 13.4.1885, IA, DC/HX 136–01. For more on the Penitentiary, see p. 199, below.

[194] 18.1.1884, IA, DC/HX 136–01.

[195] 25.1.1886, IA, DC/HX 136–01.

[196] 31.3.1891, IA, DC/HX 057–01.

[197] IA, DC/HX 060–02; IA, DC/HX 265–06, IA, DC/HX 272–02.

Very few case records were kept in respect of the Town Hospital's lunatics. The only surviving document affording an insight into their illnesses is an 1850s asylum register which briefly recorded causes of admission.[198] This also shines a revealing light on Victorian concepts of mental disorder. Over the five years between 1853 and 1858, causes of admission were recorded in a total of sixty-six cases. These fell into three main categories: firstly, admissions attributed to 'dementia', a catch-all term which seemed to encompass everything from idiocy to senility; secondly, admissions for delirium tremens, and, thirdly, admissions for episodes of 'acute mania'. Between them, and evenly split, 'dementia' and delirium tremens accounted for about 40 per cent of admissions (with most cases of 'dementia' involving people under 30, and hence a preponderance of idiocy over senility). Almost all of the remaining 60 per cent of admissions were described as being due to episodes of 'acute mania'.

In a majority of admissions for 'acute mania', the manic episode was attributed to a bout of excessive drinking. This was the case for 58-year-old Mrs McAllister, who was admitted in a 'raving state' in 1856, and for 31-year-old John Sauvage, admitted in 1857. The next most frequently attributed cause of acute mania was, interestingly, over-exposure to religion. In 1854, the manic episode suffered by 40-year-old Abraham Noel was blamed on 'listening to religious ranters'. Other causes ascribed to manic episodes were, variously, the 'irritation of neighbours and family' (38-year-old Thomas Heaume, 1855); the 'prospect of emigrating to Australia' (28-year-old Mrs Guilbert, 1854), 'attempts to cure deafness' (Mrs Arthur, 1858), and 'shock at the sudden death of her mother' (Mrs Hodder, 1856). There was also one case of puerperal mania. Two further admissions were simply attributed to 'melancholia', and two to epilepsy.

Patients admitted with acute mania or delirium tremens did not stay long in the asylum. Most were discharged within weeks. As might be expected, dementia sufferers of various sorts dominated the ranks of long-stayers. Amelia Le Roy first entered the asylum at the age of 20 in 1854 – 'idiotic with a disposition to nymphomania'. She was still in the asylum when her death was reported some forty years later.[199]

To begin with, the Town Hospital asylum accommodated not only St Peter Port's pauper lunatics but also pauper lunatics from the country parishes whom the Country Hospital found difficult to manage. For these, a weekly fee of 12s 6d was charged.[200] In 1882, however, the Country Hospital built a detached lunatics' annexe of its own, and the sending of rural lunatics ceased.

Non-pauper patients of whatever origin were received in the Town Hospital asylum throughout its existence. For such private patients, a fee of either 25s or 42s weekly was charged. In return, they enjoyed superior comforts, including a more varied diet, individual bedrooms and, for those on the highest tariff, private sitting rooms.[201] Many patients from Guernsey's middle and upper classes passed through

---

[198] IA, DC/HX 062–02.
[199] IA, DC/HX 060–03; 14.3.1894, IA, DC/HX 066–03.
[200] 19.4.1852, 4.10.1852, IA, DC/HX 075–02.
[201] 13.5.1853, IA, DC/HX 130–04; IA, DC/HX 272–08; IA, DC/HX 274–012.

the asylum, including Lilla Tupper and Philip Brock, both of patrician family; clergyman's daughter Miss Frances de Saint-Dalmas; former Town Hospital chaplain the Reverend William Valrent; doctor's son Montague Bisson; Mary Hutchinson, the wife of Poor Law Board President Elisha Hutchinson; and De Vic Tupper, who had served as Poor Law Board President himself.[202]

Private patients and non-parochial paupers comprised on average about a quarter of asylum inmates in its first three decades (although their numbers dropped significantly from the 1880s). Poor Law Board accounts show that, in the forty-four years between 1858 and 1901, lunatic asylum fees contributed an average of £477 a year to Town Hospital finances, reaching their peak in 1874, when, at £1,027, they accounted for 29 per cent of Hospital revenue.[203]

With a substantial amount of space devoted to fee-payers' bedrooms (and the supervisors' apartment), the communal quarters occupied by pauper lunatics were relatively restricted. In 1861, they consisted essentially of two dormitories and a block of cells. The asylum's thirteen pauper women were assigned to a first floor dormitory measuring 19ft by 16ft, and its eleven pauper men to a dormitory on the ground floor measuring 14ft by 16ft.[204] Material conditions for the asylum's paupers were primitive, washing and bathing facilities in particular: as late as 1934, the asylum possessed only two fixed wash-hand basins and two fixed bathtubs for the use of pauper patients and attendants alike.[205] Flea, louse and rat infestations were a recurrent problem in dormitories and cells.[206]

Aside from airings in the yards and the performance of chores around the asylum, men and women passed the day largely in their rooms. Men might be asked to pick oakum if they were able to; women to sew, knit or mend.[207] The idea of 'treating' patients never arose. Untrained supervisors and keepers saw their primary role as one of containment. Coercive and often painful methods of management were the norm for agitated or disruptive patients. It was common to quieten (or punish) them with water jetted from a special apparatus; by holding their heads under running water; or by putting salt in their mouths.[208] Much use was made of cells for patients who caused trouble, particularly at night. Six such cells were still in nightly use as late as 1910.[209] These unheated lock-ups contained no bedsteads, and their stone floors were covered with only a loose litter of seaweed.[210] Confinees judged to be at risk

---

[202] 25.8.1858, IA, DC/HX 130–04; 17.1.1865, IA, DC/HX 127–01; 3.7.1857, 25.7.1857, IA, DC/HX 130–04; 12.12.1865, 28.10.1870, IA, DC/HX 127–01; 5.12.1889, IA, DC/HX 157–01.

[203] IA, DC/HX 272–02.

[204] 4.1.1861, IA, DC/HX 054–05.

[205] *Billet*, 9.5.1934.

[206] 1.12.1881, IA, DC/HX 136–10; 26.3.1888, IA, DC/HX 136–02; 14.8.1916, IA, DC/HX 080–05.

[207] 4.1.1861, IA, DC/HX 054–05.

[208] 8.5.1854, IA, DC/HX 130–04; 13.7.1865, IA, DC/HX 136–07; 13.2.1883, IA, DC/HX 136–10; 16.2.1883 IA, DC/HX 062–03.

[209] 1.1.1910, IA, DC/HX 005–01.

[210] On 4 January 1909, the temperature as measured in the cells was 6 degrees celsius (4.1.1909, IA, DC/HX 080–01).

of suicide were denied any clothing or bedding.[211] Dr Maurice Craig, an English mental health specialist visiting in 1903, remarked:

> I saw one of the most painful sights that I had ever witnessed in an asylum in your institution. This was an apparently elderly woman sitting in a corner of a cell which had, as I am informed, a cement floor, and the sole covering which she had was seaweed.[212]

Mechanical restraints such as chains, straps and straitjackets were in daily use at the asylum well into the twentieth century. In the United Kingdom, the influence of John Conolly and others had led to the progressive disuse of such restraints from the mid-nineteenth century onward.[213] In 1890, a Lunacy Act passed by the Westminster parliament forbade all use of mechanical restraints save during surgical operations or where a patient was at risk of injuring himself or others.[214] On assuming oversight of Guernsey's Hospitals in 1901, the Royal Court passed a similar ordinance.[215] Nevertheless, an account of the asylum written by Dr Francis Edwards, another English expert visiting in 1903, suggests that this ordinance was liberally interpreted:

> even whilst in the open air and taking exercise, mechanical restraint was resorted to without any disguise … several men and women had their wrists confined by bracelets which were fastened to belts around their waists … One old woman was confined in a camisole, the arms drawn tightly round the body, and fastened to the back of a fixed stay. In one or two cases, the ankles were confined by a contrivance preventing them walking freely.[216]

Pressure for reform

By progressive early twentieth-century lights, the situation at the Town Hospital asylum was clearly unsatisfactory, and the visits of these English experts were themselves one manifestation of an intermittent campaign for reform whose origins can be traced back to the previous decade. One of the first matters to attract attention had been certification. When the asylum opened in 1851, Hospital authorities had resolved that no-one should be admitted unless a doctor 'deemed it necessary', but there was no formal statutory procedure for certification. Not until thirty-eight years later did the Royal Court finally pass a certification law, and this seems to have been motivated less by matters of principle than by practical concern over the high-profile case of 57-year-old former Poor Law Board President and current Jurat, De Vic Tupper, who had been showing alarming signs of aberrant behaviour throughout 1889.[217] Two ordinances on the subject were passed in the autumn of that year. The

---

[211] 1.4.1905, IA, DC/HX 254–10.

[212] Dr Maurice Craig to St Peter Port Poor Law Board, 10.2.1904, TNA, HO 45/16850.

[213] John Conolly had himself written a seminal work entitled *The Treatment of the Insane without Mechanical Restraints* (London, 1856).

[214] Jones, *Mental Health Services*, p. 178; Bartlett, *Poor Law of Lunacy*, p. 220.

[215] Ord, 21.12.1901.

[216] Dr Francis Edwards to Commissioners in Lunacy, 8.3.1904, TNA, HO 45/16850.

[217] For more on the Tupper case, see R.P. Hocart, *An Island Assembly: The Development of the States of Guernsey, 1700–1949* (Guernsey, 1988), p. 82.

ordinance of 30 September 1889 laid down a formal procedure for the confinement of patients in Guernsey's Hospitals on grounds of insanity. Henceforth, this was to be done on the basis of certificates from two doctors, both countersigned by one of the Crown law officers and also the patient's husband, guardian, *curateur* or *tuteur*.[218] The ordinance of 2 November 1889 related to the discharge of lunatics, making this the exclusive prerogative of the Hospital authorities, providing the asylum doctor confirmed the patient was no longer ill.[219]

On the basis of the new law, Jurat De Vic Tupper was confined to the Town Hospital asylum in December 1889.[220] Tupper's forcible confinement in an institution over which he had once presided must have been a blow to his dignity and hardly beneficial to his mental state. However, he recovered and was discharged a few weeks later. In 1890, he retaliated against Guernsey's authorities by launching a vigorous campaign against the new laws, which included the dispatch of a memorial to the Queen in Council.[221] In this memorial, Tupper voiced strenuous objections to the involvement of the Crown law officers in the certification process, alleging that their participation conflated 'insanity with crime'. He also pointed out that, in the particular case of the Town asylum, the new procedure opened an opportunity for nefarious collusion, in that the chief law officer, HM *Procureur* Thomas Godfrey Carey, and the current asylum doctor, Francis Carey, were brothers.[222]

The Tupper affair reached the British press and aroused curiosity in British mental health circles. One of the first of many experts drawn to visit the Town Hospital asylum was Dr Daniel Hack Tuke, Governor of Bethlem Hospital, who privately inspected the facility in 1891.[223] As the negative reputation of the asylum grew, others followed in Tuke's footsteps, including Drs Maurice Craig and Francis Edwards in 1903. Craig, who was Assistant Medical Director of Bethlem Hospital, admitted that he had been 'anxious' to visit the asylum as he had 'frequently been told by Physicians experienced in Mental Disease that I should find in it methods which date back to the Middle Ages'.[224] Following his visit, Dr Craig wrote a highly

---

[218] *Curateurs* were appointed by the Court to manage the affairs of the incapacitated; *tuteurs* to manage those of the under-age.

[219] These two ordinances represented a curious amalgam of the two streams of legislation then governing the admission and discharge of private and pauper lunatics in England and Wales. While the absence from the admission process of any role for poor law officers made it broadly analogous to that governing admissions to private asylums in England and Wales, the Hospital authorities' sole power to discharge was more akin to the prerogative exercised over paupers by the Committees of Visitors of county and borough asylums (fee-paying patients in private asylums could be discharged at will by their next-of-kin). For more on these matters, see Jones, *Mental Health Services*, pp. 147–8; Bartlett, *Poor Law of Lunacy*, pp. 4–7, 48.

[220] 5.12.1889, IA, DC/HX 157–01.

[221] D.V. Tupper, *Memorial presented by De Vic Tupper, Esq., Colonel (retired list) and Jurat of the Royal Court of Guernsey* (Guernsey, 1890). See also De Vic Tupper to St Peter Port Poor Law Board, 29.11.1890, IA, DC/HX 054–07.

[222] Westminster's 1890 Lunacy Act, passed in March of that year, had set out detailed regulations on prohibited relationships between signatories of certificates (Jones, *Mental Health Services*, p. 178).

[223] 21.8.1891, IA, DC/HX 054–07.

[224] M. Craig to Town Hospital House Committee, 22.9.1903, IA, DC/HX 274–001.

critical report on the asylum which he sent to the Commissioners in Lunacy, who in turn forwarded it to the Home Office.[225] Francis Edwards, who was Medical Director of Camberwell Asylum, submitted a similarly damning report which followed the same route.[226] Responding to these reports, the Home Office arranged for Under-Secretary of State Sir Mackenzie Chalmers and Lieutenant Governor Major General Barrington Campbell to make an unannounced visit to the asylum in the autumn of 1904.[227] The visit did not result in any specific action, but the Home Office decided to keep a watching brief, and a file was opened on the Town Hospital asylum.

In December 1904, for the first time since the facility opened, St Peter Port's Poor Law Board appointed an outsider as asylum physician.[228] Dr William Duncan, an Englishman, began work in January 1905, and his arrival inaugurated the most turbulent chapter in the facility's history.[229] Earnest (and hot-tempered), Duncan was astonished at what he found in the asylum and, early in his tenure, put on record his resolve 'faithfully and fearlessly' to expose 'every form of abuse and unkindness and neglect'.[230] He bombarded the Poor Law Board with a succession of complaints regarding inhumane treatment, insanitary conditions, staff ineptitude, irregularities in certification and non-existent record-keeping.[231] When these complaints proved unavailing, Duncan personally invited Home Office officials on to the premises, causing the parochial authorities to retreat into a defensive mentality.[232] Eventually, Duncan's relationship with the Poor Law Board completely broke down. The Board requested him to resign, and, when he refused, they simply closed the asylum doors to him in May 1906.[233] By way of a parting shot, Duncan sent a scathing report to the British Lord Chancellor, calling on him to 'appoint an Inspector to investigate the whole system'.[234] This report found its way into the thickening Home Office file.

Of itself, Duncan's confrontational approach did nothing to advance the cause of St Peter Port's mentally ill. During his tenure, however, a States' committee set up to review Guernsey's entire poor law system put forward vigorous recommendations for the establishment of a States' asylum.[235] Such proposals had been made many

[225] 10.2.1904, TNA, 45/16850. The Home Office was responsible for dealing with the United Kingdom's relations with the Channel Islands between 1782 and 2001 (D.M. Ogier, *The Government and Law of Guernsey* (Guernsey, 2005), p. 108).

[226] 8.3.1904, TNA, 45/16850.

[227] 3.10.1904, IA, DC/HX 056–04.

[228] 5.12.1904, IA, DC/HX 056–04.

[229] For more on Dr Duncan, see L.G.H. Craske, 'Two complementary Guernsey physicians', in Jeffs (ed.), *One Hundred Years of Health*, p. 136.

[230] 1.4.1905, IA, DC/HX 254–10.

[231] 27.1.1905, IA, DC/HX 056–04; 1.4.1905, 1.7.1905, 30.9.1905, IA, DC/HX 254–10; 26.5.1905, 1.4.1905, 27.11.1905, 30.11.1905, IA, DC/HX 080–02; 31.12.1905, TNA, HO 45/16850.

[232] 6.4.1905, IA, DC/HX 179–05.

[233] 8.9.1905, 17.5.1906, IA, DC/HX 056–04.

[234] 31.12,1905, 22.1.1907, TNA, HO 45/16850.

[235] *Billet*, 5.7.1905.

times before to no avail, but, on this occasion, the States proved more receptive.[236] The committee's recommendations were accepted in principle and, by 1908, the States had both purchased a suitable site and commissioned plans for a new public asylum.[237] Two years later, matters were also advanced on the legislative front by the passage of an updated certification law.[238] This law was broadly based on Westminster's 1890 Lunacy Act, adopting analogous provisions for medical certification, which included bans on specified relationships between signatories.[239]

Nevertheless, mental health was low on the list of States' priorities, and no further developments followed the 1910 law. When, two years on, the Home Office became aware of the lack of progress, they suggested that matters might be hastened by a visit from one of the Commissioners in Lunacy.[240] The offer was accepted and, in August 1913, Commissioner Edward Marriot Cooke inspected facilities at both the Town and Country Hospitals. Unfortunately, Cooke's visit resulted in no more than a report reiterating criticisms made a decade earlier, since any further action which might have arisen was stymied by the outbreak of World War I.[241] From this point onward, with unprecedented calls on States' finances, plans for a new asylum were put indefinitely on ice.[242]

It was not until 1923 that matters were tentatively taken up again. In this year, the site purchased for a new asylum in 1908 was sold (on advice that its steep slopes made it unsuitable for building) and a States' Asylum Committee was appointed.[243] This was followed by a rather more momentous change in 1925, when the States' assumption of poor law funding and Hospital ownership brought the two existing asylums under States jurisdiction.[244] Although the asylums continued to be run by parochial authorities as part of the Hospitals, co-ordination by the new States' Central Poor Law Board produced a degree of improvement. In 1926, the severely mentally handicapped were removed from the Hospital asylums and sent at States' expense to homes run by Hampshire County Council.[245] In 1929, all Guernsey's male lunatics were moved to the Country Hospital and all female lunatics to the Town Hospital.[246] Nevertheless, the States' acquisition of the Hospital asylums seems to have ended all further thought of a new-build – at least as far as members

---

[236] Emboldened, perhaps, by their experience of running a States' isolation hospital since 1903, or encouraged by pressure from Westminster.

[237] 6.2.1907, IA, AS/MB 023–02; *Billet*, 16.9.1908.

[238] O in C, 11.6.1910.

[239] Like the 1889 ordinance, this law eschewed the involvement of poor law officers, leaving patients' relatives responsible for instigating committal proceedings, as under section 5 of the English statute. For more on the 1890 Lunacy Act, see Jones, *Mental Health Services*, pp. 176–81.

[240] *Billet*, 11.12.1912.

[241] *Billet*, 3.12.1913.

[242] For the States' financial situation at this time, see Hocart, *Island Assembly*, pp. 91–2.

[243] *Billet*, 18.7.1923.

[244] O in C, 24.7.1925.

[245] *Billet*, 18.5.1926.

[246] 8.4.1929, 26.4.1929, IA, DC/HX 051–01.

of the Central Poor Law Board were concerned, since, as a next step, they advanced proposals to upgrade the existing facilities.[247]

Asked to investigate these proposals, the States' Asylum Committee were unhappy. They raised the objection that the existing Hospital buildings would not admit of sufficient improvement to justify the high cost involved in altering them. The Committee engaged Dr Thomas Good, superintendent of Oxford Mental Hospital, to advise them on possible alternatives and, early in 1933, they submitted his report to the States. Dr Good provided the States with yet another grim account of deficiencies in facilities for lunatics at the Hospitals, apprised them of the revolution in approaches to mental illness in Britain since the passage of the 1930 Mental Treatment Act, and strenuously recommended that they appoint a mental health specialist of their own 'to study local conditions, and then report ... as to the best steps which should be taken'.[248] On this point the States decided to accede, and it is this decision which more than anything else provided the final impetus to the long-delayed building of an asylum.

In May 1933, Dr William McGlashan, a 45-year-old former deputy medical superintendent of Derby County Mental Hospital, was engaged by the States on temporary contract.[249] Within months, McGlashan, seemingly an inspirational character, had submitted plans for the construction of a state-of-the-art mental hospital on a site at Le Vauquiédor in St Andrews.[250] Fired by his enthusiasm, the States agreed in 1935 to fund his plans, at the same time giving him permanent tenure as their 'Mental Officer'.[251]

While the new hospital was in the course of construction, the States also passed an entirely fresh law placing the whole matter of mental health on an up-to-date footing.[252] Based on Westminster's 1930 Mental Treatment Act, the new law introduced similar innovations. As in the United Kingdom, the terms 'lunatic' and 'lunatic asylum' were officially abolished (replaced by 'persons of unsound mind' and 'mental hospital'), and three categories of patient were introduced – voluntary, temporary and certified.[253] Guernsey's certification procedure was also aligned more closely than previously with that laid out in Westminster's 1890 Lunacy Act (which continued to govern certification in England and Wales).[254] A third major innova-

---

[247] *Billet*, 25.1.1933.

[248] *Billet*, 25.1.1933.

[249] 1.5.1933, TNA, 45/16850. For a photograph of McGlashan, see Plate 9.

[250] *Billet*, 9.5.1934. In the interim, McGlashan had also assumed the post of medical officer to the Town Hospital asylum, which now contained thirty-six women (11.12.1933, IA, DC/HX 051–01).

[251] *Billet*, 27.2.1935. The Home Office file on Guernsey's lunatic asylums ends with an account of this development, observing that the new hospital would 'close the page on a crying disgrace to the island' (10.5.1935, TNA, 45/16850).

[252] O in C, 5.9.1939. This law remained in force, as amended, for three-quarters of a century. It was replaced by the Mental Health (Bailiwick of Guernsey) Law, 2010, which was ratified by the Privy Council in 2011 and came into force in 2013.

[253] For more on the 1930 Mental Treatment Act, see Jones, *Mental Health Services*, pp. 249–52.

[254] Although again eschewing the involvement of poor law officers.

tion of the 1939 law was the establishment of a dedicated States' Mental Health Services Board.

Early in 1940, the Vauquiédor Mental Hospital was completed and, on 6 March, forty-three women were transferred from the Town Hospital, along with twenty-one men from the Country Hospital. The new facility was staffed chiefly by attendants from the former Hospital asylums, and William McGlashan was given the post of 'Hospital Administrator'. By December 1940, the Vauquiédor Hospital held 111 patients. These were a mixture of pauper patients who had their fees paid for them and private patients who were invoiced for their care.[255]

Unfortunately, however, the new mental hospital lasted scarcely a year. Attracted by its modernity, the German forces which had occupied the island in 1940 soon appropriated it as a military hospital, and, in July 1941, the mentally ill were moved back to their dismal quarters at the Hospitals.[256] The following year, Dr McGlashan himself was deported to Germany along with other United Kingdom natives removed from the island *en masse*. He remained in Germany until 1945, interned at Dorsten and, later, Biberach prison camps.

By the time the war was over and McGlashan had returned, the climate in Guernsey had changed. A full-scale reorganisation of insular medical facilities was under way and, under the constraints of post-war austerity, mental health had been relegated to the bottom of the priority list. The Mental Health Services Board was abolished, and, as Guernsey's most modern facility, the Vauquiédor Hospital was earmarked as the island's new general hospital. As a replacement facility for the mentally ill, it was decided that the former Country Hospital would be converted into a mental home.[257] However, States' funds were limited and conversion work was delayed, so that the old Town Hospital lunatic asylum continued in use for another few years, now under the jurisdiction of the Board of Health. On 9 November 1951, with the 'new' mental home substantially complete, the old St Peter Port premises were finally vacated.[258] They had served the mentally ill for just over a century – far too long, many would have said, for a facility which was never 'a proper asylum'.

---

[255] *Billet*, 16.5.1941.
[256] *Billet*, 10.6.1942.
[257] *Billets*, 17.10.1945, 11.12.1946, 25.1.1950.
[258] *Billet*, 20.2.1952.

8

People

This chapter concerns the various categories of people associated with the Town Hospital. These people will be considered not from a statistical point of view but in terms of their individual personalities, their relationships with one another, their contribution to the institution and their interaction with wider society. The first section will look at the Hospital's administrators and staff. Following that, the focus will move to inmates, examining the various discrete groups in turn. Children will be discussed first, proceeding to adult women and men, and then the elderly. Strangers, always accorded a distinct status, will be considered last.

Administrators and staff

Administrators

In the period from its foundation to the Second World War, the Town Hospital was variously administered by a Board of Directors (1743–1852); by the House Committee of the St Peter Port Poor Law Board (1853–1925); by the Executive Committee of the St Peter Port Poor Law Board (1925–37); and, lastly, by the Hospital Board of the States' Public Assistance Authority (1938–70). With these bodies rested responsibility for day-to-day decisions concerning the Hospital and its inmates.[1] Membership of the original Board of Directors varied from twenty-one in 1743 to more than forty in the 1840s.[2] Members of the post-1853 House Committee numbered just seven, those of the post-1925 Executive Committee numbered eight, and members of the post-1938 Hospital Board numbered sixteen.[3] Seats on these bodies were subject to a property qualification, in that they could be held only by ratepayers.[4] All Board and Committee members served *gratis*.

---

[1] After 1853, major policy decisions of the House Committee, Executive Committee and Hospital Board were taken in full session with their parent body.
[2] 28.9.1743, IA, DC/HX 079–01; *Rapport du Comité nommé par les Chefs de Famille de la Ville et Paroisse de Saint Pierre-Port le 5 Avril 1849*, PL. For more detail, see section on 'Governance', Chapter 6.
[3] O in C, 28.12.1852; O in C, 24.7.1925; O in C, 22.10.1937.
[4] After 1853, Poor Law Board Presidents and Vice-Presidents were required to have a minimum of thirty quarters of property.

For the majority of pre-1853 Directors, duties were not onerous. The greatest burdens were borne by the Treasurer and, from 1813, the Vice-Treasurer.[5] From the beginning, the Hospital was provided with a well-appointed boardroom in which Directors met once a week.[6] Board meetings were the principal call upon Directors' time, although few Directors attended all of the meetings, which by the 1780s had been reduced to one a month.[7] In addition, Directors might occasionally be required to perform tours of inspection at the Hospital or to visit the outdoor poor. Such duties were, however, sporadic. They were usually instituted in a drive to cut expenditure or improve discipline, and lapsed after the initial urgency had passed.[8] The smaller Committees to whom management was entrusted after 1853 were expected to be more proactive. The 1853 House Committee met weekly and rostered its seven members to perform rounds at the Hospital four times a week – a regime which seems to have been consistently observed over the next seven or eight decades.[9]

The social complexion of Boards/Committees changed greatly across the eighteenth and nineteenth centuries. At the meeting of the Hospital Board on 3 January 1774, sixteen Directors were present.[10] These men represented the elite of local society. Most of them belonged to the twenty or so 'armigerous families of ancient Guernsey lineage' whom Gregory Stevens Cox has identified as 'the insular aristocracy'.[11] In addition, many of them were, or had been, substantial merchant-shipowners in their own right: Matthew De Sausmarez; Daniel De Lisle; Thomas, Nicolas and Pierre Dobrée; William Brock; Charles De Carteret; Jean Carey and Henry Le Mesurier.[12] Within a decade or so of 1774, however, elite interest in parochial poor law waned as the Hospital's original founders all died or retired. Patrician disengagement from parish matters generally was accelerated from the 1820s, as members of the 'aristocratic' caste increasingly forsook all types of parochial office and concentrated their civic involvement in the Royal Court and States.[13] For a time, a residual link between the Hospital and the insular elite was maintained through the granting of *ex-officio* seats to Jurats on the Hospital Board, but this practice ceased when the new Poor Law Board was instituted in 1853.

By the 1870s, membership of St Peter Port's poor law authorities had for the most part devolved to the town's middling social strata. Only two of the 'ancient' insular

5   1.2.1813, IA, DC/HX 079–02.
6   28.9.1743, IA, DC/HX 079–01. The boardroom, which underwent periodic refurbishment, was described in the late nineteenth century as 'a very handsome room, warmly carpeted, with a large table placed in the centre [and] several old oil paintings of benefactors on the walls' (*Star*, 29.10.1896).
7   2.8.1784, IA, DC/HX 079–01.
8   See, for instance, 5.6.1805, IA, DC/HX 079–02 and 7.2.1825, IA, DC/HX 135–02.
9   January 1853, IA, DC/HX 054–05.
10 3.1.1774, IA, DC/HX 079–01.
11 G. Stevens Cox, *The Guernsey Merchants and their World* (Guernsey, 2009), p. 94.
12 For information on the commercial activities of these individuals, see Stevens Cox, *Guernsey Merchants*, pp. 176, 178, 182, 183, 185, 195.
13 R.-M. Crossan, *Guernsey, 1814–1914: Migration and Modernisation* (Woodbridge, 2007), pp. 188–9.

dynasties were represented on the 1875 Poor Law Board – the Le Mesuriers and the Careys, in the form of the President, Nicholas Le Mesurier, and the Vice-President, Charles Carey.[14] These top-level posts tended to be reserved for what remained of the patriciate, and Messrs Le Mesurier and Carey were gentlemen of leisure, living on investment income. However, by far the majority of the 1875 Board were working members of St Peter Port's business community – wholesalers, such as Peter Le Lievre (a wine merchant) and Nicholas Martel (a salt merchant), or retailers, such as John Valpied (a draper), Thomas Agnew (an ironmonger), James Langlois (a bookseller) and Henry Cumber (a druggist).[15] All six of the above were serving members of the House Committee and thus directly in charge of the Hospital.

Le Lievre, Agnew, Cumber and company probably considered their prestige augmented and their commercial interests furthered by service as House Committee members, and they seem voluntarily to have put themselves up for election. By contrast, the more onerous offices of Poor Law Board President and, earlier, Hospital Treasurer, were not always so willingly sought. As the consent of 'candidates' was not mandatory, a number of individuals elected to these roles declined to serve. Notwithstanding an ordinance of 1759 which made it compulsory to serve as Treasurer when elected, Jean Le Mesurier flatly refused to do so in 1765, and apparently escaped sanction while two Directors jointly performed his work until fresh elections the next year.[16] In 1880, the Poor Law Board remained similarly leaderless when President-elect Archibald Armstrong rejected the office, protesting that voters had never ascertained his 'willingness or ability to serve'.[17]

On the positive side, there were several who embraced the Treasurership or Presidency enthusiastically, and who voluntarily stood for re-election when their original terms were over. Some of the Treasurers of the immediate post-Condamine period – Daniel De Lisle, Hilary Rougier, Nicolas Maingy, William Collings – stand out as unusually engaged. Among these, the two latter were especially notable.[18] William Collings, a successful entrepreneur in his own right, was an energetic and efficient manager, attempting to set the Hospital on a more businesslike footing by instituting new rules and new enterprises.[19] Nicolas Maingy was conspicuous for his diligence in supervising staff. Unlike some other incumbents, he stood firm in insisting that basic standards were observed in the face of staff indifference. In 1823, Maingy threatened master Thomas Mauger with dismissal when it became apparent that he was evading his duty to supervise inmates' meals.[20] In 1825, he formally reprimanded Mauger once again for neglecting to keep the Hospital clean.[21]

[14] For 1875 Poor Law Board members, see 1875 accounts in IA, DC/HX 272–02.
[15] G.W.J.L. Hugo, born in 1862, describes some of these individuals in his *Guernsey as it Used to Be; Some Aspects of the Island in my Boyhood, Youth, and Early Manhood, with Allusions to Well-known Persons* (Guernsey, 1933).
[16] Ord, 23.4.1759; 21.2.1765, IA, DC/HX 079–01.
[17] 28.1.1880, 20.4.1880, IA, DC/HX 054–06.
[18] IA, DC/HX 079–02; IA, DC/HX 135–02.
[19] See section on 'Income', Chapter 6.
[20] 1.4.1823, IA, DC/HX 135–02.
[21] 7.2.1825, IA, DC/HX 135–02.

One reason why service as a Director or House Committee member was actively prized by some was that, in the words of a student of eighteenth-century English workhouses, 'supply of goods to workhouses provided a golden opportunity for outright corruption'.[22] For St Peter Port's merchants and tradesmen, a place on the Board was a way of securing extra business, although they would not have viewed this as 'outright corruption'. In England and Wales, venality was curbed when the 1834 Poor Law Amendment Act formally prohibited all poor law office-holders from being concerned in any contract to supply goods either to workhouses or for any other poor law purpose. In the Town Hospital, eighteenth-century Boards had unfettered discretion over what was purchased, from whom and at what price. In 1809, following the forced resignation of Treasurer Jean Condamine (over whose probity an unspecified shadow was cast), a new rule made it mandatory to solicit sealed bids for the supply of staples by advertisement in the local press.[23] There was, however, no specific prohibition on the supply of goods by members of the Hospital Board, and records show that these frequently supplied bulk commodities themselves. In the 1840s, Vice-Treasurer and brewer Joseph Gullick provided the workhouse with most of its beer; St Peter Port *Procureur* and soap chandler Joshua Ahier furnished it with soap and candles, and other Board members Thomas Clugas, Thomas Greenslade and John Valrent were supplying sugar, groceries and spirits respectively.[24] Such practices continued unquestioned until 1887, when the Poor Law Board resolved that none of its members should henceforth furnish supplies to the Hospital.[25] There was an immediate outcry from the many small businessmen on the Board, and the resolution was rescinded in 1888.[26] Again, years passed and, by 1904, the main supplier of the Hospital's sugar, tea, coffee, cocoa, haricot beans, onions, sago, oatmeal and vinegar was none other than the House Committee chairman himself, wholesale grocer William Murdoch.[27] At a parish meeting in 1909, objections to such arrangements were raised by a number of rate-payers. However, the Poor Law Board, by now almost exclusively commercial in complexion, resolved to let the practice continue, its only concession being that members should henceforth be barred from adjudicating over their own tenders.[28] In the event, it was not until 1930, five years after the assumption of poor relief funding by the States, that official regulations finally prohibited members of the St

---

22 T.V. Hitchcock, 'The English workhouse: a study in institutional poor relief in selected counties, 1696–1750' (unpub. DPhil thesis, Oxford University, 1985), p. 137.

23 5.4.1809, IA, DC/HX 079–02. The range of commodities for which sealed tenders were mandatory was extended in 1821 and 1855 (28.6.1821, IA, DC/HX 079–02; 12.2.1855, IA, DC/HX 130–04).

24 IA, DC/HX 081–01; IA, DC/HX 020–01.

25 7.2.1887, 4.4.1887, IA, DC/HX 054–06.

26 13.2.1888, IA, DC/HX 054–07.

27 21.3.1904, IA, DC/HX 127–02. Mr Murdoch, who ran Murdoch's Stores at 48 and 49 the Bordage, was adept at interweaving business with civic life, later serving as St Peter Port Constable, President of the Chamber of Commerce and Grand Treasurer of the Masonic Province of Guernsey and Alderney. See obituary in *Guernsey Weekly Press*, 23.4.1921. Murdoch is fifth from the right, front row, Plate 4.

28 27.5.1909, IA, DC/HX 046–01.

Peter Port Poor Law Board Executive Committee from contracting or tendering for Hospital supplies.[29]

Staff

The Hospital, at least in theory, required high moral standards of its employees from the outset. The earliest rules stipulated that the *gouvernante*, or mistress, of the house, should be 'sober, modest, pious and scrupulous in the performance of all her duties'.[30] In its first years, the establishment was headed by a woman, with a paid staff of three working under her. Female heads were common in France, where most *hôpitaux* were run and staffed by nuns.[31] They were less common in England, where only smaller houses tended to be run by women. That a woman was chosen in St Peter Port might reflect French influence, but it is more likely to have reflected the fact that the institution was at first populated predominantly by women and children.

The first two *gouvernantes* were respectable middle-aged matrons. Marianne Regnault served between 1743 and 1746, and Sarah Messervy between 1746 and 1753. Little is known of Mme Regnault, but Mme Messervy was from a well-to-do Jersey family. When she died in office in 1753, the Town Hospital Treasurer acted as chief mourner at her funeral and the Directors as her pall-bearers.[32] Her will, in which she bequeathed £50 to the Hospital, survives in the Jersey Archive.[33] The *gouvernante*, who had custody of the Hospital keys, was in overall charge of the institution's day-to-day running. Her duties included dealing with suppliers, keeping accounts and writing up the daybooks.[34] Her three staff comprised one man and two women. The *maître*, or master, initially Mathieu Pezet, oversaw everything which pertained to the male inmates. He supervised their dormitories and their work. In addition, he maintained discipline throughout the institution, supervised inmates' meals, catechised the children and gave them the rudiments of education. The *sous-gouvernante* (under-mistress), initially Rachel Le Lacheur, had the same pastoral responsibility for female inmates as the *maître* had for males. She was also in charge of housekeeping throughout the establishment. The third and lowest-ranking staff member, one Mrs Brock, was in charge of the Hospital's linen. She supervised the women and girls in making, mending and laundering garments and bedclothes, and she also taught the little girls to sew. All four staff lived in.

Over the two centuries in which the Hospital operated as a workhouse, these four distinct roles – leadership and co-ordination; oversight of men and boys; oversight of women and girls; supervision of housekeeping – remained the chief functions

29 IA, DC/HX 272–06.
30 *Règlements pour la Maison des Pauvres de la Paroisse de St Pierre-Port*, Vol. III, Watkins MS, LL 940 W, PL.
31 D. Hickey, *Local Hospitals in Ancien Régime France: Rationalization, Resistance, Renewal, 1530–1789* (Montreal, 1997), p. 8.
32 27.4.1753, IA, DC/HX 079–01.
33 L/C/67/F29. The will was contested, and it is doubtful that this money ever reached its target.
34 For a schedule of staff duties, see opening pages of IA, DC/HX 117–01 and T. Dicey, *An Historical Account of Guernsey* (London, 1751), pp. 189–90.

of the Hospital's core staff. However, the way these roles were distributed and the titles of the staff performing them underwent repeated change. One of the earliest changes was the eclipse of the *gouvernante* and the usurpation of her role by the *maître*. Hereafter these officers will be referred to as 'master' and 'mistress'.[35]

To begin with, as befitted her status, the mistress was paid more than the master. Their first year's salaries were £11 13s and £10 8s (sterling) respectively.[36] By 1766, however, the master was receiving £12 12s to the mistress's £10.[37] The transfer of precedence seems to have begun in the late 1740s. In 1749, Mathieu Pezet was replaced as master by the more reliable and more forceful Jean Le Page.[38] After Sarah Messervy died four years later, Directors decided to replace her from within rather than recruiting a woman of comparable stature from outside. Thus it was that Mrs Brock found herself promoted from stewardship of the linen to the rank of mistress.[39] This choice reflected an apparently intentional diminution of the authority associated with the post, and Mrs Brock's duties were henceforth limited to oversight of housekeeping and responsibility for women inmates. The master's ascendancy was fully acknowledged in 1759, when, faced with a threat of resignation from Jean Le Page unless Mrs Brock left, Directors chose to dismiss Mrs Brock.[40]

After this date, a majority of mistresses (eleven out of the seventeen between 1760 and 1927) were promoted from among women who had first served the Hospital in lowlier roles. The prestige of the post continued to diminish, and the salary gap between master and mistress grew progressively wider. By 1821, the mistress received £21 per year to the master's £55. By 1854, she was receiving just £30 to his £80.[41] £30 a year equated to a mere 11s 6d per week, which was no more than the wage of the lowest-paid labourer.[42] In the absence of staff pensions, some mistresses who survived in post to old age were obliged to continue in the institution as inmates.[43]

Most of the Town Hospital's mistresses were widows or spinsters obliged to work for a living because they lacked male support. In nineteenth-century English workhouses, it was standard practice to employ a married couple as governor and matron.[44] For a long time this was resisted in St Peter Port. In 1825, Directors

---

[35] In 1810, Hospital authorities dropped the term *gouvernante* and substituted *maîtresse* (2.4.1810, IA, DC/HX 079–02). In the 1870s, there was an attempt to introduce the English titles 'governor' and 'matron' (1877 accounts, IA, DC/HX 272–02). These titles did not, however, find favour. It was not until 1911 that the mistress was officially referred to as 'matron'. The title 'master' remained in force until both officers were redesignated 'superintendents' in 1951 (6.3.1911, IA, DC/HX 046–01; 5.5.1951, IA, AS/MB 065–02).
[36] Entries for July and August 1744, IA, DC/HX 117–01.
[37] 1766 accounts, IA, DC/HX 079–01; IA, DC/HX 165–01.
[38] IA, DC/HX 117–01.
[39] 1.5.1753, IA, DC/HX 118–01.
[40] 22.8.1759, IA, DC/HX 079–01.
[41] 12.3.1821, IA, DC/HX 079–02; 6.2.1854, IA, DC/HX 054–05.
[42] Though board and lodging in the Hospital came 'free'.
[43] Such as Fanny Gray in 1841 and Eliza Rowe in 1911 (6.12.1841, IA, DC/HX 075–01; 18.10.1911, IA, DC/HX 046–01).
[44] M.A. Crowther, *The Workhouse System, 1834–1929: The History of an English Social Institution* (1981; London, 1983 edn), p. 116.

rejected a request from master Thomas Mauger that his wife take over deceased mistress Sarah Nevis's post, attributing their refusal to the 'abuses' this might engender.[45] By 1879, attitudes had changed to the point where the St Peter Port Poor Law Board passed a formal resolution expressing readiness to countenance married couples in the role, but they did not actually recruit such a couple until 1927, when a Mr and Mrs Dorrington were appointed joint master and matron.[46] From this time until the 1960s, this arrangement became standard.

Owing, perhaps, to the more prestigious nature of the master's post, turnover of Town Hospital masters was lower than that of mistresses. Simon Fowler reports an average turnover of seven masters between 1854 and 1918 in English provincial workhouses.[47] In the Town Hospital, there were only four masters in that period and eight over the entire nineteenth century.[48] The social status of English workhouse masters has been likened to that of middle-ranking tradesmen.[49] The two Thomas Maugers, father and son, who occupied the post between 1810 and 1878, appear to have been of this rank. Their family background was in printing, and the younger Mauger had trained as a compositor before succeeding his father as master at the age of 22.[50] The funeral of Mauger senior, who died prematurely at 50, was paid for by the Hospital and attended by the Treasurer and Directors attired in formal mourning.[51]

In terms of status, the master's post probably reached its apogee with the Maugers. Following the second Mauger's demise in controversial circumstances in 1878, the Poor Law Board reduced the salary for the post from £104 per year to £80,[52] (which was, in fact, an average salary for workhouse masters in England and Wales at the time).[53] Mauger's successor, former brewer James Le Patourel, whose 'insufficient firmness of character' led to his dismissal within months, was succeeded in turn by 36-year-old Thomas Ozanne, who also began on £80.[54]

In 1915, the post of Town Hospital master sustained what was perhaps its greatest drop in status, when the institution was divided in two and control of the infirmary

---

45 1.8.1825, IA, DC/HX 135–02; IA, DC/HX 082–01.
46 21.7.1879, IA, DC/HX 054–06; 12.12.1927, IA, DC/HX 051–01.
47 S. Fowler, *Workhouse: The People, the Places, the Life Behind Doors* (Richmond, 2007), p. 80.
48 Pierre Marquand served as master until 1802 (2.6.1802, IA, DC/HX 079–02); Jean Bertram until 1809 (4.1.1809, IA, DC/HX 079–02); Isaac Marquand until 1810 (7.2.1810, IA, DC/HX 079–02); Thomas Mauger senior until 1837 (1.11.1837, IA, DC/HX 130–02); Thomas Mauger junior until 1878 (2.3.1878, IA, DC/HX 069–01); James Le Patourel until 1879 (20.5.1879, IA, DC/HX 054–06), and Thomas Ozanne until 1901 (10.9.1901, IA, DC/HX 056–04).
49 Crowther, *Workhouse System*, p. 125.
50 16.11.1837, IA, DC/HX 130–02. For the Mauger family's involvement with printing, see A. Bennett, 'A history of the French newspapers and nineteenth-century English newspapers of Guernsey' (unpub. MA dissertation, Loughborough University, 1995), pp. 12–18.
51 6.11.1837, IA, DC/HX 130–02.
52 *Star*, 19.3.1878, 2.4.1878. For the controversy surrounding Mauger's death, see section on 'Infirmary regime', chapter 7.
53 R.G. Hodgkinson, *The Origins of the National Health Service* (London, 1967), p. 541.
54 21.7.1879, IA, DC/HX 054–06.

passed to the sister-in-charge.[55] In 1920, the post's prestige fell still further, when clerical and accounting duties were transferred to a new Poor Law Board clerk.[56] From this point onwards, the master's post was a mere shadow of its former self, with duties limited to nothing more than management of supplies and oversight of a dwindling band of 'house people'. The post survived until 1963.[57]

Aside from the master and mistress, the one other employee who featured constantly on the Hospital's staff list was the under-mistress, later usually known as the second mistress. Her function was to share responsibility for domestic supervision and oversight of children and females with the mistress. In 1766, she earned £6 a year to the mistress's £10; in 1899, £25 to the mistress's £40.[58] About half of the thirteen or so women who served as second mistress during the nineteenth century went on to become mistresses in their own right.

In 1806, the second mistress's load was lightened when the Hospital engaged its first 'schoolmistress' to take over the supervision of babies, toddlers and girls.[59] Despite her title, the schoolmistress's teaching duties consisted solely of instructing the older girls at needlework.[60] Her chief functions were of a pastoral nature. Assisted by her team of women inmates, she bathed and fed her charges, mended their clothes, tended them when they were ill, and generally supplied the place of mother. In 1841, census returns show the presence in the Hospital of eleven infants and twenty-eight girls aged 15 and under, all of whom the schoolmistress, Elizabeth Guilliard, would have had in her charge.[61] Despite their low pay (the salary was set at £15 in 1806 and remained unchanged until the twentieth century), schoolmistresses tended to stay long-term. Elizabeth Guilliard herself served in this capacity for over fifty years.[62] In 1882, the schoolmistress was redesignated 'children's matron', though without ostensible change of duties.[63]

The post of under-master, or second master, was instituted in 1763, after the master became too busy to oversee the men and educate the children.[64] The first incumbent's salary, at £8 per annum, was £2 less than the mistress's.[65] This post was particularly subject to fluctuation. In the late eighteenth century, when benign economic conditions reduced the number of male inmates to insignificance, it seems to have lapsed altogether. In 1788, a master weaver, Maître Quesnel, was taken on to oversee cloth production, and some of the second master's supervisory functions

[55] 29.9.1915, IA, DC/HX 080–05.
[56] 6.4.1920, 3.5.1920, IA, DC/HX 052–01. From 1853, the master had officially been designated 'accountant and registrar' to the Poor Law Board (1877 accounts, IA, DC/HX 272–02).
[57] 31.10.1963, IA, AS/MB 065–02.
[58] 1766 accounts, IA, DC/HX 165–01; 6.11.1899, IA, DC/HX 056–04.
[59] 5.11.1806, IA, DC/HX 079–02. For more on the circumstances surrounding the appointment of this schoolmistress, see section on 'Children', below.
[60] 5.12.1853, IA, DC/HX 130–04.
[61] Enumerators' books (microfilm), PL.
[62] 2.7.1824, IA, DC/HX 135–02; 1.7.1876, IA, DC/HX 069–01.
[63] 29.3.1882, IA, DC/HX 130–03.
[64] 27.1.1763, IA, DC/HX 079–01.
[65] 1766 accounts, IA, DC/HX 165–01.

were assumed by him.[66] In the post-Napoleonic period, when the Hospital was awash with children, a new post was created which was similar in some respects to that of the old second master's, but now bore the entirely new title of 'schoolmaster'. The first person to be appointed to this post was Joseph Renouf, a 26-year-old private tutor, engaged in 1816.[67] Renouf, who held the post until his retirement at the age of 82 in 1872, was exceptional in many ways.[68] His starting salary, at £40, was unusually generous: the mistress was receiving less than half this sum at the time, and the master only £10 more.[69] Also unusually, Renouf lived outside the institution throughout his tenure. During this time he brought up five children, one of whom became an internationally renowned scholar.[70] In 1819, Renouf assumed the additional title of 'director of manufacturing', and his salary rose to £55, on a par with the master's.[71] He held this role until 1841, when his salary reverted to £40, ostensibly because there was no more manufacturing to supervise.[72] From this point on, Renouf concentrated solely on teaching. He was obliged to keep school for the Hospital's boys between 9.00 a.m. and 4.00 p.m. Monday to Friday, and to spend an additional hour every day teaching the girls reading, writing and arithmetic.[73] Unlike the schoolmistress, however, Renouf had no pastoral duties. The cleanliness, health, nutrition, clothing and recreation of boys aged from about 6 to 15 (of whom there were thirty-four in 1841) were all the responsibility of an inmate 'usher'. The use of inmates in this pastoral capacity probably dated back to the eighteenth century, but, between 1834 and 1868, the role was performed by Ernest Colbert, whose dedication and kindness towards his charges is evident from Hospital records.[74] After Colbert's death, the Poor Law Board advertised in

---

[66] 22.7.1788, IA, DC/HX 120–01.

[67] 5.8.1816, IA, DC/HX 079–02. Prior to Renouf's appointment, the Hospital had briefly experimented with sending the boys out to day school. For more on this episode, see section on 'Children', below.

[68] 6.5.1872, IA, DC/HX 054–05. For Renouf's obituary, see *Star*, 29.11.1879.

[69] Even in 1850, the average salary of an English workhouse schoolmaster was only £31 (Hodgkinson, *National Health Service*, p. 368).

[70] The Egyptologist Sir Peter Le Page Renouf, for whom see C.J. Durand, K. Brock and E.C. Ozanne (eds), *Elizabeth College Register, 1824–1873* (Guernsey, 1898), p. 92.

[71] 7.6.1819, IA, DC/HX 135–02.

[72] 1.2.1841, IA, DC/HX 075–01.

[73] 5.12.1853, IA, DC/HX 130–04.

[74] Born at the close of the Napoleonic Wars to a local woman and a foreign soldier, Colbert, who suffered from a limp and other health problems, entered the workhouse at the age of two. Evidently bright and trustworthy, the parochial authorities used him to perform clerical tasks, as well as to care for the boys, from his late teens (27.6.1838, IA, AQ 0965/02). The fact that inmates named children after him (as did Mr and Mrs Millman their 'Ernestine Colbert Millman' in 1852), suggests that he was generally held in esteem (4.17.1852, IA, DC/HX 075–02). His work with the boys was initially unremunerated, but the new Poor Law Board officially designated him 'assistant schoolmaster' in 1853, rewarding him with £5 a year, a half-day's leisure weekly, and the privilege of taking his meals with the staff (5.12.1853, IA, DC/HX 130–04). Colbert appears to have saved most of his earnings, and he bequeathed them to the Hospital when he died aged 54 in 1868 (7.2.1870, IA, DC/HX 054–05). His funeral was attended by the entire Poor Law Board and all the ambulant inmates (4.11.1868, IA, DC/HX 127–01).

the local press for 'an under-schoolmaster to live in the House, and give all his time to the Hospital'. Notwithstanding that they had paid Colbert only £5 for doing precisely this, the Board advertised the post at £25. Initially, however, they received no responses.[75] Some time later, they succeeded in recruiting one James Sarre, and then went through another three under-schoolmasters before the post lapsed altogether in 1879.[76] Thereafter, no further attempt was made to educate the boys internally, and they were all sent instead to the nearby National School.[77] The post of second master was then formally resurrected, and subsequent incumbents combined responsibility for the boys' pastoral needs with management of the Hospital stores.[78]

In an earlier reapportionment of duties, a series of 'labour masters' or 'work superintendents' had been engaged from 1854. As well as overseeing able-bodied men's work, these officers were also given responsibility for their discipline and supervision of their sleeping quarters.[79] This post survived until 1920, when the last labour master was not replaced on his retirement, and the second master incorporated supervision of the few remaining able-bodied men with his various other duties.[80]

Ancillary staff were few to begin with, since inmates did the bulk of the physical work. From the 1850s and 1860s, however, the supply of able-bodied inmates began to shrink as economic conditions improved, and increasing numbers of casual workers were engaged to perform functions such as tailoring, shoemaking, hair-cutting and porterage.[81] By the time the States took over poor law funding in 1925, the Town Hospital had a total of thirty-one waged employees, including cooks, laundresses, kitchen maids and ward maids, as well as paid nurses and lunatic attendants.[82] As a consequence, the proportion of St Peter Port's poor law expenditure absorbed by Hospital wages grew from 10 per cent in 1858 to 18 per cent in 1924, and the absolute amount increased from £404 to £2,090.[83]

For most of the eighteenth and nineteenth centuries, staff had been expected to devote virtually their whole lives to their work. All save one or two exceptions lived in, and they were required to leave any family they had outside the institution.[84] Their working day stretched from rising to bedtime, and time off from Hospital duties was extremely limited. As late as the 1870s, even the master had only three evenings off a week, together with alternate Sundays.[85] Leave of absence was, more-

---

75   8.2.1869, IA, DC/HX 054–05.

76   5.4.1869, 8.6.1871, IA, DC/HX 059–01; 25.4.1877, IA, DC/HX 069–01; 5.6.1877, 20.5.1879, IA, DC/HX 054–06.

77   9.7.1879, IA, DC/HX 054–06.

78   24.7.1890, IA, DC/HX 136–02; IA, DC/HX 272–04.

79   5.2.1855, IA, DC/HX 054–05.

80   9.8.1920, IA, DC/HX 052–01.

81   1.4.1852, IA, DC/HX 272–02; 25.10.1852, IA, DC/HX 075–02; 14.3.1853, 12.9.1854, IA, DC/HX 130–04; 16.7.1888, IA, DC/HX 136–02.

82   4.1.1926, IA, DC/HX 051–01.

83   IA, DC/HX 272–02.

84   Mrs Beaugy, engaged as under-mistress in 1753, found separation from her young daughter too hard to bear and tendered her resignation within months (13.5.1753, IA, DC/HX 079–01).

85   15.11.1870, IA, DC/HX 054–05.

over, not a right but a concession, rarely granted. When master Thomas Mauger's request to go on holiday to France was granted in 1863, it was a mark of his stature in the institution.[86] A similar request from mistress Sophia Langlois in 1884 was refused, and the House Committee put it on record that 'that leave of absence from the island is not thought desirable by the Committee, and they trust that no further applications will be made'.[87]

Real improvement in staff conditions came only in the early twentieth century after the Royal Court's assumption of Hospital supervision. By 1903, all staff were allowed a fortnight's annual leave.[88] From 1913, those who had accrued a set amount of service were additionally entitled to four weeks' sick pay. Off-duty hours nevertheless remained minimal, and on the eve of World War I junior workhouse staff were still restricted to two free Sundays a month.[89]

Such close and prolonged confinement had both positive and negative effects. On the positive side, a conjuncture of compatible personalities could produce a sense of community. The masters and mistresses who were admonished in 1832 for singing and dancing until midnight evidently enjoyed each other's company and may have performed well as a team.[90] On the negative side, personal antipathies could soon explode into open warfare. After only four months in post, new mistress Sophia Langlois' escalating clashes with second master William Corbet led to his dismissal in 1883, notwithstanding that he had served the Hospital for four years.[91]

Of course, if the job was not to their liking, staff were always free to leave. Inmates, however, did not have this choice. From the Hospital's opening until the twentieth century, their discharge depended not on their own wishes but on the pleasure of the Hospital authorities.[92] Their confinement was thus even more complete than that of staff, and they too constituted a community apart. In the next section, the component groups in this community will be scrutinised in turn.

Inmates

Children
In her study of London's Holborn workhouse in the 1860s, Anne Crowther found that the vast majority of child inmates came from households which, for one reason or another, lacked a father.[93] Many of these children were illegitimate, born to unwed mothers in the workhouse itself. Statistics on illegitimacy in respect of Guernsey's

---

[86] 16.9.1863, IA, DC/HX 136–07.
[87] 25.8.1884, 8.9.1884, IA, DC/HX 136–01.
[88] 27.7.1903, IA, DC/HX 080–03. It is unclear whether this was paid.
[89] IA, DC/HX 272–04.
[90] 9.7.1832, IA, DC/HX 135–03.
[91] 2.5.1883, IA, DC/HX 054–06.
[92] Note that, under the post-1834 system in England and Wales, all an inmate had to do if he wished to leave was to give three hours' notice (Crowther, *Workhouse System*, pp. 44, 208–9).
[93] Crowther, *Workhouse System*, p. 228.

Town Hospital were kept only between 1853 and 1901.[94] During the 1850s and 1860s, an average of twenty illegitimate children were resident at each year's end, comprising about a third of all children present. After 1870, absolute numbers of illegitimate children present at mid-winter dropped to about nine, although, as overall child numbers declined in tandem, their proportion of the child cohort remained the same. Very few illegitimate children were actually born in the Hospital during the period covered by statistics because of the carceral policy adopted from the 1840s toward unmarried women giving birth in the house.[95]

A small number of those recorded as illegitimate were foundlings, such as the female new-born deposited anonymously at the Hospital gate in the summer of 1850.[96] Most illegitimate children, however, were placed in the Hospital's care by lone mothers who identified themselves. One such mother was Mary Anne Stephens, from whom a letter requesting admission for her daughter was transcribed verbatim in an 1826 register: 'if you please to take mi Child in the house as she is in want of a friend, for i cannot keep er any longer, it is out of my power, and sorry i ham to part with har, Bot what ham i to do'.[97]

Illegitimacy was not, of course, the only cause of fatherlessness, and the Hospital also sheltered a large number of fatherless children who had been born in wedlock. In some cases, the loss of a father might be temporary. Elizabeth De Jersey's son was admitted for a short time in 1822 while her husband was at sea.[98] In other cases, the loss was permanent. The three Tucker children were admitted in 1870 after the family had been deserted by their father.[99] The two Andrews children entered in 1914 after their father had died.[100]

In addition to the above, many children from families with two parents living and present were taken into the Hospital. Some entered on a short-term basis to tide their families over periods of poverty, such as Henry Le Cheminant's two children, admitted in 1831 because his outdoor relief was insufficient to maintain them at home.[101] A further proportion were taken into the house at the behest of the Constables. Some, such as nine-week-old Joseph McBride in 1825, had been removed from neglectful or abusive parents.[102] Others, such as 10-year-old James Le Lacheur in 1845, were brought in to 'correct' their delinquent propensities.[103] Yet others, such as 13-year-old Amelia Farley in 1853 and 14-year-old Bridget Quin in 1882, were compulsorily admitted for the treatment of sexually transmitted diseases.[104]

St Peter Port's poor law authorities sought to minimise the number of children

---

94   IA, DC/HX 272–02.
95   See section on 'Policy and regime', Chapter 6.
96   21.6.1850, IA, DC/HX 075–02.
97   9.5.1826, IA, DC/HX 135–02.
98   2.9.1822, IA, DC/HX 135–02.
99   8.8.1870, IA, DC/HX 127–01.
100 2.3.1914, IA, DC/HX 046–01.
101 6.6.1831, IA, DC/HX 135–03.
102 In this case, the baby's parents were alleged to have 'cruelly and inhumanly neglected and starved him' (7.3.1825, IA, DC/HX 135–02).
103 18.7.1845, IA, DC/HX 130–01.
104 29.10.1853, IA, DC/HX 130–04; 10.6.1882, IA, DC/HX 130–03.

taken into and kept within the Hospital, and used various strategies towards this end. There was no formal boarding-out policy, but if a relative could be found to take on a child who had come to the authorities' notice, the child would normally be deposited with them. Payment was sometimes offered in return. In 1851, Louisa Brouard's uncle was paid a flat fee of £2 to take care of her until she came of age.[105] Informal adoptions by non-relatives were also arranged. In 1875, 6-year-old Frank Green was 'adopted' in this way by a Mrs Engelhart; in 1879, 8-year-old Alice Brooks was similarly 'adopted' by a Mrs Duplain.[106] The first adoption by legal agreement appears to have been that of Eleanor Rolls, adopted by a Mrs Richards in 1901.[107]

A more drastic way of offloading children, resorted to in varying degrees over time, was despatch overseas. This was particularly favoured in the Hospital's first decades, facilitated by the trading activities of Guernsey's eighteenth-century merchants. Many Hospital children were simply committed to the care of departing sea captains, such as the fourteen entrusted to Captain Flight on his departure for New England in 1752, and the six sent with Captain Andress to Newfoundland in 1765.[108] In 1767, Hospital Directors formally resolved to send to Canada and other British colonies as many children as could be persuaded to go.[109]

In the early nineteenth century, the decline of maritime trade brought something of a lull in child emigration. However, by the 1840s, it had picked up again and, over the next four decades, it proceeded in full spate. Well into the 1870s, the Hospital regularly sent out mixed parties of inmates to Canada, the United States and, to a lesser extent, Australia. These groups invariably included a large proportion of children, who were usually related to their adult companions. In the group of twenty-seven despatched to Quebec in the spring of 1862, there were no fewer than sixteen under-13s.[110] After the 1870s, the Hospital ceased sending out inmates in groups, and the number of children sent abroad greatly diminished. In the late nineteenth and early twentieth centuries, only one or two a year were selected for despatch overseas, and these were usually sent via United Kingdom agencies which specialised in child emigration. In 1892, 14-year-old Theresa Fenwick was sent to Canada under the scheme set up in England by Annie Macpherson and Maria Rye; in 1907, Robert Wright and Walter Sarre were also despatched to Canada via Barnardo's.[111]

---

[105] 4.9.1851, IA, DC/HX 075–02.

[106] 27.4.1875, 17.6.1879, IA, DC/HX 069–01.

[107] 21.6.1901, IA, DC/HX 136–05.

[108] IA, DC/HX 117–02; IA, DC/HX 119–01. In the New England case of 1752, Captain Flight had undertaken to place the girls in service and the boys in apprenticeships. F.B. Tupper, writing a century later, quotes an advertisement which appeared in Boston that year: 'To be sold, Guernsey boys and girls, for a term of time, on Board the sloop Two Brothers' (F.B. Tupper, *The History of Guernsey and its Bailiwick* (Guernsey, 1854), p. 362).

[109] 21.4.1767, IA, DC/HX 079–01.

[110] 10.5.1862, IA, DC/HX 127–01.

[111] 4.1.1892, 25.2.1892, IA, DC/HX 136–03; 29.4.1907, IA, DC/HX 080–01. For Macpherson and Rye, Barnardo's and other child emigration agencies, see Fowler, *Workhouse*, p. 170 and H. Hendrick, *Child Welfare: England, 1872–1989* (London, 1994), p. 80.

By far the most common way the Hospital unburdened itself of children, however, was to bind them out to external employers. In 1748, the Royal Court accorded the Hospital Board the right to bind out any children taken into care without reference to parents or relatives.[112] This prerogative was inherited by the St Peter Port Poor Law Board in 1853 and freely exercised until as late as 1915, from which point the consent of any living parents or guardians had to be obtained.[113]

Until the last third of the nineteenth century, Hospital children were usually bound out at the age of 11 or 12. After this time, the typical age for binding out rose to 13 or 14. Records of child placements were not systematically kept, but one of the first daybooks recorded a total of twenty-five bindings-out in 1744.[114] An abstract of accounts for 1821 showed twenty.[115] Later abstracts recorded an average of seven new bindings-out annually until 1850, dropping to two or three in the last years of the century.[116] Since children were bound for periods of up to seven years, records of new bindings-out reflected just a small fraction of the total of Hospital children out on placement in any particular year.

In both the eighteenth and nineteenth centuries, the vast majority of boys were bound out to employers within the island of Guernsey. For the fortunate few, proper apprenticeships were found – as bakers, tailors, gardeners, etc. – but more usually they were sent out as unskilled hands, often to farms, as Charles Rooks to Jean Sarre in Torteval in 1830, or James Guernier to Alfred Tostevin of the Castel in 1900.[117] More rarely, boys might be sent in similar capacities to employers in Jersey, Sark or Alderney, although this seems to have ceased by about 1850.

An alternative option for boys, especially in the eighteenth century, was binding out to sea. In 1788, for instance, Nicolas Capelain was bound to a Captain Le Messurier to serve five years in the Newfoundland cod fishery.[118] Again, there was a lull in this practice as maritime trade declined in the first two decades of the nineteenth century. By the 1820s, however, the Hospital had negotiated a standing arrangement to supply boys to colliers operating from North and South Shields and, for the next few years, considerable numbers of Hospital boys were employed in the coal fleet.[119] More exotically, for a period between the 1820s and 1870s boys might be bound out to overseas-based Guernsey merchants to serve in stores and counting-houses: 13-year-old Peter Claypole was sent out to Peter Bonamy in Rio

---

[112] Act of Court, 16.1.1748, IA, DC/HX 180–14.

[113] 15.12.1914, IA, DC/HX 272–04. This unconstrained power may be contrasted with the situation in England and Wales, where, under the 1847 Consolidated General Order of the Poor Law Commission, no child under 16 could be bound without the consent of the father (or, in his absence, the mother), and indentures in duplicate had to be signed by both child and parent (J.F. Archbold (ed.), *The Consolidated and other Orders of the Poor Law Commissioners and of the Poor Law Board* (London, 1859), pp. 54, 57).

[114] IA, DC/HX 117–01.

[115] IA, DC/HX 045–01.

[116] IA, DC/HX 178–01; IA, DC/HX 272–02.

[117] 5.7.1830, IA, DC/HX 135–03; 9.4.1900, IA, DC/HX 136–05.

[118] 5.4.1788, IA, DC/HX 120–01.

[119] 4.2.1822, IA, DC/HX 079–02; 6.6.1825, IA, DC/HX 135–02.

de Janeiro in 1821; 13-year-old William Le Sauvage to Saumarez Carey in Alicante in 1861.[120]

Where possible, boys were bound for six or seven years. On a few occasions, premiums were paid by the Hospital when a boy was apprenticed to a trade or craft, such as the £5 paid for a lad to learn hairdressing in 1869.[121] Usually, however, the Hospital required payment from the employers themselves, reflecting the fact that the boys' prime purpose was to supply labour. In 1900, 5s was charged for James Guernier in his first year on Alfred Tostevin's farm, rising to £8 in his sixth.[122]

For girls, the one and only option was domestic service, as low-cost maids-of-all-work. As with boys, their usual placements were in Guernsey, but up to the mid-1800s they might also be sent to employers in other Channel Islands. In addition, for a brief spell in the post-Napoleonic period, some girls were sent out to serve British families in France.[123] A handful, including 14-year-old Rosa Foy in 1866, were also sent to England, although this was rare, and they were usually sent to expatriate Guernsey families, as, in Rosa's case, a Mr Le Page of London.[124]

The usual practice was to bind girls out for three years in the first instance. Payment was required from all employers, as there was no question of apprenticeship. In 1817, 50s was charged for girls in their first year of service, 55s in their second and 60s in their third and any subsequent years.[125]

Children's wages were held by the Hospital on the children's behalf and paid to them when they came of age or finished their term.[126] Cash held in their name might be used to pay for breakages or thefts from their employers, and could also fund their emigration. Any child who ran away, or whose employers returned them for misconduct, automatically forfeited all they had earned.[127]

In most cases, a trial period with prospective employers was allowed, following which employers would commit to the agreed term if they found the child acceptable. For a variety of reasons, however, by no means all terms were completed. Hospital children had a poor reputation for behaviour and reliability, and those taking them on usually did so because they could not afford any better. The Hospital was often hard put to find takers for its children, and periodically advertised the services of its boys and girls in local newspapers.[128] In 1830, Directors discussed making girls' employment contracts 'unbreakable'. Ultimately, however, they decided not to pursue this course lest removal of the facility for easy return deterred potential employers altogether.[129] In England and Wales, poor law

---

[120] 17.8.1821, IA, DC/HX 124–01; 24.6.1861, IA, DC/HX 130–04.

[121] IA, DC/HX 272–02.

[122] 9.4.1900, IA, DC/HX 136–05.

[123] See, for example, 21.12.1820, IA, DC/HX 124–02.

[124] 23.10.1866, IA, DC/HX 136–07.

[125] 23.6.1817, IA, DC/HX 079–02.

[126] The register labelled 'Children's Wages, 1872–1916' (IA, DC/HX 169–09) shows that a bank account was opened to hold the money in 1872.

[127] Money from a fund made up of forfeited wages was used by the Hospital authorities to furnish their new chapel in 1896 (14.9.1896, IA, DC/HX 136–11).

[128] See, for instance, 27.1.1817, IA, DC/HX 079–02 and 11.12.1912, IA, DC/HX 080–06.

[129] 7.6.1830, IA, DC/HX 135–03.

authorities reported in 1862 that a fifth of workhouse children bound to outside employers were returned.[130] No statistics exist for the Town Hospital, but day-to-day records give the impression of a greater proportion than this. Most children appear to have been returned at least once. The experience of little Prudence Bailey in the 1880s was typical: in February 1885, the 11-year-old was sent out to service with Mrs Howe of St Peters, only to be returned to the Hospital in November. The following March, she was sent out for a second time to the Reverend Carey in St Saviours but was again returned a month later. In May 1886, she was sent out for a third time, to Mrs Langlois of the Forest, where, on this occasion, she appears to have remained long term.[131]

Young girls sent out in this manner were clearly very vulnerable. During the eighteenth and nineteenth centuries, unwanted sexual attention was a distinct occupational hazard for female servants everywhere.[132] Some of the Hospital's girls, such as 15-year-old Elizabeth Sheppard in 1879, were returned to the Hospital pregnant. Elizabeth had been sent into service with James Le Page of St Andrews and, four months after her return to the Hospital, gave birth to a son to whom she gave the second name of James.[133] With Hospital boys, similar problems might sometimes be encountered in reverse: in 1831, teenager Samuel Maingueneau was returned to the institution by Philippe Hotton of Sark after sexually molesting Hotton's 9-year-old daughter.[134]

More frequently, boys were returned on grounds of laziness, defiance, dishonesty or general mischief. William White, a 13-year-old apprenticed in 1822 to a Jersey shoemaker, was typical in being returned for lying to his master and answering back.[135] Many boys also suffered ill-treatment by their masters, ran away from them and returned to the institution themselves. In one astonishing case, Henry Catts, sent to Rio de Janeiro as a 12-year-old in 1846, found his way back to the Hospital four years later after a solo journey of 5,000 miles.[136]

Prior to 1755, children living within the Hospital had no separate quarters. They shared dormitories with adults of their own sex, sometimes sleeping in the same beds.[137] It was only after an outbreak of illness among the children, thought to have been caused by sharing with the elderly, that Directors allocated them dormitories of their own.[138] Even so, segregation from adults during daytime remained minimal. Up to the early nineteenth century, children spent only a small part of the day in

---

[130] P. Wood, *Poverty and the Workhouse in Victorian Britain* (Stroud, 1991), p. 103.

[131] 23.2.1885, 24.11.1885, 25.3.1886, 6.4.1886, 8.5.1886, IA, DC/HX 130–03.

[132] For an assessment of this hazard, see T. Meldrum, 'London domestic servants from depositional evidence, 1660–1750: servant–employer sexuality in the patriarchal household', in T.V. Hitchcock, P. King and P. Sharpe (eds), *Chronicling Poverty: The Voices and Strategies of the English Poor, 1640–1840* (Basingstoke, 1997), pp. 47–69.

[133] 20.7.1879, IA, DC/HX 069–01.

[134] 3.9.1831, IA, DC/HX 135–03.

[135] 4.11.1822, IA, DC/HX 135–02.

[136] 26.10.1850, IA, DC/HX 075–02.

[137] T. Quayle, *A General View of the Agriculture and Present State of the Islands on the Coast of Normandy subject to the Crown of Great Britain* (London, 1815), p. 292.

[138] 7.9.1755, IA, DC/HX 079–01.

education and, for the rest of their time, worked with their elders in the Hospital's manufacturing enterprises, as well as eating with them in the Hospital refectory.[139] Some adult inmates were less than savoury, and there were many opportunities for abuse. After 36-year-old Thomas Shoesmith had contrived to have 'an illicit connection' with 11-year-old Rachel Le Filliâtre and 13-year-old Sophie Squires in 1806, Directors approached some of St Peter Port's patrician ladies to take over care of the girls.[140] Lady Saumarez, Lady De Havilland, Mrs Carteret Perchard and thirteen other ladies set up a 'school of industry' on Hospital premises to train the girls in self-respect and religion, and to teach them sewing. The ladies had sole management of the school, whose expenses were partly defrayed from selling the girls' handiwork. It was at this time and for this reason that the girls were given their own schoolmistress.[141] It was for this reason, too, that, in 1809, they were provided with their own detached quarters and playground.[142]

The Town Hospital's 'school of industry' lasted for twelve years, after which the ladies withdrew following friction with Treasurer William Collings, who wished to use the girls to spin flax for his new weaving enterprise and resented the ladies' control of this branch of 'his' institution.[143] Nevertheless, the separate girls' block, which came to be known as 'Phoebe's ward', remained a permanent fixture at the Hospital, as did the schoolmistress.[144] The girls had at all times to share their block with infants and toddlers, and also with adult females during the 1820s and 1830s. The Hospital's boys remained in the main building throughout the nineteenth century.

One effect of the initial success of the girls' school of industry was to highlight deficiencies in schooling for Hospital boys, and the new Board which succeeded that of Jean Condamine resolved to send them out to day school. For this, the Board had to pay 10s per head per year.[145] By 1816, with sixty-four boys in the Hospital, the cost was deemed too high, and the decision was taken to engage the young schoolmaster Joseph Renouf to teach the boys in-house.[146]

In the 1830s, boys generally benefited from full-time education only until the age of 10 or 11, after which, if not placed out, they worked in-house 'as twine-spinners; in sail-cloth, sheeting, brown canvass making; as straw hat manufacturers, net makers, tailors, shoemakers, etc.'.[147] By 1876, the maximum age until which boys

---

[139] 7.6.1779, IA, DC/HX 079–01.

[140] 13.8.1806, 3.9.1806, IA, DC/HX 079–02. For more on Thomas Shoesmith, a long-term inmate whose surname was variously also rendered as Soosmith, Sousmith and Southsmith, see 8.7.1845, IA, DC/HX 130–01.

[141] 5.11.1806, IA, DC/HX 079–02.

[142] 10.5.1809, IA, DC/HX 079–02.

[143] 18.3.1818, 10.4.1818, IA, DC/HX 079–02; *Gazette de Guernesey*, 11.4.1818. See also 'A Statement of Facts, as connected with the Dismission of the Mistress from the Girls' School at the Town Hospital and with the Resignation of the Ladies, as Superintendents of that School, Guernsey, 8 April 1818' (printed document, IA).

[144] 17.2.1832, IA, DC/HX 135–03.

[145] 7.1.1811, 7.9.1812, 5.4.1813, IA, DC/HX 079–02.

[146] 5.8.1816, IA, DC/HX 079–02; 31.12.1816, IA, DC/HX 123–02.

[147] J. Jacob, *Annals of Some of the British Norman Isles Constituting the Bailiwick of Guernsey* (Paris, 1830), p. 149.

attended the schoolroom had risen to 14, during which time they received twenty-five hours' instruction a week in reading, writing, arithmetic and other subjects, such as geography.[148] By 1879, however, with only a dozen or so boys in long-term residence, a decision was taken to dispense with the schoolmaster and, once more, to send the boys out to day school.[149] From this time onward, no further schooling was provided to boys on Hospital premises.

The first intimation of any form of external education for girls came only in 1882, when it was resolved that they should attend Sunday School.[150] Day school attendance followed shortly afterwards. Up to this point, the girls had been at a serious educational disadvantage to the boys. Their own schoolmistress taught them only sewing, and it was never thought necessary for the schoolmaster to give them more than one hour's daily instruction in the three Rs.[151] To the House Committee, this seemed quite sufficient to prepare them 'for the position they are intended to fill in after life'.[152] However, in most cases it also ensured that they could advance no further.

The health of Hospital children was often blighted by the poor environment in which they were kept. In 1844, retiring medical officer Marc Corbin complained to the Board about the unhygienic state of the boys' schoolroom and dormitory; the lack of recreational facilities; the poor diet offered to boys; and the prevalence among them of 'a loathsome disease'.[153] Corbin later wrote that, in his first term as medical officer (1838), one third of Hospital girls suffered from 'pustular ophthalmia'.[154] Ratepayers were loath to spend more than the bare minimum on Hospital facilities, and little was done in response to these complaints.

In 1859, local philanthropist Osmond De Beauvoir Priaulx, 'disagreeably struck by the appearance of the children', devised a scheme to improve their lot. With the aim of financing the purchase of a farm, to be run by the parish, where pauper children might combine education with healthy outdoor work, Priaulx, who owned a large tenanted house in St Peter Port, arranged for the diversion of rental income from it into a special fund, whose contents would be transferred after twenty years to the parochial authorities.[155] In 1859, ratepayers had seemed well disposed to Priaulx's initiative, but when, twenty years later, they were offered the £6,000 which had accrued, they backed away, preferring not to 'saddle themselves with the matter'.

[148] 18.5.1863, IA, DC/HX 136–07; 6.3.1876, IA, DC/HX 136–09.

[149] 9.7.1879, IA, DC/HX 054–06.

[150] 5.7.1882, IA, DC/HX 054–06.

[151] 6.3.1876, IA, DC/HX 136–09.

[152] 5.7.1869, IA, DC/HX 136–08.

[153] 7.10.1844, IA, DC/HX 130–01. The disease may have been ringworm, or possibly scabies, caused by mites burrowing under the skin.

[154] *Star*, 26.2.1878. This bacterial infection, characterised by spots on the lining of the eyelids, was described by a historian of English workhouses as 'the trademark of workhouse children' (N. Longmate, *The Workhouse: A Social History* (London, 1974), p. 198).

[155] O. De B. Priaulx to St Peter Port *Douzaine*, 29.4.1859, IA, AQ 0966/01. Priaulx, who lived in London, may have been inspired by the Philanthropic Society's innovative Farm School, which opened at Redhill, Surrey in 1849; this was itself based on the boys' *colonie agricole* at Mettray in France (Fowler, *Workhouse*, p. 170).

Their chief objection was that £6,000 would stretch only to buying and stocking a farm, 'leaving its maintenance a permanent charge upon the ratepayers'.[156]

After the mid-1800s, Hospital children did experience some improvements to their lives, but most of these were financed by private charity and came at no cost to ratepayers. From the 1840s, children were allowed out to enjoy free treats provided by visiting entertainers, such as Mr Hay, who invited them to see his 'Panorama of the Afghan War' in 1843.[157] From the 1860s, well-wishers were permitted to bring in toys and other extras for the children at Christmas time.[158] From the 1870s, bene-factors were allowed to take the children out for tea, for picnics, for rides around the island and even for day-trips to Sark and Herm.[159] In the last decade of the century, the Hospital itself began to organise more activities for its children. In 1890, the House Committee decreed that youngsters could be taken out to bathe during the school holidays, and even provided them with 'bathing frocks'.[160] In 1897, it bought musical instruments and set up a band for the boys.[161]

To an extent, the late nineteenth-century easing of the children's regime mirrored a change in attitudes towards child workhouse inmates which had set in across the Channel three decades earlier. However, the change in English attitudes had long proceeded from mere easing to a complete reassessment of the desirability of keeping children in workhouses. As early as 1862, the Poor Law Commission had authorised guardians to transfer suitable children to non-poor law institutions at the expense of union funds.[162] In the 1890s, the Local Government Board decreed that no new workhouse should henceforth provide accommodation for children. In 1900, the Board issued a circular recommending the removal of all children from workhouses and, in 1913, it outlawed the keeping of any children over the age of 3 in institutions containing adults.[163]

From the 1890s, St Peter Port's Poor Law Board had tentatively experimented with sending some of its charges, at parish expense, to non-poor law institutions in England.[164] However, in all other respects, children remained an integral part of the Hospital population well into the twentieth century. Continuing laxity of supervi-sion, moreover, led to just the type of incident English legislation was intended to avoid. Hospital authorities did little when 56-year-old long-term inmate James Sarre indecently assaulted 8-year-old Bertie Minchinton in 1907, and their subsequent failure to institute safeguards facilitated a second assault by Sarre on little Bertram

[156] 5.11.1879, IA, AQ 940/02; *Star*, 6.11.1879.
[157] 13.7.1843, IA, DC/HX 130–01.
[158] 4.1.1867, IA, DC/HX 127–02.
[159] 30.6.1871, 1.7.1874, IA, DC/HX 059–01; 3.8.1876, IA, DC/HX 069–01.
[160] 28.7.1890, IA, DC/HX 136–02.
[161] 14.3.1897, 12.4.1897, IA, DC/HX 136–11.
[162] Crowther, *Workhouse System*, p. 70.
[163] Fowler, *Workhouse*, p. 172; Wood, *Poverty and the Workhouse*, pp. 176–7.
[164] In 1893, 14-year-old Nellie Allen was sent to a Salvation Army Home in London; in 1903, Frederick Taylor was sent to a Barnardo's Home; in 1906, Louisa Carter was sent to Dr Stephenson's Home in Birmingham (18.4.1893, IA, DC/HX 057–01; 15.6.1903, IA, DC/HX 127–02; 18.6.1906, IA, DC/HX 080–02).

Cleal a few years later. On the latter occasion, Sarre was convicted of sodomy and sentenced to three years in prison.[165]

In parallel with its change of policy towards workhouse children, the Westminster parliament had passed a series of much broader statutes designed to protect all children from ill-treatment, neglect and exploitation. These statutes, which included the 1872 and 1897 Infant Life Protection Acts and the 1889 Prevention of Cruelty to Children Act, were consolidated into the landmark 1908 Children Act, which, among other things, imposed penalties on parents who neglected or abused their children, and made poor law authorities responsible for dealing with victims of cruelty and neglect.[166] Somewhat belatedly, Guernsey's authorities followed this lead, and, in 1917, the Law on the Protection of Children and Young People was passed.[167] This law closely followed Westminster's 1908 Children Act, making modifications to suit local circumstances and incorporating additional provisions embodied in earlier British legislation, such as those relating to the employment of children. In St Peter Port, a sub-committee of the Poor Law Board was assigned to deal with cases of cruelty and neglect arising under the 1917 law.[168] In the law's first year of operation, as many as ten children were removed from their homes and placed under the care of the Board. This, almost inevitably, meant transfer to the Town Hospital and contributed to the wartime rise in children's admissions.[169]

A few years earlier, in 1906, the Town Hospital boys had finally joined the girls in the detached block, and this had been redesignated the 'Children's Home'.[170] At around this time, the Country Hospital had also erected its own 'Children's Home' adjacent to the King Edward VII hospital. In 1926, the States came into possession of both Children's Homes when they assumed ownership of the Hospitals. The Country Home occupied a salubrious situation in green fields far from the main workhouse, and, in order to rationalise provision for Guernsey's children, the States decided to convert it into an all-island facility to be run by themselves.[171] Accordingly, a law was passed in 1928 instituting a dedicated States' Children Board and allocating funds to extend the Country Hospital Home.[172] Works were completed within two years and, in December 1930, the Town Hospital's children finally left their old block for a new home in the country.[173]

The opening of the States' Children's Home removed all cared-for children from Hospital jurisdiction and was thus vaunted as obliterating the 'workhouse taint from child life'.[174] It did not, however, mark the severing of children's residential care from

[165] 19.7.1907, IA, DC/HX 080–01; 24.8.1914, IA, DC/HX 080–05; 26.9.1914, IA, DC/HX 254–04.
[166] For more on this statute, see Hendrick, *Child Welfare*, pp. 46, 53–5, 121–6.
[167] O in C, 24.1.1917.
[168] 7.5.1917, IA, DC/HX 052–01.
[169] See section on 'Patterns of occupation', Chapter 6.
[170] 2.2.1906, IA, DC/HX 080–02.
[171] *Billet*, 15.6.1927. In 1923, the States had accepted in principle that care of children should pass from the Hospital authorities to themselves (*Billet*, 21.3.1923).
[172] O in C, 24.11.1928; *Billet*, 12.9.1928.
[173] 31.12.1930, IA, DC/HX 253–03.
[174] *Billet*, 24.2.1928.

the poor law, for the Children Board established in 1928 was a sub-committee of the Central Poor Law Board and, from 1937, of the Public Assistance Authority. The connection was in fact broken only in 1970. In this year, the old Children Board was dissolved and replaced with an entirely freestanding non-poor law Children Board.[175] We might note that this development occurred more than two decades later than the same transition in England and Wales.[176]

Women

Until the last third of the nineteenth century, the Hospital's typical female inmates were women, of all ages, whose destitution was caused by a lack of male support. Many were spinsters or widows. There were also deserted wives, prisoners' wives, wives of sick or disabled men, wives of sailors away at sea, even wives of deportees. Because these are too numerous and too varied to analyse in any detail, we shall instead focus on a group which accounted for only a minority of women, but whose presence threw into relief many of the intrinsic disadvantages faced by females in the eighteenth and nineteenth centuries.

Younger female age-groups in the Hospital always contained a proportion of what Thomas Dicey described as 'lewd Women, incapable of subsisting honestly'.[177] As well as a sea-port, St Peter Port was also a garrison town. Sailors on shore leave and soldiers far from home created a ready market for prostitution, and the ubiquity of female poverty ensured that there were always women to supply it. The proportion of inmates comprised by 'lewd Women' in Dicey's time is unknown, but statistics kept on cause of admission between 1852 and 1924 recorded such women's admissions under the heading 'syphilis and prostitution'.[178] Over the seventy-three years for which statistics exist, adult female admissions in this category comprised about 14 per cent of total adult female admissions, with a peak of 19 per cent in the 1850s, reducing to about 9 per cent in the 1920s. In the 1850s, this represented an average of some fifteen admissions a year; in the 1920s, about six admissions a year.

Parochial authorities had from the beginning used the Town Hospital to examine, treat and confine prostitutes. Throughout the eighteenth and nineteenth centuries, Constables, or their assistants, would simply arrive at the gates with street girls, who, like 17-year-old Mary Green in 1833, would then be subjected to unspecified 'examinations'.[179] On occasion, several might be brought in at a time, as the six '*garces*' (sluts) admitted in July 1846.[180] No warrant was offered or sought for this. However, where forced confinement was the object, the Royal Court adopted the expedient from around 1810 of consigning street women to the care of the *Procureur des Pauvres*.[181] In 1897, the States attempted to put matters on a firmer footing by promulgating an Order in Council which empowered the Court to issue ordinances

---

[175] O in C, 30.9.1970.
[176] Hendrick, *Child Welfare*, p. 218.
[177] Dicey, *Historical Account*, p. 190.
[178] IA, DC/HX 060–02; IA, DC/HX 265–06; IA, DC/HX 272–02.
[179] 17.12.1833, IA, DC/HX 130–02.
[180] 23.7.1846, IA, DC/HX 130–01.
[181] See section on 'Policy and regime', Chapter 6.

mandating the examination and confinement of prostitutes.[182] Surprisingly, it was not until 1912 that the first such ordinance was passed.[183] The ordinance was largely irrelevant, however, since prostitutes continued both before and after its passage to be managed in much the same way as the past.

The treatment of street girls once inside the Hospital was harsh and punitive. Until at least the 1870s, many were compelled to wear '*l'habit de disgrâce*' – distinctive attire, which varied over time from the yellow bedgown and skirt worn by Anne Marquis in 1820 to Ann Hughes' dress of blue and yellow stripes in 1866.[184] From the early 1800s, prostitutes were segregated in a ward of their own, initially known as '*le dortoir de la Madeleine*' and later as the 'lock ward', where they were not allowed visitors.[185] In the 1830s and 1840s, this ward was located above a cesspit whose odour permeated the room. When, in 1844, Dr Marc Corbin complained to a Director about the stench, the Director retorted that this was 'quite good enough for such creatures'. This particular Director, as Corbin pointed out, had the reputation of having himself been an 'unbridled devil' in his youth.[186]

These young street women were among the Hospital's most challenging inmates. Resistance to staff was perhaps the only mode of self-affirmation open to them, since they were otherwise powerless and could be detained in the institution indefinitely.[187] They nevertheless paid a high price for their defiance. Mary Miller was rewarded with twenty days in the Hospital's cells when she struck the mistress in 1761.[188] When Jane Bell appeared in the girls' dormitory exhorting disobedience to staff in 1831, she was confined alone in an attic for a fortnight, and thereafter treated with unremitting severity.[189] A year on from this, a more significant female rebellion occurred, which seems to have at least partly prompted the building of the house of separation. Early in 1832, Treasurer John Mansell and his Board had refused 24-year-old Mary Ann Jones permission to 'visit her parents', fearing she might return pregnant. When Jones opportunistically attacked Mansell in a corridor, other women joined in. This led to the intervention of the master, Thomas Mauger, and the affair escalated, culminating in a physical and verbal assault on Mauger which produced a minor injury. Jones was taken before the Court and sentenced to a month in prison, and two of the other women received a fortnight in the Hospital

---

[182] O in C, 15.1.1897. See also Crossan, *Guernsey, 1814–1914*, pp. 136–7

[183] Ord, 6.1.1912. See also J. McLellan, 'The strange case of the Maladies Secrètes ordinance of 1912', *Jersey and Guernsey Law Review*, February 2013.

[184] 26.1.1820, IA, DC/HX 079–02; 5.1.1866, IA, DC/HX 136–07. Many English workhouses had a similar policy under the old poor law, but this was officially discouraged under the new regime set up in 1834 (Crowther, *Workhouse System*, p. 195).

[185] 11.12.1805, IA, DC/HX 079–02; 21.12.1822, IA, DC/HX 135–02; 9.4.1909, 26.4.1909, IA, DC/HX 129–02.

[186] The French phrase Corbin used was '*un vrai diable déchaîné*' (Corbin was retrospectively relating his experiences as medical officer in *Star*, 26.2.1878).

[187] Unlike in England and Wales, discharge was the sole prerogative of the Hospital authorities (Chapter 6, n. 79).

[188] 30.8.1761, IA, DC/HX 079–01.

[189] 7.3.1831, IA, DC/HX 135–03.

cells on bread and water. Later that year, Jones and one of her abettors were detailed to work as nurses on the cholera ward.[190]

Many of the Hospital's 'loose women' originally acquired their status not through active choice but through ignorance or exploitation. This seems to have been the case with 16-year-old servant girl Martha McCuddy, admitted pregnant in 1797, and 19-year-old Mary McCourt, who entered the Hospital in a similar predicament in 1833. Priror to her admission, Martha McCuddy had worked for a publican named Thompson. Her daughter, whom she named Anne Thompson, was born a few months later.[191] Mary McCourt explicitly attributed her state to John Irving, the son of her employer.[192]

Once known as 'fallen', it was very difficult for these girls to recover their reputation. As Frances Finnegan observed in her study of Victorian prostitution in York, such women typically found themselves shunned by the respectable and were condemned to live out their lives on the fringes of society, with deleterious effects on their health and well-being.[193] Many girls originally admitted to the Hospital after a 'fall' went on to develop ongoing relationships with the institution, entering regularly over the years to recover from the effects of destitution, disease, drink or casual violence.

From 1822, the Hospital took a more proactive role with some of these women. It began sending the younger, less hardened ones to 'female penitentiaries' outside the island.[194] These were private charitable institutions, modelled on a small rehabilitative house set up in London in 1806. Their purpose was to enable the 'fallen' to start afresh by providing them with religious instruction, basic education, domestic training and, eventually, respectable situations in places where their antecedents were unknown.[195] Southampton County Female Penitentiary was regularly used by the Town Hospital between the 1820s and 1860s.[196] The Jersey Female Penitentiary, which was founded in 1840 and later became known as the Channel Island Female Penitentiary, was also used from 1846.[197] As befitted its name, the Channel Island Penitentiary had its own Guernsey committee as well as a committee in Jersey.[198] Between 1855 and 1874, the Hospital intermittently paid the institution a subscription.[199] Later in the century, the Town Hospital also used institutions further afield, such as the London Diocesan Penitentiary in Highgate, where 16-year-old Maud

---

[190] 11.1.1832, 12.1.1832, 22.10.1832, IA, DC/HX 135–03.

[191] 28.8.1797, 5.9.1797, 10.1.1798, IA, DC/HX 079–01.

[192] 9.12.1833, IA, DC/HX 130–02.

[193] F. Finnegan, *Poverty and Prostitution: A Study of Victorian Prostitutes in York* (Cambridge, 1979), pp. 116, 124, 144, 166.

[194] 1822 accounts in IA, DC/HX 045–01.

[195] S. Mumm, '"Not worse than other girls": the convent-based rehabilitation of fallen women in Victorian Britain', *Journal of Social History*, 29 (1996), pp. 527, 533–4.

[196] For more on this institution, see J.S. Davies, *A History of Southampton* (London, 1883), p. 311.

[197] 22.9.1846, IA, DC/HX 130–01.

[198] For an account of this institution, see *Star*, 12.3.1878.

[199] 5.2.1855, IA, DC/HX 054–05; 2.2.1874, IA, DC/HX 054–06. In 1863, the Hospital also made a contribution to the 'Jersey Refuge for Fallen Women', about which less is known (9.2.1863, IA, DC/HX 054–05).

Clabby was sent in 1880.[200] By the early twentieth century, a branch of the 'Rescue and Preventive Work Society' had been established in Guernsey, and girls were channelled through the Hospital to the Society's Homes in England.[201]

For each 'fallen woman' who started afresh, however, many others simply grew old and infirm in St Peter Port, drifting in and out of the Hospital and eventually ending their days in the institution. Charlotte Backhouse, Jane Bell and Kitty Beer were all in this category.[202] Each ultimately died in the Hospital after long associations with it: Charlotte in 1834, Jane in 1867 and Kitty in 1870.[203] Kitty's entrances and exits had spanned more than half a century. The workhouse officer who recorded her death in the winter of 1870 deplored what he saw as her wasted existence. If there were any mitigating circumstances, he could not see them. Her life had followed its unenviable course – emphatically – 'all because of misconduct!!!!'[204] A century-and-a-half of distance allows us to see Kitty in a different light. If such a fate such Kitty's was the inevitable outcome of sexual misconduct, why, then, had Poor Law Board President De Vic Tupper escaped unscathed from his own transgression against social mores?[205] From a modern perspective, Kitty's life course seems less a function of her lack of moral fibre than of the unequal power relationships which governed her world.

Men

When cause of admission statistics began to be kept in the 1850s, 'illness and accident' accounted for the largest proportion of the adult male intake at 44 per cent of all admissions.[206] The other three categories to which men's admissions could be assigned were 'intemperance and misconduct', 'poverty and infirmity' and 'syphilis'.[207] The category which accounted for fewest admissions was syphilis, with a steady average of only two male cases a year in the seventy-three years for which statistics exist. This represented less than 1 per cent of men's admissions over the entire period. 'Poverty and infirmity', a category reserved largely for elderly men, accounted for a small but fairly constant share of the adult male intake: 11 per cent in 1852–9, rising to 13 per cent in 1910–19. The only category whose share of admissions actually declined over the seventy-three years was 'intemperance and misconduct'. In the 1850s, at 43 per cent of men's admissions, it accounted for nearly the same proportion as 'illness and accident'. By 1910–19, however, it accounted for only 9 per cent of the adult male intake, with 78 per cent of men now

---

[200] 4.5.1880, IA, DC/HX 069–01.
[201] 26.1.1914, IA, DC/HX 080–05. For a time after World War II, a body known as the 'Moral Welfare Association' also ran its own girls' hostel in Guernsey (18.2.1948, IA, AS/MB 065–02).
[202] Charlotte's surname was also rendered as Backus, Baccus or Bacchus. Kitty's real forename was Gertrude, under which she sometimes appeared in registers. Her surname was also spelt Bear or Beare.
[203] 13.11.1834, IA, DC/HX 130–02; 7.1.1867, 30.11.1870, IA, DC/HX 127–01.
[204] 30.11.1870, IA, DC/HX 127–01. The exclamation marks are in the register.
[205] See maintenance agreement in respect of De Vic Tupper's illegitimate child with Elizabeth Thorn in Plaids de Meubles, 1863, Greffe.
[206] IA, DC/HX 272–02. See also Appendix 5.
[207] IA, DC/HX 060–02; IA, DC/HX 265–06; IA, DC/HX 272–02.

entering on medical grounds. The turning point came in the last two decades of the nineteenth century, with a steep drop in the proportion of admissions attributed to 'intemperance and misconduct' from 35 per cent in the 1870s to 18 per cent in the 1880s, after which the decline continued at an accelerating rate. This category is particularly significant, in that it was the category to which able-bodied men of working age were primarily assigned. As such, it merits closer scrutiny.

Outside periods of extreme distress, few healthy working-age men were admitted to the Hospital simply on grounds of unemployment. If considered 'deserving', such men were normally provided with short-term outdoor relief rather than maintained in the Hospital. If the choice was made to admit an able-bodied man rather than give him outdoor relief, it was a sign that he was viewed as 'undeserving', and that there were reasons why his difficulties might be deemed his own doing. It is this, essentially, that caused the attribution of so many male admissions to 'misconduct'. We shall examine some of the principal groups to whom this characterisation was applied.

Throughout the eighteenth and nineteenth centuries, the Hospital contained a small core of youthful louts, often brought in by the Constables because of their heavy drinking and disorderly behaviour. These caused more trouble than most other inmates and loomed large in the records. Such prominence gives a misleading impression of their actual numbers. They were at their most numerous between the 1820s and 1840s, when the Royal Court used the establishment in a quasi-penal fashion, but even then they probably amounted to less than 5 per cent of adult male inmates.[208] Many were merely passing through a turbulent phase in their late teens and early twenties. Typically, they were admitted and discharged repeatedly for a few years, disappearing once they had matured. Samuel Hospin (or Hopin), first admitted aged 21 in 1822 and associated with the Hospital for the next ten years, is a typical instance.[209]

Aside from these young reprobates, there were a larger number of slightly older males who, though ostensibly able-bodied, had some underlying problem which made it hard for them to hold down jobs. Something which was not widely recognised as an illness before the twentieth century was long-term alcohol addiction. The Town Hospital always had its complement of chronic alcoholics, who might be associated with the institution for as long as four or five decades. Isaac Le Lacheur, described in the records as 'a good mason but a drunkard', spent repeated spells in the Hospital throughout his adulthood, and eventually hanged himself in a Hospital cell at the age of 64.[210]

Other able-bodied regulars appear to have been mentally or emotionally disturbed. One such was Daniel Morris, whose abandonment by his mother and upbringing in the Hospital seem to have inspired him with a desire for revenge on both. Register

---

[208] See section on 'Policy and regime', Chapter 6.

[209] Hospin's colourful association with the Hospital has been described in A. Glendinning, *Eye on the Past in Guernsey* (Jersey, 1993), pp. 68–70.

[210] Directors appeared to feel some sympathy for Le Lacheur, whom they permitted a Christian burial notwithstanding his suicide, on the grounds that he had been 'out of his wits' (3.11.1823, IA, DC/HX 135–02).

entries concerning Morris span 1823 to 1855.[211] His violence and disruptiveness drove the Hospital authorities to various expulsive expedients: forced emigration to Nova Scotia, forced enlistment in the Royal Navy, consignment to prison and to English lunatic asylums. Each time, however, Morris returned to plague them again. Eventually he was transported to Australia for burglary, where he finished his troubled existence in the Swan River Colony in 1862, aged only 39.[212]

For other regulars, an unstated physical impairment was clearly the root cause of wider social problems. William Gore died in the Hospital in 1909 after a long series of entrances and exits beginning in 1885. Violent, unmanageable and usually jobless, he alternated spells on the street with spells in prison and spells in the house. The Hospital never cited this as a causative factor and did not admit him on grounds of illness, but, as incidental information in registers reveals, Gore was profoundly deaf.[213]

The late nineteenth-century fall in male admissions ascribed to 'misconduct' arose essentially because growth in the island's economy increased job opportunities even for society's most marginal. The effect of this development was that the relatively small intake for 'misconduct' in twentieth-century decades was more exclusively composed of men with serious social and psychological problems than the much larger intake in this category in the 1850s and 1860s.

After the Royal Court undertook to regulate the island's workhouses in 1901, St Peter Port's ratepayers called for the Town Hospital to be split into two institutions, one for the respectable, the other for 'homeless and destitute vagabonds, often habitual drunkards, morally degraded and vicious'.[214] Though unwilling to set up a separate institution, the Poor Law Board responded by introducing a new regime for 'drunkards and vagabonds' analogous to that in use with 'casuals' in English workhouses.[215] From July 1903, such people were not to be admitted to the body of the Town Hospital but offered a cell for the night, with a blanket which they had to wash the next morning and a loaf to see them through the day.[216] A 'Casuals Log' shows the new regime to have been well-used at first, with nine regulars making frequent stays in 1904. Usage soon tailed off, however, and by 1913 only ten 'casual' stays were logged in the whole year.[217] The reason for this was that, unlike English casuals, St Peter Port's 'vagrant' population was stationary, composed of homeless

211 The first and last are 1.12.1823, IA, DC/HX 135–02 and 19.11.1855, IA, DC/HX 130–04. Morris's history is recounted in detail in J.H. Lenfestey, 'Extracts from books of the Town Hospital regarding Daniel Morris', *The Review of the Guernsey Society*, 46 (1987), pp. 34–7, and Glendinning, *Eye on the Past in Guernsey*, pp. 70–5.
212 http://www.conviz.info; http://www.fremantleprison.com.au, accessed 23.1.2012.
213 24.3.1885, 10.8.1886, 5.1.1888, IA, DC/HX 130–03; 12.3.1888, IA, DC/HX 136–02; 24.2.1891, IA, DC/HX 057–01; 16.3.1891, IA, DC/HX 136–03; 19.5.1909, IA, DC/HX 129–02.
214 *Guernsey Evening Press*, 7.5.1903.
215 In England and Wales, 'casuals' (vagrants, tramps and similar itinerants) had had their own separate quarters and regime within the workhouse since the 1840s (Longmate, *The Workhouse*, p. 232; Crowther, *Workhouse System*, pp. 247–66).
216 6.7.1903, IA, DC/HX 056–04.
217 IA, DC/HX 180–13.

alcoholics and others with intractable problems. Having no other long-term shelter, they could not be excluded permanently and had perforce to be readmitted to the wards.

As time went on, alcoholics and down-and-outs (mostly male) came to make up nearly all of the 'house' population. Although, by the 1940s, they comprised no more than a fifth of the Town Hospital's inmates, their presence cast a shadow over the whole institution, which rendered residence there for non-house groups distasteful.[218] Among those who felt this distaste most keenly were the elderly, and the next section will look in detail at them.

The Elderly

Anyone who had not laid up a sufficient store for old age in the eighteenth and nineteenth centuries stood a fair chance of ending their lives in a workhouse. Thus, although the Town Hospital's elderly population was dominated by those who had always been poor, it also contained many who had known better days. Among these were retired Hospital staff and their relatives, such as ex-mistress Fanny Gray, and Judith Sleque, the widow of former master Thomas Mauger.[219] There were also retired sea captains, such as Edwin Lytton;[220] impoverished ex-schoolteachers, such as Miss de Jausserand;[221] and former white-collar workers, such as retired journalist J.G. Hamilton.[222] Even those who had held parochial office were not exempt: 70-year-old ex-*Douzenier* André Cohu, admitted 'in want' in 1860, was not the only former office-holder to enter the Hospital as an old man.[223]

Much more common, however, were old folk with long associations with the Hospital, such as Charlotte Backhouse, Kitty Beer and William Gore, mentioned earlier, who all ended lifetimes of poverty with spells as septuagenarian inmates. Many of those who had begun their lives as Hospital children also ended them in the institution, sometimes after absences of many decades. Sophie Stokes, first admitted as a baby in 1810, spent long years of marriage and widowhood outside the institution, but was ultimately readmitted, blind and infirm, in 1892.[224] Compilers of Hospital registers often noted the deaths of these elderly inmates alongside entries relating to them as children.

Registers give the impression that, in the Hospital's first decades, a permanent place in the house was more highly prized by the elderly than it came to be subsequently. Many old people applied for admission on their own account. In 1750,

---

[218] IA, DC/HX 051–01; IA, DC/HX 015–04; IA, AS/MB 065–05.

[219] 1.8.1849, IA, DC/HX 075–02; 7.9.1879, IA, DC/HX 059–01.

[220] 17.5.1909, IA, DC/HX 080–01.

[221] 11.4.1871, IA, DC/HX 136–08.

[222] James Hamilton, who did much of the Hospital's book-keeping in the first two decades of the twentieth century, appears to have belonged to the Hamilton family, involved in newspaper publishing in Guernsey since the early nineteenth century (25.7.1919, IA, DC/HX 249–02; Bennett, 'History of the French newspapers', pp. 26ff).

[223] 20.12.1860, IA, DC/HX 130–04.

[224] IA, DC/HX 053–01; IA, DC/HX 060–03.

Rachel Bazin had to apply twice before Directors eventually agreed to accept her.[225] By the nineteenth century, however, there is little doubt that the majority of elderly inmates entered reluctantly. Most were admitted at the instigation of the poor law authorities, often after having previously received outdoor relief. It also became increasingly common for elderly people to be admitted on doctor's orders, ill and enfeebled, at the very end of their days. The case of 83-year-old Elizabeth Guilbert, who died within five days of admission in 1876, was fairly typical.[226] In this, St Peter Port was part of a trend encompassing the wider British Isles. David Thomson has noted a marked increase in English workhouse death rates over the second half of the nineteenth century, and has concluded that a rising proportion of all aged persons were dying in the workhouse.[227] Town Hospital death rates also rose over this period (from an average of thirty-two per year in 1850–9 to forty-six per year in 1910–19), and the increasing frequency of cases like Mrs Guilbert's probably contributed to this phenomenon.[228]

In his article on residential care, David Thomson remarked that entry to a work-house in England and Wales was voluntary, in that the law did not allow anyone to be forcibly admitted or detained.[229] This was not the case in Guernsey, where public law was lacking and parochial authorities arrogated broad powers to themselves. An element of coercion is clearly discernible in many elderly admissions to the Town Hospital. In 1889, 70-year-old Susanne Ingrouille was brought in against her will by the Constables, who considered her to be neglecting herself.[230] In 1890, the Poor Law Board withdrew Mrs Hayes' pension in order to 'induce her' to accept admission.[231] Once admitted, inmates could not, of course, discharge themselves.

Unless they were fee-paying boarders, 'able-bodied' elderly inmates were expected to contribute to their keep through work, as all other inmates. An informal census of inmates taken in 1870 shows that twenty-seven out of the Hospital's seventy-two over-65s had regular jobs. Of the men, a 69-year-old and a 71-year-old cracked stone; a 66-year-old, a 75-year-old and an 85-year-old served as ward orderlies; and several other old men were employed in the coal store, porter's lodge, bakery and shoemaker's and tailor's shops. Of the women, a 70-year-old and an 80-year-old looked after infants in the Hospital nursery; a 67-year-old minded older children in the girls' department; and other old ladies knitted and sewed in the dayrooms.[232] In addition, elderly inmates might be sent to perform tasks outside the Hospital. In the 1860s, for instance, retired prostitute Kitty Beer was regularly despatched to lay out the corpses of deceased outdoor paupers.[233] In this, the Hospital was not only

[225] 13.5.1750, 28.12.1750, IA, DC/HX 079–01.
[226] 16.2.1876, IA, DC/HX 069–01.
[227] D. Thomson, 'Workhouse to nursing home: residential care of elderly people in England since 1840', *Aging and Society*, 3 (1983), pp. 62–3
[228] IA, DC/HX 060–02; IA, DC/HX 265–06; IA, DC/HX 272–02.
[229] Thomson, 'Workhouse to nursing home', p. 44.
[230] 8.6.1889, IA, DC/HX 130–03.
[231] 1.4.1890, IA, DC/HX 054–07.
[232] 24.8.1870, IA, DC/HX 179–06.
[233] 28.4.1868, IA, DC/HX 136–07.

making best use of available assets, but also acting in accordance with the principle that care did not come free. Work, however, had a therapeutic value for many elderly inmates, who seemed to cherish their roles. In 1915, 72-year-old Annie Ozard had to be positively dissuaded from rising at 5.00 a.m. every day to begin her work in the Hospital.[234] When 77-year-old James Hamilton was told in 1919 that he could no longer do the institution's book-keeping, he was devastated.[235] As Anne Crowther has commented, 'in nearly every workhouse could be found aged inmates who worked without compulsion: to act as nurse, wardsman, night porter, or even voluntary cleaner, was to salvage a fragment of identity and self-respect'.[236]

By and large, the elderly were the least troublesome of inmates. Some of them developed affectionate relationships with staff, to the extent that, when they died, register entries reporting their demise expressed a sad respect. When 78-year-old Jane Kennedy died in the winter of 1826, a register reflected that she had been 'one of the best paupers in this establishment'.[237] When 98-year-old Nanon Le Page died just months after her 92-year-old husband Pierre in 1830, the register noted that they had been a conscientious hard-working couple, happily married for sixty-three years, whom infirmity had forced into the Hospital in the last years of their lives.[238]

There is no indication that the Town Hospital ever provided separate rooms for elderly married couples, as workhouses in England and Wales were officially authorised to do from 1847.[239] However, the elderly were given preferential treatment in many other ways, particularly if they were infirm. Spectacles were from time to time bought for those who could not see to read.[240] From the Hospital's opening until 1853, old folk were permitted to smoke in the grounds (though not inside).[241] These elderly smokers included women, such as 74-year-old Barbary Cook, who regularly had small amounts of tobacco bought for her in 1814 and 1815.[242] When, in the late eighteenth century, it became acceptable for inmates to drink tea, the old and infirm were allowed extra rations.[243] Formal treats for elderly inmates seem to have begun somewhat later than for children, but by the 1880s they were regularly being taken out for picnics and excursions, as well as receiving small gifts at Christmas time.[244] In the late 1880s and early 1890s, one old lady, Elizabeth Luscombe, was even allowed an annual 'holiday' in a local nursing home, her fees paid by a private benefactor.[245]

Despite these concessions, accommodating old folk alongside boisterous youngsters was often far from congenial. In 1831, an 89-year-old was told he must desist from leading elderly inmates in prayer in the refectory when two youths caused

[234] 29.12.1915, IA, DC/HX 080–05.
[235] 25.7.1919, IA, DC/HX 249–02.
[236] Crowther, *Workhouse System*, p. 201.
[237] 31.1.1826, IA, DC/HX 135–02.
[238] 31.3.1830, IA, DC/HX 135–03.
[239] Longmate, *The Workhouse*, pp. 143–4.
[240] 16.2.1792, IA, DC/HX 121–01; 14.2.1831, IA, DC/HX 135–03.
[241] IA, DC/HX 117–01.
[242] 30.7.1814, 29.5.1815, IA, DC/HX 123–01.
[243] 7.5.1787, IA, DC/HX 079–01.
[244] 2.9.1880, IA, DC/HX 069–01; 29.12.1885, IA, DC/HX 130–03.
[245] 26.9.1887, IA, DC/HX 136–01; 6.8.1890, 17.8.1891, IA, DC/HX 057–01.

uproar by throwing acorns across the room and indecently parodying a psalm.[246] In 1868, a group of boys were punished with twenty-four hours' confinement for 'continually annoying the old men in the dayroom'.[247]

With the children removed to their new States' Children's Home in 1930, this source of friction was eliminated. Nevertheless, it was not until the late 1960s that the institution became exclusively a geriatric hospital, and this final phase of its existence lasted barely two decades. The position of elderly inmates in the Town Hospital after World War II will be examined at the end of Chapter 9.

Strangers

Guernsey's stringent settlement laws made the achievement of settled status difficult for the majority of strangers and, without settled status, there was no claim to poor relief and hence no claim to a place in the Hospital.[248] For all that, the Town Hospital was seldom entirely devoid of non-locals, who, for most of its history, were admitted as a matter of discretion rather than of right.

Between 1743 and 1755, stranger inmates amounted to no more than a handful. Some, such as Mme Esther Chaboiseau and her daughter, admitted in 1750, are likely to have been Huguenot refugees.[249] The stranger intake increased after 1755, when ratepayers resolved that distressed dependants of garrison members should be relieved indoors until repatriated.[250] By 1767, there were some thirty-seven soldier's wives and children among a year-end population of 150, which equated to about a quarter of inmates.[251] This elicited a complaint from St Peter Port's poor law authorities, prompting the Royal Court to issue the first of a series of orders dividing soldiers' dependants between Town and Country Hospitals.[252] From this point onwards, the number of strangers in the Hospital declined. Once mass civilian immigration set in at the end of the Napoleonic Wars, however, the Hospital's stranger population climbed again, and censuses between 1841 and 1911 once more show a non-native proportion of around one-quarter, equating to fifty or so stranger inmates at each census.[253]

Technically, no non-settled inmate could be funded direct from the Hospital budget, as this was derived from the parochial poor rate, which did not cover the non-settled. In 1788, the States undertook to reimburse costs incurred in respect of garrison dependants, and, from time to time thereafter, the Hospital invoiced them for these costs.[254] Civilian strangers were the responsibility of the Constables and

---

[246] 21.11.1831, IA, DC/HX 135–03.

[247] 9.11.1868, IA, DC/HX 136–08.

[248] See section on 'Settlement and deportation legislation', Chapter 4.

[249] 23.9.1750, IA, DC/HX 079–01.

[250] 22.7.1755, St Peter Port Délibérations des Chefs de Famille, 1715–79, PL.

[251] 1.1.1767, IA, DC/HX 165–01.

[252] 7.3.1767, IA, DC/HX 180–14.

[253] 1841–1901 enumerators' books (microfilm), PL; http://www.1911census.co.uk.

[254] *Acte*, 19.4.1788. For accounts issued in respect of States-funded strangers (which later also included Chelsea and Greenwich pensioners and shipwrecked mariners), see IA, DC/HX 013–01; IA, DC/HX 013–02.

funded from the Constables' tax (chiefly used for street cleaning and lighting) so that Constables, too, were separately billed for strangers admitted at their request.[255] A few non-natives entered as boarders and paid their own fees, and a further few had their stays funded remotely by their parishes of settlement.[256] In addition to these, a very small number of strangers (no more than half a dozen at any one time) were admitted 'as natives' under a scheme formalised in 1810.[257] Under this arrangement, Constables could apply to the *Douzaine* for permission to remove particularly 'deserving' strangers from their outdoor list and have them enter the Hospital long-term, from which point they would be funded from the institution's own budget.[258] Typical of these were the 78-year-old Cornishman John Symons and his 74-year-old wife Ann, admitted as permanent inmates in 1831 after more than fifty years' residence in St Peter Port.[259]

By far the majority of strangers in the Hospital were not long-term inmates, however, but merely passing through. A small number were in for short-term medical treatment, but most (in the eighteenth century) were garrison dependants awaiting repatriation or (in the nineteenth century) civilian strangers earmarked for deportation.[260] Given that this was the ultimate fate of perhaps three-quarters of the strangers who sojourned in the Hospital, the remainder of this section will be devoted to an examination of the conditions under which deportations from the institution took place. The cases which follow are typical of nineteenth-century deportations from the Town Hospital. None of them were illegal in Guernsey (because the modalities of deportation were not defined in any law), but many would not have been permitted in England.

In England and Wales, the sick were precluded by law from being removed.[261] Guernsey law was silent on such matters, and people were often deported from the island in questionable mental or physical states. Ann Williams was in the last stages of pregnancy when put on the boat to Plymouth in February 1841 and ultimately suffered a stillbirth.[262] In 1852, 33-year-old Sarah Ellis was despatched to Torquay just three days after attempting suicide.[263] In 1871, 54-year-old John Brennan was shipped to Alderney in the terminal stage of an illness and died the day after arrival.[264]

Couples and families were often parted by selective deportation. The removals

[255] IA, DC/HX 013–01; IA, DC/HX 013–02.
[256] Such as Jane Johns, for whom Megavissey were paying 2s weekly in 1832 (6.8.1832, IA, DC/HX 135–03).
[257] 7.5.1810, IA, DC/HX 079–02.
[258] This practice was continued under the new St Peter Port Poor Law Board from 1853, with permission now required from the Board rather than the *Douzaine* (January 1853, IA, DC/HX 054–05).
[259] 4.7.1831, IA, DC/HX 135–03.
[260] For more on Guernsey's deportation policy, see section on 'Settlement and deportation legislation', Chapter 4.
[261] Hodgkinson, *National Health Service*, p. 19.
[262] 23.2.1841, 25.2.1841, IA, DC/HX 075–01.
[263] 10.7.1852, IA, DC/HX 075–02.
[264] 15.4.1871, IA, DC/HX 059–01; *Star*, 22.4.1871.

of Samuel Roberts and his wife Elizabeth in the 1870s took place at an interval of more than six years.[265] In 1890, Guernsey-born Emma Goubert was despatched to her father's parish in Normandy after becoming pregnant at the age of 17, while the rest of her family remained in the island.[266]

Children in general could be deported at any age and in any circumstances. Margaret Stevens (15) and Jane Hutton (14) were expelled from the island alone after being admitted to the Hospital as suspected prostitutes in 1825 and 1830 respectively (the former was pregnant).[267] Six-year-old Louisa Dillon was also ostensibly alone when she was sent from the Hospital to Jersey in 1848.[268] Necessity, however, dictated that the orphaned baby despatched to its father's parish in Berkshire in 1868 was carried by an attendant.[269]

Neither was extreme old age a bar to deportation. In the summer of 1853, 87-year-old Guernseywoman Marthe Lenfestey (widow Griffin) was sent to the Town Hospital from St Helier, where she had lived for many years. Because she had been married to an Englishman, the Hospital kept her only two days, the Constables having arranged for her to be shipped out on the next boat to Lyme.[270] When 89-year-old Anne Harris (widow Couch) was admitted 'in her second childhood' in the spring of 1855, her arrival coincided with the despatch of an emigrant party travelling via Plymouth. Without further ado, the 89-year-old was sent off on the boat with them, again because her husband had been English.[271]

On many occasions, it was clear that strangers were held in the Hospital against their will for no other reason than to give Constables time to arrange a desired departure. In February 1863, 48-year-old Henry Crang's urgent request for discharge was refused because 'measures were in hand' to deport him, and he was duly confined until he could be despatched to Plymouth.[272] In 1881, following the death of her Nottinghamshire husband, Minnie Smith (née Rouget), a Guernseywoman, was admitted to the Hospital with her son pending deportation to her late husband's parish. While in the Hospital, she received an offer of marriage from St Peter Port resident John Harland, which would have allowed her to stay in her native island. The House Committee, however, refused to allow Mrs Smith out of the Hospital to marry, and kept her and her child in detention until the Constables were able to deport them as per their original plan.[273]

Disputes over settlement (especially with Jersey and France, where the law in this area was undeveloped) sometimes led to protracted bouts of back-and-forth shuttling which deportees must have found exhausting. Between 1849 and 1852, 24-year-old Louisa Bucknell (née Carr) and her children were sent from Jersey

[265] 12.1.1871, 14.1.1877, IA, DC/HX 059–01.
[266] 19.11.1890, 4.2.1891, 8.9.1891, IA, DC/HX 057–01.
[267] 27.6.1825, IA, DC/HX 082–01; 13.12.1829, 4.1.1830, IA, DC/HX 135–03.
[268] 1.9.1848, IA, DC/HX 130–01.
[269] 8.12.1868, IA, DC/HX 127–01.
[270] 27.6.1853, 29.6.1853, IA, DC/HX 130–04.
[271] 13.4.1855, IA, DC/HX 130–04.
[272] 11.2.1863, 31.3.1863, IA, DC/HX 136–07.
[273] 26.9.1881, 17.10.1881, IA, DC/HX 136–10; 7.11.1881, IA, DC/HX 069–01.

to Guernsey three times and returned twice from Guernsey to Jersey.[274] In 1863, 48-year-old Mary Peadon (née Hawkins) was sent from Jersey to Guernsey, returned from Guernsey to Jersey, returned again from Jersey to Guernsey and was finally despatched from Guernsey to Somerset.[275] Between November 1892 and October 1896, 58-year-old Victor Petit was sent once from Jersey to Guernsey, twice from Guernsey to France, twice from France back to Guernsey and twice from Guernsey to Jersey – all without any court involvement.[276] To modern observers, such treatment of the vulnerable would seem a gross infringement of human rights. However, Guernsey law vouchsafed few rights to paupers, and those taken into parochial charge effectively forfeited their autonomy.

The extent of public concern regarding pauper deportation in nineteenth-century Guernsey is unclear. Now and again, charitable individuals would support potential deportees to preserve them from the parish, as the ladies who maintained elderly Irish shopkeeper Hugh McCoubrey in the early 1900s.[277] Public subscriptions were also occasionally raised to forestall impending deportations, such as the fund organised by the Reverend Clark on behalf of the widowed Mrs Marsh and her seven children in 1903.[278] There is nevertheless little evidence of active opposition to the deportation regime, save on the part of two outspoken individuals: Anthony de Saint-Dalmas and Thomas Brock. Saint-Dalmas, born in 1810, was a businessman who served as a St Peter Port Overseer and treasurer of the Guernsey committee of the Channel Island Female Penitentiary.[279] His father Henry, a prominent evangelical Anglican, had been an active visitor and champion of Town Hospital inmates.[280] His aunt Frances had been a fee-paying patient in the Hospital's lunatic asylum.[281] Thomas Brock, born in 1816, was the long-serving vicar of St John's Anglican church, in a working-class district of St Peter Port. He was active in social philanthropy and helped set up the Girls' Industrial School.[282] In the 1860s, Saint-Dalmas contested the deportation of two old ladies in the Royal Court, and he supported one of them from his own pocket for years when his suit proved unsuccessful.[283] Saint-Dalmas vigorously pressed for the repeal of Guernsey's summary expulsion

[274] 6.12.1849, 27.12.1849, 27.3.1850, 6.3.1851, 2.4.1852, IA, DC/HX 075–02.

[275] Although Mrs Peadon was born in Guernsey, her deceased husband had been settled in Chard (17.8.1863, IA, DC/HX 136–07).

[276] Petit, whose parents were French, was born in St Peter Port, but had moved to Jersey in his childhood. He would not have had a settlement in Jersey, since this was determined by birth alone. Neither would he have had a settlement in Guernsey, since, under the law of 1867, strangers' children could only earn this through twenty years' unbroken residence (11.11.1892, 29.11.1892, 2.12.1892, 6.12.1892, 27.10.1893, 2.1.1894, 8.10.1896, 13.10.1896, IA, DC/HX 057–01).

[277] 16.1.1906, IA, DC/HX 249–01.

[278] *Star*, 12.5.1903.

[279] 1860 accounts, IA, DC/HX 272–02; *Star*, 12.3.1878; A.H. Ewen, 'A Guernsey family from Piedmont', *Quarterly Review of the Guernsey Society*, 21 (1965), pp. 51–4.

[280] 21.5.1832, IA, DC/HX 135–03.

[281] 3.7.1857, IA, DC/HX 130–04.

[282] *Star*, 19.2.1870.

[283] *Star*, 9.9.1865, 23.12.1865; 11.9.1871, IA, DC/HX 059–01.

laws, which he deemed to 'disgrace our statute-books', and he was outspokenly critical of the Poor Law Board's 'sad desire … to grind the poor'.[284] Thomas Brock, an assiduous correspondent to the press, used this forum to air misgivings over deportation. In particular, he lodged a forthright protest against John Brennan's 1871 removal to Alderney, which he publicly indicted as an 'act of cruelty'.[285] The protests of Brock and Saint-Dalmas were, however, unsupported by any strong wish for change among the general public, and they ultimately achieved nothing.

Deportations from the Hospital continued relatively unabated throughout the late nineteenth and early twentieth centuries. They then diminished as immigration to Guernsey tailed off after World War I. Following developments in the new field of social security after World War II, poor law deportations became rare. Nevertheless, the Town Hospital continued until the 1960s to be used as short-term shelter for foreigners in transit. A case in point is that of the fifty Turkish sailors briefly accommodated when their vessel, the 'Edirne', was wrecked off Guernsey in February 1950.[286] With this innocuous survival from a darker past we conclude our survey of individuals whose lives were marked – more often negatively than positively – by their passage through St Peter Port's workhouse. The following chapter, the last on the Town Hospital, will focus in detail on the substance of their experience as inmates.

---

[284] *Star*, 7.9.1865, 8.2.1866.
[285] *Star*, 22.4.1871.
[286] 22.2.1950, IA, AS/MB 065–02.

9

Daily Life

Town Hospital registers are rich in the sort of domestic detail not often found in historical documents. Copious evidence is preserved on the minutiae of everyday life, from the beds inmates slept in and the clothing they wore to the food they ate and the punishments they suffered. This chapter will examine such minutiae in depth. The intention is a dual one: to recover something of the lived experience of past human beings, and to illuminate the norms of the society to which they belonged.

Routines and rhythms

From the outset, regimentation was key to Hospital life. The passage of the day was marked by the ringing of a bell. It rang out the hours of rising and retiring, of beginning and ending work and of the three daily meals. Under the rules of 1743, the summer timetable was as follows:

6.00 a.m. – rise
6.30 a.m. – breakfast
7.00 a.m. – begin work
1.00 p.m. – break for dinner
7.00 p.m. – finish work/assemble for supper
9.00 p.m. – retire.[1]

Subsequent rules introduced minor variations, but a similar timetable obtained as late as World War I.[2] Prayers preceded breakfast and followed supper every day. From 1743 until the end of the nineteenth century, inmates were locked into their dormitories at night.[3]

For most of their waking hours, inmates were bound by Hospital rules to do any

---

[1] In winter, inmates rose an hour later and retired an hour earlier. Sunday was a day of rest (*Règlements pour la Maison des Pauvres*, Vol. III, Watkins MS, LL 940 WAT, PL).

[2] For later timetables, see Hospital rules in 20.8.1817 and 6.10.1817, IA, DC/HX 079–02; 21.2.1853, IA, DC/HX 054–05; IA, DC/HX 272–04. These rules are the source of all other information in this section without specific attribution.

[3] This was a practice banned in English workhouses from the 1830s (D.R. Green, 'Pauper

work deemed suitable to their age, sex and physical condition.[4] In the 1700s and early 1800s, inmates of both sexes and all ages worked in the Hospital's manufacturing enterprises as well as performing all the chores of the house. By the mid-1800s, most formal manufacturing had been discontinued, but a census of inmates dating from August 1870 shows that more than two-thirds of the Hospital's inmates still had a regular domestic occupation: as cooks, laundresses, nurses, store-keepers, porters, messengers and much else.[5]

Aside from their work indoors, inmates were also used to perform *ad hoc* tasks around the parish. For a few years the Hospital supplied St Peter Port with its town crier.[6] Gangs of Hospital men and boys were regularly sent out to clean St Peter Port's streets, cemeteries and parks, sometimes in a distinctive 'striped frock'.[7] Inmates staffed the public soup kitchen, occasionally helped the fire brigade and even distributed *Billets d'Etat* in advance of States meetings.[8] They were rewarded for their pains by small 'gratuities' in the form of alcohol, tobacco (when permitted) or pocket money.

For those inmates whose conduct was considered satisfactory, the monotony of the daily grind might be punctuated by visitors from outside or leave of absence from the institution. In the 1820s, visits were allowed on two afternoons weekly. In addition to this, the well-behaved were entitled to one Sunday afternoon outside the Hospital per month, plus a few hours' discretionary liberty on high days and holidays.[9]

Within the institution itself, there was at first little provision for leisure. Such free time as inmates had was spent chatting to their fellows, or, at best, smoking a pipe in the grounds. By 1810, however, a 'library' had been installed for inmates in the Hospital parlour, and in 1817 a new set of rules allowed inmates to engage in any 'innocent exercise which might be useful to their health'.[10] By the 1830s, periodicals such as *The Instructor* and *The Weekly Visitor* were being purchased for inmates' use.[11]

As the numbers of infirmary patients rose, more thought was given to activities which might enhance their lot and, by the 1860s, such things as garden chairs and board games were acquired specifically for them.[12] Two decades on, with the sick and infirm in an outright majority, there was a general relaxation of the Hospital

protests: power and resistance in early nineteenth-century London workhouses', *Social History*, 31 (2006), p. 153).

4   The first regulations on work date from 1742 and are set out in IA, DC/HX 079–01; the last date from 1939 and are to be found in IA, DC/HX 272–13.

5   24.8.1870, IA, DC/HX 179–06.

6   In 1831, the Hospital took in nearly £19 for this service (IA, DC/HX 178–01).

7   For street-cleaning, see 30.7.1832, IA, DC/HX 135–03; for cemeteries, see 9.8.1886, IA, DC/HX 054–06; for parks, 22.4.1907, IA, DC/HX 080–01; for striped frocks, 2.4.1867, IA, DC/HX 136–07.

8   27.2.1867, IA, DC/HX 136–07; 24.9.1887, IA, DC/HX 136–01; 8.12.1902, IA, DC/HX 080–03.

9   5.1.1824, IA, DC/HX 135–02. See also 28.3.1853, IA, DC/HX 136–02.

10   24.1.1810, 6.10.1817, IA, DC/HX 079–02.

11   10.9.1838, IA, DC/HX 075–01.

12   29.4.1867, 22.7.1867, IA, DC/HX 136–07.

regime, with all inmates enjoying such occasional entertainments as the German band which was allowed to perform in the yard in the mid-1880s or the play staged in the Hospital by an amateur dramatic society in the same decade.[13] The early 1900s saw further improvements to amenities in the form of a piano and a gramophone bought for inmates' entertainment.[14] Smoking (banned from 1853) was once more permitted from 1903.[15] These changes did not, however, alter the underlying ethos of the institution – at least as far as the workhouse department was concerned – and, even in 1914, all house people who could work remained obliged to do so, and lights-out was strictly at 9.00 p.m.[16]

Living conditions

In the eighteenth century, inmates too ill or too old to work remained in their dormitories day and night. Dayrooms for the sick and infirm were not introduced until 1809.[17] For most of the Hospital's history, all dormitories, wards and dayrooms had bare stone or wooden floors and whitewashed walls, on which religious texts were sometimes hung. There is no indication of any alternative décor until 1901, when it was decided to paint the women's wards a 'light terracotta' and lay cork matting on the floors.[18]

Originally, some of the Hospital's inmates were accommodated in garrets over the main building. Until 1809, these garret dormitories had no ceilings and were exposed to heat, cold, damp and draughts coming through the roof slates.[19] In 1847, the garrets were described as having been 'for too long the disgrace of this institution'. The building was reroofed and the garrets transformed into proper rooms.[20]

To begin with, although the sexes slept separately, different categories of inmates were indiscriminately mixed in the same dormitories, where bed-sharing was the norm. The first move towards separation came in 1755, when the children were given their own quarters.[21] In 1805, 'bad' inmates were segregated from 'good', and, in 1810, the girls were moved into a detached building walled off from the main premises.[22] In 1817, the Hospital's sick were transferred into their own purpose-built extension.[23] Finally, in 1822, the entire inmate cohort was divided into six

---

[13] 3.9.1885, IA, DC/HX 130–03; 7.6.1886, IA, DC/HX 136–01.
[14] 2.10.1905, IA, DC/HX 056–04; 25.12.1905, IA, DC/HX 129–02.
[15] 21.2.1853, IA, DC/HX 054–05; 16.10.1903, IA, DC/HX 080–03.
[16] IA, DC/HX 272–04.
[17] 24.1.1810, IA, DC/HX 079–02.
[18] 5.18.1901, 11.12.1901, IA, DC/HX 136–05.
[19] T. Quayle, *A General View of the Agriculture and Present State of the Islands on the Coast of Normandy subject to the Crown of Great Britain* (London, 1815), p. 294.
[20] 27.10.1847, IA, DC/HX 130–01.
[21] 7.9.1755, IA, DC/HX 079–02.
[22] 11.12.1805, 7.1.1811, IA, DC/HX 079–02.
[23] 15.7.1817, St Peter Port Délibérations des Chefs de Famille, 1780–1817, PL.

'classes' and allocated separate quarters accordingly.[24]

By the early nineteenth century, the Hospital's sixty-year-old wooden bedsteads had become 'rotten and full of dirt and vermin' and were replaced with iron bedsteads.[25] Straw-filled mattresses were laid on sacking stretched across the bedframes, and inmates slept on these between coarse linen sheets, covered with blankets and rugs. A cheap seaweed stuffing sourced from France replaced straw in mattresses in 1855, and iron slats replaced sacking bases in 1878.[26] In 1904, it was resolved gradually to phase out seaweed mattresses and replace them with modern sprung mattresses, but the Hospital was still purchasing seaweed as late as 1924.[27]

The purchase of new bedsteads in 1809 did not eliminate the practice of bed-sharing. An inventory of Hospital fixtures made two years later reveals that there were only 132 bedsteads for 218 inmates.[28] Indeed, a decision to give each boy his own bed in 1904 indicates that bed-sharing, at least among children, persisted into the twentieth century.[29] In English and Welsh workhouses, bed-sharing by any inmates over the age of seven was prohibited from the 1840s.[30]

For the Hospital's first century and a half, inmates' quarters were lit only by rush lights, candles and oil lamps. In 1831, Hospital Directors rejected as too costly an offer by the Guernsey Gas Company to install gas lighting, and the Hospital's lighting was not fully converted to gas until 1883.[31] In 1922, gas lighting was replaced by electric lighting.[32]

Cast-iron stoves were installed in the new dayrooms introduced in 1809, but not all of the Hospital's dormitories appear to have been heated.[33] As late as 1959, there were complaints that the 'complete lack of heating' in the sleeping quarters of house people was causing illness.[34] Some of the wards used for the elderly still had open fires as late as 1968.[35] In 1980, it was observed that the Town Hospital had never had 'a proper heating system'.[36]

Drainage and water supply were for a long time extremely primitive. Before 1824, the Hospital's latrines were housed in outbuildings. These were essentially sheds containing benches with holes cut in them. Excreta fell into trenches cut into the soil under the benches. Liquid content seeped away, and the semi-solidified residues were periodically dug out – by inmates or, sometimes, by contractors – and

---

[24] 1.7.1822, IA, DC/HX 135–02.
[25] 7.6.1809, IA, DC/HX 079–02.
[26] 24.9.1855, IA, DC/HX 130–04; 11.3.1878, IA, DC/HX 136–09.
[27] 8.4.1904, IA, DC/HX 056–04; 11.4.1904, IA, DC/HX 080–02; IA, DC/HX 272–02.
[28] 31.12.1811, IA, DC/HX 122–01. See also IA, DC/HX 123–01.
[29] 24.9.1904, IA, DC/HX 080–02.
[30] J.F. Archbold (ed.), *The Consolidated and other Orders of the Poor Law Commissioners and of the Poor Law Board* (London, 1859), p. 75.
[31] 5.8.1831, IA, DC/HX 135–03; 9.10.1883, IA, DC/HX 062–03.
[32] 1.5.1922, IA, DC/HX 052–01. The lunatic asylum had benefited from electric lighting since 1916 (21.2.1916, IA, DC/HX 080–05).
[33] 7.1.1811, IA, DC/HX 079–02.
[34] 21.1.1959, IA, AS/MB 065–02.
[35] *Billet*, 27.11.1968.
[36] 14.11.1980, IA, BH 52–14.

either buried in the Hospital garden or removed from the premises.[37] Indoor privies of some sort were installed in the new wing of 1824, but their contents were allowed to accumulate in one or more cesspits close to, or under, the building. In 1831, as a precautionary measure against the impending cholera epidemic, Directors had a limited length of drain laid from the 1824 latrines to the sea.[38] Nevertheless, a portion of the Hospital's sewage continued to accumulate in pits, and when victims of the 1849 cholera were again received in the Hospital, it was thought that drinking water contaminated by these pits had infected otherwise healthy inmates.[39] This led to further improvements in drainage and the installation of indoor self-acting water closets in 1850.[40]

The Hospital's water supply originally came from a spring in the Hospital garden, later supplemented by a second spring located at Les Vauxlaurens.[41] To begin with, this water was stored in outdoor cisterns and had to be fetched in pails. In 1809, Directors installed a limited system of internal pipes and tanks.[42] This could not have been extensive, since, in 1845, a medical officer complained that male inmates were exposed to the 'inclemency of the weather' in having to wash out of doors.[43] Although indoor washing facilities were introduced at the same time as water closets in 1850, it was not until 1895 that the institution was finally connected to the town's piped water supply.[44]

These infrastructural deficiencies arose from ratepayers' reluctance to fund improvements. Staff laxity engendered further shortcomings. Aside from initially stipulating a weekly change of inmates' under-linen, eighteenth-century Hospital registers evinced little concern for hygiene.[45] By the early 1800s, decades of neglect had resulted in an institution characterised by 'filth, noise and disorder', and those who ousted Jean Condamine in 1809 lost no time in instituting new sub-committees to enforce 'Cleanliness and Salubrity' and 'Personal Cleanliness'.[46] Staff inertia, however, soon trumped the Board's resolutions, and any improvements these sub-committees might have achieved were short-lived. By the 1840s, ex-medical officer Marc Corbin described the Hospital as 'an Augean pig-stye', urging Directors to compel regular cleaning of 'wards, landing-places, staircases, windows, etc.', as they were 'excessively filthy' and allowed vermin to flourish.[47] While there is no evidence of a proactive response to Corbin's complaints, a further change of regime

---

[37] For instances of this operation, see 15.3.1755, IA, DC/HX 118–01; 8.4.1817, IA, DC/HX 079–02.

[38] 5.8.1831, 5.9.1831, DC/HX 135–03.

[39] S.E. Hoskins, 'The origin and progress of cholera and small-pox in Guernsey', *The London Medical Gazette*, 12 (1851), p. 384. See also 6.8.1849, IA, DC/HX 075–02.

[40] 9.1.1850, 27.2.1850, St Peter Port Délibérations des Chefs de Famille, 1844–66, PL; *Star*, 10.1.1850, 26.2.1850, 28.2.1850.

[41] 14.5.1779, IA, DC/HX 119–04.

[42] 24.1.1810, IA, DC/HX 079–02; Quayle, *General View*, p. 294.

[43] 6.1.1845, IA, DC/HX 130–01.

[44] 21.1.1895, IA, DC/HX 136–04.

[45] IA, DC/HX 117–01.

[46] Quayle, *General View*, p. 292; 7.2.1810, IA, DC/HX 079–02.

[47] 7.10.1844, 6.1.1845, IA, DC/HX 130–01. See also *Star*, 26.2.1878.

in 1853 led to new rules stipulating that dormitories were to be swept daily and scrubbed weekly, and that inmates were to be 'cleansed' on admission, their clothes disinfected in a 'steaming machine'.[48] Once more, staff indifference overcame good intentions and, by the 1870s, the house was again reported as infested with vermin, 'the genera Pulex, Cimex and Pediculus being all liberally represented'.[49] In response to such observations, the House Committee instituted an annual spring-clean which consisted of disinfection, fumigation, white-washing and painting.[50] Although the spring-clean became a regular fixture, extreme instances of ignorance and neglect persisted well into the twentieth century. In 1912, it emerged that the Hospital cook was in the habit of boiling her soiled underwear in a pan she used for inmates' vegetables.[51] In 1917, an inspection visit by the Medical Officer of Health revealed that a nurse had been sluicing the contents of her chamber pot down the operating theatre sink.[52] At the root of such laxity, for both management and staff, was a fundamentally relativistic attitude to the conditions experienced by paupers. As a pair of visiting Jurats asserted in 1904, middle-class standards simply did not apply, since 'practically all the inmates are of the pauper class, and … well-being and comfort are relative terms'.[53]

Eating and drinking

Food and drink were always the largest single item in the Town Hospital's budget. Accounts covering the period 1858 to 1924 show that they absorbed, on average, almost 50 per cent of the institution's annual expenditure.[54] From the beginning, the Hospital had a purpose-built refectory, where all food (save that served to the sick and infirm) was to be consumed under the supervision of one of the masters or mistresses. Early nineteenth-century rules indicate that no meal was to last longer than thirty minutes. Grace was to be said before and after every meal. Males and females sat on different sides of the refectory, and no talking was permitted before, during or after meals.[55]

In the eighteenth century, Hospital tableware consisted of wooden trenchers, earthenware bowls and mugs, and metal spoons and knives.[56] For breakfast and supper, inmates were served bread and butter. For dinner, the main meal of the day, they were usually served soup, also accompanied by bread.[57] Since bread was

48 21.2.1853, IA, DC/HX 054–05; 17.5.1853, 5.12.1853, IA, DC/HX 130–04.
49 1.3.1878, IA, DC/HX 281–25; *Star*, 19.2.1878.
50 19.5.1884, IA, DC/HX 136–01.
51 29.8.1912, IA, DC/HX 080–06
52 M.o.H. to House Committee, January 1917, IA, DC/HX 253–01.
53 G.E. Kinnersley and G.H. Le Mottée to Home Office, 24.5.1904, TNA, HO 45/16850. The Jurats, both doctors, were responding specifically to criticism of lunatics' quarters.
54 IA, DC/HX 272–02.
55 20.8.1817, 6.10.1817, IA, DC/HX 079–02.
56 IA, DC/HX 117–01.
57 T. Dicey, *An Historical Account of Guernsey* (London, 1751), p. 191.

the institution's single most important dietary item, the Hospital had a bakehouse in which it made its own supply.[58] The Hospital managed the entire bread-making process from grain to loaves. Raw wheat or barley, received in payment of *rentes* or purchased wholesale, was sent to be milled externally, with inmates used for transport and handling. Flour was returned in several grades, according to the type of grain used and the fineness of the milling. The best grades were made into loaves for staff and the sick, intermediate grades were used for inmates' breakfast- and supper-time bread, and the coarsest grades were kept to eat with soup.

Eighteenth-century inmates received between a third and a half pound of butter every week to eat with the bread served to them at breakfast and supper.[59] Cheese, which normally accompanied bread at these meals in English workhouses, was never served, as Guernsey had no tradition of cheese-making.[60] Inmates were not, however, given Guernsey butter, but, from at least the 1760s, cheap salted butter imported from France.[61] The local variety, which sold at a premium, was reserved exclusively for staff.

Gruel, the standard dinner-time fare in English workhouses, was also absent from ordinary Town Hospital diets. Soup was islanders' traditional staple and, in the eighteenth century, Town Hospital inmates had it for dinner almost every day.[62] Boiled up in a cauldron over an open fire, its main ingredient was water. To this were added various permutations of dried pulses, root vegetables, cabbage and animal derivatives. An almost continuous record exists of daily dinner menus between 1763 and 1796.[63] In the summer, fish was occasionally served when cheap local mackerel or conger became available.[64] Less frequently, portions of boiled beef or salt pork might be served with a vegetable.[65] This, however, was exceptional. For weeks and months on end, the only real variation was in the principal ingredient of the soup, which might be peas, hogslard, beans or 'meat'. Only twice yearly was the culinary monotony relieved, when, at Christmas and midsummer, inmates were regaled with a meat dinner accompanied by cider or ale, and followed by a desert of *gâche*.[66]

From the beginning, staff, whose food was part of their remuneration, enjoyed

[58] The bakehouse remained in operation until 1883, from which point the Hospital bought bread from commercial bakers (20.2.1883, 13.8.1883, IA, DC/HX 136–10).

[59] See Appendix 9. Guernsey weights are used throughout this section. The Guernsey pound, which was based on the Rouen *livre*, was two ounces heavier than the English pound (W. Berry, *The History of the Island of Guernsey* (London, 1815), p. 119).

[60] Perhaps this was because Guernsey milk so readily turned to butter. As William Berry said, 'the peculiar richness of the milk renders it unnecessary that it should stand for cream to make butter; the milk itself is churned, and the butter it produces incomparably good' (Berry, *Island of Guernsey*, p. 286).

[61] See 1766 accounts, IA, DC/HX 165–01.

[62] For islanders' soup-based diet, see Berry, *Island of Guernsey*, p. 299.

[63] IA, DC/HX 120–02; IA, DC/HX 120–03; IA, DC/HX 120–04.

[64] See, for example, July 1770 (IA, DC/HX 120–02).

[65] See August 1782 (IA, DC/HX 120–03).

[66] *Gâche* was a generic Guernsey term for cake or sweetmeat; sometimes it came in the form of fruit cake, sometimes as plum pudding. For examples of festive dinners, see 25.12.1756, IA, DC/HX 118–01; 17.7.1773, IA, DC/HX 119–03.

a richer and more varied diet than inmates. They ate together at a staff table, and the 1766 accounts show them consuming eggs, poultry, mutton, fresh fish, English cheese and exotic vegetables such as artichokes. The sick and infirm, whose food was brought to their bedsides, were also better provided for, with fresh milk, oatmeal, sugar and light meats all featuring in infirmary accounts.[67]

It has been calculated that, in eighteenth-century Britain, up to a fifth of an average person's daily energy needs was supplied by beer.[68] Just as it had a bakehouse, the Town Hospital also had a brewhouse, where it brewed its own small beer for table use.[69] Adult inmates were allowed a pint at every meal, including breakfast.[70] Strong beer, used only as a tonic for the sick or a 'gratuity' for workers, was normally purchased externally. Cider, which was more expensive than beer, was also bought from time to time, and small amounts were made from the Hospital's own apples.[71] This beverage was, however, kept strictly for special occasions.[72]

Tea, to begin with, was reserved exclusively for staff and the sick. It was an expensive commodity, imported from China, and its consumption by poor people generally was frowned upon.[73] When inmates began to brew their own tea in the 1750s, Directors placed a blanket ban on its use (unless medically indicated) on pain of eight days in the cells.[74] At first, the ban was rigorously policed, with inmates confined and their 'tinpots' confiscated.[75] However, as public attitudes softened, tea-drinking by inmates was gradually accepted and, by 1806, apparatus was purchased to make tea for the whole institution.[76]

This was not the only early nineteenth-century change. The new Board which replaced Jean Condamine and his colleagues in 1809 re-equipped the kitchen along lines promoted by Count Rumford, a well-known Georgian innovator in mass catering.[77] The Board also acquired a winnowing machine, two hand-mills and a

[67] IA, DC/HX 165–01.
[68] J. Burnett, *Liquid Pleasures: A Social History of Drinks in Modern Britain* (London, 1999), pp. 3, 114.
[69] 12.10.1748, IA, DC/HX 117–02.
[70] Children were given water from the spring in the Hospital grounds (Dicey, *Historical Account*, p. 191).
[71] 3.12.1781, IA, DC/HX 119–04.
[72] The use of cider at Christmas persisted until the early nineteenth century (25.12.1819, IA, DC/HX 124–01).
[73] In the mid-1700s there was an ongoing debate in the British Isles over the lower-class consumption of tea. Social observers such as John Wesley and Jonas Hanway feared that the poor would ruin themselves by wasting limited funds on tea (J. Wesley, *A Letter to a Friend, concerning Tea* (London, 1748), p. 12; J. Hanway, *A Journal of Eight Days Journey … To Which is Added an Essay on Tea* (London, 1756), pp. 271–6). Other commentators saw a social threat in the lower ranks' emulation of upper-class habits and wished forcibly to confine their consumption to the traditional beverages thought to befit their station (D. Valenze, 'Custom and humanity: changing attitudes towards the poor in eighteenth-century England', in J. Garnett and C. Matthew (eds), *Revival and Religion since 1700* (London, 1993), pp. 70–2).
[74] 4.12.1752, IA, DC/HX 079–01.
[75] See, for instance, 3.2.1753 and 6.12.1753, IA, DC/HX 079–01.
[76] 2.4.1806, IA, DC/HX 079–02.
[77] Quayle, *General View*, p. 294.

boulting machine, partly so that some grain could be processed on Hospital prem-ises, partly to serve a disciplinary purpose. The coarse flour produced by inmates was used for soup bread.[78] In addition, the new Board introduced a number of dietary changes. Milk became a more important item in the Hospital's budget, as its use was extended beyond the sick to children, whose breakfast it became, mixed with bread in a sop.[79] More reliance was also placed on the potato, formerly just one of many roots used in soups. As wheat prices soared amid the international grain shortages of 1809–11, potatoes temporarily replaced bread as a staple.[80] Their use declined when the crisis was over but never reverted to previous low levels.

Over the hard-pressed years from 1814 to 1850, further changes were made, usually in the form of retrenchments. Rations generally were cut back.[81] Over the 1820s and 1830s, the use of pork was phased out entirely as its price climbed relative to beef.[82] From the 1830s, fresh fish virtually disappeared from inmates' diets, replaced by dried Newfoundland cod.[83] From 1840, the ultra-cheap (and often rancid) *beurre de Bazouges* was imported in barrels from Brittany, and became standard fare until 1916.[84] By 1846, the consumption of beer was restricted to dinnertime only and, by 1848, it had ceased to be brewed on the Hospital site.[85]

All these retrenchments were consolidated in the official house dietary published in 1853 by the House Committee of the new St Peter Port Poor Law Board.[86] According to this dietary, both breakfast and supper, seven days a week, were to consist of 8oz of bread with a smearing of butter and a pint of tea.[87] Dinner, four days out of seven, was to consist of a pint and a half of soup. On Sundays and Wednesdays, stew was to be served instead of soup. On Fridays, inmates were to have dried codfish and potatoes. Women were to have one ounce less bread for breakfast and supper than men, and under-twelves were to have half adult rations.[88]

The distinction between 'soup' and 'stew' in the 1853 dietary seems to have been that soup was meatless (containing only such ingredients as potatoes, turnips, pearl barley and onions), while stews were made with the addition of cheap cuts of beef such as shin, head or brisket.[89] Originally, all dinners were to be accompanied by

---

78 7.1.1811, IA, DC/HX 079–02.

79 6.6.1814, IA, DC/HX 079–02. See also J. Jacob, *Annals of Some of the British Norman Isles Constituting the Bailiwick of Guernsey* (Paris, 1830), p. 148.

80 5.4.1809, IA, DC/HX 079–02.

81 See Appendix 9.

82 The Hospital kept its own pigs until the 1860s; however, the meat from these was not eaten by inmates but was sold to supplement Hospital finances.

83 18.9.1832, IA, DC/HX 173–05; 5.8.1839, IA, DC/HX 181–01; although see 15.3.1838, IA, DC/HX 081–01 for inmates enjoying a rare treat of ormers, a local marine mollusc.

84 26.5.1840, IA, DC/HX; 14.2.1916, IA, DC/HX 080–05.

85 27.10.1846, IA, DC/HX 130–01. Malt and hops disappeared from Hospital accounts after 1848 (IA, DC/HX 020–01).

86 A copy of the dietary is to be found with the Poor Law Board's 1872 accounts in IA, DC/HX 272–02.

87 Cocoa was initially offered as an alternative, but accounts show that purchases of it all but ceased after 1858 (IA, DC/HX 272–02).

88 Infirmary extras remained at the discretion of doctors.

89 For purchases of these items, as also a recipe for soup, see IA, DC/HX 166–01.

4oz of dry bread, but, a few weeks into the new regime, the House Committee attempted to withdraw the bread on 'meat days'. There was a revolt, after which ten inmates were incarcerated in the cells, but it is unclear whether the bread allowance was reinstated.[90]

The 1853 dietary was silent on the matter of beer, but evidence from Hospital accounts suggests that its use at dinner had by now also ceased: annual spending on this commodity dropped from £139 in 1846 to £16 in 1854.[91] From this point on, the routine consumption of beer was limited to staff and infirmary patients, although it was still given as an occasional 'gratuity' to inmate workers and served to other inmates as a Christmas treat.[92]

Tea, rather than beer, became inmates' standard drink during the second half of the century.[93] The Hospital's purchases of this commodity increased from less than an ounce per head weekly in the 1850s to nearly six ounces in the 1890s.[94] In respect of this item, Town Hospital inmates were perhaps more fortunate than their counterparts in England and Wales, where water was the everyday beverage under the post-1834 regime, and tea did not become regular fare until the 1870s.[95] This was due to the lack of a tea duty in Guernsey, which meant that the parish was able to buy it for less than half of its price in England.[96] In other respects, foodstuffs served in the Town Hospital and amounts per inmate were roughly comparable to those served in English workhouses over the mid-nineteenth century.[97]

From the 1880s, however, Town Hospital inmates were at a distinct dietary disadvantage *vis-à-vis* English counterparts. In the United Kingdom, prices of staples fell by over a third between 1874 and 1896 with the onset of bulk imports from the new world.[98] This permitted workhouses to serve larger rations and more varied fare than had previously been possible.[99] Guernsey's unusual position as regards food imports precluded it from reaping the full benefit of these trends. Of five staples bought by the Town Hospital – beef, potatoes, butter, tea and sugar – only butter and sugar came down in price between 1874 and 1896, and the cost of other commodities actually rose.[100] The last decade of the century was thus marked by further retrenchment and, in 1890, inmates' daily bread allowances were cut by 20 per cent.[101]

[90] 3.3.1853, IA, DC/HX 130–04.
[91] IA, DC/HX 020–01.
[92] In the early 1850s, the serving of beer at Christmas had also been suspended, but it resumed a few years later (23.12.1851, 20.12.1852, IA, DC/HX 075–02).
[93] At first, it was consumed without milk and sugar, though these additions were allowed from 1883 (8.1.1883, IA, DC/HX 054–06).
[94] Appendix 9.
[95] V.J. Johnston, *Diet in Workhouses and Prisons, 1835–1895* (London, 1985), pp. 119, 142.
[96] In the 1840s, the Town Hospital bought tea for 1s 6d per lb, while the cheapest tea cost at least 3s per lb in England (IA, DC/HX 020–01; J. Burnett, *A History of the Cost of Living* (1969; Aldershot, 1993 edn), pp. 212–13).
[97] Johnston, *Diet in Workhouses*, p. 123.
[98] Burnett, *Cost of Living*, p. 204.
[99] Johnston, *Diet in Workhouses*, p. 228.
[100] IA, DC/HX 272–02.
[101] 10.3.1890, 20.3.1890, 21.7.1890, IA, DC/HX 136–02.

In the event, it was not until after the Hospital had been brought under Royal Court supervision in 1901 that was there any departure from the strictest frugality. Under pressure to improve 'deserving' inmates' lot, the Hospital introduced a new dietary in 1902, modelled explicitly on a dietary issued by the English Local Government Board the previous year.[102] Unprecedentedly, all the institution's children, sick and elderly were henceforth to be served a much more varied diet containing mutton, bacon, eggs, cheese, jam, golden syrup, porridge, steamed and milk puddings. For inmates in the 'house' department, the changes were, however, less exciting, the only departures from the 1853 dietary being bacon in the place of dried fish, and one serving of pudding per week. Beer virtually disappeared from the Hospital at this point. Payments in beer to workers ceased in the summer of 1902, and the same year also saw the withdrawal of employees' Christmas beer, matching its yuletide withdrawal from inmates in 1891.[103]

Clothing

At the time the Town Hospital was founded in the 1740s, clothing was expensive relative to labouring incomes and often comprised the largest part of a poor person's possessions. It is unclear whether eighteenth-century entrants to the Town Hospital were allowed to retain the clothes they arrived in, but such garments as they owned would necessarily have been threadbare and quick to wear out, so that the Hospital was obliged, from the beginning, to provide clothing for its inmates.

The institution had its own shoemaker's shop, which turned out a regular supply of leather shoes made to measure for individual male and female inmates. It also had a tailor's shop, where the coats, waistcoats and breeches worn by men and boys were sewn by hand. These shops were staffed by a master tailor and master shoemaker with two or three assistants. Assistants were invariably drawn from within the institution, as were masters, if inmates with appropriate skills were available; if not, tradesmen were paid to come into the institution to work.

The Hospital's female inmates were responsible for most of the clothing not made by the tailors. Under the supervision of the second mistress, they knitted woollen stockings for inmates of both sexes, sewed shirts for the men and boys and made shifts, petticoats, gowns, aprons, neckerchiefs and caps for the women and girls.[104] Items whose manufacture required specialist skills, such as women's stays and men's hats, were bought in from outside.[105]

---

[102] 3.11.1902, IA, DC/HX 056–04; 1902 accounts in IA, DC/HX 272–02; Johnston, *Diet in Workhouses*, p. 32.

[103] 21.12.1891, IA, DC/HX 136–03; 23.6.1902, 15.12.1902, IA, DC/HX 080–03.

[104] Dicey, *Historical Account*, pp. 188–91; IA, DC/HX 117–01. Inmates did not have separate nightwear until the early 1900s, and slept in their shirts and shifts. Drawers, usually made of flannel, were worn only by elderly male inmates in the eighteenth century.

[105] For details of the articles of eighteenth-century clothing mentioned above, see J. Styles, *The Dress of the People: Everyday Fashion in Eighteenth-Century England* (London, 2007), pp. 35–6, 38, 41–2, 45, 55, 182–4, 363.

Initially, the Hospital purchased externally all the cloth required by its tailors and seamstresses. However, after weaving was introduced to the Hospital in the 1750s, external supplies were supplemented with textiles woven by inmates themselves.[106] By the early nineteenth century, the Hospital was making petticoats and aprons with its own grogram, shirts and shifts with its own shirting, men's suits with its home-made grey cloth and women's gowns with its home-made blue stuff.[107] From 1817, the Hospital even supplied inmates with headgear from its own straw hat manufactory.[108]

Although this coarse grey and blue clothing constituted a recognisable house livery, the Hospital had never dressed its inmates in an actual uniform. In the early nineteenth century, some, indeed, were allowed to wear garments of their own, as evidenced by the ban on white waistcoats and neckcloths in 1824.[109] Such toler-ance ceased in 1832, however, when, as part of a general hardening of the regime, new regulations compelled all inmates (save fee-paying boarders) to wear a specific costume: grey Hospital-issue suits were now mandatory for men and boys and, for women and girls, a brown gown, black neckerchief and plain white linen cap or black straw bonnet. The new rules also provided for special badges to distinguish those exhibiting exemplary behaviour.[110]

The Hospital uniform was, however, short-lived, for the cessation of weaving and hat-making at the Hospital in the late 1830s made it difficult to preserve strict homo-geneity, and inmates' clothing gradually diversified. In 1837, Directors purchased a large quantity of cheap blue-printed cotton to make gowns and frocks for women and girls.[111] Fustian, an inexpensive cloth with a cotton weft and linen warp, was also purchased for male outerwear, which now consisted of a jacket, waistcoat and ankle-length trousers.[112] In 1862, the boys were made coats on the same pattern as those worn by Guernsey postmen.[113] In 1882, the girls were provided with ulsters and, in 1895, their cotton frocks were supplemented with warm winter dresses.[114] All clothing nevertheless continued to be made by the institution's own tailors and needlewomen, from fabrics chosen by the House Committee. Price remained the Committee's chief criterion and, even at the turn of the twentieth century, their purchases – 'grey calico', 'olive jean', 'army cloth', 'drab fustian', 'black worsted', 'blue striped linen' – indicate that inmates would have remained conspicuous by the texture and colour of their garb.[115] Since 1853, inmates had been formally obliged to surrender their own clothes on admission, and these were kept in a locked cupboard

---

[106] 19.6.1757, IA, DC/HX 079–01. For a history of weaving in the Hospital, see section on 'Income', Chapter 6.

[107] IA, DC/HX 139–10.

[108] 8.4.1817, IA, DC/HX 079–02.

[109] 3.5.1824, IA, DC/HX 135–02.

[110] 11.7.1832, IA, DC/HX 135–03; *Star*, 12.7.1832.

[111] 17.7.1837, 9.10.1837, IA, DC/HX 130–02.

[112] 7.6.1838, IA, DC/HX 075–01. See also IA, DC/HX 096–02.

[113] 8.12.1862, IA, DC/HX 136–07.

[114] 11.12.1882, IA, DC/HX 136–10; 11.11.1895, IA, DC/HX 136–04. Ulsters, first produced in Belfast in 1867, were distinguished by an integral cape covering the shoulders.

[115] 17.4.1900, IA, DC/HX 136–05.

until discharge.[116] One distressed early twentieth-century inmate is recorded as having begged to have his original garments restored to him when going out, because it was 'most difficult for a man in hospital clothes to be civilly spoken to'.[117]

By this time, Hospital staff were also recognisable by their dress. Limited staff uniforms had first been introduced in 1871 and, over the next few years, black merino dresses with white aprons and caps became mandatory for senior female employees, while, for males, the uniform consisted of double-breasted reefer jackets and peaked caps bearing a pelican badge.[118]

The in-house making of inmates' clothing continued unquestioned until the early twentieth century. At this point, changing economics forced a change of policy. With the dearth of able-bodied inmates, the Hospital's master tailor and shoemaker were both waged employees, and the calculation was made that, inclusive of labour and materials, it was now costing the Hospital as much as £1 17s 10d for a man's suit and 12s 9¼d for a pair of men's shoes.[119] On St Peter Port's High Street, by contrast, men's suits could be bought off the peg for 30s, and men's boots purchased ready-made for 8s.[120] Thus, at the end of 1903, the Hospital finally took the decision to cease manufacturing inmates' clothing and footwear in-house.[121]

Doubtless, inmates' off-the-peg garments were still purchased with economy in mind, but, since they were now bought from the same sources as those used by ordinary working people, inmates must have felt themselves less painfully conspicuous. One can only speculate as to the feelings of Hospital boys emerging from the institution in 1862 dressed as postmen. Those who, in 1908, went off to school in trousers, guernseys and flat caps will have blended more seamlessly with their peers.[122]

Discipline

For most of the eighteenth and nineteenth centuries, the Hospital population contained disruptive elements. These might be unruly children, delinquent adolescents, drunkards, street women, even petty criminals. With just six or seven staff in charge of 200–300 inmates, the potential for disorder was huge and discipline was correspondingly strict. Until 1852, ultimate responsibility for adjudicating over offences and handing down punishments rested with the Board of Directors; after that date it rested with the House Committee. The range of offences was broad

---

[116] 17.5.1853, IA, DC/HX 130–04

[117] 28.12.1903, IA, DC/HX 080–03.

[118] 27.11.1871, IA, DC/HX 136–08; 7.11.1887, IA, DC/HX 054–06; 11.6.1894, IA, DC/HX 136–04; 11.6.1900, IA, DC/HX 136–05; 2.6.1902, IA, DC/HX 056–04. The pelican, piercing its breast to feed its young with its blood, was an ancient symbol of charity. It featured prominently on the Hospital's entrance archway and was adopted as corporate livery (17.10.1904, IA, DC/HX 080–02). See staff members in back and middle rows, Plate 4.

[119] IA, DC/HX 135–06.

[120] 30.4.1904, DC/HX 127–02; 10.6.1904, DC/HX 080–02.

[121] 2.11.1903, DC/HX 056–04.

[122] 9.11.1908, IA, DC/HX 080–01.

and fluid. A set of rules from 1817 mentions swearing, blasphemy, absconding and drunkenness, but also the more nebulous 'insubordination' and 'querulousness'.[123]

To punish perceived misbehaviour, Hospital administrators had at their disposal a graduated scale of sanctions. The simplest was to expel a trouble-maker, and, in the institution's early years, summary expulsion was frequently used. Many of the first inmates prized the guarantee of food and shelter the Hospital offered. Thus it came as a blow to 63-year-old Jonathan Mauger when he was ejected for 'malversations' in 1750, and he gladly returned when the Directors relented.[124] Directors knew their inmates, and were aware even at this early date that there were some to whom ejection would be positively welcome. At the other end of the scale, therefore, they also used prolonged detention. After a group of nine inmates misbehaved when out on leave in 1764, they were collectively denied the privilege of going out for a year.[125] Confinement for these nine was within the Hospital precincts, but more serious offenders were detained in the institution's *cachots* – purpose-built lock-ups or cells. Children as well as adults could be sentenced to solitary confinement in the cells, usually on dry bread and water. Sentences normally varied between two days and one month, but some could be much longer. In 1788, Mary Holt was sentenced to an indefinite term when it was discovered she was trading in Hospital food.[126]

In terms of physical punishments, *l'abot* (or *le billot*) was often imposed for attempts at escape. This was a heavy impediment, known in English as a 'clog' or a 'hobble', which was affixed to an inmate's leg by means of a chain. When the usual wooden hobble failed to prevent Judith Le Moigne making an unscheduled exit in 1791, her leg chain was attached to a lump of metal.[127] Stocks were added to the Hospital's repertoire in the 1760s.[128] These consisted chiefly of two horizontal planks; miscreants sat on the ground and rested their lower legs in half-moons cut into one plank, while the other was secured on top. In 1764, Marie Maissend and Elizabeth Le Lacheur spent three undignified afternoons in this apparatus as part of a punishment for threatening to burn down the Hospital.[129]

Hobbles and stocks were uncomfortable, but they were probably not unduly painful. The same cannot be said of flogging. This was most frequently used on boys, but occasionally on girls and adults too. The operation was usually performed in front of other inmates, often by inmates themselves. In 1755, 52-year-old Daniel Bott was flogged in front of the whole Hospital after he stole the Bailiff's silver teapot.[130] In 1806, 11-year-old Rachel Le Filliâtre and 13-year-old Sophie Squires were given an exemplary caning in front of the girls after their 'illicit connection' with a 36-year-old male inmate.[131]

---

[123] 6.10.1817, IA, DC/HX 079–02.
[124] 7.8.1750, 2.9.1750, IA, DC/HX 079–01.
[125] 1.2.1764, IA, DC/HX 079–01.
[126] 2.6.1788, IA, DC/HX 079–01.
[127] 13.9.1791, IA, DC/HX 121–01.
[128] 2.8.1763, IA, DC/HX 079–01.
[129] 21.8.1764, IA, DC/HX 079–01.
[130] 17.3.1755, IA, DC/HX 118–01.
[131] 13.8.1806, 3.9.1806, IA, DC/HX 079–02.

Severity intensified as St Peter Port's economy deteriorated in the early nine-teenth century, and there was almost a paroxysm of harshness between the late 1820s and 1840s, when the Royal Court used the Hospital to detain social deviants and petty criminals.[132] In 1830, four pairs of handcuffs were acquired to add to the institution's disciplinary equipment.[133] One of their first uses was to punish 38-year-old escapee James Todd, whose leg was continuously chained to a hobble for a month while he also spent three hours each day with his arms handcuffed behind his back.[134] Women were also increasingly subjected to hair-shearing at this time, as Mary McCourt, Marie De France and Carterette Herivel, who had their heads shaved for insulting the mistress in 1831.[135] Neither does any distinction appear to have been made as to categories of inmate liable to punishment, with infirmary patients subjected to it as well as the able-bodied. Jean Torode, recovering from an operation in Lazarus Ward, received a punishment for fighting on the ward in 1839.[136]

It is difficult to assess the frequency of early nineteenth-century punishments, since these were not separately logged until a much later time. Some idea is never-theless provided by a random year-end tally surviving in a 1820s minute-book, which shows that a total of seventy-one punishments was meted out in 1826. This equated to an average of one or two punishments per week.[137]

Paradoxically, in tandem with the increased harshness of this period, a parallel strand of more temperate punishments was simultaneously evolving. In the 1820s, clothes of bright and conspicuous colours began to be used to distinguish offending inmates from the well-behaved. Yellow and red were favourite colours, sometimes with black or blue stripes. Thomas Jeffreys (38), who impregnated a fellow inmate in 1822, was made to wear a yellow and black jacket for a year. Marie Batiste (23), his partner in the offence, was sentenced to wear a rimless cap and yellow dress for the same period.[138] As we saw earlier, prostitutes, too, were obliged from around this time to wear distinctive dress.[139] The punitive use of colour-coding appears to have continued until the 1870s.[140]

As a variant on this theme, offending inmates might also be made to wear plac-ards emblazoned with the name of their offence, such as that inscribed *MENTEUR* (liar) suspended round the neck of William White in 1822.[141] In addition, a *table de disgrâce* was instituted in the refectory, where low-level transgressors of all ages could be set apart to eat their bread and water 'in shame', as did 62-year-old Ursula Robil-liard for three days in February 1830 after she was discovered trying to sell Hospital

---

[132] See section on 'Policy and regime', Chapter 6.
[133] 8.2.1830, IA, DC/HX 135–03.
[134] 4.3.1830, IA, DC/HX 135–03.
[135] 7.3.1831, IA, DC/HX 135–03.
[136] 8.2.1839, IA, DC/HX 075–01.
[137] 8.1.1827, IA, DC/HX 135–02.
[138] 1.7.1822, IA, DC/HX 135–02.
[139] Section on 'Women', Chapter 8.
[140] For a late example, see 28.6.1870, IA, DC/HX 136–08.
[141] 4.11.1822, IA, DC/HX 135–02.

soap.[142] The punitive use of task work, such as a spell on the corn mill, also increased in the 1820s and 1830s, as did formal demotion from responsible jobs and loss of corresponding gratuities.

How, we might ask, did inmates as a body react to such punishments? Did they accept them as legitimate, or did they rebel? In an English context, historian David Green has detected the operation of a 'moral economy' in nineteenth-century workhouses, whereby inmates might collectively challenge punishments they felt to be inappropriate, unjustified or excessive.[143] Challenges of this sort were not unknown in the Town Hospital. In 1822, for example, male inmates refused to flog 14-year-old Henry Ball when they were ordered to do so by Directors. The boy had been bound to a South Shields captain and was no longer resident in the Hospital. His ship was in port and the captain wished to have him punished for an offence committed on board. Evidently, Ball's former companions found the captain's request unwarranted and their own involvement even more so. Their refusal to carry out the punishment resulted in the confinement of their ringleaders for a week, but the point was conceded and Henry Ball rejoined his boat without a whipping.[144]

From the late 1840s, when the Court's penal use of the Hospital was abandoned, handcuffs, chains, clogs and hobbles vanished from the institution for good. Nevertheless, women's hair continued to be shorn, and both children and adults continued to be confined in the *cachots* and denied leave of absence from the Hospital for long periods. Flogging also continued, but, by the late nineteenth century, it was restricted to boys and performed by the master, rather than by fellow inmates.[145]

In 1842, the Poor Law Commission of England and Wales had issued a set of regulations which codified in detail the different categories of offence within the workhouse and specific punishments applicable thereto.[146] No such codification was undertaken in Guernsey until after the Royal Court assumed supervision of the Hospitals in 1901, and, up to this date, Hospital authorities had almost unfettered discretion as to what they deemed an offence and how they punished it. Moreover, the disciplinary regime as eventually codified remained more rigorous than that in force in England and Wales. In the latter jurisdiction, it had not been permissible since 1842 to confine inmates on reduced fare for more than twenty-four hours. St Peter Port's 1914 disciplinary code allowed inmates to be confined for as much as seven days, during which they might spend up to forty-eight consecutive hours on reduced rations.[147]

After the institution of Royal Court supervision, the Town Hospital finally began to keep a separate log of adult punishments.[148] The log shows that, by this time,

142 1.2.1830, IA, DC/HX 135–03. The punishment was recorded under Ursula's maiden name – probably Gueho or Guegen – which the Hospital spelt in a variety of ways.
143 Green, 'Pauper protests', pp. 137–59.
144 8.7.1822, 12.7.1822, 5.8.1822, IA, DC/HX 135–02.
145 For a late nineteenth-century example of the master caning boys, see 8.2.1892, IA, DC/HX 136–03.
146 Archbold (ed.), *Consolidated and other Orders*, pp. 80–2.
147 15.12.1914, IA, DC/HX 272–04.
148 IA, DC/HX 122–05.

punitive sanctions consisted exclusively of sentences to the cells, loss of gratuities and deprivation of leave. In 1902, there were twenty punishments in the entire year. These punishments – for drunkenness, absconding, refusal to work and refusal to attend church – were now entirely restricted to house people. Punishments continued to tail off as the Hospital's workhouse function faded. By 1923, the number had dropped to just five in the year. By 1951, the last year for which any sanctions were recorded, one single punishment was logged. This final punishment – loss of gratuities and deprivation of leave – was imposed on a male inmate for attempting to escape while under Public Assistance Authority 'care'.

Religion

When the Town Hospital opened in 1743, Anglicanism was Guernsey's only religion, having acquired *de facto* established status after Charles II's suppression of Presbyterianism in 1662. Outside the garrison, dissenting sects and Roman Catholicism had no local presence until the late eighteenth century. Quakers and Methodists were the first dissenters to establish permanent local outposts in the 1770s and 1780s, and Catholicism was reintroduced by French refugees only in the 1790s.[149]

The Town Hospital's founders seem to have been influenced by literature published by the Anglican-run Society for Promoting Christian Knowledge (SPCK), and, in accordance with the Society's recommendations, they erected their Hospital on a foundation of Anglicanism.[150] The Hospital's first regulations specified that prayers from the Anglican prayerbook were to be read at the beginning and end of each day, and children were to be instructed in the Anglican catechism thrice weekly.[151] In addition, the Hospital was allocated sixty-two sittings at the Town Church, and ambulant inmates were to attend Anglican divine service every Sunday.[152]

Such formalities aside, however, religion was seldom mentioned in the Hospital's eighteenth-century registers. There was no permanent chaplain, and religious attitudes within the Hospital appear to have been relatively relaxed. This approach was abandoned with the ousting of Treasurer Jean Condamine and the casting-off of the old order in 1809. New Directors were of a more earnest turn of mind and wished to expunge the laxity which, they felt, had crept in over past decades. They may have been influenced by the growth of the evangelical tendency within the wider Anglican church, evident in Guernsey since the 1780s.[153] One of the first actions of the 1809 Board was to purchase new copies of the Anglican prayerbook for inmates' use.[154] Shortly afterwards, they instituted a Sunday prayer service within

[149] J. Marr, *The History of Guernsey: The Bailiwick's Story* (1982; Guernsey, 2001 edn), pp. 52–7.
[150] Section on 'Foundation', Chapter 6.
[151] IA, DC/HX 117–01.
[152] For number of sittings, see 23.1.1885, IA, DC/HX 054–06.
[153] An evangelical proprietary chapel, Holy Trinity, had opened in St Peter Port in 1789 (Marr, *History of Guernsey*, p. 40).
[154] 10.5.1809, IA, DC/HX 079–02.

the Hospital for ill-behaved inmates who had been banned from church, and they engaged two Anglican ministers to take it in turns to preach to them.[155] Feeling, at length, the lack of a chaplain of their own, Directors resolved in 1813 to replace the two visiting ministers with a permanent salaried chaplain in the person of Anglican clergyman William Chepmell.[156] From this time onward, the chaplain's post became a fixture, although the Hospital sometimes had difficulty filling it.

The duties of the Hospital's chaplain were relatively light, consisting essentially of a Sunday service for those who could not attend church, prayers on a Wednesday and Friday, occasional funerals and pastoral visits to inmates.[157] Initially, the chaplain's stipend was set at £20 per year, increasing by £10 or so each decade until it reached £50 in the 1830s. It then remained at around that level until 1918. For a Hospital post, this was reasonable pay. In the mid-1800s, medical officers also received £50 for rather more onerous jobs.[158] Nevertheless, this stipend was worth appreciably less than a parochial living, and the Hospital post tended to be filled either by young clergymen without charge or as a supplement to another appointment.[159] As Norman Longmate observed of workhouse chaplaincy posts in England and Wales, they 'tended to attract the worst-off members of the profession'.[160] In the century between 1813 and the First World War, twenty clergymen worked as chaplains in the Hospital, with short interregnums in most decades as one resigned and another was sought.[161] The longest-serving chaplain was Henry Clark (also vicar of St John's), who occupied the post between 1886 and 1914.[162]

For many decades, the Hospital managed without a dedicated chapel, and services were conducted in the refectory or, occasionally, on a ward.[163] There were suggestions in the 1860s and 1870s that a room should be set aside and fitted up as a chapel, but this was rejected as 'too expensive' by the House Committee of the day.[164] In 1894, a Mrs Maria Wells of Boulogne left a legacy of £489 to the Hospital in memory of her brother Robert Keil, a failed music teacher who had once been an inmate. Although she did not specify how the money should be spent, St Peter Port's Poor Law Board resolved to spend it on a chapel, which soon became a prestige project

[155] 3.9.1810, 7.10.1812, IA, DC/HX 079–02.
[156] 1.2.1813, IA, DC/HX 079–02.
[157] 1.3.1824, IA, DC/HX 135–02; 11.7.1836, IA, DC/HX 130–02.
[158] 31.1.1853, IA, DC/HX 054–05.
[159] In 1836, Guernsey's Anglican parochial livings yielded an average income of £107 per year each (*Comet*, 19.9.1836).
[160] N. Longmate, *The Workhouse: A Social History* (London, 1974), p. 100.
[161] The twenty were, in order of service, W.J. Chepmell, J.S. Sabonadière, R. Potenger, J.S. Lys, T. Grut, C.J. Belin, H. Benwell, T.D. Ozanne, T. King, W.M. Valrent, F.W.B. Bouverie, W. Manning, T.W. Sidebotham, A. Morris, R.J. Ozanne, J. Thurstan, J.W. Popplewell, C.R. De Havilland, G.R. Bigge and H. Clark. Two of these – John Lys and William Valrent – also had spells in the institution as lunatics (26.3.1836, IA, DC/HX 130–02; 27.7.1849, IA, DC/HX 130–04).
[162] 1.2.1886, IA, DC/HX 054–06; 8.2.1914, IA, DC/HX 046–01.
[163] 12.9.1829, 8.10.1832, IA, DC/HX 135–03.
[164] 4.10.1869, 3.7.1876, IA, DC/HX 136–09.

for the local businessmen composing the Board.[165] By the time it was finished, the chapel had cost £990 in total, with Mrs Wells' legacy supplemented by a special tax, and furnishings paid for out of forfeited apprentices' wages.[166] Named the 'Wells Memorial Chapel' (though the original bequest had been in memory of Robert Keil), it opened to great fanfare in 1896 with a service attended by the Lieutenant Governor, Bailiff and other dignitaries.[167] In the early 1900s, elaborate Harvest Festival services in the chapel became a fixture on St Peter Port's social calendar. Edwardian prestige did not, however, stand the test of time, and in 1979 the chapel was converted into a ward.[168]

All twenty clergymen serving the Hospital between 1813 and 1914 were Anglican. Nevertheless, even when the first of these was appointed, St Peter Port's religious complexion was already undergoing transformation. Nonconformity, particularly Methodism, had made many converts among local people since the late eighteenth century and, in the post-Napoleonic period, yet more Nonconformists had arrived from south-west England and French Catholics from Normandy. By 1830, St Peter Port possessed one Catholic and eight Nonconformist places of worship to just four Anglican churches.[169] The retreat of Anglicanism continued and, by the end of the century, the number of Nonconformist and Catholic places of worship had increased to eighteen, while that of Anglican churches stood at only six.[170]

Despite such changes, the Town Hospital remained resolutely Anglican, continuing to use the Anglican prayerbook and to instruct its children in the Anglican catechism.[171] In the early 1820s, while Catholicism and Nonconformity were still relative novelties, some small concessions appear to have been made to other denominations. In 1821, for instance, Directors co-operated with St Peter Port's Roman Catholic priest, André Navet, in arranging the transfer of Mary Gaiter, a Catholic inmate, from the Country to the Town Hospital, so that Navet could minister to her spiritual needs.[172] However, in parallel with the general tightening of regime over the late 1820s and 1830s, such tolerance evaporated. In 1832, informal Sunday evening prayer sessions conducted by Nonconformists were stopped.[173] In 1841, all clergymen other than the chaplain were banned from the Hospital without Directors' express permission.[174] In 1848, Directors publicly supported their chaplain when he prevented Catholic priests from visiting a sick member of their congregation.[175] This

[165] For a photograph of Board members at the laying of the chapel's foundation stone in 1895, see Plate 3.

[166] 2.4.1894, IA, DC/HX 054–07; 14.9.1896, IA, DC/HX 136–11; IA, DC/HX 272–02.

[167] 18.11.1896, IA, DC/HX 057–01.

[168] IA, BH 52–13.

[169] W.R. Chapman, *His Praise in the Islands* (1984; Guernsey, 1995 edn), pp. 116–26.

[170] *Comet*, 15.7.1893.

[171] From 1822, prizes of silver-clasped prayerbooks were awarded to the most proficient boy and girl in end-of-year catechism examinations (2.12.1822, IA, DC/HX 135–02).

[172] 1.10.1821, IA, DC/HX 079–02.

[173] 8.10.1832, IA, DC/HX 135–03.

[174] 18.10.1841, IA, DC/HX 075–01.

[175] 9.9.1848, IA, DC/HX 075–01; *Gazette*, 23.9.1848; *Star*, 28.9.1848, 30.9.1848.

stance accorded with a strong current of anti-Catholicism in the island at this time, and was not without its parallel in the Country Hospital.[176]

The first half of the nineteenth century also saw a tightening of policy on inmates' church attendance. Under regulations issued in 1817, any able-bodied inmate, of any creed, refusing to attend Anglican Sunday service at the Town Church was prohibited from otherwise leaving the Hospital that day.[177] New rules instituted in 1853 added that non-attenders were also to be confined in the cells for twenty-four hours on bread and water.[178] This was very different from the mid-century situation in England and Wales, where the 1834 Poor Law Amendment Act had laid down that no workhouse inmate could be obliged to attend a service contrary to his religious principles, and non-Anglicans had been allowed out to attend their own services since the late 1830s.[179]

In 1859, there was a minor relaxation of the Hospital's anti-Catholic stance when a decision was taken finally to allow Catholic priests to conduct the burials of deceased Roman Catholic inmates and outdoor paupers, and an old paupers' vault in the Strangers' Cemetery was reopened for exclusive Catholic use.[180] However, this lenity was not extended to the living. Requests by parish priests in the early 1880s that Roman Catholic inmates be excused Town Church services and allowed to attend their own met with repeated refusals.[181] Requests for the discharge of Catholic children so that they could be sent to Catholic orphanages and schools in England were also denied.[182] In 1889, chaplain Henry Clark had all suitably aged children confirmed in the Anglican faith irrespective of their antecedents.[183] In 1898, a request by the Sisters of Mercy to provide Catholic instruction in the Hospital was refused.[184] Again, all this was very different from the situation in England and Wales. Here, it had been illegal to educate any workhouse child in a religious creed other than that of his parents since 1834, and, from the 1850s, large numbers of Catholic children had been educated away from the workhouse in denominational schools, their fees paid by the guardians.[185]

As with many other aspects of Hospital life, the first real easing of religious policy came after the Royal Court's assumption of oversight. By 1903, although Catholic inmates were still compelled to be present at daily Anglican prayers, they were now

---

[176] On anti-Catholicism in the Country Hospital and Guernsey generally, see R.-M. Crossan, *Guernsey, 1814–1914: Migration and Modernisation* (Woodbridge, 2007), pp. 198–201.

[177] 6.10.1817, IA, DC/HX 079–02.

[178] 31.1.1853, 21.2.1853, IA, DC/HX 054–05. This was despite the fact that O in C, 28.12.1852 had ostensibly secularised St Peter Port's poor law regime.

[179] Archbold (ed.), *Consolidated and other Orders*, p. 2; M.A. Crowther, *The Workhouse System, 1834–1929: The History of an English Social Institution* (1981; London, 1983 edn), p. 129.

[180] 7.2.1859, IA, DC/HX 054–05; 1.9.1859, IA, DC/HX 130–04. See also loose sheet in IA, DC/HX 060–02.

[181] 27.6.1881, 18.9.1882, IA, DC/HX 136–10.

[182] 10.12.1883, IA, DC/HX 136–10. See also correspondence from 1884 in IA, DC/HX 062–03.

[183] 13.5.1889, IA, DC/HX 136–02.

[184] 21.3.1898, IA, DC/HX 136–11.

[185] Archbold (ed.), *Consolidated and other Orders*, p. 2; A. Brundage, *The English Poor Laws, 1700–1930* (Basingstoke, 2002), p. 96.

permitted to go to Mass on a Sunday rather than attend the Town Church or a Hospital service.[186] Within the next year or two, a Catholic priest was given leave to baptise two Hospital children, and a Methodist minister was allowed to baptise a third.[187]

Matters eased even further after 1909, when Henry Ollivier became Poor Law Board President.[188] Ollivier was a prominent Nonconformist and had served as Vice-Dean of Preachers in Guernsey's French Methodist circuit. In a complete break with past practice, the Reverend J.D. Stevens, a Methodist minister, applied for the Hospital chaplaincy when it fell vacant a few years into Ollivier's tenure.[189] Although Stevens' candidature proved unsuccessful, he would probably not have stood without Ollivier's encouragement. New Hospital rules drawn up under Ollivier in 1914 formalised far-reaching changes in the institution's religious regime. While maintaining the requirement for able-bodied inmates to attend a religious service on Sundays, the new rules confirmed their free choice of church. These rules also explicitly permitted all inmates to be buried by their own clergymen, and specified that religious instruction would henceforth 'have due regard to the religious persuasion of the child'. In addition, clergymen of all denominations were to be allowed unrestricted access to inmates from their congregations and, although inmates still had to attend twice-daily prayers, the word 'Anglican' was conspicuously omitted.[190]

Henry Ollivier remained head of the St Peter Port Poor Law Board until poor relief was brought under States' auspices in 1925. Thereafter he presided over the States' Central Poor Law Board and over the Public Assistance Authority from its inception in 1938 to his death in 1941. His long tenure in office brought further relaxations to the Town Hospital's religious regime. In 1923, the Roman Catholic parish priest of St Peter Port, Father Thomas Hickey, became an Overseer and, in 1925, was elected a member of the Hospital's House Committee.[191] In 1929, permission was granted for Nonconformist services to be held in the Hospital chapel.[192] In 1938, the compulsion on able-bodied inmates to attend a religious service every Sunday was finally lifted.[193]

As regarded its chaplains, however, the Town Hospital remained unshakeably Anglican until late in the twentieth century. Other Methodist ministers followed the Reverend Stevens in applying for the chaplaincy after 1914 and, in 1930, one of them, the Reverend A. Claxton, was actually appointed. His appointment was, however, annulled after three months, when the Royal Court ruled that only an Anglican could serve the institution as chaplain.[194] For nearly forty years this stance was maintained. Finally, in 1969, on the resignation of the last Anglican monopolist,

---

[186] 3.8.1903, IA, DC/HX 056–04; 4.8.1903, IA, DC/HX 267–22; *Guernsey Evening Press*, 11.8.1903.
[187] 17.10.1904, IA, DC/HX 080–02; 10.9.1906, IA, DC/HX 129–02.
[188] 13.12.1909, IA, DC/HX 056–04. For a photograph of Ollivier, see Plate 8.
[189] 2.3.1914, IA, DC/HX 046–01.
[190] 15.12.1914, IA, DC/HX 272–04.
[191] 18.12.1923, IA, DC/HX 052–01; 12.1.1925, IA, DC/HX 051–01.
[192] 6.5.1929, IA, DC/HX 051–01.
[193] 4.12.1938, IA, DC/HX 015–04.
[194] 6.1.1930, 21.3.1930, IA, DC/HX 051–01.

Canon S.W. Gerhold, the post was split into three and shared between an Anglican (Reverend K. Cadman), a Nonconformist (Reverend G. Grice) and a Roman Catholic (Canon J. Rea). However, in a last nod to establishmentarianism probably not reflective of residents' affiliations, the Anglican chaplain received double the stipend of the other two.[195]

Language

At the time of the Town Hospital's foundation, most St Peter Port parishioners would have transacted their daily business in a variant of Norman French which had established itself locally after the island became part of Normandy in the tenth century. It differed in many ways from 'standard' French, which was based on the Parisian dialect. If called upon to distinguish their local tongue from standard French, eighteenth-century Guernseymen might possibly have called it *guernesiais* or, adopting a standard French term, *patois*.[196]

Guernsey *patois* had no written form. To begin with, Latin was used for official documents, but, at some time in the fourteenth century, it was superseded in this context by a writing system based essentially on standard French.[197] In the sixteenth century, standard French also became the language of insular religion when the francophone clerics who introduced Calvinism substituted French for Latin in local churches. Over time, the use of standard French was extended to most other formal contexts – government, the judiciary, education – while *guernesiais* remained ubiquitous in private communication and domestic life.[198] In the eighteenth century, all social classes had some knowledge of both. Although the common people spoke only *guernesiais*, they heard French in church and were taught French reading and writing in their parish schools. Islanders higher up the social scale used *guernesiais* with servants, tradesmen and the lower orders generally. Those who lived in the countryside also spoke *guernesiais* among themselves. Urban patricians, some of whom were educated in francophone countries or had francophone tutors, used standard French for record-keeping and correspondence, and may perhaps also have spoken it with their peers.

Such, broadly speaking, was the situation in 1743. However, the foundation of the Hospital coincided with the beginnings of linguistic change in St Peter Port. Over the next 150 years, there was to be a shift away from the *guernesiais*/French diglossia towards English monolingualism. This shift was caused by the town's

---

[195] 9.4.1969, IA, AS/MB 068–01.

[196] The word *patois* (archaically rendered *patrois*) is derived from the low Latin *patriensis*, meaning 'of the fatherland'.

[197] This paralleled the replacement of Latin with standard French in similar contexts in mainland Normandy. Since Guernsey's legal system was based on Norman law, most local lawyers travelled to Normandy for their professional education and seem to have adopted practices current there.

[198] Linguists would term this division of roles between two languages, or variants of a language, a diglossia.

increasing exposure to English influence through trade and commerce and to English people through the garrison and immigration. A linguistic analysis of Town Hospital registers over the century and a half from 1743 throws a valuable sidelight on the progress of this shift.

From the very beginning, the Hospital's official records were kept in standard French, as was the case for all of Guernsey's official records. However, close inspection of surviving registers reveals that 'standard' was a relative notion. Daybooks were kept by the Hospital's salaried staff, who did not necessarily have an advanced education. Their orthography was variable and, for the most part, phonetic: *coueffe* for *coiffe* (cap); *sirurgien* for *chirurgien* (surgeon); *galtat* for *galetas* (garret).[199] Often they used *guernesiais* words for common domestic items with different renderings in modern French: *caboche* for *chou* (cabbage); *cadot* for *couvre-lit* (counterpane); *baheur* for *bahut* (chest). They regularly substituted *guernesiais* base-ten numerals (*septante, octante*) for the base-twenty forms normal in standard French. Their sentence construction, too, exhibited Norman grammatical and syntactic features not seen in standard French.[200] These features most commonly comprised the routine anteposition of adjectives of colour (*le verd cadot*); the use of *ès* instead of *aux* for *à + les*, and the use of *ils* (or *i*) instead of *elles* as feminine third person plural subject pronoun. Some of these features were also present in the Hospital's early minute-books, which were usually written up by Treasurers, who were of high social rank. Strikingly, in a 1749 letter to the Hospital's *gouvernante*, Nicolas Dobrée himself, St Peter Port's leading townsman, consistently used the pronoun *ils* when referring to a pair of girls.[201] On the balance of evidence, we may therefore conclude that, although eighteenth-century staff and administrators were certainly francophone, they were also all thoroughly permeated with the influence of Norman French.

Even at this early stage, however, registers also exhibited English influences. Right from the start and in tandem with all the foregoing, there was a conspicuous tendency to use English vocabulary for articles of fairly recent importation, presumably from England, for which there was no pre-existing *guernesiais* term. Hence yeast derived from the brewing process and sold by the Hospital was called *barm(e)*, an English term for the froth on fermenting malt liquor. In this particular instance, there was no direct equivalent in standard French.[202] However, even for articles where there was a straightforward French equivalent, English terms were used without restraint, rendered as they were spoken. Thus we find in the midst of French sentences *sospen* for saucepan; *mogs* for mugs; *jougg* for jug; *tarre* for tar; *theaketle* for tea kettle; *une paire de trozer*.

[199] These examples, and others pertaining to eighteenth-century usage in the next paragraphs are gleaned from and typical of IA, DC/HX 117–01, IA, DC/HX 117–02, IA, DC/HX 118–01, IA, DC/HX 118–02, IA, DC/HX 119–01, IA, DC/HX 119–02, IA, DC/HX 119–03, IA, DC/HX 119–04, IA, DC/HX 120–01, IA, DC/HX 120–03, IA, DC/HX 121–02.

[200] These distinctive features are summarised in M.C. Jones, *The Guernsey Norman French Translations of Thomas Martin: A Linguistic Study of an Unpublished Archive* (Leuven, 2008), pp. 33–5.

[201] Nicolas Dobrée to Sarah Messervy, 10.8.1749, L/C/67/F3, Jersey Archive.

[202] George Métivier glosses it as '*fleur de bière*' in his *Dictionnaire Franco-Normand ou Recueil des Mots particuliers au Dialecte de Guernesey* (London, 1870).

Such were the beginnings. However, with the turn of the nineteenth century came signs of more fundamental change. Registers continued to be kept in French, but the Directors who replaced Jean Condamine and his colleagues in 1809 chose English titles for their new sub-committees: 'Education and Morals', 'Cleanliness and Salubrity', and so on.[203] This preference underlines the advance of cultural anglicisation among St Peter Port's elite, many of whom were now attending English schools and marrying into English families. Usage among the lower ranks in the first decades of the century also reflects a state of transition. Only half of the new prayerbooks ordered for inmates in 1813 were in French; the others were in English.[204] In 1822, anglophones were separated from francophones in the infirmary so that each group might pray in its own language.[205] In 1823, an account in French of an escape bid by Marie Pallot and Jeanne Le Page explicitly recorded their cry of 'death or liberty' as being in English.[206] Perhaps the best encapsulation of the linguistically intermediate state of the Hospital at this time is the punitive placard worn by James Lihou in 1825: 'IVROGNE ET DRUNK'.[207]

Over the following twenty years, Town Hospital registers reveal a more decisive shift towards English. Metalinguistic evidence shows that, although 'French' remained the official language of record, English was the language in which compilers now habitually thought and spoke. An official account in French of a fight between inmates in 1839 was marginally annotated 'a load of blackguards!'[208] Sentence construction now followed not Norman French but English norms, with French vocabulary inserted into the slots of an underlying English syntax. This is evident in such phrases as, in 1845, '*il eut une cuisse amputée*', which is a literal translation of 'he had a thigh amputated', where a more idiomatic French rendering would be '*il fut amputé d'une cuisse*'.[209] Sometimes, moreover, the 'French' words used were not French at all, but pseudo-French calques of English words: *satisfactoire* instead of *satisfaisant*; *lunatique* instead of *aliéné*.[210] In 1850, a register entry revealed that reports were now initially drafted in English before being translated into French for the official record.[211] Seven years later, efforts to keep registers in what had become an unfamiliar tongue were abandoned and, from 1857 onwards, Poor Law Board minutes and Hospital daybooks were kept entirely in English.[212]

This shift in Hospital record-keeping summed up the linguistic shift which had taken place in St Peter Port generally. Regular steamship services to England since 1824 had greatly accelerated the dissemination of English books, newspapers,

203 7.2.1810, IA, DC/HX 079–02.
204 5.7.1813, IA, DC/HX 079–02.
205 25.10.1822, IA, DC/HX 124–02.
206 15.10.1823, IA, DC/HX 135–02.
207 6.4.1825, IA, DC/HX 135–02.
208 8.2.1839, IA, DC/HX 075–01.
209 8.7.1845, IA, DC/HX 130–01.
210 4.5.1846, IA, DC/HX 130–01; 19.4.1852, IA, DC/HX 075–02.
211 19.7.1850, IA, DC/HX 075–02.
212 2.2.1857, IA, DC/HX 054–05. House Committee minutes were however kept in French until 1890.

fashions, practices and ideas.[213] The sustained influx of English migrants since 1816 had also transformed the town's ethnic make-up, so that, by 1851, non-natives, mostly English, comprised 39 per cent of civilian parishioners and over half of 20- to 55-year-olds.[214] The inevitable outcome of these processes, as a mid-nineteenth-century newspaper observed, was that 'the language of the people' had been transformed 'from French into English'.[215]

In the last third of the nineteenth century, a campaign to restore French to its former status in island life was initiated by a group of prominent Guernseymen. In 1867, these individuals founded a *Société Guernesiaise* to promote the use of French, and over the next few years exerted their influence to ensure that educational links with the British government were cut and that the learning of French was made compulsory in all local primary schools.[216] Hospital records contain a dim reflection of this era. In 1870, the request of the Hospital chaplain to abolish religious services in French was refused.[217] In 1871, the House Committee instituted a special prize for children's proficiency in French.[218]

Both inside and outside the Hospital, however, such measures were ineffectual. Within little more than two decades, the States had conceded the ubiquity of English in local life by accepting English as an official language of debate in the assembly.[219] In the Hospital, this acknowledgement had its parallel in a final tidying up of linguistic loose ends. In 1894 and 1900 respectively, house rules and then the Poor Law Board constitution were for the first time officially published in English.[220] In 1903, the corporate notepaper of the House Committee and Poor Law Board acquired an English heading, and, from 1904, Poor Law Board meetings opened and closed with prayers in English rather than the traditional French.[221]

The distinct variant of *guernesiais* spoken in St Peter Port became extinct around 1900.[222] By this point, most French, standard or *patois*, heard in town would have been spoken by French immigrants or incoming rural parishioners. In 1911, census enumerators' books show that the Town Hospital accommodated just eight French inmates and fifteen from the country parishes in a total complement of 181.[223] We may therefore surmise that, by World War I, Hospital corridors, too, echoed largely to the sounds of English speech.

---

[213] Crossan, *Guernsey, 1814–1914*, p. 105.

[214] 1851 census enumerators' books (microfilm), PL. See also Crossan, *Guernsey, 1814–1914*, pp. 70, 209.

[215] *Comet*, 28.12.1848.

[216] Crossan, *Guernsey, 1814–1914*, pp. 252–5; R.-M. Crossan, 'The retreat of French from Guernsey's public primary schools, 1800–1939', *TSG*, 25 (2005), pp. 861–5.

[217] 8.8.1870, 15.11.1870, IA, DC/HX 054–05.

[218] 23.2.1871, IA, DC/HX 136–08.

[219] Crossan, *Guernsey, 1814–1914*, pp. 272–3.

[220] 26.2.1894, IA, DC/HX 136–04; 5.11.1900, IA, DC/HX 056–04.

[221] 6.7.1903, 11.3.1904, IA, DC/HX 056–04.

[222] E. Martel, 'Philological report', *TSG*, 17 (1965), p. 709.

[223] http://1911census.co.uk.

Epilogue

We will conclude our survey of the Town Hospital firstly with some general observations on the nature of the Hospital, and then with an account of the institution's final years.

The view is sometimes heard in Guernsey that the Town Hospital was never a workhouse. This may be partly due to its title, and partly, perhaps, to a wish to distance it from the English institutions which have attracted so much opprobrium. Yet this is how its founders first conceived it, and how later administrators also referred to it.[224] In essence, the Town Hospital served a very similar function to any medium-size workhouse in England, and – almost definingly – it subjected its inmates to the same obligation to work. Where the similarity with England ends, however, is that the Town Hospital's inmates did not have any of the protections which English workhouse inmates derived from belonging to a national system supervised by a central bureaucracy and regulated by law. The law accorded inmates rights and provided mechanisms for their enforcement. The bureaucracy, removed from the pressures of ratepayer politics, enforced basic standards and provided the momentum for reform. In Guernsey, there was no regulation and no supervision until the twentieth century, and parochial authorities had free rein to treat inmates of their workhouses as they wished. In consequence of this, not only did inmates of the Town Hospital endure all the hardships which attracted opprobrium in England, but they suffered many more besides. Town Hospital inmates' basic living conditions took decades longer to improve than those of their counterparts across the Channel. Town Hospital authorities exercised powers of detention, expulsion and tutelage over inmates which were completely unknown to English guardians. The disciplinary regime to which inmates were subject was more arbitrary and more oppressive than that in force in England and Wales.

One characteristic, however, which the Town Hospital did have in common with kindred institutions all over Britain was that it continued to exist late into the twentieth century. Also like them, its role underwent mutations as that century progressed. After the advent of the welfare state in 1948, many former English and Welsh poor law institutions became homes for the elderly.[225] So, eventually, did the Town Hospital, but the process was protracted over more than two decades. The year 1948 marked a milestone for the Town Hospital as well as for the British welfare state, so we shall resume the history of the institution in that year.

In 1948, the Town Hospital, now States-funded, remained under the Public Assistance Authority and retained its poor law status.[226] By this time, it had become

---

[224] See, for instance, Treasurer Thomas Clugas in a letter dated 24.5.1843 (IA, DC/HX 130–01).

[225] Crowther, *Workhouse System*, p. 153; S. Fowler, *Workhouse: The People, the Places, the Life Behind Doors* (Richmond, 2007), p. 259.

[226] Proposals had been made at the end of World War II to bring the Hospital under the jurisdiction of the States' Board of Health, but these had been rejected by the Public Assistance Authority, whose Hospital Board wished to retain oversight of the institution (19.12.1945, 23.1.1946, IA, AS/MB 065–05).

Guernsey's only repository for people of limited means who required residential care. These included the elderly, the infirm, the chronically ill and down-and-outs. In May 1948, after a period of instability at the helm of its infirmary, the Hospital Board appointed 26-year-old Leeds-trained Celine Bones as sister-in-charge.[227] The dual management structure instituted in 1913 continued in force, and, although Sister Bones was given sole jurisdiction over the infirmary, the master and matron remained in charge of the workhouse.

In 1951, the title of matron fell vacant when the couple in charge of the house were redesignated 'superintendents'.[228] Seven years later, Celine Bones was herself accorded the title of matron, though the superintendents continued in post.[229] This exacerbated friction arising from the division of responsibilities, which eventually led to the resignation of the superintendents in 1963.[230] Bowing to pressure from Matron Bones and her staff, the Hospital Board did not replace them, and officially abolished the post of superintendent in the autumn of that year, giving Matron Bones exclusive charge of the whole institution.[231]

By 1963, house people numbered only seven, and Matron Bones pressed vigorously for the complete abolition of the workhouse department.[232] The incompatibility of infirmary and house had been officially acknowledged as early as 1960 and, in September 1967, the workhouse department was finally closed down.[233] As well as marking the belated demise of the workhouse as a living institution in Guernsey, its closure also signalled the end of the Hospital's long transformation into a home for the elderly.

This transformation had come about by default rather than design. For more than a decade after the war, there had been no clarity as to the Hospital's mission and it had continued to serve as a catch-all institution for those requiring long-term care who could not be accommodated elsewhere. Only in 1956, after Sister Bones had questioned the propriety of admitting a 9-year-old, was the decision taken actively to prioritise the elderly, 'particularly those unable to remain in their own homes'.[234] From this time onwards, fewer chronically ill people were admitted to the Hospital's wards, but it was to be another decade before the institution's population was exclusively composed of the old. Having, however, finally attained this position, the Hospital passed another significant milestone. In 1970, it was removed from the

[227] 15.5.1948, IA, AS/MB 065–02.

[228] 5.5.1951, IA, AS/MB 065–02.

[229] 22.10.1958, IA, AS/MB 065–02.

[230] 25.3.1963, IA, AS/MB 065–02.

[231] 31.10.1963, IA, AS/MB 065–02. Miss Bones remained in charge of the Town Hospital until its closure in 1986. For a résumé of her career, see *Guernsey Press*, 20.5.2010.

[232] 22.1.1964, IA, AS/MB 065–02.

[233] *Billet*, 20.4.1960; 23.11.1960, IA, AS/MB 065–02; 25.9.1967, IA, AS/MB 068–01. The remaining house people were relocated to the Hospital's former lunatic asylum, transformed into a 'welfare hostel', to be run by the Central Outdoor Assistance Board under the name of St Julian's House.

[234] 24.10.1956, IA, AS/MB 065–02.

domain of the poor law altogether and transferred to the jurisdiction of the newly instituted Geriatric Committee of the States' Board of Health.[235]

The name of the Hospital had by this time officially been changed to the 'St Peter Port Hospital', but little could be done about its fabric. With its stone-flagged floors and rows of iron bedsteads, it still smacked of its past. Nine years later, now a scheduled 'ancient monument', the Hospital was described as 'archaic, costly to maintain and difficult to run'.[236]

By 1979, Guernsey's States were funding a total of 250 long-stay beds for the elderly, of which 108 were in the Town Hospital.[237] In that year, the States were advised that their 250 beds equated to proportionately double the number of local authority long-stay beds in the United Kingdom. They were also informed that closure of the Town Hospital would save them £132,000 a year. This prompted the passage of a resolution in principle to close the institution down.[238]

For a while, nothing was done. Problems in finding alternative accommodation for patients ensured that the Hospital remained operational, though with minimal maintenance. In 1983, growing concerns over fire safety finally persuaded the Board of Health that plans for closure must be implemented and, the following year, residents began to be moved out.[239] It took months to relocate all the Hospital's patients, but, by the end of October 1986, the last twenty-six of them had gone.[240] Following their departure, the Hospital was emptied of equipment and eventually relinquished by the Board of Health in July 1987.[241] After a brief spell housing the Island Archives (during which the records on which this book is based were found), work began to prepare the building for a quite different role. Suitably modified – although, appropriately, still containing its old cells – the 250-year-old building reopened as Guernsey's police headquarters in 1993.

---

[235] 1.5.1970, IA, AS/MB 067–09.
[236] *Billet*, 12.12.1979.
[237] *Billet*, 12.12.1979.
[238] *Billet*, 12.12.1979; *Guernsey Evening Press*, 10.12.1979, 13.12.1979.
[239] 23.3.1983, 5.12.1984, IA, BH 52–14.
[240] *Guernsey Evening Press*, 24.9.1986; 4.11.1986, IA, BH 52–14.
[241] 14.7.1987, IA, BH 52–14.

IV

Twentieth Century and Beyond

10

From Parishes to States

This chapter will chart the growth of States' involvement in social welfare after 1900. Its chief source will be the *Billets d'Etat* containing agendas for States' meetings and background information on proposals. It will also use contemporary newspaper accounts of States' meetings and press articles on States' policies. The first section will deal with the development of a system of social security over the first two-thirds of the twentieth century. The second section will focus on the evolution of a health service.

Towards social security

1900–1940

Prior to the late nineteenth century, public welfare all over Europe was largely controlled by municipalities or communes. The wider state seldom had a role and, where it did – as in England – it was one of co-ordination rather than direct funding or provision. Towards the end of the nineteenth century, as economic competition between nations intensified, a debate arose in northern Europe concerning the desirability of state intervention in securing the well-being of national populations and, one by one, central governments increased their welfare activities. In most European countries, the first government measures concerned the welfare of the national work-force. In 1871, Germany, the pioneer in this field, passed an Employers' Liability Act making employers in mines, quarries and factories liable to pay compensation for workplace injuries or deaths caused by their negligence.[1] In 1880, the United Kingdom took its own first steps down this path with a similarly titled but more limited Act giving injured workers the faculty of suing their employers.[2] It was also in this area that Guernsey made an initial foray into what might broadly be termed 'welfare' legislation, although twenty years later and in slightly different form. The 1900 Law on Compensation to Families of Persons killed in Accidents empowered

---

[1] J. Tampke, 'Bismarck's social legislation: a genuine breakthrough?', in W.J. Mommsen and W. Mock (eds), *The Emergence of the Welfare State in Britain and Germany, 1850–1950* (London, 1981), p. 74.

[2] The Employers' Liability Act, 1880 (43 and 44 Vic., c.42) codified the common law liability of employers for workplace injuries sustained through their negligence.

executors or administrators of the estate of any person whose death had been caused by negligence to sue the negligent party for damages on behalf of the deceased's family.[3] Although this law was not restricted merely to workplace accidents, it was explicitly described in a local newspaper as 'an adaptation of the [United Kingdom] Employers' Liability Act'.[4] Use of the law was not widespread owing to the cumbersome legal process involved, but its passage showed an awareness of developments elsewhere and a nascent acknowledgement that government might have a role, however indirect, in protecting the interests of the disadvantaged.

Although Guernsey's States passed no further such legislation for the next twenty-five years, pressures associated with World War I forced them to intervene in other ways. Living costs rose exponentially during the war, producing unrest among Guernsey workers even while hostilities continued. When the war ended and local servicemen began to be repatriated, not only did the cost of living remain high but there were serious shortages of both jobs and housing. The immediate post-war situation demanded urgent measures and, in December 1918, the States established a 'Homes for Workers Committee' to tackle the housing crisis.[5] Five months later, they also set up a 'Committee for Works of Public Utility' to organise relief work for the jobless.[6] These two Committees were to have a significant impact on the insular community over the inter-war decades, so their work will be examined in detail.

In 1919, the States granted the Committee for Works of Public Utility £2,000 to employ men to clear cemeteries and parks, cut cliff paths and build and repair roads.[7] Though there were models for this north of the Channel,[8] the provision of relief work by Guernsey's States was unprecedented. Further grants to the Committee were provided in 1923 and 1926, and again in the early 1930s as unemployment flared.[9] By 1932, more than 500 men were employed on an extensive works programme which now included the construction of a major road.[10] By the time the road was opened in 1935, the worst of the crisis was over and the scheme was discontinued (though it was revived under the States' Labour and Welfare Committee in the post-war period).

The Homes for Workers Committee set up in 1918 was originally charged with investigating remedies not only to the housing shortage but to 'deplorable' housing

3   O in C, 13.12.1900. All local laws of relevance to this chapter are listed in Appendix 10.
4   *Star*, 10.11.1900. The newspaper explained that the law was 'the outcome of an accident which had occurred a year or two ago, the results of which had occupied the Royal Court without satisfaction to the plaintiff'.
5   *Billet*, 18.12.1918.
6   *Billet*, 21.5.1919.
7   *Billet*, 21.5.1919.
8   Notably Westminster's 1905 Unemployed Workmen Act, which had provided for the establishment of relief work schemes at local level (P. Murray, *Poverty and Welfare, 1830–1914* (London, 1999), p. 100).
9   *Billets*, 10.1.1923, 27.10.1926, 20.1.1932, 19.10.1932, 18.12.1932.
10 This was le Val des Terres, an arterial route linking St Peter Port to the south of the island. For details of relief projects, see *Billet*, 2.12.1932 and *Guernsey Weekly Press*, 9.1.1932.

conditions generally.[11] In their first report (strongly influenced by the social housing programme inaugurated in Britain by the post-war Lloyd George government) the Committee made three main recommendations: first, the immediate erection of a minimum of twelve 'model cottages'; second, the introduction of low-interest loans to workers wishing to build their own homes; and, third, the institution of a law compulsorily enforcing the repair of sub-standard houses.[12] The States rejected the first recommendation but adopted the two latter, and a limited loans scheme and compulsory repair scheme became operational in 1920.[13]

The ostensible reason for the States' rejection of the Committee's proposal for model cottages was that they had no wish to become house-builders. However, with the housing crisis unabated, necessity soon forced them into house-building of a sort. In 1921, to cope with families facing eviction from temporary homes in militia arsenals, the States gave the Homes for Workers Committee £5,000 to erect a number of prefabricated wooden dwellings, which they subsequently let at between 5s and 7s 6d per week.[14] The breaching of this psychological barrier seems to have freed the States to embark on more ambitious social housing projects. In 1922, they allocated the Committee a further £10,000, this time to build proper houses of bricks and mortar.[15] Further grants and further developments followed over the next few years, such that, by 1937, 1,817 islanders were living in States' houses and flats.[16]

Aside from this and the public works scheme, early twentieth-century States' initiatives in the realm of public welfare were few in comparison with those of other northern European jurisdictions. By World War I, Austria, Belgium, Denmark, France, Germany, the Netherlands, Romania, Sweden and the United Kingdom had all instituted welfare programmes encompassing cover for sickness, for workplace accidents and for old age.[17]

In the United Kingdom, much important welfare legislation was passed by the Liberal government of 1906–14. Partly from a wish to limit the influence of the Labour Party after late nineteenth-century franchise extensions, the Liberals introduced a Workmen's Compensation Act in 1906, an Old Age Pensions Act in 1908 and a National Insurance Act in 1911. These schemes were facilitated by the institution of an unprecedentedly redistributive system of taxation in Lloyd George's 'People's Budget' of 1909, which introduced a new supertax on the very wealthy, a new graduated income tax and increased duties on alcohol, tobacco and motoring.[18]

---

[11] *Billets*, 18.12.1918, 19.2.1919.
[12] *Billet*, 30.12.1919. For more on Westminster's post-war housing policy, see J. Burnett, *A Social History of Housing, 1815–1970* (1978; London, 1983 edn), pp. 216–22.
[13] R.P. Hocart, *An Island Assembly: The Development of the States of Guernsey, 1700–1949* (Guernsey, 1988), p. 100.
[14] The arsenals had been used as emergency accommodation between the suspension of the local militia in 1916 and its revival five years later (Hocart, *Island Assembly*, p. 100).
[15] *Billet*, 6.12.1922.
[16] Hocart, *Island Assembly*, p. 100.
[17] M. Cousins, *European Welfare States: Comparative Perspectives* (London, 2005), p. 81.
[18] D. Gladstone, *The Twentieth-Century Welfare State* (Basingstoke, 1999), pp. 18, 98–9.

The passage of the United Kingdom Workmen's Compensation Act in 1906 had attracted the attention of the Guernsey Reform Association, which was at that time lobbying for local social and political modernisation. The 1906 Act differed from the United Kingdom's 1880 Employer's Liability Act in that it obliged employers to pay compensation for workplace injuries on a no-fault basis, without the need to sue through the courts.[19] With serious maimings and even deaths a regular occurrence in Guernsey's quarrying industry, the Reform Association felt that such a measure was urgently needed in Guernsey. Immediately following the passage of the Act, the Association wrote to Labour MP Keir Hardie, asking him 'to do his utmost to have the Workmen's Compensation Act extended to Guernsey'.[20] This resulted in a Home Office suggestion to Guernsey's Royal Court that it might be advisable to adopt the Act, but the Court demurred on the grounds that it was unsuited to local conditions. The Court added, however, that it approved the principle of workmen's compensation and would be prepared in due course to recommend it to the States in more appropriate form.[21] This marked the beginning of a long process which finally culminated in Guernsey's first piece of mainstream welfare legislation.

For six years after this exchange of correspondence, the issue of workmen's compensation was left on the back-burner. However, a group of twenty-nine States members and others took it up again during a period of labour unrest in 1912. Petitioning the States for a local workmen's compensation scheme, they asserted that the support offered by parish or charity was 'barely sufficient to provide the meanest necessities of life, and … an accident may doom a Worker and his dependants to lives of misery from … no fault of their own'.[22] The States appointed a committee to look into the matter and, after eighteen months of research, this committee submitted a set of proposals for a workmen's compensation law in 1914.[23] The States, however, found these proposals unsatisfactory and, after amendments in 1915 failed to allay their misgivings, the matter was suspended for the duration of the First World War.[24] This suspension was further compounded by delays in the post-war period and, in the event, it was not until 1924 that a Workmen's Accident Compensation Law was finally approved – a full eighteen years since its first mooting.[25]

The Guernsey Workmen's Accident Compensation Law of 1924 was, in its final form, a hybrid law, exhibiting affinities with Britain's 1911 National Insurance Act as well as with the 1906 Workmen's Compensation Act. Part One of the National Insurance Act had made it compulsory for employees on less than £160

---

19 The principle of no-fault liability had already been established in the Workmen's Compensation Act of 1897, of which the 1906 Act was an extension and elaboration.

20 *Star*, 27.11.1906.

21 *Hansard*, House of Commons Debates, 28.5.1906, vol. 158, c.68; Home Office to Lieutenant Governor, 26.1.1907, TNA, HO 45/12918.

22 *Billet*, 22.5.1912. A later publication claimed that the move was partly prompted by an incident where a man had been badly injured attempting to stop a bolting horse and was thereafter reduced to parish relief (P. Dorey, *Official Opening of Edward T. Wheadon House* (Guernsey, 1985), p. 5).

23 *Billet*, 4.3.1914.

24 *Billet*, 30.6.1915.

25 O in C, 9.10.1924. For detail on post-war delays, see Hocart, *Island Assembly*, pp. 100–1.

a year to pay a weekly fourpenny 'stamp' towards a scheme paying doctors' bills, with complementary contributions from employers and the state.[26] The Guernsey law (though its object was not doctors' bills) also adopted the insurance principle, compelling the participation of all employees earning less than £156 a year. The employee's contribution was in Guernsey's case set at 1d, supplemented by 2d from the employer and 1d from the States. Amounts payable in respect of female workers were slightly less. Any employee earning up to £312 yearly could join voluntarily. The scheme applied only to Guernsey, and not to other Bailiwick islands. All contributions paid into the scheme were to be directed to a standing insurance fund, from which benefits would be drawn. This arrangement was quite different from Britain's 1906 Workmen's Compensation Act, which left employers wholly responsible for funding compensation payments by whatever means they saw fit. The reason why it was found necessary to introduce the insurance principle in Guernsey was that the 1924 Workmen's Accident Compensation Law, in its final form, encompassed a far broader sphere than simply the workplace, providing cover for injury and loss of life arising through any accident whatsoever, in the workplace or outside of it. Benefits available under the new law consisted of allowances to the injured in respect of time off work by reason of temporary incapacity, pensions for the permanently disabled, funeral expenses to families in case of an insured person's death and pensions for widows and orphans.

The 1924 Accident Compensation Law came into force on 17 January 1925. The scheme was administered by a newly created States' 'Insurance Authority'. The Authority's first President was Edward Wheadon and its first 'Administrator' Ambrose Robin, both of whom were subsequently to play an important role in shaping Guernsey's social security system.[27] Over the course of 1925, some 9,286 males and 4,400 females joined the new scheme, and 523 claims were successfully processed, 111 of them in respect of stone-workers.[28] Illustrating the local prevalence of low pay, the 9,286 men who enrolled equated to roughly two-thirds of Guernsey males over school-leaving age, and the 4,400 women to one-quarter of females in the same bracket.[29]

An important factor facilitating the passage of Guernsey's 1924 law was the introduction of income tax in 1919, which had provided the States with a consistent and reliable revenue stream.[30] The States' growing confidence in their revenue is reflected in another decision taken in 1924, this time in respect of old age pensions. By 1924, state old age pensions had been available in the United Kingdom for sixteen years and, with each passing year, demand had increased for a similar scheme in Guernsey. Elections to the States were held at the end of January 1924, and, according to the *Star*, 'practically every candidate made the provision of such pensions a plank in his

---

[26] 1 and 2 Geo. V., c.55.
[27] See Plates 10 and 11.
[28] *Billet*, 28.4.1926.
[29] *Census 1921: Jersey, Guernsey and Adjacent Islands* (London, 1924).
[30] O in C 20.12.1919. Note that Jersey, which did not introduce income tax until 1928, had to wait until 1935 for a similar scheme (M. Phillips, *Poor People* (Jersey, 2001), pp. 134, 140).

election platform'.[31] It is notable that this was only the second general election since the States' reform of 1920 had increased the number of Deputies to eighteen and extended the franchise to non-ratepayers.

In March 1924, with a cohort of newly elected Deputies in place, the States agreed in principle to the introduction of old age pensions.[32] The States then appointed a committee to investigate possible schemes, and this committee reported back the following year. Emphasising that the introduction of pensions would 'save' the States at least £4,000 in terms of the poor law costs they had just taken on, the committee submitted proposals for a scheme based explicitly on the United Kingdom's 1908 Old Age Pensions Act.[33]

In contrast to the insurance-based pension schemes favoured in continental Europe, Britain's 1908 Old Age Pensions Act had set up a non-contributory and means-tested old age pension scheme. Under this scheme, people aged 70 and over with incomes below a certain threshold received the full allowable pension, and those with incomes between that threshold and an upper limit qualified for proportionately reduced amounts.[34] The States' Old Age Pensions Committee felt that a non-contributory scheme would also be best for Guernsey, judging that a majority of islanders would 'resent' any compulsion to contribute to an insurance scheme because – with life-expectancy 'far below 70' – few would ever reap any benefits.[35]

The States accepted the committee's proposals, and Guernsey's first Old Age Pensions Law was passed in 1926.[36] Just as in the United Kingdom, recipients had to be over 70.[37] If an individual's income was under £12 per year, he or she qualified for the full pension of 8s a week. For those with incomes between £12 and an upper limit of £40, pensions were reduced on a sliding scale. The law was to be administered by a new States' 'Old Age Pensions Authority', and monies paid out to pensioners were to be drawn entirely from States' general revenue. A few years later, blind persons aged 50 and over were made eligible for means-tested pensions on the same terms as the over-70s.[38]

In the new Old Age Pensions scheme's first six months of operation, 862 individuals were awarded pensions, most of them at the full rate.[39] As testimony to both the small size and poverty of Guernsey's older generation in the mid-1920s, these 862

[31] *Star*, 6.3.1924.
[32] *Billet*, 12.3.1924.
[33] *Billet*, 14.1.1925.
[34] 8 Edw. VII, c.40. Further Acts in 1911, 1919 and 1924 introduced minor amendments.
[35] *Billet*, 14.1.1925.
[36] O in C, 19.3.1926. Like the 1924 Accident Insurance Law, the 1926 Old Age Pensions Law applied only to the island of Guernsey, and not the whole Bailiwick.
[37] They had also to have been British subjects for at least the previous ten years. All British subjects had additionally to have lived in Guernsey for twelve years since attaining the age of 50, and all naturalised foreigners to have lived in Guernsey for twenty years since the age of 45. These provisions were analogous to those set out in the United Kingdom Old Age Pensions Acts passed between 1908 and 1924.
[38] O in C, 1.10.1931.
[39] *Billet*, 25.2.1927.

people equated to approximately 40 per cent of all the island's over-70s.[40]

A mere two years after the passage of the 1926 Old Age Pensions Law, dissatisfaction with its operation began to emerge. Ambrose Robin, now in charge of both the Old Age Pensions and Insurance Authorities, submitted a report in 1928 which pointed out the deficiencies of the new law. The main problem, in his view, was that 8s a week was 'obviously inadequate to provide complete subsistence'. Many pensioners were therefore still having to seek poor law help and were ending up as Hospital inmates at 'three times [the cost] of the maximum pension'.[41] Robin's report did not elicit any response from the States, and the same misgivings were forcibly restated three years later in a joint letter to the States from the Presidents of the Insurance and Old Age Pensions Authorities.[42] Castigating the non-contributory scheme as an extremely costly 'glorified system of relief', they petitioned for an investigation of possible new insurance-based pensions which would also cover widows and orphans. The States consented, and there followed a period of research during which the assistance of the British Government Actuary's Department was enlisted. Finally, in 1933, formal proposals were submitted to the States for a comprehensive contributory scheme similar in its scope to that which had already been established in the United Kingdom by the 1925 Widows', Orphans' and Old Age Contributory Pensions Act, but which would also include the element of accident insurance presently offered under the Guernsey Workmen's Accident Compensation Law of 1924.[43]

The 1925 United Kingdom Widows', Orphans' and Old Age Contributory Pensions Act had been passed because of dissatisfactions with the 1908 non-contributory Old Age Pensions Act similar to those Guernsey had experienced with its own law. The 1925 Act had set up an entirely new state pension scheme in which all employees earning £160 a year or less were compulsorily obliged to enrol.[44] Weekly contributions were required of both employees and employers, and the government's contribution came in the form of an Exchequer grant to the fund from which pensions were paid. The maximum pension, now payable from the age of 65, was 10s per week.[45] Benefits were also available to widows of deceased contributors with young children. Since these pensions and benefits had been 'earned' through contributions to a scheme, they were all provided without means-testing.

In 1934, Guernsey's States accepted the proposals which had been laid before them for a contributory scheme of their own and, the following year, the island's new Contributory Pensions and Accident Insurance Law was passed.[46] This law, which came into force on 30 June 1935, made enrolment compulsory for all employed people over school-leaving age whose earnings did not exceed £156 per

[40] *Census 1921: Jersey, Guernsey and Adjacent Islands* (London, 1924).
[41] *Billet*, 24.2.1928.
[42] *Billet*, 16.9.1931.
[43] *Billet*, 29.11.1933.
[44] 15 and 16 Geo. V., c.70.
[45] For technical reasons, the 1925 scheme paid old age pensions only between the ages of 65 and 70, after which pensioners went on to the 1908 scheme, but without means-testing.
[46] O in C, 6.6.1935.

year.[47] Each male employee contributed a weekly 5d, his employer 4d and the States 8d. Contributions in respect of females were slightly lower.[48] The maximum rate for an old age pension was set, as in the United Kingdom, at 10s weekly, although, unlike the United Kingdom, pensionable age remained 70. In addition to pensions, the 1935 law also provided all the benefits formerly available to accident victims and their dependants under the 1924 Workmen's Accident Compensation Law, which it repealed and replaced. Thus a single unified contributory scheme now provided all working-age islanders on low pay with cover for both accidents and old age.

Given the unitary nature of the 1935 scheme, the former States' Insurance and Old Age Pensions Authorities were merged into a single States' Insurance Authority, again under the presidency of Edward Wheadon. The Authority's staff numbered just seven – six clerks, and Ambrose Robin, the Administrator. The new Authority's first report stated that a total of 16,272 individuals were enrolled in the Contributory Pensions and Accident Insurance scheme as at 1 June 1936. Most were transfers from the defunct Accident Compensation scheme. Payment of old age pensions had been deferred for two years from the commencement of the 1935 law and was subject to payees having made a qualifying number of contributions. Non-contributory pensions continued to be paid under the 1926 Old Age Pensions Law (as amended) to those too old to accrue sufficient contributions. The Authority anticipated that about ninety people would be receiving pensions under the new scheme in 1937, and that numbers on non-contributory pensions would 'decrease fairly rapidly' over the next few years.[49]

Such was the situation on the eve of World War II. In comparative terms, Guernsey people were better off than their counterparts in Jersey, where the only social security legislation to be passed before the war was the 1935 Workmen's Compensation Law (which, unlike Guernsey's 1924 law, covered workplace accidents only).[50] They were, however, significantly worse off than their contemporaries in the United Kingdom, who benefited not only from a contributory state pension scheme similar to theirs but also from contributory unemployment and health insurance schemes first introduced under the 1911 National Insurance Act. Some 60 per cent of United Kingdom workers were covered by the state unemployment insurance scheme by the mid-1930s, and unemployed people who were not covered could claim a means-tested dole from the Unemployment Assistance Board.[51] In 1932, Guernsey's States had rejected a petition from the Transport and General Workers' Union to consider creating a States' unemployment insurance scheme, leaving Guernsey with no statutory provision for unemployment, and the unemployed with no recourse but the

---

[47] Compulsory contributors ceasing to meet these criteria were also given the opportunity of continuing to be insured voluntarily.

[48] The States additionally agreed to make an annual grant of £21,900 to the insurance fund given that its income would initially be insufficient to meet outgoings.

[49] *Billet*, 7.10.1936.

[50] Phillips, *Poor People*, p. 140.

[51] H. Makower, J. Marschak and H.W. Robinson, 'Studies in mobility of labour: analysis of Great Britain, part one', *Oxford Economic Papers*, 2 (1939), p. 73; A. Brundage, *The English Poor Laws, 1700–1930* (Basingstoke, 2002), p. 152.

parish.[52] Similarly, while over 40 per cent of Britain's 1930s population benefited from free medical treatment under the state health insurance scheme,[53] there was no equivalent in Guernsey, and islanders unable to pay their own medical bills again had little choice but to apply to their *Procureur*.[54]

1940–2000s

Unsurprisingly, the period of German Occupation between 1940 and 1945 produced little by way of welfare legislation. The one exception was the introduction of Child Benefit in 1943.[55] Edward Wheadon had originally petitioned the States to this effect in 1940, but the 1943 measure seems to have been principally inspired by pressure from the Occupiers, in whose homeland Family Allowances had been introduced by the Nazi government in 1935,[56] and who had overseen the introduction of a similar scheme in Jersey the previous year. By virtue of the Children's Allowances Law of 18 September 1943, every compulsory contributor under Guernsey's 1935 Old Age Pensions and Accident Insurance Law became eligible for a means-tested allowance of up to 4s per week for each dependent child under school-leaving age. The law was extended in January 1944 to cover children other than those of compulsory contributors.

While Guernsey languished under German occupation, welfare matters were high on the agenda across the Channel in the United Kingdom. Amid growing public demand for more generous provision and recognition by politicians that reform was overdue, debate was in progress over the best means to achieve this. Much of this debate centred on proposals which William Beveridge had set out in his 1942 *Report on Social Insurance and Allied Services*. Three years later, in the general election which followed the war, the Labour Party put Beveridge-style reform at the heart of its manifesto and was swept to a landslide victory. Having received an unequivocal mandate, the new government then set about preparing three statutes based on Beveridge's ideas, which effectively inaugurated the modern British welfare state. First, the 1946 National Insurance Act introduced a universal system of social insurance with compulsory flat-rate contributions, which provided flat-rate benefits covering unemployment, sickness, maternity, funeral expenses, widows' pensions and old age pensions.[57] Second, the 1946 National Health Service Act instituted a free comprehensive state health service, transferring hospitals to the jurisdiction of the Ministry of Health and introducing state-salaried consultants.[58] Third, the 1948 National Assistance Act created a new National Assistance Board to provide

---

[52] *Billet*, 20.1.1932.

[53] P. Murray, *Poverty and Welfare, 1830–1914* (London, 1999), p. 124.

[54] With the one exception that, under the 1935 Pensions and Accident Insurance Law, the Insurance Authority was obliged to pay for the first medical consultation received by an insured person after an accident.

[55] *Billet*, 9.8.1943.

[56] T. Mason, 'Women in Germany, 1925–1940: family, welfare and work, part one', *History Workshop*, 1 (1976), pp. 97–8.

[57] 9 and 10 Geo. VI, c.67.

[58] 9 and 10 Geo. VI, c.81.

means-tested help to those whose resources, including National Insurance benefits, were insufficient to meet their needs.[59] All three of these statutes came into effect on 5 July 1948.[60]

Many of the 23,000 Guernsey people evacuated to Great Britain in 1940 absorbed British wartime welfare aspirations. Some joined Jersey evacuees in publishing a survey of the Islands which criticised pre-war social policies and echoed the Beveridgian view that 'release from the fear of want, in sickness, unemployment and old age, are the pre-requisites for creative living'.[61] In January 1945, anticipating the end of Occupation and perhaps aware of the British mood, Guernsey's States themselves resolved to commission 'a comprehensive report regarding changes which are desirable in our social services'.[62] Five months later, days after the German surrender, the Insurance Authority contacted the British government in quest of information on proposed welfare changes as well as copies of the Beveridge Report and government White Papers. The Authority's President and Administrator then travelled to London to meet the Government Actuary and accepted his offer of 'an outline of a comprehensive scheme'.[63] In the relief of liberation, optimism predominated and, in an important decision made in November 1947, the States agreed to the drafting of a *projet de loi* relating to a comprehensive social insurance scheme along the lines of the Actuary's recommendations.[64]

A further important decision taken by the States in these first few post-war months was to replace the 1943 Children's Allowances Law with a law broadly modelled on the United Kingdom's 1945 Family Allowances Act. Guernsey's new scheme, which came into force in May 1948, was universal and non-means-tested, giving all insular families a set allowance for each child from general revenue.[65] Unlike the United Kingdom law, however, the new Guernsey law provided for allowances in respect of all children below school-leaving age, rather than for second and subsequent children only. The law was soon repealed and replaced by another which, as well as also covering Alderney, conformed more narrowly to United Kingdom practice in restricting payments to families with two or more children and providing no allowance for the first.[66] Ostensibly, post-war Guernsey was set to follow Westminster fairly closely down the welfare route.

Nevertheless, by the time the proposed 'National Insurance (Guernsey) Law' was submitted to the States at the end of 1949, the apparent initial consensus had begun to fade. Friendly societies had declared their opposition to the law, as had a large

---

[59] 11 and 12 Geo. VI, c.29. This Act also officially abolished the poor law.

[60] The National Insurance (Industrial Injuries) Act, which provided benefits for workplace injuries and industrial diseases, also came into force on this date. For more detail on these statutes and their genesis, see Gladstone, *Twentieth-Century Welfare State*, pp. 40–6.

[61] Anon., *Nos Iles: A Symposium on the Channel Islands* (Teddington, 1944), p. 84.

[62] *Billet*, 10.7.1946.

[63] *Billet*, 10.7.1946.

[64] *Billet*, 24.11.1947.

[65] The Family Allowances Law, 1947 (O in C, 24.2.1948).

[66] The Family Allowances (Guernsey) Law, 1950 (O in C, 25.4.1950). This law remains in force at the time of writing, although an ordinance of 1980 reinstated the payment of allowances in respect of all of a family's children (Ord, 24.9.1980).

number of Guernsey's small employers and many politically conservative islanders wary of what they saw as 'socialism'.[67] Negativity was compounded by economic uncertainty as Guernsey continued its recovery from occupation. On 30 November 1949, a motion not to proceed with the scheduled debate on the Insurance Law was carried by twenty-nine votes to twenty-six.[68] This effectively barred further progress on the new law. Edward Wheadon, still at the helm of the Insurance Authority, was prompted to ask whether the earlier courage of the States had turned into 'fatty degeneration of the heart'.[69]

After sixteen months of political manoeuvring, the draft law was resubmitted to the States unaltered in April 1951.[70] On this occasion, the debate was allowed to proceed and the law was approved, but only by the casting vote of the Bailiff, Sir Ambrose Sherwill. Unhappy at this state of affairs, Sherwill had the *projet* submitted again the following month, and this time it was passed by a clear majority of two.[71] The new law – which provided for universal contributory unemployment and sickness benefit, maternity grant, attendance allowance, maternity allowance, widow's benefit, retirement pension and death grant – was then sanctioned in the usual manner by the King in Council.[72] This having been done, the States' Insurance Authority made a statutory instrument appointing 3 March 1952 as the day when the scheme would come into operation. The law's opponents, however, remained as determined as ever to block it, and it was at this very last stage that they ultimately succeeded in their aim. The next paragraphs will describe the tactics they used.

Throughout this period, controversy had also been raging in Jersey over its own 'Insular Insurance Law', similarly inspired by Westminster and comparable to the proposed Guernsey law. Newspapers in each island carried reports of the progress of each other's laws, and a degree of reciprocal influence was brought to bear.[73] Ultimately, Jersey's Insular Insurance Law gained Privy Council sanction in 1950, and 10 September 1951 was appointed as the day it would come into force. Just like the Guernsey law, Jersey's Insurance Law remained unacceptable to some islanders, and a vigorous last-ditch campaign was mounted to persuade the States to annul the Appointed Day Order. A petition was organised to this effect, and 18,000 signatures were garnered in support.[74]

It was this strategy which Guernsey's own anti-law lobby replicated in 1952, collecting some 14,314 signatures as the starting date for the National Insurance Law drew near. These signatures were then presented to the States in support of a motion put by Deputy Clifford Moullin in February 1952 to annul the Insurance

---

[67] *Star*, 1.12.1949.
[68] *Billet*, 30.11.1949.
[69] *Star*, 1.12.1949.
[70] *Billet*, 25.4.1951.
[71] *Billets*, 23.5.1951. This majority was later attributed to the two Alderney representatives (*Billet*, 30.7.1952).
[72] O in C, 11.7.1951. In this year, Edward Wheadon, now aged 76, relinquished his presidency of the Insurance Authority.
[73] For inter-island coverage, see Phillips, *Poor People*, p. 183.
[74] Phillips, *Poor People*, pp. 183–90.

Authority's statutory instrument. When Moullin's motion was put to the vote, he and his fellow petitioners met with the success they desired.[75] This was perhaps the more surprising as the Jersey petition of 1951 had failed, and Jersey's Insular Insurance Law had entered into force as planned.

It is possible that the Jersey law owed its ultimate acceptance to its omission of cover for unemployment. This was a contentious issue in both islands, since its provision was held to encourage the work-shy. If the proposed Guernsey law had similarly omitted this item, we may speculate that its fate might have been different. In July 1952, Clifford Moullin and fourteen other States members sought to complete their task by lodging a petition to have the National Insurance (Guernsey) Law formally repealed. They were, however, unsuccessful. The law remained in limbo, on the statute book but unenforced.[76]

Thus Jersey acquired a reasonably comprehensive modern social security scheme in 1951 while Guernsey was left indefinitely with pre-war legislation. One problem much in evidence in Guernsey by this time was that the non-universal nature of the 1935 Pensions and Accident Insurance scheme had left a significant proportion of islanders totally without cover for incapacity or old age. Further, cover which had been earned under the scheme was often inadequate, being based, as it was for many, on intermittent contributions. Such problems had made it impossible to close the 1926 non-contributory pension scheme. However, benefits under this scheme had by this time declined to the extent that they did not yield anything like a living income.

Poverty therefore remained an acute problem for some sections of the Guernsey community in the early 1950s, and this was acknowledged by the States, who, with the failure of the National Insurance Law, set up an 'Indigence Relief Investigation Committee'.[77] To begin with, the Committee was tasked only with finding ways to make parochial relief more acceptable to those who had hitherto shunned it. This brief was found to be too narrow and, in 1952, the Committee was reconstituted as the 'Non-Contributory Relief Investigation Committee' with a mandate to devise an entirely new non-contributory scheme.[78] The result was the Non-Contributory Pensions (Guernsey) Law, 1955.[79]

This new scheme, based broadly on United Kingdom National Assistance, provided means-tested assistance to men over 70; women over 60; widowed, divorced or deserted women incapable of self-support through physical or mental infirmity; the handicapped, and persons over school-leaving age incapacitated by illness or injury for more than six months. It was to be administered by the States' Insurance Authority, and its benefits were to be drawn from States' general revenue. The new law repealed and replaced the 1926 non-contributory pension scheme, and all remaining beneficiaries were transferred to the 1955 scheme. The 1935

[75]   *Billet*, 20.2.1952.
[76]   *Billet*, 30.7.1952; *Star*, 31.7.1952.
[77]   *Billet*, 16.4.1952.
[78]   *Billet*, 20.5.1953.
[79]   O in C, 27.8.1955.

Contributory Pensions and Accident Insurance scheme remained in place; however, those with partial cover due to insufficient contributions could now claim top-ups under the new law.

The Non-Contributory Pensions (Guernsey) Law came into force on 1 November 1955. Its first effect was to reduce the numbers claiming parochial relief. In recognition of the diminished workload, St Peter Port cut its number of Overseers from ten to six.[80] In 1957, the Insurance Authority issued a review of the new non-contributory scheme. Within a few months of commencement, some 1,303 long-term pensions were being paid under the scheme. For a majority of recipients, this pension was their sole income. Fewer than half received any pension at all from the contributory scheme, and three-quarters had made no alternative provision for their old age. This situation disturbed the Administrator, who predicted that, unless this trend was reversed, future calls on States' general revenue would greatly exceed the level foreseen.[81] Correspondence from this period between the Insurance Authority and the British Government Actuary's Department also shows that, since the maximum pension which could be paid under the 1935 Contributory Pensions and Accident Insurance scheme was less than half that payable under the 1955 Non-Contributory Pensions scheme, the Authority was anxious that demand might mount for the abandonment of the contributory principle altogether.[82]

It was this that ultimately caused the resurrection of the abandoned National Insurance project. Alarmed by the Authority's predictions, the States in 1959 requested it to investigate afresh the cost of a comprehensive social insurance scheme.[83] With the assistance of the Government Actuary's Department, the Authority then spent three years researching and drafting a completely new scheme. This time, wishing to avoid a repetition of 1952, its proposals were relatively unambitious, leaving male pensionable age at 70 and providing no cover for unemployment.[84]

The States were scheduled to debate the new proposals in May 1963. In the weeks immediately preceding the debate, the Authority took the precaution of publicising its case in twenty-one public and private meetings. Coverage in television and press was positive, reflecting the buoyant mid-1960s mood.[85] Guernsey had changed profoundly since the austere days of 1952 and, when the proposals were finally submitted, the States not only approved them but directed the Insurance Authority to investigate further enhancements, addressing in particular the questions of male pensionable age and unemployment benefit.[86] Early in 1964, the Insurance Authority returned to the States with a second, rather more ambitious, scheme. It was favourably received and, in a complete reversal of events twelve years

80 *Billet*, 3.4.1957.
81 *Billet*, 23.1.1957.
82 TNA, ACT 1/1495.
83 *Billet*, 29.7.1959.
84 *Billet*, 29.5.1963.
85 *Billet*, 29.5.1963.
86 *Guernsey Evening Press*, 30.5.1963.

earlier, a comprehensive and universal compulsory States insurance scheme was finally voted in.[87]

The Social Insurance (Guernsey) Law, 1964 came into force on 4 January 1965.[88] Modelled on the United Kingdom's 1946 National Insurance Act and applicable to Alderney as well as Guernsey, it obliged all residents over school-leaving age and under 65, whether employed, self-employed or non-employed, to pay a flat-rate contribution.[89] Employers and the States also contributed, and benefits were payable from a newly created 'Guernsey Insurance Fund'. Benefits available under the new scheme encompassed retirement pension, widow's pension, guardian's allowance, sickness benefit, limited medical benefit, industrial disablement benefit, industrial medical benefit and, at long last, unemployment benefit.[90]

The new Social Insurance Law repealed both the 1935 Contributory Pensions and Accident Insurance Law and the ill-fated 1951 National Insurance Law, while leaving the 1955 Non-Contributory Pensions Law untouched. Six years later, however, this law, too, was repealed and replaced by the Supplementary Benefit (Guernsey) Law, 1971.[91] In this case, the change was chiefly terminological, following the lead set by the United Kingdom when it abolished National Assistance and replaced it with Supplementary Benefit in 1966. Guernsey's 1971 Supplementary Benefit Law retained very similar provisions to the 1955 Non-Contributory Law and continued to fulfil the same role. The chief modifications embodied in the new law were the reduction of the qualifying 'old' age for men to 65 and – significantly – the admission to benefits of unmarried mothers and pregnant women not living with a spouse or partner. This law, as amended, is the law under which non-contributory means-tested benefits continue to be administered in Guernsey today.

A further United Kingdom change replicated locally in the 1970s was the move from flat-rate to earnings-related contributions as the basis for National Insurance. Necessitated by increasing inflation, this change was accomplished in the United Kingdom by means of the 1973 Social Security Act. Jersey moved to an earnings-related scheme the following year.[92] In the autumn of 1974, Guernsey's States' Insurance Authority observed that it was 'becoming increasingly difficult in times of inflation to provide a worthwhile rate of benefit in a scheme … financed by

---

[87] *Billet*, 29.1.1964.

[88] O in C, 25.9.1964.

[89] Though the self-employed and non-employed with incomes of less than £208 could apply for exemption.

[90] Limited medical benefit was defined as 'medical, surgical or pharmaceutical aid, the supply and renewal of artificial limbs and surgical appliances, payment for hospital accommodation and travelling expenses'. Unemployment benefit was payable in the first instance only for 180 days, whereafter the claimant had to 'requalify' by paying 13 contributions of the relevant class. Pensionable age was 65 for both sexes, but, this being a 'retirement' pension, it would not become payable until the individual had substantially stopped work, up to a ceiling of 70. In 1970, the States resolved to delete all references to 'retirement pensions' and replace them with 'old age pensions', leaving open the right to defer until 70.

[91] O in C, 5.4.1971.

[92] Anon., *Continuity and Change: A Review of the Social Security and Health Insurance Schemes in Jersey* (Jersey, 1995), p. 9.

flat-rate contributions' and reported that it had secured British government help in developing its own earnings-related scheme.[93] The idea was to eliminate the 'regressive' character of the flat-rate scheme, whereby the low-paid contributed a greater proportion of their earnings than those with higher incomes, while also supporting enhanced benefit levels through increased contributions from the better-off. In 1975, the States gave their formal approval to the earnings-related principle, and in 1978 a new earnings-related social insurance law replaced that of 1964.[94] The range of benefits remained essentially the same, but the Social Insurance (Guernsey) Law, 1978 removed the right to defer old age pensions until 70 while leaving pensionable age at 65 for both sexes. This law, which came into force on 1 January 1979, remains the law under which Guernsey's social insurance scheme is presently administered.

Throughout this protracted period of modernisation, parochial relief had continued to operate in the time-honoured way. Though States-funded since 1925 and styled 'public assistance' since 1937, it was still dispensed in the nine country parishes by *Procureurs des Pauvres*, and by Overseers in St Peter Port. The chief reason for its continuation was a technical one. Although the 1964 Social Insurance Law had introduced unemployment benefit, this benefit was contributions-based, with the inevitable result that there were always a small number of individuals with insufficient contributions to be covered, or whose entitlement was exhausted. In the United Kingdom, people in a similar situation were eligible for National Assistance or, later, Supplementary Benefit. In Guernsey, however, under the terms of the 1955 Non-Contributory Pensions Law and, after it, the 1971 Supplementary Benefit Law, able-bodied people of working age requiring help on grounds of unemployment alone were ineligible for assistance. It was thus primarily of this class of people that late twentieth-century public assistance claimants were composed.

In 2004, a major restructuring of Guernsey's government took place, under which a single new 'Social Security Department' assumed sole responsibility for social insurance, supplementary benefit and public assistance. In taking over public assistance from the now defunct Public Assistance Authority, one of the new Department's first acts was to seek to integrate this benefit with those it already administered as the successor of the Guernsey Social Security Authority.[95] The Department submitted its proposals for the integration of benefits to the States in April 2005.[96] It pointed out that, as at February that year, there were just 153 public assistance claimants (more than 40 per cent of them teenagers) compared with 1,975 on supplementary benefit. Moreover, though public assistance rates were notionally uniform and on a par with supplementary benefit, Overseers and *Procureurs* retained discretion to adjust them, which resulted in inconsistent treatment of claimants. Describing public assistance as 'a relic of the Poor Laws which sits uncomfortably in the social security provision of a developed society', the Department then proposed an amendment to the 1971 Supplementary Benefit Law in order to extend eligibility

---

93 *Billet*, 25.9.1974.
94 *Guernsey Evening Press*, 5.6.1978; O in C, 13.6.1978.
95 Into which the States' Insurance Authority had been transformed in 1993 (Ord, 29.9.1993).
96 *Billet*, 24.4.2005.

to 'persons under 60 … who are capable of work but are either partly or wholly unemployed and not entitled to unemployment benefit, or whose unemployment benefit entitlement is exhausted or who need a top-up of unemployment benefit'. Opposition to this measure was minimal, and the change was achieved through the Supplementary Benefit (Amendment) Ordinance, 2005, which came into force on 30 June that year. With virtually all cases of non-insured need now provided for through supplementary benefit, existing public assistance structures were dismantled by the Public Assistance (Amendment) Law, 2006.[97]

This did not, however, quite spell the end of the parish as a dispenser of welfare. Though they no longer disbursed States' funds, many parishes still possessed charitable funds of various provenance, and some felt they required an officer to distribute them. Therefore, while the 2006 Amendment Law abolished the Outdoor Assistance Boards, as also the office of Overseer in St Peter Port, it did not abolish the office of *Procureur*. Parishes were instead left the option of electing up to two *Procureurs*, with provision for Constables to perform the office's functions where none was elected.[98] For such time as this law stands, and as long as the island's parishes remain civil entities, no final line can be drawn under the poor law in Guernsey.

Medical services

In order to begin our account of medical services, we must now revert to 1945. A few months after the German Occupation had ended, a trio of medical experts was sent over by the Home Office to advise the States on the reorganisation of medical provision. These advisors straightforwardly assumed that the States were intending 'to assimilate all health services to the unified standard and structure of those contemplated in England'.[99] One of their first recommendations was that Le Vauquiédor Hospital (built in the late 1930s as a mental hospital) should be converted into a new general medical and surgical hospital serving the whole community. They also proposed that the wartime 'Emergency Hospital' (formerly the Country Hospital) should take over as the island's mental hospital, and that the Victoria Cottage Hospital should be purchased by the States and transformed into a maternity unit.[100] Some of these measures had already been considered by the States prior to the Occupation. Late in 1946, they were all approved without difficulty, and conversion work on Le Vauquiédor Hospital began in short order.[101] The following year, the States further debated the possibility of 'a Health Services

---

[97] It was decided not to repeal the 1937 Public Assistance Law in its entirety because it contained powers (such as those for repatriation) which the Social Security Department still found useful. There was nevertheless an anticipation that the law would be fully repealed once its remaining useful provisions had been 'incorporated into other social security legislation' (*Billet*, 24.4.2005).

[98] *Billet*, 6.12.2006.

[99] *Billet*, 17.4.1946.

[100] *Billet*, 17.4.1946.

[101] *Billet*, 11.12.1946.

Scheme' which would provide financial help with 'medical and hospital treatment for all persons in the community'.[102] However, action on this was postponed in order to give the Insurance Authority time to observe Britain's new National Health Service in operation.

On 26 July 1949, Le Vauquiédor Hospital reopened as the Princess Elizabeth Hospital, a modern 150-bed community hospital.[103] Though the States owned and ran the facility, they initially employed only the hospital's nursing and ancillary staff. Medical services were provided by the island's general practitioners, who came into the wards to treat their own patients in the cottage hospital tradition. Patients were billed directly by their doctors for the treatment they had provided, and then received a separate bill from the States for hospital services such as food, accommodation, nursing, pathological analyses and x-rays.[104] In the continued absence of the 'Health Services Scheme' mooted in 1947, the cost of protracted or extensive medical treatment in the new hospital could be onerous. A minority of islanders subscribed to private medical insurance or friendly societies, but, for most, the only assistance came in the form of the voluntary abatement of bills by GPs and, for the worst-off, parochial help.

Ultimately, the States' Insurance Authority submitted proposals for the 'Health Services Scheme' in 1951. Unfortunately, by this time, controversy was raging over Guernsey's National Insurance Law, and the beleaguered Authority felt able to propose only a limited contributory scheme covering GP and hospital expenses for those whose annual incomes did not exceed £468.[105] Such was the climate, however, that, despite the modesty of these proposals, they were not accepted by the States.

For the next few years, the pre-war *status quo* regarding payment of medical expenses remained largely in place. The only minor exception was that, from 1955 onwards, recipients of the new States' non-contributory pensions could be given discretionary help with their doctors' bills. This was done under section 6 (1) of the 1955 law, which permitted the Insurance Authority to provide qualified claimants with 'a grant in money by way of single payment to meet an exceptional need'.[106]

Throughout the 1950s and 1960s, the States' Insurance Authority and Board of Health conducted intermittent negotiations with local doctors' representatives in which various options for insurance were explored.[107] These, however, yielded nothing, and the only tangible changes in these decades came in the form of the States' abolition of their own charges for hospital radiology and pathology services in

---

[102] *Billet*, 24.11.1947.

[103] B. Seth-Smith, The post-war period', in D.A. Jeffs (ed.), *One Hundred Years of Health: The Changing Health of Guernsey, 1899–1999* (Guernsey, 1999), p. 104.

[104] The hospital had a pathology laboratory from its opening, and an x-ray department from 1952. Though the former was run by a laboratory technician until 1973, the latter employed a consultant radiologist from the year of its establishment (Seth-Smith, 'Post-war period', pp. 104–5).

[105] *Billet*, 7.3.1951. See also S.R. Langford, 'Paying for health', in Jeffs (ed.), *One Hundred Years of Health*, pp. 122–3.

[106] Discretionary help with medical bills continued under the 1971 Supplementary Benefit Law, into which this section was incorporated verbatim.

[107] Langford, 'Paying for health', pp. 123–5.

1959 and their further abolition of all nursing, accommodation and other ancillary charges in the public wards of the Princess Elizabeth, Maternity and Mental Hospitals in 1969.[108] The 1964 Social Insurance Law also introduced some improvements, but their impact was not widespread: qualified insured persons suffering an industrial injury or contracting an industrial disease became entitled to 'industrial medical benefit', which paid all their medical expenses, while those suffering a non-industrial accident received a grant-in-aid towards such expenses.

By the late 1960s, with the increasing range and sophistication of drug therapies, it was recognised that their cost, borne in full by islanders, was becoming burdensome. The States therefore turned their attention to a pharmaceutical scheme and, in due course, passed the 1972 Health Service (Pharmaceutical) (Guernsey) Law.[109] This law entitled old age pensioners and supplementary benefit recipients to free medicines, and reduced the cost of medicines to other islanders to a nominal fixed prescription charge. The scheme was financed from a new 'Guernsey Health Service Fund' created from a combination of social security contributions and prescription charges and supplemented by a grant from States' general revenue.

The remainder of the 1970s saw no further advances, and the 1980s were even less eventful, seeing only the introduction of two relatively minor measures affecting small sub-groups of islanders. The first was the 1984 Attendance and Invalid Care Allowances (Guernsey) Law, which provided non-contributory allowances to the severely disabled needing constant care, as also to their carers. The second was the establishment in 1988 of the Medical Expenses Assistance Scheme, a limited non-statutory scheme of discretionary means-tested loans and grants to those on low incomes whose medical costs were not otherwise covered by supplementary benefit, public assistance or industrial medical benefit.[110]

For the generality of islanders, however, medical costs remained substantial throughout the 1970s and 1980s, since those who lacked private insurance still paid full market prices for all surgery consultations and hospital treatment. In 1990, this situation changed in limited fashion with the passage of the Health Service (Benefit) (Guernsey) Law, which reduced the costs of primary care by introducing a universal flat-rate States' co-payment towards GP and nurse consultations in the surgery and at home.[111] While such help was welcome, the new law did not, however, address the issue of hospital treatment. By this time, each of Guernsey's six medical practices contained not only GPs but also specialists with higher medical qualifications.[112] These specialists were using hospital facilities to a greater extent than ever before and, with increasingly complex procedures available, a referral for surgery could cost islanders thousands of pounds. For the 40 per cent of islanders who lacked specialist

108 Langford, 'Paying for health', pp. 124–5.
109 O in C, 26.9.1972.
110 *Billet*, 27.5.1987.
111 The law also repealed the 1972 Health Service (Pharmaceutical) Law and re-enacted it in similar terms in respect of pharmaceutical benefit.
112 R.E. Irvine, 'Health services in Guernsey', *The Review of the Guernsey Society*, 46 (1990), pp. 19–21.

insurance cover,[113] this might entail a substantial depletion of savings, or even going into debt. Moreover, as use of the hospital increased, the 1969 decision to abolish hospital charges was proving a significant drain on States' general revenue.

With concerns over these issues mounting during the 1980s, the States commissioned a number of reports on Guernsey's healthcare arrangements. These included a report from a team led by Sir Douglas Black in 1985, and one from the accountancy firm Peat Marwick Mitchell in 1987.[114] Both reports stressed the urgent need to tackle burdens placed on States' general revenue and on individual patients by escalating healthcare costs. The latter additionally set out three different costed options for island-wide health insurance schemes.

With both the Insurance Authority and Board of Health vigorously pressing the need for such a scheme, the States in 1989 resolved in principle that health insurance should be made compulsory for all Guernsey and Alderney residents.[115] The Insurance Authority were charged with bringing forward detailed proposals and, partly to assist with costing, the Board of Health recommended that Guernsey's specialist doctors should form a separate practice with its own tariff-setting powers.[116] The specialists had already recognised that modern medicine would have no future in the island without major reorganisation, and they lost no time in implementing the Board of Health's suggestion.[117] Thus, in January 1992, a new 'Medical Specialist Group' opened in St Sampsons with a total of nineteen founding partners, most of whom came from the original general practices.[118]

Four months after the opening of the new practice, the Insurance Authority returned to the States with proposals for a comprehensive compulsory insurance scheme covering acute primary and secondary medical costs. Having already put the scheme out to tender, the Authority identified Norwich Union Healthcare Ltd as its preferred insurer.[119]

The proposed insurance scheme had been well publicised at public meetings and in the media, but it was not universally popular. Local insurance companies and friendly societies were against it, and the local division of the British Medical Association opposed the inclusion of primary care. Immediately prior to the States' debate on the Insurance Authority's proposals, a petition against the scheme was presented to the assembly by Deputy Pat Mellor.[120] In the event, the States withheld their approval and, highlighting their own concerns over potential costs and the surrender of administrative responsibility to a commercial company, they directed the Authority to report back with a modified scheme which would address these

---

[113] Figure from States of Guernsey, *Guernsey Census, 1991* (Guernsey, 1992), p. 31.

[114] *Billets*, 29.5.1985, 29.7.1987. Sir Douglas Black was a past president of the Royal College of Physicians who had co-authored the 1980 'Black Report' on health inequalities.

[115] *Billet*, 29.11.1989.

[116] *Billet*, 31.10.1990.

[117] R. Allsopp, 'Pressures for change – a specialist view', in Jeffs (ed.), *One Hundred Years of Health*, p. 116.

[118] Allsopp, 'Pressures for change', pp. 116–17.

[119] *Billet*, 29.4.1992.

[120] *Guernsey Evening Press*, 30.4.1992.

issues.[121]

In January 1994, the Guernsey Social Security Authority (as it now was) duly returned to the States with a smaller-scale and less costly scheme. The revised scheme covered specialist care only and was to be administered by the States themselves, with contributions collected through the existing social security apparatus. In order to contain costs, the Social Security Authority also suggested that the States might wish to enter into fixed-price, fixed-term contracts with one or more providers of specialist medical services.[122] On this occasion, States approved the Authority's proposals, and requested it to finalise the operational details of the scheme.

Once States' approval had been secured, the Authority entered a period of intensive negotiations with the Medical Specialist Group, and a fixed-price contract was signed the following year. On 1 January 1996, the new States' Specialist Health Insurance Scheme came into operation, a full seven years after the idea of compulsory health insurance was first approved. The extent of deferred need for specialist treatment was demonstrated by the 20 per cent surge in demand experienced in the scheme's first operational year.[123]

Guernsey's Specialist Health Insurance scheme remains in operation at the time of writing. It covers residents of all Bailiwick islands except Sark. All specialist treatment and associated physiotherapy are now free at the point of delivery to people with a minimum of thirteen weeks' residence. Treatment costs are paid from the Guernsey Health Service Fund.[124] All residents over school-leaving age and above a minimum income threshold are required to pay contributions into the Fund of just over 1 per cent of assessable income, to which is added a grant from States' general revenue. In thus spreading financial burdens, the Specialist Health Insurance scheme has guaranteed access to high-level secondary care for all sections of the community, including the uninsurable and those whose low incomes would always have precluded the purchase of private insurance.

At the time of writing, the position as regards primary care remains unaltered since 1990. The only universally available States' assistance towards GP consultations remains the flat-rate co-payment introduced in that year. This grant has not been uprated for some time and now equates, at best, to 21 per cent of the GP consultation fee.[125] Islanders on higher incomes continue to purchase primary care cover from private insurers, or receive it as part of a salary package. Those on the lowest incomes are entitled to assistance through supplementary benefit. For the

[121] *Billet*, 29.4.1992.
[122] *Billet*, 26.1.1994.
[123] Langford, 'Paying for health', p. 133.
[124] This Fund was first established under the 1972 Health Service (Pharmaceutical) Law. It was modified under the 1990 Health Service (Benefit) Law, and further modified by the 1995 and later Health Service (Specialist Medical Benefit) Ordinances.
[125] In 2015, the co-payment for a consultation with a doctor was £12, which left some £45 still payable by the patient for an ordinary surgery visit. Far larger sums were payable for home and out-of-hours visits, as the £213.95 quoted by one of Guernsey's three GP practices for a home visit between 11.00 p.m. and 8.00 a.m. on Saturdays and Sundays (http://www.eqrmp.com, accessed 16.2.2015).

uninsured and unassisted, however, the prospect of large GP bills continues to militate against optimal care.[126]

Twenty-first century

It remains to give an account of the one major development in Guernsey's social welfare arrangements instituted since the turn of the millennium. This concerns long-term elderly care. We should first observe by way of context that, between 1901 and 2001, the proportion of Guernsey's population aged 65 or over grew from about 6 per cent to nearly 16 per cent, and absolute numbers more than tripled from some 2,700 to 9,366.[127] In the nineteenth and early twentieth centuries, nearly all elderly islanders requiring residential care were accommodated in the Town and Country Hospitals. Consequently, when the States assumed ownership of these Hospitals in 1926, they were effectively also assuming responsibility for the residential care of Guernsey's elderly. The Country Hospital was lost as a facility for the elderly just prior to World War II. However, as the number of elderly islanders began to increase in line with rising life expectancy in the post-war period, the States made up this loss, and indeed added to the stock of available beds, by building new facilities and by co-operating with and financially assisting the three post-war voluntary homes (the Hostel of St John, Le Platon Home and Les Côtils Home).

By 1979, nearly 7 per cent of the island's over-65s were living in care homes. A small handful were in commercial homes,[128] but by far the majority were accommodated in eleven States' or voluntary establishments. The three voluntary homes provided 124 beds between them, with a further twenty at the Victoria Homes, which was run by a charitable trust. The States provided 402 beds. Most of these beds were in facilities administered by the Board of Health: the St Peter Port and Castel Hospitals (the latter now a mental hospital, but accommodating elderly dementia cases); the King Edward VII Hospital (increasingly converted to geriatric use since 1966) and the Duchess of Kent House, opened in 1974. In addition to these, the Housing Authority ran Longue Rue House and Maison Maritaine, opened in 1963 and 1971 respectively as a form of sheltered housing. St Julian's House, a welfare hostel run by the States' Public Assistance Authority, also accommodated a number of elderly residents.[129]

The above analysis shows that, on the threshold of the 1980s, public sector

---

[126] A survey conducted as part of a 2015 review of primary care in Guernsey found that 42 per cent of respondents had no insurance or friendly society cover, and 50 per cent of respondents had put off visits to the GP because of their cost (Channel Islands Competition and Regulatory Authorities' Review of the Guernsey Primary Healthcare Market, 11.2.2015, accessed at http://www.cicra.gg).

[127] PP 1903 LXXXIV; States of Guernsey, *Report on the 2001 Guernsey Census* (Guernsey, 2002), p. 17.

[128] In 1982, Guernsey's private homes were listed as 'Westcroft' in Queen's Road, 'St Louis' in Doyle Road, 'Château du Village' in St Martins and 'Mon Repos' at Cobo (Hospitals File, PL).

[129] *Billet*, 12.12.1979.

beds accounted for over 75 per cent of Guernsey's total elderly care provision. The proportion in the United Kingdom at this time was around 60 per cent. However, a change in British government policy in 1983 promoted a major expansion of the private sector so that, by 1999, the proportion of public sector elderly care beds in the United Kingdom had dropped to just 16 per cent.[130] Aware of United Kingdom developments, Guernsey's Board of Health itself discussed the desirability of promoting private elderly care in 1983.[131] While some expansion did occur after this time, it was not on the same scale as in the United Kingdom, and States' beds still accounted for 43 per cent of Guernsey's total provision in 1999.[132]

By this point, a consensus had formed in the higher echelons of the Board of Health, Social Security Authority and Housing Authority that the operation of Guernsey's elderly care sector was unsatisfactory. An inter-departmental working party undertook a root-and-branch review of provision in the late 1990s and presented its report to the States in November 1999.[133] Much of the report concerned funding.

All of Guernsey's elderly care beds were subject to fees, whether run by the Board of Health, the Housing Authority or independent operators. The States, however, provided means-tested help to residents in all types of establishment. Residents of Board of Health and Housing Authority facilities were eligible for a means-tested abatement of the institution's fee. Residents of commercial and voluntary homes were obliged to pay full fees, but could apply for supplementary benefit, which would top up the resident's own resources to provide the sum required. One of the report's central points was that the Social Security Authority, Housing Authority and Board of Health all used different means tests, and disparities between these were creating a structural imbalance in the take-up of care. The chief anomaly concerned the capital value of residents' real property. While both the Housing and Social Security Authorities took account of this in their assessments, the Board of Health disregarded it. This meant that, though residents of Housing Authority and independent homes 'almost inevitably' had to sell any property they owned in order to finance long-term care, the assets of Board of Health residents were protected. A 'strong incentive' was thus created for home-owners to enter Board of Health accommodation, as also for 'bed-blocking', when those referred for assessment resisted subsequent transfer. It was felt that the predilection for Board of Health care produced an unwarranted double drain on States' general revenue: not only was taxpayers' money already subsidising Board of Health beds (whose fees were below true cost) but the provision of asset protection to their occupants was also depleting general revenue.

---

[130] The main reason for this was that, after 1983 (and until 1993) it became possible for the Department of Health and Social Security to fund private care from uncapped supplementary benefit payments (R. Robinson, 'The finance and provision of long term care for elderly people in the UK: recent trends, current policy and future prospects', p. 34, accessed at http:www.ipss.go.jp/webj-ad/webjournal.files/socialsecurity/2002/02dec/robinson.pdf).

[131] 14.6.1983, IA, BH 52–14.

[132] *Billet*, 24.11.1999.

[133] *Billet*, 24.11.1999.

With Guernsey's over-65s forecast to number 16,000 by 2036, the inter-departmental working party predicted a rise in demand for nursing and residential beds. However, they also confirmed that the Board of Health had no intention of providing them. Their vision for the future was instead predicated on the 'assumption' that the independent sector would expand to supply the extra beds. Clearly, for such an expansion to be feasible, the structural disadvantage suffered by that sector required removal. Having concluded that this could not be achieved merely by adjusting the present system, the working party turned their attention to completely new methods of funding.

In the absence of a United Kingdom model, the working party set their sights further afield. In particular, they analysed in detail social insurance schemes for long-term care lately introduced in Germany and Luxembourg. Considering that 'the principle of pooled risk [was] now well established locally', they had then decided to submit proposals for a similar scheme in the Bailiwick. At the November States meeting of 1999, members were asked to approve these proposals in principle. The response was overwhelmingly positive, and the States directed the Social Security Authority to return in due course with detailed plans for a workable scheme.[134]

Following three years of further research and drafting, the Long-Term Care Insurance (Guernsey) Law, 2002 came into operation in January 2003. Under the new law, which remains in force at the time of writing, all residents of Guernsey, Alderney, Herm and Jethou over school-leaving age and above a set income threshold pay a contribution of between 1 and 2 per cent of their assessable income through the existing social security apparatus. These contributions are directed to the Long-Term Care Insurance Fund created under the 2002 law. When in due course an islander requires long-term care, he or she must be seen by a Needs Assessment Panel, which determines the level of care required and issues a certificate of entitlement to benefit which applicants may present to a private home of their choice.[135] As at 2015, all beneficiaries are required to make a minimum co-payment of £190.75 weekly towards their own costs (a sum just under the full States' old age pension), to which the States add £422.66 for those in residential homes and £756.98 for those in nursing homes.[136] By 2011, the number of private-sector beds in Guernsey had risen by 43 per cent relative to 1999 and, in a reversal of the situation three decades earlier, non-States facilities accounted for more than 75 per cent of long-term provision.[137]

[134] *Guernsey Evening Press*, 26.11.1999.
[135] Applicants must also have a minimum of five years' continuous residence in the Bailiwick, and have been resident for at least twelve months immediately preceding the first benefit payment. Benefits provided from the Long-Term Care Insurance Fund cover only private residential and nursing homes.
[136] Anyone unable to afford the minimum co-payment remains eligible for assistance through supplementary benefit. Care providers charge a range of fees according to the facilities provided, and users are free to pay from their own resources any fees over the maximum payable under the scheme.
[137] *Billet*, 25.5.2011.

Summary – social security and medical services since 1900

Publicity surrounding the passage of the United Kingdom's founding social welfare statutes – the 1906 Workmen's Compensation Act, the 1908 Old Age Pensions Act, the 1911 National Insurance Act – was such that early twentieth-century members of Guernsey's States could not have failed to be aware of them. At this time, however, few States members would have considered passing such legislation themselves. Historically, the States had never had any involvement in welfare provision, and their overall role to date had been more one of policy formulation than active agency. Any scope for action they may have had was strictly circumscribed by both the undeveloped state of their administrative infrastructure and the comparatively small extent of their revenues, which, up to this point, had been derived almost exclusively from indirect taxation. This situation began to change only during World War I, when the States were forced by external pressures not only to intervene more pro-actively in island life but also to increase and diversify their revenues.[138] One means adopted to achieve this was the introduction of income tax, which soon proved an unprecedentedly 'convenient and easily adjusted source of revenue'.[139] The existence of this new revenue source encouraged not only the continuation but the positive growth of States' activities during the post-war period. That some of these activities were directed towards welfare also reflected the fact that, in 1920, for the first time in Guernsey's history, non-ratepayers (i.e., the non-propertied) had been admitted to the suffrage for States elections.[140]

The first important post-war welfare decision directly facilitated by income tax was that taken by the States in 1924 to assume responsibility for poor law funding.[141] This, in turn, expedited progress on long-delayed social security legislation, for, having taken on the poor law burden, it was logical for the States to minimise calls on revenue by instituting contributory schemes. It was hence not entirely by coincidence that the first States' contributory scheme – the Workmen's Accident Compensation Law – was instituted that same year.

The beginnings of States' involvement in modern social security were, however, modest and tentative, since the Accident Compensation Law, and the other landmark welfare laws which followed in 1926 and 1935, covered fewer people for fewer contingencies than contemporary British legislation. One reason for this was that the States' income tax take, though an improvement on pre-war revenue, was proportionately far below that of the United Kingdom. Inter-war Guernsey had a relatively flat tax base, in which there were few very wealthy people. Tax burdens were borne chiefly by small businessmen, farmers and growers, who were traditionally accustomed to light taxation. Unlike in the United Kingdom, there was no super tax and, while the basic British inter-war tax rate was never below 4s in

---

[138] Hocart, *Island Assembly*, pp. 89–99.
[139] Hocart, *Island Assembly*, p. 92.
[140] O in C, 13.10.1920.
[141] *Billet*, 8.10.1924.

the pound, the usual Guernsey rate was 10d or 11d.[142] There was also a limit to the social insurance contributions which could be asked of Guernsey's employers and employees. Most employers were small-scale, providing employment to just two or three workers, sometimes for only part of the year. Many employees worked only intermittently, combining seasonal jobs in quarrying or horticulture with periods of work on their own account.[143]

All these conditions persisted beyond World War II and, indeed, they were aggravated by economic uncertainty as Guernsey recovered from Occupation during the late 1940s and early 1950s. Thus, after the initial post-war optimism, the gulf between Guernsey and the United Kingdom merely widened as the latter inaugurated its new welfare state and the former remained entrenched in 1930s mode. States' accounts for 1950 show that the amount spent on health and welfare in Guernsey that year equated to just £11 per head of population, whereas the United Kingdom figure was £25 8s.[144]

Nevertheless, Guernsey was by this time on the cusp of a period of concentrated change which would leave the island a very different place a decade later. As the British economy entered its mid-1950s expansionary phase, so Guernsey's horticultural industry and tourist trade, both structurally linked to the British economy, began to revive strongly. States members, many of them small businessmen, were among the first beneficiaries, but so too was Guernsey's workforce, whose earning power increased amid conditions of full employment and low inflation. Expectations of comfort and security rose, and increasing exposure to British mass media created a demand for parity with United Kingdom contemporaries, to which States members were not unresponsive. Accordingly, when proposals for a comprehensive social insurance scheme were laid before them in 1963, the time was ripe to transcend 1930s constraints, and Guernsey finally entered the age of universal social security.

In an echo of the pre-war situation, however, Guernsey's 1960s and 1970s social welfare schemes covered fewer people for fewer contingencies than contemporary British schemes. In particular, the issue of healthcare costs had not been systematically addressed and, in the absence of any local equivalent to Britain's National Health Service, a substantial section of the population continued to suffer hardships long forgotten in the United Kingdom.

During the 1980s and 1990s, Guernsey experienced a second period of concentrated economic and social change, instigated this time by the rapid growth of the finance sector. Not only did this increase the States' tax receipts, it also altered the social structure of the population. It was the first of these changes which ultimately provided the means for a partial resolution of the healthcare costs issue, and the second which provided the impetus to find one. As finance professionals came in from outside the island and a native class of finance workers developed, Guernsey's middle class expanded. These professionals required a level of medical services for

---

[142] Gladstone, *Twentieth-Century Welfare State*, p. 101; Hocart, *Island Assembly*, pp. 107, 116–17.
[143] *Billet*, 28.4.1926.
[144] *Billet*, 20.6.1951; http:www.ukpublicspending.co.uk.

themselves and their families on a par with that available elsewhere. It became evident that an up-to-the-minute secondary healthcare system could not be provided on the basis of a minority of high-earners with the means to pay market prices, and that only the collective participation of the entire community would yield the funding required. It was arguably this underlying change which, as much as any other factor, led to the introduction of Specialist Health Insurance in 1996. The Long-Term Care Insurance scheme inaugurated seven years later may also partly be attributed to the same phenomenon, since among its main motivations was the need to protect the transmission of property.

As Guernsey entered the second decade of the new millennium, the revenue which continued to flow from the finance industry ensured that its 63,000 inhabitants were more secure and better cared for than ever before. From £11 per head in 1950, States' health and welfare expenditure had reached £4,795 per head in 2011, and a return to the situation just twenty years previously was, for most islanders, unthinkable.[145]

Postscript

Lest readers discern a whiggish tendency in this account, we should observe that, at the time of writing, the 'unthinkable' had been contemplated. In February 2015, the States' Social Security and Treasury and Resources Departments issued a joint 'Review of Benefits and Taxation'.[146] This Review had been prompted by two major challenges. The first was a structural budget deficit equivalent to 4 per cent of general revenue income caused by a change to corporate taxation in 2008.[147] The second was the impending retirement of the baby-boom generation which was forecast to double the number of over-65s between 2012 and 2050, potentially also doubling the demand for pensions, medical services and long-term care.[148]

As an opening premiss, the joint departments stated their unwillingness to tackle these problems by an increase in direct taxation. This unwillingness was ascribed to the need to maintain Guernsey's low tax status, since it was to this that the island owed its economic success.[149] Instead, the joint departments proposed placing an aggregate limit on government income of 28 per cent of GDP, so that

---

[145] 2011 figure from States of Guernsey, *Public Consultation on Personal Tax, Pensions and Benefits*, Part B (Guernsey, 2013), p. 15.

[146] *Billet*, 24.3.2015.

[147] *Billet*, 24.3.2015, appendix 1, p. 55.

[148] *Billet*, 24.3.2015, appendix 1, pp. 16–17.

[149] Wealth taxes such as inheritance tax and capital gains tax were eschewed as potentially undermining Guernsey's attractiveness to High Net Worth individuals and the island's 'tax neutral offer for financial services'. An increase in the 20 per cent headline rate of income tax, and/or the institution of higher rates for higher earners, were also rejected both as a deterrent to High Net Worth individuals and as an impediment to Guernsey's finance industry in sourcing executives from outside. The Review did, however, recommend restructuring personal taxation, raising property taxes and investigating the imposition of a Goods and Services Tax (*Billet*, 24.3.2015, pp. 367–8; appendix 1, pp. 33, 40; appendix 4, paragraph 8).

money extracted from the economy to fund public services would remain at a level consistent with Guernsey's identity as a low tax jurisdiction.[150]

In default of increased tax revenue, the joint departments put improved management of welfare spending at the centre of their strategy. The process was to start with the redirection of expenditure away from universal benefits and, to this end, the Review set out a number of far-reaching proposals.[151] Among the most significant of these was a proposal for the withdrawal of universal Family Allowances by 2025, as also for the withdrawal of the universal States' co-payment towards GP and nurse appointments by the same date. The Review further proposed removing the exemption of over-65s from prescription charges by 2020, and raising prescription charges for all islanders in 2016.[152]

However, the Review also identified two major problems of a structural nature which these measures would do nothing to remedy. These problems concerned the future funding of long-term care and old age pensions. At current rates of depletion, the Long-Term Care Insurance Fund was projected to be exhausted by the 2020s, and the Guernsey Insurance Fund, from which pensions were drawn, to be likewise exhausted by the 2040s.[153] As a palliative to this, the Review therefore also proposed a phased-in increase of the pension age to 70 by 2049, and an investigation of the possible inclusion of long-term care recipients' homes in their assessments, which might eventually incorporate 'some form of equity release'.[154]

The Review of Benefits and Taxation was debated by the States in the spring of 2015. Some proposals, such as the cap on States' income and the raising of the pension age, were approved, while others, such as the restructuring of personal taxation and the imposition of a Goods and Services Tax, were rejected. Consideration of universal benefits was deferred to an unspecified future date. The Review has lost its coherence as a package, and the long-term outlook is unclear. It is however possible that future generations may look back on the quarter-century between 1990 and 2015 as the golden age of Guernsey welfare.

---

[150] *Billet*, 24.3.2015, pp. 270, 294, 363; appendix 1, p. 9. As at 2015, the proportion for most Nordic countries was in excess of 50 per cent; and other western European countries, including the United Kingdom, typically had proportions of over 40 per cent. Even such low-tax jurisdictions as the Cayman Islands and Luxembourg had government incomes equivalent to 31 per cent and 39 per cent of GDP respectively (CIA World Factbook, accessed 17.2.2015 at https://www.cia.gov).

[151] *Billet*, 24.3.2015, p. 288.

[152] Proposals were also made for the withdrawal of benefits not directly related to health or welfare, such as the provision of free television licences to the over-75s (*Billet*, 24.3.2015, pp. 365–6).

[153] *Billet*, 24.3.2015, pp. 287, 307, 298; appendix 1, p. 18.

[154] *Billet*, 24.3.2015, pp. 303, 307–8, 364–5.

Conclusion

Robert Montgomery Martin's remark that Guernsey had 'no poor laws, and no paupers requiring relief' was not uncharacteristic of early nineteenth-century writing on the island.[1] This claim was originally made by leading islanders wishing to portray their land tenure system in a positive light, and it was subsequently taken up by British authors to make a political point about their own tenurial systems in an era, just before the introduction of new poor laws in England, Wales and Ireland, when the problem of rural poverty was high on the United Kingdom agenda.[2] The assertion is in two parts, and we shall tackle them in reverse order.

There was no great wealth in Guernsey's country parishes, but, in an economy based on peasant agriculture, those who lived most comfortably were those with the largest farms. In 1851, there were about 500 farms of more than ten acres in Guernsey.[3] With a rural population of some 2,500 households, this meant that approximately 80 per cent of families lived on holdings of less than that size.[4] Those who lived on the smaller holdings usually led hand-to-mouth existences, supplementing their own produce with earnings from trade or labour. Even after quarrying and horticulture had increased rural work opportunities in the nineteenth century, life for such families was tough and unpredictable. In earlier centuries, poor harvests and/or high food prices exposed them intermittently to hunger.

St Peter Port, unlike the country parishes, did accommodate an opulent class, particularly between the mid-1700s and mid-1800s. Nevertheless, the well-off were just a small minority and, in overall terms, property ownership in St Peter Port was less widespread than in the country. Owning nothing of their own, most parishioners relied on waged work for a living and paid market prices for shelter and subsistence. This rendered their incomes vulnerable to external economic fluctuations and their budgets vulnerable to high urban rents and food prices. In addition to this, they had also to contend with social problems which rural parishioners were largely spared, since the town bore the brunt of migratory influxes, and paid the price – widows,

---

[1] R. Montgomery Martin, *History of the British Colonies*, 5 vols (London, 1835), 5, p. 478. For more on Martin, see Appendix 1, n. 1.

[2] For more detail on these authors and their writings, see Appendix 1.

[3] PP 1852–3 LXXXVIII gives the number of such farms in the Bailiwick as 509 (out of a total of 821). It is probably safe to assume that almost all of the farms of more than ten acres were in Guernsey.

[4] PP 1852–3 LXXXVIII gives the total population of Guernsey's nine country parishes as 12,687. I have calculated the approximate number of households by dividing this total by five.

unwed mothers, orphans and bastards – attached to its role as Guernsey's main port and garrison base.

For all of these reasons, poverty was an omnipresent feature of Guernsey life, both before and after the period when literary denials as to 'paupers requiring relief' were first made. Confirmation that paupers existed comes in the straightforward circumstance that, by the 1820s, there was not one of Guernsey's parishes which did not raise poor rates.

In the claim that there were 'no poor laws', there is, however, more substance, for it was a fact that Guernsey did not have a corpus of poor laws such as had developed since the 1500s in England and Wales. Guernsey's Royal Court had periodically issued ordinances relating to the poor since early modern times, but these had never been built into any consistent body of law. Instead, the insular welfare system was based on a set of customary practices shaped and moulded by the church, and poor relief was not fully secularised until 1926.[5] This represents a major point of difference from the English welfare system, and it prompts us to revisit some of the questions originally posed in the introduction to this book: specifically, can we identify further divergences with England besides this one and, if we can, are there corresponding affinities with continental welfare systems?

In an article which takes a macro-level view of factors influencing the development of European welfare states, Jose Harris has usefully recapitulated features which characterised many nineteenth-century continental welfare systems while simultaneously differentiating them from the English system.[6] The principal features typical of continental welfare stand out as: elision of the ecclesiastical with the secular, and of poor relief with charity;[7] decentralisation and local autonomy;[8] amateurism in administration and delivery;[9] social control; the exercise of powers to confine and restrain.[10] Other features included a predominance of urban over rural relief; a preference for residential over domiciliary relief; the strongly residual nature of all relief; and the harsh treatment of itinerants.[11]

As shown in Chapters 3–9, almost all of these features were also characteristic of Guernsey, not least the primacy of the Hospitals and their administrators' wide-ranging powers of tutelage and detention. Adopting Professor Harris's perspective, it seems clear that Guernsey's primary affinities lay not with England, but with its neighbours to the south. Indeed, it was precisely this which enabled contemporary observers to deny the existence in Guernsey of English-style pauperism.

Affinities with the continent in the 1500s are unsurprising, since Guernsey's welfare structures were imported direct from Geneva. However, these affinities

5 O in C, 30.4.1926.
6 J. Harris, 'From poor law to welfare state? A European perspective', in D. Winch and P. O'Brien (eds), *The Political Economy of British Historical Experience, 1688–1914* (Oxford, 2002), pp. 409–27.
7 Harris, 'From poor law to welfare state', pp. 420–22.
8 Harris, 'From poor law to welfare state', pp. 419–20.
9 Harris, 'From poor law to welfare state', pp. 420, 423.
10 Harris, 'From poor law to welfare state', pp. 412, 424–6.
11 Harris, 'From poor law to welfare state', pp. 416–26.

remained in evidence until the twentieth century. Are we then to infer that Guernsey continued actively to model itself on continental practice long after the Genevan links had been lost?

Paradoxically, all the evidence suggests that islanders looked not towards Europe but in the opposite direction. Poor-related ordinances issued in the sixteenth and seventeenth centuries already demonstrated a knowledge of English legislation. This intensified in the eighteenth century, when parochial poor rates were adopted along with the concept of settlement. The building of Guernsey's workhouses appears to have been directly inspired by SPCK literature from England. The 1834 Poor Law Amendment Act and the 1870s 'crusade' against outdoor relief were not without oblique influence in Guernsey, and neither were late nineteenth-century British attitudinal changes towards the deserving poor. What is striking, moreover, is that Guernsey's eighteenth- and nineteenth-century records yield no corresponding evidence of continental influence. This appears to have ended – as it began – with the late sixteenth-century adoption by Guernsey's Presbyterian church of Calvin's Ecclesiastical Ordinances.

The paradox of Guernsey's enduring 'continental' affinities thus remains unresolved. At this point, it may be helpful to exchange Jose Harris's 'macro' view for an alternative perspective proposed by Steven King. Professor King has suggested a more 'ground-level' approach, identifying similarities and differences among European regions on the basis not of national legal contexts but of variation in 'local practice, sentiment and experiences of the poor'.[12] Such a perspective has enabled King to discern affinities between the Manchester region and Belgium; between industrial Lancashire and urban Austria; between north Wales and Italy; and between Scotland and Spain.[13]

On the basis of his findings, Professor King has set out a four-fold typology for classifying local and regional welfare regimes. Of his four ideal types – 'entitling', 'obligatory', 'disciplinary' and 'exclusionist' – Guernsey's would seem to be a compound of the latter two, which were distinguished by their arbitrary, deterrent, minimalistic and residual nature.[14] In locating English regions on the spectrum from 'entitling' to 'exclusionist', Professor King identified a *prima facie* correlation between a region's distance from the centre and its position towards the 'exclusionist' end of the scale. Hence eastern and south-eastern England exhibited features of an 'entitling' regime, while northern and western England were more inclined to be 'exclusionist'.[15] This ties in with earlier joint work by King and John Stewart, where 'peripherality' was identified as a potential 'organising principle' for welfare systems, and it was suggested that 'there was something about being "peripheral" that helped create distinctive welfare structures'.[16]

---

[12] S.A. King, 'Welfare regimes and welfare regions in Britain and Europe, c.1750s to 1860s', *Journal of Modern European History*, 9 (2011), p. 55.

[13] King, 'Welfare regimes', pp. 50, 53, 56.

[14] King, 'Welfare regimes', pp. 59–61. The four-fold model was designed primarily for an English context, and King conceded that continental regimes would require more categories.

[15] King, 'Welfare regimes', pp. 53, 62.

[16] S.A. King and J. Stewart, 'Welfare peripheries in modern Europe', in S.A. King and J. Stewart

It is in this perspective that we shall now attempt to locate Guernsey's position within the narrower context of welfare in the British Isles. Not unsurprisingly, Guernsey's closest welfare affinities were with its fellow Channel Islands, since the welfare structures of all the Islands evolved in similar environments and under similar circumstances.[17] For the next closest match, we must, however, travel north around the British periphery, since it is the Scottish system, at least under the old Scottish poor law, which exhibits the clearest congruence with Guernsey.[18]

At first sight, given the geographical distance and lack of contact, this seems implausible. However, affinities between the Scottish and Guernsey welfare systems are less surprising if we consider their common origins. Both were derived from Geneva along with the Reformed faith. Initial similarities engendered by this fact of history were then sustained by the prolonged retention of both systems within the ecclesiastical domain. The lack of governmental input meant that both systems remained for long periods under the autonomous control of local oligarchies. This in turn engendered administrative parallels. In Scotland, welfare was the joint responsibility of a rural parish's 'kirk session' and its 'heritors'.[19] The kirk session comprised the minister and elders and was analogous to Guernsey's Presbyterian consistories. Heritors were the parochial landowners, whose estates were charged for the upkeep of parish church and school, and any levies which might be made in respect of the poor. The heritors' counterparts in Guernsey (albeit on a smaller scale) were the *Chefs de Famille*. These, too, were parochial landowners whose properties were charged for parish burdens. In both rural Scotland and the Channel Islands, the co-location of decision-making powers and financial responsibility in a small group of property-owners had similar effects. Firstly, there was a protracted resistance to the levying of any rates at all.[20] Secondly, when circumstances made these inescapable, there was a drive to set them at the lowest possible level. This in turn led to residualism and chronic insufficiency, with the inevitable effect that primary reliance was placed on private charity.[21]

In the final analysis, many of the commonalities between Guernsey and Scotland are traceable to the strength of localism in both jurisdictions. The same could be said of features identified by Jose Harris in many parts of mainland Europe. It is

---

(eds), *Welfare Peripheries: The Development of Welfare States in Nineteenth and Twentieth Century Europe* (Bern, 2007), pp. 22–31, 34.

[17] For the welfare arrangements of Jersey, Alderney and Sark, see Appendix 3.

[18] The old Scottish poor law operated until 1845, when Westminster's passage of a new poor law for Scotland aligned it more closely with England, Wales and Ireland, for whom new poor laws had been enacted in 1834 and 1838. Comparison for the present purposes is primarily with Scotland's rural parishes, since burghs evolved differing arrangements. For more on the pre-1845 Scottish system, see R. Mitchison, 'The making of the old Scottish poor law', *Past & Present*, 63 (1974), pp. 58–93; R.A. Cage, *The Scottish Poor Law, 1745–1845* (Edinburgh, 1981); R. Mitchison, *The Old Poor Law in Scotland: The Experience of Poverty, 1574–1845* (Edinburgh, 2000).

[19] Cage, *Scottish Poor Law*, pp. 5–7.

[20] In pre-1845 Scotland these were usually termed 'stents'.

[21] For the role of charity in Scotland, see Cage, *Scottish Poor Law*, pp. 41–3, 68. For Guernsey, see 'Conclusion', Chapter 4, above.

also true of features identified by Steven King in outlying parts of northern and western England. Peripherality is the key factor in all of these cases. The further removed from the control of a strong centre, the greater the tendency for local elites to prioritise their own sectional interests, primarily in minimising outlays, but also in enforcing social control. This was perhaps the essence of the 'distinctive welfare structures' which peripherality helped to create.

From the late 1800s, the impact of peripherality on welfare matters declined all over Europe as central governments began to assume responsibilities which had traditionally rested with localities. Steven King pinpoints the beginning of this trend in the 1860s, Jose Harris in the 1880s. They nevertheless agree that variability both within and between countries reduced sharply towards the end of the nineteenth century as governments emulated each others' best practice and national policies gradually converged.[22] Guernsey, however, was so peripheral as to be beyond the reach of any 'national' government. Convergence, therefore, took longer. As the 1920s opened, the only public source of welfare assistance in Guernsey remained parish relief, funded and dispensed in the age-old way by ten separate bodies, and regarded by all islanders who considered themselves respectable as profoundly demeaning. Only in 1924 did the ancient *status quo* finally begin to yield. In this watershed year, two important changes were enacted: the decision was taken to transfer poor relief funding from parishes to States, and the first States' social insurance scheme was approved.

Key to this development were the democratisation of insular government and change in taxation which occurred at the end of World War I. Acting in combination, these two factors eventually yielded a universal and stigma-free system of social security in 1965, with the reforms of that decade arguably producing a greater degree of social cohesion than the island had ever experienced. By the second decade of the twenty-first century, however, the crest of the hill had been reached. The generation which had benefited most from the mid-twentieth-century reforms was now threatening to overburden the system, and a decision had to be made either to provide more funding or to cut the system back. In February 2015, Guernsey's authorities advanced far-reaching proposals for the latter, having identified protection of the finance sector as the priority to which all else must yield.

Without the finance sector, twenty-first-century islanders would probably not have enjoyed the benefits of a first-rate secondary healthcare system or even a long-term care insurance scheme. However, the industry had exerted negative as well as positive impacts on island life. Its presence had raised living costs to levels which bore hard on those outside the higher echelons of finance. In putting cut-backs before burden-sharing, Guernsey's authorities appeared to have discounted the debt of compensation owed to islanders for such negative impacts. In seeking to revert to a welfare system based upon residualism, they also risked reinstating social clefts.

---

[22] King, 'Welfare regimes', p. 42; Harris, 'Poor law to welfare state?', pp. 427–8.

Appendix 1

Writings on Peasant Proprietorship in Guernsey

Daniel De Lisle Brock, Bailiff of Guernsey 1821–42, was proud of Guernsey's distinctiveness and always happy to furnish enquirers with particulars of its unique regime.
During the 1820s, he supplied information of this sort to two young men who went
on to make use of it in their own publications. The first was Robert Montgomery
Martin, whom Brock met in London while on States' business in 1821.[1] The second
was Frederic Hill, with whom Brock became acquainted when Hill visited Guernsey
in 1826.[2] Hill used material supplied by Brock in an article for the London *Examiner* published in September 1832 which was subsequently reproduced in several
other periodicals.[3] Hill's article focused on the benefits of Guernsey's widely diffused
landownership, contending that this resulted in increased crop yields, a spirit of
self-reliance and an absence of pauperism. In 1835, Robert Montgomery Martin's
five-volume *History of the British Colonies* appeared. In his section on Guernsey in
the fifth volume, he vaunted the advantages of the insular land tenure system in a
similar way to Hill, going so far as to assert that there were 'no poor laws, and no
paupers requiring relief'. His closing paragraph speculated on how the introduction
of a system such as Guernsey's might palliate 'the poverty and barbarism of the
Irish'.[4] Dublin-born Martin had already published two books on the problems of his
native country,[5] and the theme of Irish poverty was very much a live one at the time

[1]   Robert Montgomery Martin was an Anglo-Irish author who published widely on the economics
     of the British Empire. Later in life, he served as Colonial Treasurer of Hong Kong. See F.H.H.
     King, *Survey our Empire! Robert Montgomery Martin (1801?–1868), a Bio-bibliography* (Hong
     Kong, 1979).
[2]   As a young man, Frederic Hill served as parliamentary secretary to the Whig MP Sergeant
     Wilde and campaigned vigorously for the 1832 Reform Bill. He was later a member of HM
     Inspectorate of Prisons. One of his brothers was the postal reformer Rowland Hill, and another
     brother, Matthew Hill, became a Whig MP. See C. Hill (ed.), *Frederic Hill: An Autobiography
     of Fifty Years in Times of Reform* (London, 1893).
[3]   For a copy of the article, see Hill's *Autobiography*, where details are also given of his 1826 visit
     to Guernsey (pp. 63–6). An annotated version of Hill's article was published in *The Guernsey
     and Jersey Magazine*, 5 (1838), pp. 152–9.
[4]   R. Montgomery Martin, *History of the British Colonies*, 5 vols (London, 1835), 5, pp. 484–90.
     In these pages, Martin describes his 1821 meeting with Daniel De Lisle Brock.
[5]   R. Montgomery Martin, *Poor Laws for Ireland, a Measure of Justice for England; or Humanity
     to the People of both Islands* (London, 1833) and *Ireland before and after the Union with Great
     Britain* (London, 1833).

he wrote his piece on Guernsey. During the 1820s, there had been an outpouring of pamphlet literature on the subject, stimulated in particular by the Irish potato crop failure of 1823 and the rural disturbances of 1825. The problem was felt to lie in the monopoly of land by a small and often exploitative class of proprietors, a situation which condemned most rurals to live as labourers, often solely in return for the produce of plots held from their employers.[6] Press interest in Ireland continued throughout the 1830s, sustained by the appointment in 1833 of the Royal Commission on the Condition of the Poorer Classes in Ireland, the publication of its report in 1836 and the introduction in 1838 of a new poor law for Ireland.[7]

The 'Irish problem' struck a chord with Jonathan Duncan, an English writer and businessman resident in Guernsey between the 1820s and 1840s. It is possible that Duncan's interest may initially have been ignited by the author Henry Inglis when Inglis visited Guernsey in the early 1830s to research his book on the Channel Islands.[8] Inglis had lately also been conducting research in Ireland, on whose problems he entertained strong views. These views were published in an influential study which appeared shortly after the publication of his book on the Channel Islands.[9] Jonathan Duncan was himself of a radical political cast, openly deploring the 'grasping squirearchy' which dominated English Tory heartlands.[10] He also enjoyed friendly relations with Daniel De Lisle Brock – an 'eminent statesman', according to Duncan, 'whose fitting station would have been in Downing-street, were personal merit and usefulness the recommendation to office'.[11]

In the mid-1830s, Jonathan Duncan edited *The Guernsey and Jersey Magazine*. Between 1836 and 1838, four lengthy articles appeared in the magazine making explicit comparisons between Guernsey and Ireland and again extolling the benefits of 'peasant' landownership in Guernsey. Most seem to have been penned by Duncan himself, but, significantly, one was written by Daniel De Lisle Brock.[12] In 1839, Jonathan Duncan went on to write a piece for *Tait's Edinburgh Magazine* which bore the heading 'A new remedy for the distresses of Ireland'.[13] He also reverted at length to this subject in his 1841 *History of Guernsey*, reproducing large sections of

---

6   J. Innes, 'The distinctiveness of the English poor laws, 1750–1850', in D. Winch and P. O'Brien (eds), *The Political Economy of British Historical Experience, 1688–1914* (Oxford, 2002), pp. 400–2.

7   L. Patriquin, 'Why was there no "Old Poor Law" in Scotland and Ireland?' *The Journal of Peasant Studies*, 33 (2006), p. 238.

8   H.D. Inglis, *The Channel Islands*, 2 vols (London, 1834).

9   H.D. Inglis, *Ireland in 1834* (London, 1835).

10 J. Duncan, *The History of Guernsey* (London, 1841), p. 301.

11 Duncan, *History of Guernsey*, p. 279.

12 The first article, in the form of a review of Montgomery Martin's chapter on Guernsey in his *British Colonies*, was published in *Guernsey and Jersey Magazine*, 1 (1836), pp. 176–82; the second was headed 'Ireland & Guernsey' and appeared in *Guernsey and Jersey Magazine*, 2 (1836) pp. 65–74; there followed Brock's piece on 'The agriculture of Guernsey' in *Guernsey and Jersey Magazine*, 4 (1837), pp. 235–42, and finally an article on 'Irish poor laws and Guernsey landed tenure' in *Guernsey and Jersey Magazine*, 5 (1838), pp. 1–9.

13 *Tait's Edinburgh Magazine*, 4 (1839), pp. 137–46.

Hill's *Examiner* article and Brock's piece in *The Guernsey and Jersey Magazine*.[14] Over the next few years, the ideas expressed by Frederic Hill, Robert Montgomery Martin and Jonathan Duncan were taken up and reproduced in magazines and journals all over the English-speaking world.[15] Their ultimate parenthood can be traced back to Daniel De Lisle Brock.

These ideas also surfaced repeatedly in the work of serious thinkers and writers. In 1848, the theme of peasant proprietorship was taken up by the economist William Thornton, who had visited Guernsey 'to test the accuracy of some of the statements of preceding writers'.[16] Thornton seems not to have been disappointed, filling seventeen pages with a roseate account closely based on passages from Duncan's *History*. Jerseyman Charles Le Quesne also published on the subject in 1848, his endeavours perhaps motivated by a wish that Jersey, which had a similar landholding regime, should share in the favourable publicity.[17]

The next to echo these ideas was no less a figure than John Stuart Mill, who included them in the second and subsequent editions of his *Principles of Political Economy*. Mill, who does not seem to have felt a need to visit the island personally, lifted his text almost verbatim from William Thornton.[18] Frederick Blackwood (Lord Dufferin) also recycled the ideas – and the words – in his 1867 book on Irish land tenure.[19] Many others who dallied with this theme doubtless remain to be discovered. The last mainstream author we shall mention is the Scottish self-help advocate Samuel Smiles, who held up the self-reliance of Guernsey countryfolk as 'an example to English workpeople' in his best-selling *Thrift* of 1875.[20] Smiles had evidently read previous writers on the subject, but, like Mill, never seems to have visited the island. The image of Guernsey he offered his readers was thus no more than a hackneyed piece of lore.

Perhaps the healthiest contribution to this theme was that offered by Edward Denison, Liberal MP for Newark and a founder member of the Charity Organization Society, who came to Guernsey in 1869 expressly 'to explore the mysteries of peasant proprietorship'. His conclusions were published posthumously in 1872. The independent-minded Denison was not nearly so impressed as his predecessors. He acknowledged the self-reliance of Guernsey's farmers but found their frugality extreme. In his view, such frugality had led them 'to reduce their diet to the very lowest point consistent with health'. Denison thought this frugality motivated by 'excessive desire of gain'. Far from being a lifestyle fit for emulation, the MP felt that

[14] Duncan, *History of Guernsey*, pp. 300–13.
[15] A search in Google Books under 'Guernsey peasant proprietorship' yields articles in such unexpected quarters as the *Connecticut Common School Journal* in 1842 and *Littell's Living Age* of Boston in 1866.
[16] W.T. Thornton, *A Plea for Peasant Proprietors: With the Outlines of a Plan for their Establishment in Ireland* (London, 1848), p. 97.
[17] C. Le Quesne, *Ireland and the Channel Islands* (London, 1848). Le Quesne was an acquaintance of Jonathan Duncan's who had previously contributed to *The Guernsey and Jersey Magazine*.
[18] J.S. Mill, *Principles of Political Economy*, 2 vols (1848; London 1849 edn), 1, pp. 333–5.
[19] F.H.T. Blackwood, *Irish Emigration and the Tenure of Land in Ireland* (London, 1867), p. 336.
[20] S. Smiles, *Thrift* (London, 1875), pp. 33–6.

English landlords would be 'hooted at' for advocating it even to their cottagers.[21] His appraisal introduced a salutary note of realism into a theme which had always been overstated, and – by dint of uncritical repetition – had long lost any relationship it might ever have had with the truth.

[21] B. Leighton (ed.), *Letters and other Writings of the Late Edward Denison* (London, 1872), pp. 141–50.

Appendix 2

Poor Rates, Indoor and Outdoor Relief Spending, St Peter Port, 1724–1924

Year	Poor rate (£)	Indoor spending (£)	Outdoor spending (£)
1724	285	0	c.500
1734	285	0	n/a
1751	285	c.360	n/a
1766	285	665	c.40
1776	571	n/a	n/a
1784	429	n/a	n/a
1795	571	n/a	n/a
1804	1,000	n/a	n/a
1812	1,800	3,874	300
1821	4,706	2,665	600
1831	4,172	3,834	800
1841	4,351	4,081	1,000
1854	4,750	3,730	1,835
1864	3,400	2,978	1,604
1874	5,340	2,547	2,865
1884	5,700	3,765	2,524
1894	3,800	3,994	1,673
1904	6,030	4,779	2,185
1914	6,750	4,960	2,618
1924	no rate	11,359	4,833

Sources: T. Dicey, *An Historical Account of Guernsey* (London, 1751), p. 186; IA, AQ 1002/03, 1003/02, 1003/03, 1003/04, 1004/02, 1004/03, 1005/01; IA, DC/HX 020–01, 045–01, 165–01, 165–01, 272–02; St Peter Port Délibérations des Chefs de Famille, 1844–66, PL.

Appendix 3

Parochial Poor Relief in Other Channel Islands

Bailiwick of Guernsey

Sark and Alderney

Throughout the period covered by this book, Sark and Alderney were under the nominal superintendence of Guernsey but enjoyed substantial administrative and legislative autonomy. In the sixteenth and seventeenth centuries, both were members of the Presbyterian Church of the Channel Islands and subscribed to the Discipline drawn up in 1576.[22] It was this Discipline which embodied their original welfare arrangements, based on those prescribed by John Calvin in his Ecclesiastical Ordinances. After the imposition of Anglicanism on the Bailiwick in 1662, Sark and Alderney each became parishes in the Deanery of Guernsey. Their welfare arrangements then evolved in ways similar, but not identical, to those of the larger island.

At some point in the post-Anglican era, the deacons of Sark and Alderney's Presbyterian churches came to be known as *Collecteurs*. However, like their Guernsey counterparts, they continued to perform essentially the same duties with regard to the poor. Each island appears originally to have had four *Collecteurs*, but, by the time John Jacob wrote his study of the Bailiwick in the late 1820s, Sark's four had become two.[23] Interestingly, at the time Jacob was writing, neither Alderney nor Sark appears to have had an officer bearing the title *Procureur*.

Initially, the *Collecteurs* of Sark and Alderney funded their welfare activities from voluntary sources such as church collections, donations and bequests. By at least the early nineteenth century, however, both islands had begun intermittently to levy taxes for the poor.[24] As in Guernsey, islanders were assessed on the value of their capital assets, expressed in terms of wheat. The precise mechanics of taxation varied with each island. Beginning with Sark, we shall examine the systems of both islands as they operated during the nineteenth century.

---

[22] See section on 'The Presbyterian era, 1560s–1660s', Chapter 3.

[23] J. Jacob, *Annals of Some of the British Norman Isles Constituting the Bailiwick of Guernsey* (Paris, 1830), pp. 45, 82.

[24] In Sark, Dr Richard Axton has found records of sporadic one-off levies for the poor dating back as early as the seventeenth century (Chief Pleas meetings of 13.10.1624, 8.2.1625 and 4.5.1636, Sark Court Records, series 4, Seigneurie Archive Bb 1.4, Société Sercquaise). For levies in Alderney, see Jacob, *Annals*, pp. 45–6.

Sark's sole legislative body was its 'Chief Pleas', and it was this body which determined whether or not a poor tax was needed and set the sum to be raised. A committee of Chief Pleas, composed of the principal inhabitants and known as the *Douzaine*, was responsible for drawing up the tax list and assessing the property of ratepayers.[25] Sark's Constable, a minor officer concerned with public order, appears to have collected the tax.[26] This procedure, followed in raising taxes for all communal purposes, was enshrined in an ordinance of 1899.[27] At some time in the early decades of the twentieth century, Sark's two *Collecteurs* came to be known as *Procureurs*. The reason for this is unclear, but it was perhaps an alignment with practice in Guernsey, which abolished *Collecteurs* as part of the poor law apparatus in 1925.[28] Their duties as primary dispensers of welfare remained unaltered.

Until the Second World War, Alderney had three legislative bodies: the States, the Court and the Court of Chief Pleas, with the States foremost among them.[29] The island also had a *Douzaine*, which, unlike Sark's, was a parochial body fulfilling many of the same functions as a Guernsey parochial *Douzaine*.[30] As in Sark, the amount to be raised in tax, both for the poor and for other purposes, was set by Chief Pleas, and the *Douzaine* drew up the tax list and assessed ratepayers' property.[31] *Collecteurs* collected the poor rate, while Constables collected taxes for other purposes.[32]

In 1822, Alderney's *Collecteurs* were joined by a new officer, elected by the parish for a term of three years to take charge of the poor and superintend Alderney's small poorhouse. John Jacob termed this officer an 'Overseer', but in due course he seems to have assumed the title of *Procureur*, playing a co-ordinating role in welfare throughout the rest of the century.[33] Also, at some point after 1853, Alderney decided to emulate St Peter Port in establishing a 'Poor Law Board' to administer welfare.[34] This was an outgrowth of the parish, and comprised the *Procureur*, the four *Collecteurs* and the Churchwarden. The *Procureur* chaired meetings and kept accounts, and the Board's activities were funded by parish rates, as previously.[35]

Neither Alderney nor Sark were mentioned in any Guernsey settlement legislation

---

[25] Note that this was not a *Douzaine* in the Guernsey parochial sense, as Sark never had a separate civil parochial administration.

[26] J.N. van Leuven, 'History and practice of parochial taxation in Sark and Guernsey', *Guernsey Law Journal*, 24 (1997), pp. 117–18; J.L.V. Cachemaille (ed. L.E. Hale), *The Island of Sark* (London, 1928), pp. 221–3.

[27] van Leuven, 'Parochial taxation in Sark and Guernsey', pp. 119–20.

[28] See section on 'Administration of relief – personnel', Chapter 4.

[29] J.N. van Leuven, 'Constitutional relationships within the Bailiwick of Guernsey – Alderney', *The Jersey Law Review*, June 2004, paragraphs 27 and 28; *Report of the Committee of the Privy Council on the Island of Alderney, October 1949* (Cmd 7805), p. 16.

[30] *Report of the Committee of the Privy Council on Alderney*, pp. 20–1.

[31] *Second Report of the Commissioners appointed to enquire into the State of the Criminal Law of the Channel Islands* (London, 1848), pp. 195–6.

[32] *Report of the Committee of the Privy Council on Alderney*, pp. 21, 28.

[33] Jacob, *Annals*, pp. 45–6.

[34] Since Alderney's public records were lost during the German Occupation, it has not been possible to determine precisely when this Board was created.

[35] *Report of the Committee of the Privy Council on Alderney*, p. 26.

prior to 1867. However, perhaps because they were parishes in the Deanery of Guernsey, Guernsey's authorities appear to have applied the various pre-1867 criteria for acquiring and changing settlements to natives of Sark and Alderney in the same way as they did to Guernseymen and *vice versa*.[36] The Order in Council of 26 June 1867, which regulated settlement for the whole Bailiwick, explicitly put natives of all three islands on precisely the same footing. Nevertheless, since the requirements for earning new settlements in Guernsey were onerous, many migrants from Alderney and Sark failed to acquire them, which put them at a disadvantage if they fell into distress. On occasion, problems were solved by the provision of non-resident relief. In the 1830s, for instance, the Alderney *Procureur* maintained an Alderney family in the Town Hospital.[37] In the 1860s, one of Sark's *Collecteurs* requested St Peters' *Procureur* to provide a Sarkee with a weekly loaf at Sark's expense.[38] However, summary deportations were also frequently resorted to by both islands. Where these were challenged, protracted disputes could arise, and more of the letter-book kept by St Peter Port's nineteenth-century *Procureurs* is devoted to inter-island disputes over welfare responsibilities than to any other topic.[39] From at least 1885, Sark had its own poor law representative in Guernsey, whose job it was to liaise with Guernsey's parochial authorities and generally act for and on behalf of fellow islanders.[40] Alderney did not appoint a Guernsey welfare representative until 1918.[41]

Alderney's Poor Law Board remained in operation until World War II, when the island's entire civilian population was evacuated. When the evacuees returned in 1945, the Board resumed its activities for a brief period.[42] However, under a law of 1948 which restructured Alderney's system of government, the *Douzaine* was abolished and the parish of Alderney ceased to have any secular administrative functions, which also entailed the end of the Poor Law Board.[43]

From 1949, the States of Guernsey assumed responsibility for all major components of Alderney's infrastructure and services, including education, police, health and social services. In return, the inhabitants of Alderney began to pay Guernsey income tax and gained two representatives in Guernsey's States. The remodelled Alderney States however retained responsibility for ancillary matters. These included public assistance, which henceforth came under the mandate of the States' Health, Welfare and Education Committee and was funded on a non-statutory basis out of Alderney's general revenue. As Guernsey's social security system developed in the 1950s and 1960s, laws on health and welfare matters were extended to Alderney,

36 Cachemaille, *Island of Sark*, p. 224.
37 10.12.1837, IA, DC/HX 081–01.
38 6.1.1863, IA, AQ 0458/03.
39 IA, DC/HX 072–02.
40 In 1885, this was Thomas Baker of Victoria Road, St Peter Port (24.9.1885, IA, DC/HX 072–02).
41 The first appointee was Ira Ozanne. In return, St Peter Port appointed W.R. Gaudion as their poor law representative in Alderney (6.5.1918, 1.7.1918, IA, DC/HX 052–01).
42 *Report of the Committee of the Privy Council on Alderney*, p. 26.
43 van Leuven, 'Constitutional relationships', paragraphs 36–41, 47.

whose residents paid into the same schemes as their Guernsey counterparts and received the same benefits. Therefore, when, in 2005, Guernsey's supplementary benefit law was amended to include categories of claimant hitherto restricted to public assistance, these amendments also applied to Alderney.[44] This obviated the need for Alderney's non-statutory assistance scheme, and it ceased operation thereafter. At the time of writing, the only welfare services which Alderney continues to fund and administer are of a minor nature, such as a home help and meals-on-wheels service. In other respects, its health and welfare arrangements have become subsumed into Guernsey's social security schemes.

In Sark, the present-day situation is quite different. Islanders are not represented in Guernsey's States and do not pay Guernsey taxes or Guernsey social security contributions. Sark has, however, never evolved social insurance of its own and, instead, continues to operate an assistance scheme based essentially on nineteenth-century poor law structures. The island retains a *Procureur* and deputy *Procureur*, who work in tandem with the *Douzaine* to provide assistance to those in need, which is funded out of a property tax. Residents of Sark currently number some 600. The *Procureurs'* budget allocation for 2015 stood at £150,000, or about £250 per head.[45]

Herm and Jethou

These small islands, each of which was historically leased to a single tenant, lie about three miles to the east of St Peter Port.[46] They form part of the Deanery of Guernsey's St Peter Port ecclesiastical district, but not of the parish of St Peter Port. Hence residents of these islands were not called upon to contribute to parochial taxation in St Peter Port.[47] The unfortunate *quid pro quo* in poor law terms was that residents (or former residents) of Herm had no claim on St Peter Port for relief unless they had acquired a settlement in the town parish in ways prescribed in Guernsey settlement legislation. Thus the Touzeau family, Herm born and bred, received a negative response when they applied for assistance in St Peter Port after quitting Herm in 1838.[48] This left them in a difficult position, because, unlike Sark and Alderney, Herm had no welfare structures of its own and did not possess the public wherewithal to relieve anyone.

Although Herm remains extra-parochial to this day, it became more securely incorporated into Guernsey's all-island administrative structures during the

---

[44] Supplementary Benefit (Amendment) Ordinance, 2005.

[45] *Guernsey Press*, 3.7.2014.

[46] The larger, Herm, has an area of three-quarters of a square mile. Herm's nineteenth-century population averaged no more than fifty, save for a period in the 1820s and 1830s when the island's granite quarries were intensively exploited, and quarry workers and their dependants numbered nearly 200 (R.-M. Crossan, *Guernsey, 1814–1914: Migration and Modernisation* (Woodbridge, 2007), pp. 119–21).

[47] Nevertheless, a decision of the Privy Council established in 1837 that Herm – and by analogy Jethou – were part of Guernsey for the purposes of the *impôt*, a duty on spirits which went into States' general revenue (E.F. Moore (ed.), *Reports of Cases Heard and Determined by the Judicial Committee and the Lords of His Majesty's Most Honourable Privy Council, 1836–1837* (London, 1838), pp. 307–32).

[48] 16.5.1838, IA, AQ 0965/02.

twentieth century. A law of 1948 formally placed Herm and Jethou within St Peter Port for electoral purposes; Herm (though not Jethou) is explicitly included in Guernsey's modern income tax law, and both Herm and Jethou are included in Guernsey's social insurance laws.[49] In terms of their entitlement to health and social security benefits, residents of both of these islands are now indistinguishable from residents of Guernsey.

Bailiwick of Jersey

Jersey and its adjacent reefs form a Bailiwick of their own, which has been politically separate from the Bailiwick of Guernsey since the fifteenth century. Like the other islands, Jersey became a member of the Channel Islands Presbyterian Church in the second half of the sixteenth century, and adopted the Presbyterian Discipline, out of which the welfare system which operated in its twelve parishes subsequently evolved.[50] In its 'mature' years between the eighteenth and twentieth centuries, Jersey's parochial welfare system differed from the system which operated in Guernsey in four major respects: administrative personnel; mechanics of taxation; the role and status of the workhouse; and the treatment of strangers. We shall explore these differences in sequence.

In terms of personnel, the main welfare officers in each Jersey parish were the two parochial *Surveillants* (Churchwardens) who took the lead in co-ordinating and distributing welfare, and had oversight of *la Charité* (a fund akin to Guernsey's *Bien des Pauvres*).[51] Thomas Quayle, writing in the early nineteenth century, likened them to English overseers.[52] The *Surveillants* were assisted in their activities by two parochial *Collecteurs d'Aumônes* (Almoners), who took church collections and helped distribute their proceeds.[53] Jersey's parishes also had officers known as *Procureurs du Bien Publique*, but these, unlike Guernsey's parochial *Procureurs*, had no special welfare role, and acted as parish trustees and representatives in all financial matters.

Uniquely among Jersey parishes, St Helier in 1908 replaced the traditional welfare apparatus with a purpose-designed body which it called its 'Poor Law Commission'.[54] This body, which consisted of the Rector, the Constable, the two *Surveillants*, the two *Procureurs du Bien Publique* and six ratepayers, was reminiscent of the 'Poor Law Board' established fifty years earlier in St Peter Port.

[49] D.M. Ogier, *The Government and Law of Guernsey* (Guernsey, 2005), pp. 101–2.
[50] Note that Anglicanism was imposed on Jersey by James I in 1620, some forty years earlier than in Guernsey (T. Thornton, *The Channel Islands, 1370–1640: Between England and Normandy* (Woodbridge, 2012), pp. 140–1).
[51] C. Le Quesne, *A Constitutional History of Jersey* (London, 1856), p. 10; P. Falle, *Caesarea: Or, an Account of Jersey* (1694; London, 1734 edn), pp. 323–4.
[52] T. Quayle, *A General View of the Agriculture and Present State of the Islands on the Coast of Normandy* (London, 1815), p. 60. *Surveillant* literally means 'supervisor' and is the direct lexical if not functional equivalent of overseer.
[53] Le Quesne, *Constitutional History*, p. 11.
[54] M. Phillips, *Poor People* (Jersey, 2001), p. 127.

To begin with, Jersey's parochial welfare funds were derived exclusively from voluntary sources: church-door collections, the church poor-box, donations and legacies. In 1597, Jersey's States authorised the levying of rates in parishes where voluntary poor funds proved insufficient,[55] but this does not seem to have been acted upon, and there is no evidence that taxation was resorted to for poor relief purposes until the late eighteenth century.[56] After this time, most parishes levied poor rates intermittently. By the 1830s, according to the Reverend Edward Durell, all twelve of Jersey's parishes levied a poor rate every year.[57]

Just as in Guernsey, Alderney and Sark, Jersey's poor rates were levied on a rate-payer's capital assets, valued in terms of quarters of wheat.[58] Unlike the other islands, however, Jersey's parishes did not have *Douzaines*. Thus it was the parish assembly which drew up the tax list, assessed parishioners' assets and set the rate.[59] This body, which Thomas Quayle likened to an English vestry, was composed of a number of *ex-officio* members and the *Principaux* of the parish.[60] To qualify as *un Principal*, a ratepayer had to own property beyond a certain value, which varied over time and between parishes. Much discretion was exercised in admitting parishioners to the ranks of *Principaux*, not least because of Jersey's factional politics, which led factions holding parochial power to manage lists of *Principaux* in such a way as to retain it.[61] In an effort to reduce political interference, the task of assessing parishioners for rates had, by the early twentieth century, passed from parish assemblies to thir-teen-member parochial taxation committees, and experts were appointed to value ratepayers' property.[62]

In 1815, Thomas Quayle reported a general reluctance among Jersey's parish-ioners to apply for relief: 'every effort is made to preserve themselves and their nearest connexions from that necessity ... the stigma on a family, from the acceptance [of relief] ... is not speedily forgotten'.[63] Those who did apply addressed themselves in the first instance to the *Surveillants*, who were authorised to grant temporary relief until the next meeting of the parish assembly, which would either confirm or coun-termand the grant.[64] In the country parishes especially, outdoor relief appears to

[55] B. Lander, 'The relief of the poor in Jersey', *Economic Journal*, 46 (1902), p. 193.
[56] Lander, 'Relief of the poor', p. 196.
[57] E. Durell, *An Account of the Island of Jersey by the Rev. Philip Falle to which are added Notes and Illustrations* (Jersey, 1837), p. 456.
[58] *Report of the Commissioners appointed to inquire into the Civil, Municipal, and Ecclesiastical Laws of the Island of Jersey* (London, 1860), p. lxiv.
[59] *First Report of the Commissioners appointed to inquire into the State of the Criminal Law in the Channel Islands* (London, 1847), p. x.
[60] Quayle, *General View*, p. 60; Le Quesne, *Constitutional History*, pp. 6, 8.
[61] *Report from His Majesty's Commissioners for Inquiring into the Administration and Practical Oper-ations of the Poor Laws* (London, 1834), Appendix A, p. lx. These factions, which arose in the mid-eighteenth century, were originally known as Charlots and Magots, and later as Laurels and Roses. Charlots/Laurels were broadly conservative and their counterparts broadly liberal (C. Platt, *A Concise History of Jersey: A New Perspective* (Jersey, 2009), pp. 64, 86).
[62] Lander, 'Relief of the poor', p. 201.
[63] Quayle, *General View*, p. 60, 205.
[64] *Report into the Administration of the Poor Laws*, Appendix A, p. 232. By the early twentieth century, responsibility for admitting recipients to long-term relief had passed from the parish

have been minimal, often taking the form of hand-outs in kind, which allowed some of the smaller parishes to fund their outdoor expenditure exclusively from *la Charité* and church-door collections, even in the nineteenth century. Parishioners who had no other source of support and whose circumstances were unlikely to improve – the physically and mentally handicapped, the chronically sick, lunatics, old people – were usually admitted to the General Hospital and, as in Guernsey, it was on indoor relief that the bulk of rate-derived funds were spent.[65]

Like Guernsey's Town and Country Hospitals, Jersey's General Hospital was essentially a workhouse. However, it differed significantly from the two Guernsey institutions in that it was, from the outset, a States' rather than a parochial enterprise. The Hospital's history began in 1741, when a Jersey widow left 50,000 *livres tournois* to build and endow a house for the poor. Under sanction of an Order in Council, Jersey's States assumed a co-ordinating role in the project, and when the Hospital opened in the early 1770s, the States' committee which had overseen construction transformed itself into the Hospital's governing body. The institution, which was situated in St Helier, continued thereafter to be run by the States and served the whole island.[66] Parishes who admitted paupers to the institution were invoiced directly for their keep on a fee-per-head-per-day basis.[67]

Just as Guernsey's Town and Country Hospitals developed a medical role alongside their poor law role, so too did Jersey's General Hospital. In Jersey, however, the Hospital's medical role came to outweigh its poor law role more rapidly than in Guernsey, as significant sections of its clientele were transferred to other States' residential institutions in the second half of the nineteenth century. In 1862, the Hospital's girls began to be moved to the Jersey Female Orphans' Home at Grouville. At about the same time, its boys were transferred to a rented farm at Anne Port and then, in 1867, to a purpose-built industrial school at Haut de la Garenne. Similarly, the Hospital's lunatics were removed in 1868 to a new lunatic asylum built and run by the States.[68] As in the case of Hospital inmates, the fees of paupers who resided in these institutions were met by their respective parishes.[69] As the Hospital's poor law function faded, so its medical role steadily increased, to the extent that, by 1900, it was providing short-term treatment to nearly 400 patients a year in its medical and surgical wards.[70] Although it still possessed a small poor law section

assembly to a committee consisting of Rector, Constable, *Centeniers* and *Surveillants* (Lander, 'Relief of the poor', p. 197).

[65] Phillips, *Poor People*, p. 68.

[66] Phillips, *Poor People*, pp. 46–54.

[67] Admissions were usually at the instigation of parish Constables (*Report into the Civil, Municipal, and Ecclesiastical Laws of Jersey*, p. lxvi).

[68] Mary Phillips identifies a major fire at the Hospital in 1859 as the catalyst for these changes (Phillips, *Poor People*, pp. 98, 100).

[69] Some of the Hospital's poor law load was also taken up by charitable residential institutions, such as the Barnardo Home, the Westaway Creche and the Sacré Coeur Orphanage, and, for the elderly, the Home for Aged and Infirm Women, the Home for Aged Women, the Gardner Home for Elderly Men and St Augustine's Home (Phillips, *Poor People*, pp. 107, 133, 182). It should be noted that voluntary homes were far more numerous in Jersey than in Guernsey.

[70] Lander, 'Relief of the poor', p. 199.

(accommodating chiefly the elderly) until at least the late 1940s, the Hospital was regarded as primarily a medical institution from the 1930s onwards.[71]

In contrast to Guernsey, Jersey was completely lacking in settlement laws providing mechanisms whereby non-natives might acquire eligibility for relief.[72] Birthplace alone conferred settlement, thus only those born in Jersey parishes were entitled to claim relief in them.[73] Any stranger applying for parochial relief was referred to private charities. If this proved unavailing, the parish Constable would simply despatch the destitute stranger to the General Hospital, where he would await deportation – which, as in Guernsey, was the usual mode of dealing with non-native paupers.[74]

It is important to note, however, that parishes were not invoiced directly for the strangers they sent to the Hospital, as they were for their own parishioners. As early as 1777, the States had established an arrangement whereby the costs of accommodating and repatriating strangers were met by a fixed levy imposed on each parish in the same proportions as they contributed to insular general taxation.[75] It was partly in order to fund this levy that Jersey's parishes began in the late 1770s to raise regular poor rates.[76]

In the mid-1840s, non-native paupers were being deported from Jersey at the rate of about 800 a year.[77] Nevertheless, strangers deemed particularly 'deserving' were occasionally received as long-term inmates of the Hospital, in addition to which the Hospital Board also paid discretionary allowances to a number of strangers living outside the institution. The latter amounted to some fifty or sixty in the early 1830s, chiefly the widows of British soldiers and sailors.[78] Because their costs were borne by the entire insular community, non-natives supported internally or externally by the Hospital Board came to be known as the 'island poor'.[79]

By the early twentieth century, the normal procedure for a non-native seeking relief was to apply directly to the Hospital Board. Taking each case on its merits, the Board would then exercise its discretion to admit them to the institution long-term, provide them with a small outdoor allowance, or repatriate them.[80] In 1906, the Hospital Board, which had always been a committee of the States, was renamed the States' Public Assistance Committee, but its remit remained restricted to the

[71] *Jersey General Hospital, 1863–1963* (Jersey, 1963), p. 11 (Jersey Archive, L/F/11/5); Phillips, *Poor People*, pp. 172–3, 182.
[72] For Guernsey's laws, see section on 'Settlement and deportation legislation', Chapter 4.
[73] *Report into the Administration of the Poor Laws*, Appendix A, p. 230; *Report into the Civil, Municipal, and Ecclesiastical Laws of Jersey*, p. lxv.
[74] *Report into the Administration of the Poor Laws*, Appendix A, p. 232.
[75] Phillips, *Poor People*, p. 58. This appears to have been done for reasons analogous to those which motivated Guernsey's States to take on the costs of relieving and repatriating garrison-associated strangers in 1788 (see section on 'States' involvement in poor relief', Chapter 4).
[76] Lander, 'Relief of the poor', p. 196.
[77] *First Report into the State of the Criminal Law in the Channel Islands*, p. 206.
[78] *Report into the Administration of the Poor Laws*, Appendix B2, p. 273.
[79] *Report into the Civil, Municipal and Ecclesiastical Laws of Jersey*, p. lxvi.
[80] Lander, 'Relief of the poor', p. 198.

Hospital and to strangers as before.[81] In the early 1940s, with Jersey under German occupation, the parishes themselves began directly to dispense non-native relief. The funds for such relief, however, still came from the States.[82]

In the nineteenth and early twentieth centuries, Guernseymen would have figured significantly among non-natives in Jersey (and *vice versa*) as there was a significant interchange of people between the two islands.[83] However, it was impossible for a Guernsey-born person to gain a settlement in his own right in Jersey, and difficult for a Jerseyman to gain a settlement in Guernsey.[84] From time to time, arrangements were made between parishes of the two islands to provide non-resident relief, as in the late 1890s, when St Peter Port agreed to send a regular remittance to 88-year-old retired shoemaker Helier Le Maitre and his 50-year-old consumptive daughter, both Guernsey-born but resident in St Helier for four decades, and St Helier returned the favour by providing an allowance to 73-year-old John King and his wife, both born in Jersey but living in St Peter Port.[85] Far more often, however, deportation was the preferred solution, and this frequently resulted in the protracted inter-island shuttling of paupers such as Victor Petit, who, though born in Guernsey and resident for decades in Jersey, had the misfortune to lack a settlement in either island, and indeed anywhere else.[86]

Fortunately for the successors of people like Victor Petit, the parochial welfare systems of both Guernsey and Jersey began to be marginalised as a system of social security gradually developed over the middle decades of the twentieth century. In 1935, Jersey's States passed a Workmen's Compensation Law.[87] In 1948, they introduced a non-contributory pension scheme for the over-70s and blind people over 40.[88] Finally, in 1950, they enacted an Insular Insurance Law under which everyone of working age contributed to a scheme providing benefits in case of sickness, accident, maternity, widowhood and retirement.[89]

This did not, however, spell the end of parochial welfare in Jersey, since the 1950 Insular Insurance Law did not cover all contingencies (unemployment in particular), and the parish system continued to function as a sort of supplementary benefit system for a further six decades.[90] Ultimately, the Income Support (Jersey) Law,

---

81 *Opinion de Messieurs les Officiers de la Couronne sur la Position Légale au sujet de la Séparation de l'Hospice des Pauvres de l'Hôpital* (Jersey, 1930), p. 20 (Jersey Archive, D/Z/D/A/5).
82 Phillips, *Poor People*, p. 148.
83 Crossan, *Guernsey, 1814–1914*, pp. 116–18.
84 See section on 'Settlement and deportation legislation', Chapter 4.
85 See correspondence from January 1898 in IA, DC/HX 179–04, also 3.1.1898, IA, DC/HX 054–07 and 4.12.1899, IA, DC/HX 056–04.
86 For the case of Victor Petit, and those of Louisa Bucknell and Mary Peadon who were also despatched repeatedly from one island to the other, see section on 'Strangers' in Chapter 8.
87 Phillips, *Poor People*, p. 140.
88 Phillips, *Poor People*, pp. 180–1.
89 Phillips, *Poor People*, pp. 1, 195, 197–205.
90 Throughout this time, assistance to natives continued to be funded from parochial rates and to non-natives by the States. From 1950, non-natives became eligible for help after just five years' residence, and, from 1953, parishes of residence (rather than birth) became liable for the payment of native relief (Anon., *Continuity and Change: A Review of the Social Security and*

2007 instituted a comprehensive States' income support scheme which included out-of-work benefits. In rendering the parish system redundant, this law, which came into force at the beginning of 2008, brought Jersey's parochial poor law history to a close.

Health Insurance Schemes in Jersey (Jersey, 1995), pp. 23, 66, 135, 177; Phillips, *Poor People*, p. 135).

Appendix 4

Average Year-end Head-counts and Average Annual Admissions and Discharges, Town Hospital, 1700s–1900s

Period	Av. year-end no.	Admissions p.a.	Discharges p.a.	Admissions as % of year-end no.
18th c	121	? 46	? 47	? 38%
1800–09	152	73	63	48%
1810–19	238	120	112	50%
1820–29	252	195	200	77%
1830–39	275	275	266	100%
1840–49	267	230	259	86%
1850–59	240	240	239	100%
1860–69	221	230	229	104%
1870–79	206	207	209	100%
1880–89	207	178	180	86%
1890–99	173	179	177	103%
1900–09	172	245	247	142%
1910–19	181	243	245	134%
1920–24	179	230	225	128%

Sources: IA, DC/HX 053–01, 053–02, 057–02, 060–02, 060–03, 117–01, 117–02, 118–01, 118–02, 119–01, 119–02, 119–03, 119–04, 120–01, 121–01, 121–02, 121–03, 121–04, 122–01, 123–01, 123–02, 124–02, 272–02.

Appendix 5

Adult Admissions Ascribed to Illness and Accidents, Town Hospital, 1852–1919

Period	Men	Women	All adults
1852–59	337 (44%)	218 (33%)	555 (39%)
1860–69	497 (46%)	254 (35%)	751 (44%)
1870–79	556 (54%)	296 (41%)	852 (52%)
1880–89	566 (65%)	361 (51%)	927 (59%)
1890–99	586 (66%)	340 (57%)	926 (62%)
1900–09	720 (66%)	865 (63%)	1,585 (66%)
1910–19	765 (78%)	601 (78%)	1,366 (78%)

Sources: IA, DC/HX 060–02, DC/HX 265–06, DC/HX 272–02.

Note: percentages are of the total number of admissions in the relevant category.

Appendix 6

Relative Proportions of Men and Women in Year-end Head-counts and Annual Admissions, Town Hospital, 1750–1919

Period	Men as % of adults at yr-end	Women as % of adults at yr-end	Men's admissions as % of adult admissions	Women's admissions as % of adult admissions
1750–59	31%	69%	n/a	n/a
1760–69	27%	73%	n/a	n/a
1770–79	34%	66%	n/a	n/a
1780–89	30%	70%	n/a	n/a
1790–99	28%	72%	n/a	n/a
1800–09	37%	63%	n/a	n/a
1811–19	39%	61%	37%	63%
1820–29	41%	59%	52%	48%
1830–39	46%	54%	58%	42%
1840–49	43%	57%	55%	45%
1850–59	39%	61%	54%	46%
1860–69	45%	55%	60%	40%
1870–79	48%	52%	59%	41%
1880–89	51%	49%	56%	44%
1890–99	51%	49%	61%	39%
1900–09	54%	46%	55%	45%
1910–19	56%	44%	58%	42%

Sources: IA, DC/HX 053–01, 053–02, 057–02, 060–02, 060–03, 272–02.

Appendix 7

Annual Averages of Child Admissions and Year-end Numbers, Town Hospital, 1756–1919

Period	Boys year-end	Girls year-end	All children year-end	Child proportion year-end	No. of children admitted
1756	27	36	63	42%	n/a
1760–7	44	29	73	45%	n/a
1770–79	26	24	50	38%	n/a
1780–89	11	12	23	25%	n/a
1790–99	28	27	55	43%	n/a
1800–09	28	32	60	40%	n/a
1810–19	59	55	114	48%	43
1820–29	56	44	100	39%	50
1830–39	53	41	94	34%	58
1840–49	41	30	71	27%	46
1850–59	39	28	67	28%	50
1860–69	27	24	51	23%	46
1870–79	15	15	30	15%	34
1880–89	16	12	28	14%	21
1890–99	15	8	23	13%	29
1900–09	14	8	22	13%	58
1910–19	17	16	33	18%	74

Sources: IA, DC/HX 053–01, 053–02, 057–02, 060–02, 060–03, 117–01, 117–02, 118–01, 118–02, 119–01, 119–02, 119–03, 119–04, 120–01, 121–01, 121–02, 121–03, 121–04, 122–01, 123–01, 123–02, 124–02, 272–02.

Appendix 8

Over-60s as a Proportion of all Inmates, and Composition by Sex of Over-60s Cohort, Town Hospital, 1756–1911

Year	Over-60s as % of all inms	Females 60+ as % of all 60+	Males 60+ as % of all 60+
1756	26%	62%	38%
1772	33%	66%	34%
1861	33%	55%	45%
1881	48%	48%	52%
1911	45%	43%	57%

Sources: IA, DC/HX 117–01, 119–02; census enumerators' books for 1861 and 1881 (microfilm, PL); http://www.1911census.co.uk.

Appendix 9

Average Weekly Amounts Purchased per Head, Town Hospital, 1760–1917

Period	Meat (lb)	Butter (lb)	Potatoes (lb)	Bread (lb)	Milk (pts)	Tea (oz)	Sugar (oz)
1760s	¾	⅓					
1770s	1	½					
1780s	1⅓	½					
1790s	1¼	½					
1811–19	1	¼	6½		1½	⅛	1½
1820–26	1	¼	8½	(5½)	1⅓	⅛	
1834–39	1	¼	6½		1½	⅓	1½
1842–45	¾	¼	7½	(6½)	1⅓	⅓	1¼
1850–59	2	⅓	4¼		1½	¾	2¾
1860–69	2	⅓	4⅓	(6¾)	1¾	1	3½
1870–79	2	⅓	4¼		2¼	1½	4⅓
1880–89	2⅓	⅓	3¾		3	1¾	5
1890–99	2⅓	⅓	3	6½		1¾	5¾
1900–09	2	½	3¾	7½		2½	10
1910–17	2	½	5	8¼		3	12

Sources: IA, DC/HX 101–01, 101–02, 109–05, 165–01, 117–01,120–02, 119–02, 119–04, 120–03, 120–01, 120–04, 045–01, 178–01, 168–01, 020–01, 274–010, 178–02, 020–01, 272–02.

Appendix 10

Timeline: Developments in Poor Relief and Social Security, 1700–2010

1724 St Peter Port levies its first poor rate

1726 Ord, 18.4.1726 establishes concept of settlement

1730 St Peter Port introduces uniforms for parochial paupers

1738 St Peter Port *Chefs de Famille* decide to build a workhouse

1743 St Peter Port's workhouse (the Town Hospital) is opened to paupers

1744 St Saviours levies a poor rate (? first in country parishes)

1752 Foundation deed of Country Hospital signed

1764 First paupers admitted to Country Hospital; most country parishes begin to levy poor rates

1788 States undertake to refund parochial relief expenses in respect of soldiers' dependants (*Acte*, 19.4.1788)

1832 Town Hospital opens its house of separation

1851 Town Hospital closes its house of separation and opens a lunatic asylum

1852 O in C, 28.12.1852 establishes St Peter Port Poor Law Board

1867 O in C, 26.6.1867 confers settlement on non-natives after 20 years' unbroken residence

1876 O in C, 27.6.1876 establishes Poor Law Boards in country parishes

1889 Ord, 30.9.1889 introduces certification for patients admitted to lunatic asylums

1892 States undertake to refund parochial relief expenses in respect of all strangers (Ord, 25.4.1892)

1899 States' Board of Health is established; first States' Medical Officer of Health is appointed

1900 Law on Compensation to Families of Persons killed in Accidents (O in C, 13.12.1900)

1901 Ord, 21.12.1901 brings Town and Country Hospitals under Royal Court supervision

1903 King Edward VII isolation hospital opens

1910 O in C, 11.6.1910 introduces new provisions for certification of patients admitted to lunatic asylums

1917 Law on the Protection of Children and Young People (O in C, 24.1.1917)

1919 States' Income Tax Law (O in C, 20.12.1919)

1920 O in C, 13.10.1920 extends franchise for States elections to non-ratepaying men over 20 and non-ratepaying women over 30

1924 Workmen's Accident Compensation Law (O in C, 9.10.1924)

1925 O in C, 24.7.1925 transfers responsibility for poor relief funding from parishes to States, and creates States' Central Poor Law Board

1926 Non-Contributory Old Age Pensions Law (O in C, 19.3.1926); O in C, 30.4.1926 makes poor relief a secular matter in all parishes; ord, 1.5.1926 transfers ownership of Town and Country Hospitals to States

1928 O in C, 24.11.1928 creates Children Board as a sub-committee of States' Central Poor Law Board, and establishes States' Children's Home

1931 O in C, 1.10.1931 modifies Non-Contributory Old Age Pensions Law to make pensions available to blind persons over 50

1934 Public Health Law (O in C, 26.2.1934)

1935 Contributory Pensions and Accident Insurance Law (O in C, 6.6.1935)

1937 Public Assistance Law (O in C, 22.10.1937) creates Public Assistance Authority and its sub-committees (Hospital Board, Children Board, Stranger Poor Assistance Committee, Central Outdoor Assistance Board); also creates Parochial Outdoor Assistance Boards

1939 Mental Treatment Law (Guernsey), 1939 (O in C, 5.9.1939)

1939 Country Hospital becomes Emergency Hospital

1940 Le Vauquiédor Mental Hospital opens

1941 Le Vauquiédor Mental Hospital is requisitioned by occupying forces

1943 Law of 18.9.1943 introduces Children's Allowances

1947 Family Allowances Law, 1947 (O in C, 24.2.1948)

1949 Princess Elizabeth Hospital opens

1950 Family Allowances (Guernsey) Law, 1950 (O in C, 25.4.1950)

1951 National Insurance (Guernsey) Law, 1951 (O in C, 11.7.1951) (not implemented)

1951 Country Hospital reopens as a mental hospital

1955 Non-Contributory Pensions (Guernsey) Law, 1955

1964 Social Insurance (Guernsey) Law, 1964

1967 Town Hospital's workhouse department closes; house people are moved to St Julian's House, and Town Hospital becomes geriatric hospital

1970 Town Hospital transferred from jurisdiction of States' Public Assistance Authority to States' Board of Health

1970   O in C, 30.9.1970 dissolves Children Board of Public Assistance Authority and replaces it with non-poor law States' Children Board

1971   Supplementary Benefit (Guernsey) Law, 1971

1972   Health Service (Pharmaceutical) (Guernsey) Law, 1972

1978   Social Insurance (Guernsey) Law, 1978

1986   Town Hospital closes

1990   Health Service (Benefit) (Guernsey) Law, 1990

1993   Guernsey Social Security Authority replaces States' Insurance Authority (ord, 29.9.1993)

1996   States' Specialist Health Insurance Scheme comes into operation

2002   Long-Term Care Insurance (Guernsey) Law, 2002

2004   Creation of States' Social Security Department (SSD) and Health and Social Services Department (HSSD)

2005   Supplementary Benefit (Amendment) Ordinance, 2005

2006   Public Assistance (Amendment) Law, 2006

2010   Mental Health (Bailiwick of Guernsey) Law, 2010

Bibliography

Primary Sources

Greffe, St Peter Port, Guernsey

Jugements, Ordonnances et Ordres du Conseil, November 1745–April 1757
Livres en Crime
Ordonnances
Plaids de Meubles, 1863
Royal Court Letter Books I and III

Priaulx Library, St Peter Port, Guernsey

Actes des Etats (published volumes)
Billets d'Etat
Census Enumerators' Books, 1841–1901 (microfilm)
*Constitution et Règlement du Conseil d'Administration pour les Pauvres de la Ville et Paroisse
    de Saint Pierre-Port* (Guernsey, 1861)
Orders in Council (published volumes)
Ordinances (published volumes)
*Rapport du Comité nommé par les Chefs de Famille de la Ville et Paroisse de Saint Pierre-
    Port le 5 Avril 1848* (Guernsey, 1849)
Relief Book of the Guernsey Benevolent and Strangers' Friend Society, 1839–61
St Peter Port Délibérations des Chefs de Famille, 1715–79
St Peter Port Délibérations des Chefs de Famille, 1844–66
*The Case of the Town Parish versus the Nine Country Parishes respecting a Change in the
    Rates and Representation, appointed to be heard before the Committee of the Privy
    Council at 11 o'clock, on Thursday April 26, 1759* (Guernsey, 1843)
Town Church Marriage Registers (microfilm)
Victoria Cottage Hospital Minutes, 1888–1946
Watkins MS

Island Archives, St Peter Port, Guernsey

AQ 0115/01 – St Pierre du Bois Procureur's Accounts, 1873–8
AQ 0116/01 – St Saviours Tax Book, 1662–1767

AQ 0116/02 – St Saviours Tax Book, 1760–1810
AQ 0141/14 – St Andrews Procureur's Accounts, 1888–99
AQ 0208/08 – St Andrews Parish Register, 1717–98
AQ 0299/16–2 – Société Charitable de l'Ile de Guernesey, 1837 annual report
AQ 0397/05 – Vale Payments to Poor, 1863–1927
AQ 0397/11 – Vale Payments to Poor, 1748–1840
AQ 0399/17 – Vale Procureur's Accounts, 1930–38
AQ 0402/04–01 to AQ 0402/04–06 – 1832 Cholera Relief Fund records
AQ 0452/02 – St Pierre du Bois Parish Register, 1757–80
AQ 0452/03 – St Pierre du Bois Tax Book, 1780–1815
AQ 0458/02 – St Pierre du Bois Procureur's Accounts, 1854–77
AQ 0459/02 – St Pierre du Bois Revenus des Pauvres
AQ 0507/04 – Vale Tax Register, 1778–1810
AQ 0511/04 – St Saviours Parish Book, 1734–1818
AQ 0517/24 – St Martins Procureur's Accounts, 1845–7
AQ 065/12 – St Peter Port Pier Accounts, 1603–55 (microfilm)
AQ 0670/02 – records of Holy Trinity Church, St Peter Port
AQ 0685/01 – Register of the Guernsey Pawnbroking Company, 1920–34
AQ 0735/31 – Torteval Procureur's Accounts, 1822
AQ 0767/10 – St Martins Churchwardens' and Collecteurs' Accounts, 1627–1754
AQ 0778/85 – Articles et Règlements de l'Union Charitable de la Paroisse de St Pierre du Bois
AQ 0824/01 – records of Victoria Road Methodist Chapel
AQ 0941/02 – St Peter Port Stranger Cautions, 1765–1807
AQ 0941/03 – St Peter Port Stranger Cautions, 1785–8
AQ 0942–02 – St Peter Port Constables' Accounts, 1762–94
AQ 0942/03 – St Peter Port Constables' Accounts, 1779–1808
AQ 0964/01 – St Peter Port Douzaine Deliberations, 1732–83
AQ 0964/02 – St Peter Port Douzaine Deliberations, 1783–1815
AQ 0965/01 – St Peter Port Douzaine Deliberations, 1815–28
AQ 0965/02 – St Peter Port Douzaine Deliberations, 1828–47
AQ 0966/01 – St Peter Port Douzaine Deliberations, 1848–73
AQ 0974/01 – Return of Dwelling Houses in St Peter Port, 1853
AQ 0988/01 – St Peter Port Constables' Book of Ordinances, 1581–1766
AQ 0991/05 – St Peter Port Grand Livre de Police, 1832
AQ 0998/02 – St Peter Port Règles Etablies par la Douzaine, 1772–1801
AQ 0999/01 – St Peter Port Register of Persons Sent out of the Island, 1842–80
AQ 40/01 – Guernsey Chamber of Commerce Minute Book, 1808–39
AQ 40/04 – Guernsey Chamber of Commerce Minute Book, 1849–89
AQ 40/06 – Guernsey Chamber of Commerce Minute Book, 1911–17
AQ 44/05 – Guernsey Chamber of Commerce Minute Book, 1889–1902
AQ 804/77 – Nicolas Dobrée Correspondence
AQ 804/79 – Nicolas Dobrée Correspondence
AQ 807/20 – Nicolas Dobrée Correspondence
AQ 807/32 – Nicolas Dobrée Correspondence

AQ 807/40 – Nicolas Dobrée Correspondence
AQ 807/52 – Nicolas Dobrée Correspondence
AQ 807/53 – Nicolas Dobrée Correspondence
AQ 940/02 – St Peter Port Délibérations des Chefs de Famille, 1866–1906
AQ 1000/65 – St Peter Port Stranger Poor Journal, 1848–91
AQ 1002/03 – St Peter Port Tax Book, 1715–40
AQ 1003/01 – St Peter Port Tax Book, 1740–62
AQ 1003/02 – St Peter Port Tax Book, 1762–80
AQ 1003/03 – St Peter Port Tax Book, 1780–8
AQ 1003/04 – St Peter Port Tax Book, 1789–97
AQ 1004/01 – St Peter Port Tax Book, 1797–1803
AQ 1004/02 – St Peter Port Tax Book, 1803–10
AQ 1004/03 – St Peter Port Tax Book, 1810–23
AQ 1005/01 – St Peter Port Tax Book, 1823–39
AQ 1005/02 – St Peter Port Tax Book, 1840–56
AQ 1006/01 – St Peter Port Tax Book, 1857–77
AQ 1007/01 – St Peter Port Tax Book, 1878–93
AQ 1008/01 – St Peter Port Tax Book, 1894–1907
AQ 1009/01 – St Peter Port Tax Book, 1908–17
AQ 1051/01 – St Peter Port Rentail des Pauvres, 1751–1945
AQ 1059/14 – St Peter Port First Class Tax Book, 1913–19
AQ 1132/045 – Vale Tax List, 1796
AS/MB 011–05 – States' Poor Law Enquiry Committee Minutes, 1936–40
AS/MB 023–04 – States' Poor Law Enquiry Committee Minutes, 1903–12
AS/MB 024/01 – States' Committee Meetings, 1914
AS/MB 024–06 – States' Parochial Taxation and Poor Law Administration Committee
    Minutes, 1920
AS/MB 065–02 – Public Assistance Authority Hospital Board Minutes, 1948–65
AS/MB 065–05 – Public Assistance Authority Hospital Board Minutes, 1942–7
AS/MB 067–09 – States' Board of Health Geriatric Committee Minutes, 1969–73
AS/MB 068–01 – Public Assistance Authority Hospital Board Minutes, 1966–70
BH 52–13 – States' Board of Health Geriatric Hospital Group File, 1976–80
BH 52–14 – States' Board of Health Geriatric Hospital Group File, 1980–8
DC/HX 005–01 – Town Hospital Lunatic Asylum Medical Officer's Visitation Book
    21.12.1909–04.01.1910
DC/HX 013–01 – Town Hospital Accounts issued to Constables and States in respect
    of Strangers, 1810–38
DC/HX 013–02 – Town Hospital Accounts issued to Constables and States in respect
    of Strangers, 1838–60
DC/HX 015–04 – Public Assistance Authority Hospital Board Minutes, 1937–41
DC/HX 017–01 – St Peter Port Livre des Pauvres Honteux, 1833–6
DC/HX 018–02 – St Peter Port Livre des Pauvres Honteux, 1811–22
DC/HX 020–01 – Town Hospital Treasurer's Accounts, 1838–62
DC/HX 021–03 – Permanent List of Outdoor Poor, St Peter Port, 1862–1900
DC/HX 044–01 – Country Hospital Register of Acts, 1751–1861

DC/HX 045–01 – Town Hospital Abstracts of Accounts, 1811–22
DC/HX 046–01 – St Peter Port Poor Law Board Minutes, 1907–15
DC/HX 049–02 – Outpatient Visits, St Peter Port North, 1877–84
DC/HX 049–03 – Outpatient Visits, St Peter Port South, 1877–83
DC/HX 051–01 – St Peter Port Poor Law Board Minutes, 1924–34
DC/HX 052–01 – St Peter Port Poor Law Board Minutes, 1915–24
DC/HX 053–01 – Town Hospital Admission and Discharge Register, 1809–22
DC/HX 053–02 – Town Hospital Admission and Discharge Register, 1823–36
DC/HX 054–05 – St Peter Port Poor Law Board Minutes, 1852–73
DC/HX 054–06 – St Peter Port Poor Law Board Minutes, 1873–88
DC/HX 054–07 – St Peter Port Poor Law Board Minutes, 1888–98
DC/HX 056–04 – St Peter Port Poor Law Board Minutes, 1899–1906
DC/HX 057–01 – Town Hospital House Committee Minutes, 1889–96
DC/HX 057–02 – Town Hospital Admission and Discharge Register, 1837–56
DC/HX 059–01 – Town Hospital House Committee Minutes, 1871–81
DC/HX 060–02 – Town Hospital Admissions and Discharge Lists, 1853–83
DC/HX 060–03 – Town Hospital Admission and Discharge Register, 1883–98
DC/HX 061–05 – St Peter Port Poor Relief Accounts, 1634–1701
DC/HX 062–02 – Town Hospital Lunatic Asylum Register, 1853–1903 (incomplete)
DC/HX 062–03 – Town Hospital House Committee Letter Book, 1881–9 (also
    containing Town Hospital Lunatic Asylum Register, 1852–3)
DC/HX 063–02 – Outpatients Register, St Peter Port North, 1853–62
DC/HX 066–03 – Town Hospital Lunatic Asylum Daybook, 1893–4
DC/HX 069–01 – Town Hospital House Committee Minutes, 1871–81
DC/HX 072–02 – Letter Book of St Peter Port Procureur of the Poor, 1835–1918
DC/HX 075–01 – Deliberations of the Town Hospital Board of Directors, 1838–42
DC/HX 075–02 – Deliberations of the Town Hospital Board of Directors, 1849–53
DC/HX 076–07 – Miscellaneous Town Hospital Accounts, 1838–57
DC/HX 079–01 – Deliberations of the Town Hospital Board of Directors, 1741–1801
DC/HX 079–02 – Deliberations of the Town Hospital Board of Directors, 1801–22
DC/HX 080–01 – Town Hospital House Committee Minutes, 1906–10
DC/HX 080–02 – Town Hospital House Committee Minutes, 1904–6
DC/HX 080–03 – Town Hospital House Committee Minutes, 1901–3
DC/HX 080–05 – Town Hospital House Committee Minutes, 1913–16
DC/HX 080–06 – Town Hospital House Committee Minutes 1910–13
DC/HX 081–01 – Town Hospital Daybook, 1837–46
DC/HX 082–01 – Town Hospital Daybook, 1823–5
DC/HX 083–01 – Town Hospital Daybook, 1826–8
DC/HX 088–02 – Town Hospital Patients' Diets, 1871–9
DC/HX 096–02 – Town Hospital Clothing Delivered, 1828–33
DC/HX 100–02 – Town Hospital Provisions Issued, 1866–70
DC/HX 101–01 – Town Hospital Provisions Issued, 1862–5
DC/HX 101–02 – Town Hospital Provisions Issued, 1818–23
DC/HX 109–05 – Town Hospital Provisions Issued, 1840–2
DC/HX 109–09 – Town Hospital Provisions Issued, 1889–91

DC/HX 117–01 – Town Hospital Daybook, 1741–59
DC/HX 117–02 – Town Hospital Daybook, 1747–52
DC/HX 118–01 – Town Hospital Daybook, 1752–8
DC/HX 118–02 – Town Hospital Daybook, 1758–63
DC/HX 119–01 – Town Hospital Daybook, 1764–70
DC/HX 119–02 – Town Hospital Daybook, 1770–2
DC/HX 119–03 – Town Hospital Daybook, 1772–7
DC/HX 119–04 – Town Hospital Daybook, 1778–83
DC/HX 120–01 – Town Hospital Daybook, 1784–90
DC/HX 120–03 – Town Hospital Daybook, 1777–87
DC/HX 121–02 – Town Hospital Daybook, 1794–9
DC/HX 121–03 – Town Hospital Daybook, 1800–5
DC/HX 121–04 – Town Hospital Daybook, 1806–9
DC/HX 122–01 – Town Hospital Daybook, 1810–11
DC/HX 122–05 – Town Hospital Cell Book, 1901–51
DC/HX 123–01 – Town Hospital Daybook, 1812–15
DC/HX 123–02 – Town Hospital Daybook, 1815–18
DC/HX 124–02 – Town Hospital Daybook, 1820–2
DC/HX 127–01 – Town Hospital House Committee Minutes, 1862–70
DC/HX 127–02 – Town Hospital House Committee Minutes, 1897–1905
DC/HX 128–02 – Town Hospital Admission and Discharge Register, 1857–78
DC/HX 129–02 – Town Hospital House Committee Minutes, 1905–12
DC/HX 130–01 – Deliberations of the Town Hospital Board of Directors, 1842–9
DC/HX 130–02 – Deliberations of the Town Hospital Board of Directors, 1833–7
DC/HX 130–03 – Town Hospital House Committee Minutes, 1882–9
DC/HX 130–04 – Town Hospital House Committee Minutes, 1853–61
DC/HX 135–02 – Deliberations of the Town Hospital Board of Directors, 1822–9
DC/HX 135–03 – Deliberations of the Town Hospital Board of Directors, 1829–33
DC/HX 135–06 – Town Hospital Abstracts and Minutes, 1894–1920
DC/HX 136–01 – Town Hospital House Committee Minutes, 1884–7
DC/HX 136–02 – Town Hospital House Committee Minutes, 1887–90
DC/HX 136–03 – Town Hospital House Committee Minutes, 1890–3
DC/HX 136–04 – Town Hospital House Committee Minutes, 1893–6
DC/HX 136–07 – Town Hospital House Committee Minutes, 1862–8
DC/HX 136–08 – Town Hospital House Committee Minutes, 1868–74
DC/HX 136–09 – Town Hospital House Committee Minutes, 1874–80
DC/HX 136–10 – Town Hospital House Committee Minutes, 1880–4
DC/HX 136–11 – Town Hospital House Committee Minutes, 1896–8
DC/HX 138–11 – Town Hospital Dispensary Patients, April–October 1867
DC/HX 139–10 – Town Hospital Mistress's Daybook, 1818–26
DC/HX 165–01 – Town Hospital Treasurer's Accounts, 1760–1812
DC/HX 166–01 – Town Hospital Master's Ledger, 1839–68
DC/HX 168–01 – Town Hospital Treasurer's Accounts, 1826–37
DC/HX 169–09 – Town Hospital Children's Wages, 1872–1916
DC/HX 172–02 – St Peter Port Overseers' Accounts, 1879–1908

DC/HX 175–01 – St Peter Port Payments to Outdoor Poor, 1828

DC/HX 175–02 – St Peter Port Payments to Outdoor Poor, 1837

DC/HX 178–01 – Town Hospital Abstracts of Accounts, 1825–33

DC/HX 178–02 – Town Hospital Abstract of Accounts, 1852

DC/HX 178–03 – St Peter Port Payments to Outdoor Poor, 1724–97

DC/HX 178–04 – Accounts for Work at the Town Hospital by way of Casual Relief

DC/HX 179–01 – St Peter Port Collecteurs' Accounts, 1828–39

DC/HX 179–04 – St Peter Port Poor Law Board Letter Book, 1889–1902

DC/HX 179–05 – Town Hospital Visitors' Book, 1832–1905

DC/HX 179–06 – St Peter Port Poor Law Board Vice-President's Letter Book, 1879–81

DC/HX 180–13 – Town Hospital Casuals Log, 1903–20

DC/HX 180–14 – Livre des Actes de l'Hôpital de Saint Pierre Port, 1746–1909

DC/HX 185–01 – St Peter Port Occasional Relief Ledger Sheets, 1888–1925

DC/HX 192–03 – St Peter Port Occasional Relief Ledger Sheets, 1888–1925

DC/HX 193–01 – St Peter Port Occasional Relief Ledger Sheets, 1888–1925

DC/HX 194–01 – St Peter Port Permanent Relief Ledger Sheets, 1881–1914

DC/HX 197–01 – St Peter Port Occasional Relief Ledger Sheets, 1888–1925

DC/HX 198–01 – St Peter Port Occasional Relief Ledger Sheets, 1888–1925

DC/HX 237–03 – Town Hospital Lunacy Certificates, 1905–29

DC/HX 237–04 – Town Hospital Lunacy Certificates, 1889–1925

DC/HX 239–05 – Town Hospital Correspondence, 1909–21

DC/HX 249–01 – Town Hospital Correspondence, 1895–1926

DC/HX 249–02 – Town Hospital Correspondence, 1920–6

DC/HX 251–02 – Central Poor Law Board Correspondence, 1925

DC/HX 253–01 – Town Hospital Correspondence, 1910–20

DC/HX 253–02 – Correspondence re. Town and Country Hospitals, 1920

DC/HX 253–03 – Town and Country Hospitals, Monthly Returns and Statistics, 1926–31

DC/HX 254–04 – Town Hospital Correspondence, 1902–26

DC/HX 254–10 – Town Hospital Lunatic Asylum Doctor's Quarterly Reports

DC/HX 257–02 – St Peter Port Outdoor Relief Returns, 1931

DC/HX 265–06 – Town Hospital Admission and Discharge Lists, 1849–52

DC/HX 266–03 – St Peter Port Outdoor Relief Returns, 1926–32

DC/HX 267–22 – Town Hospital Correspondence, 1902–20

DC/HX 272–02 – St Peter Port Poor Law Board Abstracts of Accounts, 1858–1925

DC/HX 272–04 – St Peter Port Poor Law Board Members' Handbook, 1914

DC/HX 272–06 – St Peter Port Poor Law Board Members' Handbook, 1930

DC/HX 272–08 – Town Hospital Lunatic Asylum Rules, 1862

DC/HX 272–10 – States' Central Poor Law Board Staff Handbook, 1925

DC/HX 272–11 – St Peter Port Poor Law Board Constitution and other documents

DC/HX 272–13 – States' Hospital Board, Outdoor Assistance Board and Children Board Members' Handbook, 1939

DC/HX 273–08 – Miscellaneous Documents, including Resolutions of the Central Poor Law Board to December 1925

DC/HX 274–010 – Town Hospital, miscellaneous papers

DC/HX 274–011 – Town Hospital, miscellaneous papers
DC/HX 274–012 – Town Hospital, miscellaneous papers
DC/HX 281–25 – Dr John Aikman's Report on the Management of the Town Hospital
from 5 September 1876 to 31 January 1878
Report of the Committee of the Privy Council on the Island of Alderney, October 1949 (Cmd
7805)

Seigneurie Archive, Sark

Sark court records, series 4

Jersey Archive, St Helier

D/Z/D/A/5 – *Opinion de Messieurs les Officiers de la Couronne sur la Position Légale au
sujet de la Séparation de l'Hospice des Pauvres de l'Hôpital* (Jersey, 1930)
L/C/67/F3 – correspondence between Nicolas Dobrée and Sarah Messervy
L/C/67/F29 – will of Sarah Messervy
L/F/11/5 – *Jersey General Hospital, 1863–1963* (commemorative brochure)

National Archives, Kew

ACT 1/1495 – correspondence re. Guernsey social insurance scheme, 1959–62
C 143/298/20 – details concerning the endowment of a new Hospital in Guernsey by
Peter de Sancto Petro, 24 Edward III
FS 1/937 – file containing information on Guernsey Friendly Societies
HO 45/9900/B19091 – correspondence re. immigration to Guernsey, 1895
HO 45/10344/140975 – correspondence re. parochial taxation, 1906
HO 45/12918 – correspondence re. Workmen's Compensation, 1907–28
HO 45/16850 – correspondence re. St Peter Port lunatic asylum, 1904–35
HO 98/88 – Guernsey statistical return for 1847
T 64/153 – report to HM Treasury by Customs Commissioner Stiles, 1800

Somerset Record Office, Taunton

D/G/Y 60/14 – Yeovil Workhouse Admission and Discharge Register, 1875–7

Isle of Wight Record Office, Newport

JER/BAR/3/4/16 – will of Nicolas Dobrée

Cambridge University Library

C1/1 – SPCK Subscription Book, 1698–1768

Parliamentary Papers

1833 XXXVII (1831 census analysis)
1844 XXVII (1841 census analysis)
1852–3 LXXXVIII (1851 census analysis)

1883 LXXX (1881 census analysis)
1893–4 CVII (1891 census analysis)
1903 LXXXIV (1901 census analysis)
A Statement of the Names of the Several Unions and Poor Law Parishes in England and Wales; and of the Population, Area, and Rateable Value thereof in 1881 (Cmd 5191)

Nineteenth- and twentieth-century Guernsey newspapers and journals

Comet
Gazette de Guernesey
Guernsey Evening Press
Guernsey Press
Guernsey Weekly Press
Le Baillage
Le Guernesiais
L'Indépendance
Le Mercure
Monthly Illustrated Journal
Star
The Guernsey and Jersey Magazine

Secondary Sources

Eighteenth-, nineteenth- and early twentieth-century published works

Allen, W. and McClure, E., *Two Hundred Years: The History of the S.P.C.K.* (London, 1898)
Almanach de la Gazette de Guernesey (Guernsey, 1874)
Almanach Journalier (Guernsey, 1862)
Anon., *The Stranger's Guide to the Islands of Guernsey and Jersey* (Guernsey, 1833)
Anon., *The Local Taxes of the United Kingdom* (London, 1846)
Anon., 'Guernsey – its present state and future prospects, part one', *The Dublin University Magazine*, 28 (1846), pp. 624–34
Anon., 'Guernsey – its present state and future prospects, part two', *The Dublin University Magazine*, 28 (1846), pp. 703–16
Anon., 'Account of the province of Guernsey', *The Freemasons' Magazine*, 8 (1868), pp. 323–7
Anon., *A Short History of the Temperance Movement in Guernsey, 1566–1900* (Guernsey, 1900)
Anon. (ed.), *French Protestant Hospital Charter and By-Laws* (1723; Rochester, 2000 edn)
Anon. (ed.), *An Account of Several Work-Houses for Employing and Maintaining the Poor* (1725; London, 1732 edn)
Anon. (ed.), *A Treatise on the History, Laws and Customs of the Island of Guernsey by Mr Warburton, a Herald and Celebrated Antiquary in Charles II's Reign* (Guernsey, 1822)

Ansted, D.T. and Latham, M.A., *The Channel Islands* (London, 1862)

Archbold, J.F. (ed.), *The Consolidated and other Orders of the Poor Law Commissioners and of the Poor Law Board* (London, 1859)

Atkin, G. (ed.), *The British and Foreign Homoeopathic Medical Directory and Record* (London, 1853)

Babeau, A.A., *Le Village sous l'Ancien Régime* (Paris, 1879)

Berry, W., *The History of the Island of Guernsey* (London, 1815)

Blackwood, F.H.T., *Irish Emigration and the Tenure of Land in Ireland* (London, 1867)

Boland, H., 'Les institutions de langue française à Guernesey', *Revue Internationale de Florence*, 8 (1885)

Boland, H., *Les Iles de la Manche* (Paris, 1904)

Booth, C., *Life and Labour of the People in London*, 2 vols (London, 1889 & 1891)

Bott, E. (ed. Const, F.) *The Laws Relating to the Poor*, 3 vols (1771; London, 1807 edn)

Bowley, A.L., 'The statistics of wages in the United Kingdom during the last hundred years, part one: agricultural wages', *Journal of the Royal Statistical Society*, 66 (1898), pp. 702–22

Bowley, A.L., *Wages in the United Kingdom in the Nineteenth Century: Notes for the Use of Students of Social and Economic Questions* (Cambridge, 1900)

Cachemaille, J.L.V. (ed. Hale, L.E.), *The Island of Sark* (London, 1928)

Carey Curtis, S., 'The currency of Guernsey in historical times' (Guernsey pamphlet, undated, PL)

Carpenter, M., *Reformatory Schools, for the Children of the Perishing and Dangerous Classes, and for Juvenile Offenders* (London, 1851)

Census 1911: Islands in the British Seas (London, 1913)

Census 1921: Jersey, Guernsey and Adjacent Islands (London, 1924)

Census 1931: Jersey, Guernsey and Adjacent Islands (London, 1933)

Clarke, L.L., *Redstone's Guernsey Guide* (Guernsey, 1841)

Collenette, B., 'Treatment of disease without alcohol', *British Medical Journal* (1871)

Colquhoun, P., *A Treatise on Indigence* (London, 1806)

Conolly, J., *The Treatment of the Insane without Mechanical Restraints* (London, 1856)

Dally, F.F., *A Guide to Jersey, Guernsey, Sark, Herm, Jethou, Alderney, etc.* (London, 1858)

Dally, F.F., *A Guide to Guernsey* (London, 1860)

Dally, F.F., *Agriculture of the Channel Islands* (Guernsey, 1860)

Davies, J.S., *A History of Southampton* (London, 1883)

Defoe, D., 'Review of the state of the English nation', 36 (25 June 1709), in McVeagh, J. (ed.), *Defoe's Review*, 9 vols (London, 2003–11), 6

De Guerin, T.W.M., 'The English garrison of Guernsey from early times', *Transactions of the Guernsey Society of Natural Science and Local Research*, 5 (1905)

Delisle, L., *Etudes sur la Condition de la Classe Agricole et l'Etat de l'Agriculture en Normandie au Moyen Age* (Evreux, 1851)

de Mandeville, B., *The Fable of the Bees* (1723; London, 1724 edn)

Dicey, T., *An Historical Account of Guernsey* (London, 1751)

Duncan, J., *The History of Guernsey* (London, 1841)

Durand, C.J., Brock, K. and Ozanne, E.C. (eds), *Elizabeth College Register, 1824–1873* (Guernsey, 1898)

Durell, E., *An Account of the Island of Jersey by the Rev. Philip Falle to which are added Notes and Illustrations* (Jersey, 1837)

Emminghaus, A. (ed. Eastwick, E.B.), *Poor Relief in Different Parts of Europe* (London, 1873)

Falle, P., *Caesarea: Or, an Account of Jersey* (1694; London, 1734 edn)

First Report of the Commissioners appointed to inquire into the State of the Criminal Law in the Channel Islands (London, 1847)

Fry, K. and Cresswell, R.E., *Memoir of the Life of Elizabeth Fry*, 2 vols (1847; London 1848 edn), 2

Guerin's Almanack (Guernsey, 1894)

Hammond, J.L. and B., *The Village Labourer, 1760–1832: A Study in the Government of England before the Reform Bill* (London, 1911)

Hanway, J., *A Journal of Eight Days Journey … To Which is Added an Essay on Tea* (London, 1756)

Hay, W., *Remarks on the Laws relating to the Poor with Proposals for their Better Relief and Employment* (London, 1735)

Heylyn, P., *A Full Relation of two Journeys: The One into the Main-Land of France, the Other into some of the Adjacent Ilands* (London, 1656)

Hill, C. (ed.), *Frederic Hill: An Autobiography of Fifty Years in Times of Reform* (London, 1893)

Hoskins, S.E., 'The origin and progress of cholera and small-pox in Guernsey', *The London Medical Gazette*, 12 (1851), pp. 382–8

Hugo, G.W.J.L., *Guernsey as it Used to Be; Some Aspects of the Island in my Boyhood, Youth, and Early Manhood, with Allusions to Well-known Persons* (Guernsey, 1933)

Inglis, H.D., *The Channel Islands*, 2 vols (London, 1834)

Inglis, H.D., *Ireland in 1834* (London, 1835)

Jacob, J., *Annals of Some of the British Norman Isles Constituting the Bailiwick of Guernsey* (Paris, 1830)

James, G.W., *The Sark Guide* (Guernsey, 1845)

Jeremie, J., *Historical Account of the Island of Guernsey* (Guernsey, 1821)

Jeremie, P., *On Real Property and Taxation in Guernsey* (Guernsey, 1841)

Jeremie, P., *On Parochial and States Taxation in Guernsey* (Guernsey, 1856)

J.W. Hill & Company's Historical Directory of the Channel Islands (Guernsey, 1874)

Lander, B., 'The relief of the poor in Jersey', *Economic Journal*, 46 (1902), pp. 192–201

Laurie Robinson, E., 'Small-pox and vaccination in Guernsey, 1894–5', *British Medical Journal* (1896)

Lee, G.E. (ed.), *Note-Book of Pierre Le Roy, Guernsey* (Guernsey, 1893)

Leighton, B. (ed.), *Letters and other Writings of the Late Edward Denison* (London, 1872)

Le Lievre's Almanack (Guernsey, 1886)

Le Quesne, C., *Ireland and the Channel Islands* (London, 1848)

Le Quesne, C., *A Constitutional History of Jersey* (London, 1856)

Lewis, S., *A Topographical Dictionary of England*, 4 vols (London, 1831), 2

Marshall, D., *The English Poor in the Eighteenth Century: A Study in Social and Administrative History* (London, 1926)

Marshall, J., *An Analysis and Compendium of all the Returns made to Parliament relating to the Increase of Population in the United Kingdom of Great Britain and Ireland* (London, 1835)

Métivier, G., *Dictionnaire Franco-Normand ou Recueil des Mots particuliers au Dialecte de Guernesey* (London, 1870)

Mill, J.S., *Principles of Political Economy*, 2 vols (1848; London 1849 edn), 1

Montgomery Martin, R., *Ireland before and after the Union with Great Britain* (London, 1833)

Montgomery Martin, R., *Poor Laws for Ireland, a Measure of Justice for England; or Humanity to the People of both Islands* (London, 1833)

Montgomery Martin, R., *History of the British Colonies*, 5 vols (London, 1835), 5

Moore, E.F. (ed.), *Reports of Cases Heard and Determined by the Judicial Committee and the Lords of His Majesty's Most Honourable Privy Council, 1836–1837* (London, 1838)

Ozanne, J., 'On the treatment of apoplexy', *The British Journal of Homoeopathy*, 5 (1847), pp. 58–67

Pitts, J.L., *Guernsey and its Bailiwick: A Guide and a Gossip* (Guernsey, 1890)

Press Directory and Almanack (Guernsey, 1913)

Press Directory and Almanack (Guernsey, 1923)

Purdy, F., 'Statistics of the English poor rate before and since the passing of the Poor Law Amendment Act', *Journal of the Statistical Society of London*, 23 (1860), pp. 286–329

Quayle, T., *A General View of the Agriculture and Present State of the Islands on the Coast of Normandy* (London, 1815)

Report from His Majesty's Commissioners for Inquiring into the Administration and Practical Operations of the Poor Laws (London, 1834), Appendices A and B2

Report of the Commissioners appointed to inquire into the Civil, Municipal and Ecclesiastical Laws of Jersey (London, 1860)

Rew, R.H., 'Local taxation in rural districts', *Journal of the Royal Agricultural Society of England*, 7 (1896), pp. 637–62

Ribton-Turner, C.J., *A History of Vagrants and Vagrancy and Beggars and Begging* (London, 1887)

Rowntree, B.S., *Poverty: A Study of Town Life* (1901; London, 1908 edn)

Second Report of the Commissioners appointed to enquire into the State of the Criminal Law of the Channel Islands (London, 1848)

Smiles, S., *Thrift* (London, 1875)

Thornton, W.T., *A Plea for Peasant Proprietors: With the Outlines of a Plan for their Establishment in Ireland* (London, 1848)

Tressell, R., *The Ragged Trousered Philanthropists* (1914; Ware, 2012 edn)

Tupper, F.B., *The History of Guernsey and its Bailiwick* (Guernsey, 1854 and 1876 edns)

Tupper, D.V., *Memorial presented by De Vic Tupper, Esq., Colonel (retired list) and Jurat of the Royal Court of Guernsey* (Guernsey, 1890)

Vulliamy, A.F., *The Law of Settlement and Removal of Paupers* (1895; London, 1906 edn)

Waring, G.E., *A Farmer's Vacation* (Boston, 1876)

Webb, S. and B., *English Poor Law History, Part I: The Old Poor Law* (London, 1927)

Webb, S. and B., *English Poor Law History, Part II: The Last Hundred Years* (London, 1929)

Wesley, J., *A Letter to a Friend, concerning Tea* (London, 1748)

Modern published works

Ahier, P., 'The house of correction in Jersey', *Bulletin of the Société Jersiaise*, 20 (1971), pp. 284–8

Allsopp, R., 'Pressures for change – a specialist view', in Jeffs, D.A. (ed.), *One Hundred Years of Health: The Changing Health of Guernsey, 1899–1999* (Guernsey, 1999)

Anon., *Nos Iles: A Symposium on the Channel Islands* (Teddington, 1944)

Anon., 'The soup kitchen', *Quarterly Review of the Guernsey Society*, 23 (1967), pp. 92–3

Anon., 'St Julian's Avenue – a centenary', *The Review of the Guernsey Society*, 28 (1972), p. 3

Anon, *Continuity and Change: A Review of the Social Security and Health Insurance Schemes in Jersey* (Jersey, 1995)

Appleby, J.C., 'Neutrality, trade and privateering, 1500–1689', in Jamieson, A.G. (ed.), *A People of the Sea: The Maritime History of the Channel Islands* (London, 1986)

Baines, D.E., *Migration in a Mature Economy: Emigration and Internal Migration in England and Wales, 1861–1900* (Cambridge, 1985)

Baines, D.E., 'The onset of depression', in Johnson, P. (ed), *Twentieth-Century Britain: Economic, Social and Cultural Change* (London, 1994)

Barry, J. and Jones, C. (eds), *Medicine and Charity before the Welfare State* (London, 1994)

Bartlett, P., *The Poor Law of Lunacy: The Administration of Pauper Lunatics in Mid-Nineteenth-Century England* (London,1999)

Baugh, D.A., 'The cost of poor relief in south-east England, 1790–1834', *Economic History Review*, 28 (1975), pp. 50–68

Beier, A.L., *Masterless Men: The Vagrancy Problem in England, 1560–1640* (London, 1985)

Belchem, J. (ed.), *A New History of the Isle of Man*, 5 vols (Liverpool, 2000), 5

Blaikie, A., 'Nuclear hardship or variant dependency? Households and the Scottish poor law', *Continuity and Change*, 17 (2002), pp. 253–80

Blaikie, A., 'Household and mobility in rural Scotland: the impact of the poor law after 1845', *Scottish Tradition*, 27 (2002), pp. 23–41

Blaikie, A., 'Accounting for poverty: conflicting constructions of family survival in Scotland, 1855–1925', *Journal of Historical Sociology*, 18 (2005), pp. 202–26

Blaug, M., 'The myth of the old poor law and the making of the new', *Journal of Economic History*, 23 (1963), pp. 151–84

Boyer, G.E., *An Economic History of the English Poor law, 1750–1850* (Cambridge, 1990)

Bradshaw, J. and Finch, N., 'Overlaps in dimensions of poverty', *Journal of Social Policy*, 32 (2003), pp. 513–25

Brewer, J. and Hellmuth, E. (eds), *Rethinking Leviathan: The Eighteenth-Century State in Britain and Germany* (Oxford, 1999)

Brigden, P. and Harris, B. (eds), *Charity and Mutual Aid in Europe and North America since 1800* (Abingdon, 2007)

Broad, J., 'Parish economies of welfare, 1650–1834', *The Historical Journal*, 42 (1999), pp. 985–1006

Brock, M., 'La maison des pauvres, St Peter's', *Quarterly Review of the Guernsey Society*, 18 (1962), pp. 4–6

Bromley, J.S., 'A new vocation: privateering in the wars of 1689–97 and 1702–13', in Jamieson, A.G. (ed.), *A People of the Sea: The Maritime History of the Channel Islands* (London, 1986)

Brundage, A., *The English Poor Laws, 1700–1930* (Basingstoke, 2002)

Burke, H., *The Poor Law and the People in Nineteenth-Century Ireland* (Littlehampton, 1987)

Burnett, J., *Plenty and Want: A Social History of Diet in England from 1815 to the Present Day* (1966; London, 1989 edn)

Burnett, J., *A History of the Cost of Living* (1969; Aldershot, 1993 edn)

Burnett, J., *A Social History of Housing, 1815–1970* (1978; London, 1983 edn)

Burnett, J., *Liquid Pleasures: A Social History of Drinks in Modern Britain* (London, 1999)

Cage, R.A., *The Scottish Poor Law, 1745–1845* (Edinburgh, 1981)

Cartwright, F.F., *A Social History of Medicine* (London, 1977)

Chalklin, C.W., *The Provincial Towns of Georgian England* (London, 1974)

Channel Islands Competition and Regulatory Authorities, *Review of Primary Healthcare Market, Guernsey* (CICRA document no. 15/04, 11.2.2015)

Chapman, W.R., *His Praise in the Islands* (1984; Guernsey, 1995 edn)

Charlesworth, L.R., 'The law of settlements and removals viewed as a model of property rights for the poor', Anglia Ruskin University Papers in Land Management, 3 (2007)

Cherry, S., *Medical Services and the Hospitals in Britain, 1860–1939* (Cambridge, 1996)

Chinn, C., *Poverty amidst Prosperity: The Urban Poor in England, 1834–1914* (1995; Lancaster, 2006 edn)

Corfield, P.J., *The Impact of English Towns, 1700–1800* (Oxford, 1982)

Cousins, M., *European Welfare States: Comparative Perspectives* (London, 2005)

Cousins, M., *Poor Relief in Ireland, 1851–1914* (Bern, 2011)

Craske, L.G.H., 'Two complementary Guernsey physicians', in Jeffs, D.A. (ed.), *One Hundred Years of Health: The Changing Health of Guernsey, 1899–1999* (Guernsey, 1999)

Crocker, R.H., 'The Victorian poor law in crisis and change: Southampton, 1870–1895', *Albion: A Quarterly Journal Concerned with British Studies*, 19 (1987), pp. 19–44

Crossan, R.-M., 'The retreat of French from Guernsey's public primary schools, 1800–1939', *TSG*, 25 (2005), pp. 851–88

Crossan, R.-M., *Guernsey, 1814–1914: Migration and Modernisation* (Woodbridge, 2007)

Crossman, V., *The Poor Law in Ireland, 1838–1948* (Dundalk, 2006)

Crossman, V., 'Welfare and nationality: the poor laws in nineteenth-century Ireland', in King, S.A. and Stewart, J. (eds), *Welfare Peripheries: The Development of Welfare States in Nineteenth and Twentieth Century Europe* (Bern, 2007)

Crowther, M.A., 'The later years of the workhouse, 1890–1929', in Thane, P. (ed.), *The Origins of British Social Policy* (London, 1978)

Crowther, M.A., *The Workhouse System, 1834–1929: The History of an English Social Institution* (1981; London, 1983 edn)

Crowther, M.A., 'Family responsibility and state responsibility in Britain before the welfare state', *The Historical Journal*, 25 (1982), pp. 131–45

Crowther, M.A., 'From workhouse to NHS hospital in Britain, 1929–1948', in Hillam, C. and Bone, J.M. (eds), *The Poor Law and After: Workhouse Hospitals and Public Welfare* (Liverpool, 1999)

Cule, J., *A Doctor for the People: 200 Years of General Practice in Britain* (London, 1980)

Curl, J.S., *The Victorian Celebration of Death* (Stroud, 2000)

Daunton, M. (ed.), *Charity, Self-Interest and Welfare in the English Past* (London, 1996)

Davis, N.Z., *Society and Culture in Early Modern France* (1965; Cambridge, 1987 edn)

Davison, L., Hitchcock, T.V., Keirn, T. and Shoemaker, R.B. (eds), *Stilling the Grumbling Hive: The Response to Social and Economic Problems in England, 1689–1750* (Stroud, 1992)

Dawes, G., *Laws of Guernsey* (Oxford, 2003)

De Garis, M., 'The parish of St Pierre du Bois and some of its inhabitants in the eighteenth and early nineteenth centuries', *TSG*, 14 (1949), pp. 479–88

De Lisle, D., 'The regional impact of population change in Guernsey', *TSG*, 24 (1999), pp. 703–13

de Vries, J., *European Urbanization, 1500–1800* (London, 1984)

Dickson, D., 'In search of the old Irish poor law', in Mitchison, R. and Roebuck, P. (eds), *Economy and Society in Scotland and Ireland, 1500–1939* (Edinburgh, 1988)

Digby, A., *Pauper Palaces* (London, 1978)

Digby, A., *British Welfare Policy: Workhouse to Workfare* (London, 1989)

Dorey, P., *Official Opening of Edward T. Wheadon House* (Guernsey, 1985)

Driver, F., *Power and Pauperism: The Workhouse System, 1834–1884* (Cambridge, 1993)

Dross, F., 'Health care provision and poor relief in enlightenment and 19th century Prussia', in Grell, O.P., Cunningham, A. and Jütte, R. (eds), *Health Care and Poor Relief in 18th and 19th Century Northern Europe* (Aldershot, 2002)

Duke, F., 'Pauper education', in Fraser, D. (ed.), *The New Poor Law in the Nineteenth Century* (London, 1976)

Dunkley, P., 'The hungry forties and the new poor law: a case study', *The Historical Journal*, 7 (1974), pp. 329–46

Dunkley, P., *The Crisis of the Old Poor Law in England, 1795–1834* (New York, 1982)

Dupâquier, J., 'Demographic crises and subsistence crises in France, 1650–1789', in Walters, J. and Schofield, R. (eds), *Famine, Disease and the Social Order in Early Modern Society* (Cambridge, 1989)

Dury, G.H., 'The population of Guernsey: an essay in historical geography', *Geography*, 33 (1948), pp. 61–9

Eagleston, A.J., *The Channel Islands under Tudor Government, 1485–1642: A Study in Administrative History* (Cambridge, 1949)

Emsley, C., *Crime and Society in England, 1750–1900* (1987; Harlow, 1996 edn)

Englander, D., *Poverty and Poor Law Reform in Nineteenth-Century Britain, 1834–1914* (Harlow, 1998)

Everard, J.A. and Holt, J.C., *Jersey 1204: The Forging of an Island Community* (London, 2004)

Ewen, A.H., 'A Guernsey family from Piedmont', *Quarterly Review of the Guernsey Society*, 21 (1965), pp. 51–4

Ewen, A.H., 'The Breton Myth', *TSG*, 21 (1982), p. 172–99

Fagan, B., *The Little Ice Age: How Climate made History, 1300–1850* (New York, 2000)

Faure, O., 'Health care provision and poor relief in 19th century provincial France', in Grell, O.P., Cunningham, A. and Jütte, R. (eds), *Health Care and Poor Relief in 18th and 19th Century Northern Europe* (Aldershot, 2002)

Feldman, D., 'Migrants, immigrants and welfare from the Old Poor Law to the Welfare State', *Transactions of the Royal Historical Society*, 13 (2003), pp. 79–104

Fideler, P.A., *Social Welfare in Pre-Industrial England: The Old Poor Law Tradition* (Basingstoke, 2006)

Finnegan, F., *Poverty and Prostitution: A Study of Victorian Prostitutes in York* (Cambridge, 1979)

Fleure, H.J., 'Guernsey: a social study', *Bulletin of the John Rylands Library*, Manchester, 26 (1941), pp. 57–81

Flinn, M.W., 'Medical services under the New Poor Law', in Fraser, D. (ed.), *The New Poor Law in the Nineteenth Century* (London, 1976)

Floud, R., Fogel, R.W., Harris, B. and Hong, S.C., *The Changing Body: Health, Nutrition, and Human Development in the Western World since 1700* (Cambridge, 2011)

Fowler, S., *Workhouse: The People, the Places, the Life Behind Doors* (Richmond, 2007)

Fraser, D. (ed.), *The New Poor Law in the Nineteenth Century* (London, 1976)

Fraser, D., 'The English poor law and the origins of the British welfare state', in Mommsen, W.J. and Mock, W. (eds), *The Emergence of the Welfare State in Britain and Germany, 1850–1950* (London, 1981)

Fraser, W.H., *The Coming of the Mass Market, 1850–1914* (London, 1981)

French, K., Gibbs, G. and Kümin, B. (eds), *The Parish in English Life, 1400–1600* (Manchester, 1997)

Gaggs, A., 'Mental health services', in Jeffs, D.A. (ed.), *One Hundred Years of Health: The Changing Health of Guernsey, 1899–1999* (Guernsey, 1999)

Gallienne, W., 'The Victoria Cottage Hospital (Amherst)', in Jeffs, D.A. (ed.), *One Hundred Years of Health: The Changing Health of Guernsey, 1899–1999* (Guernsey, 1999)

Garnett, J. and Matthew, C. (eds), *Revival and Religion since 1700* (London, 1993)

Gaskell, S.M. (ed.), *Slums* (Leicester, 1990)

Gazeley, I. and Newell, A., 'Poverty in Edwardian Britain', *The Economic History Review*, 64 (2011), pp. 52–71

Genicot, L., *Rural Communities in the Medieval West* (Baltimore, 1990)

Girard, P.J., 'Development of the bulb and flower industry in Guernsey,' *TSG*, 13 (1939), pp. 284–97

Girard, P.J., 'The Guernsey grape industry,' *TSG*, 15 (1951), pp. 126–44

Girard, P.J., 'Country life and some insular enterprises of the late 19th century', *TSG*, 19 (1972), pp. 88–105

Gladstone, D., *The Twentieth-Century Welfare State* (Basingstoke, 1999)

Glendinning, A., *Eye on the Past in Guernsey* (Jersey, 1993)

Goose, N., 'Workhouse populations in the mid-nineteenth century: the case of Hertfordshire', *Local Population Studies*, 62 (1999), pp. 52–69

Gordon, D. et al., *Poverty and Social Exclusion in Britain* (York, 2000)

Gordon, D., et al., *Anti-Poverty Policies – A Range of Possible Options for Guernsey* (Bristol, 2002)

Gorsky, M., 'The growth and distribution of English friendly societies in the early nineteenth century', *The Economic History Review*, 51 (1998), pp. 489–511

Gosden, P.H.J.H., *The Friendly Societies in England, 1815–1875* (Manchester, 1961)

Gosden, P.H.J.H., *Self-Help: Voluntary Associations in Nineteenth-Century Britain* (London, 1973)

Gray, P., *The Making of the Irish Poor Law, 1815–43* (Manchester, 2009)

Greaves, R.L., 'The social awareness of John Knox: the problems of poverty and educational reform', *Renaissance and Reformation*, 12 (1976), pp. 36–48

Green D.R., 'Medical relief and the new poor law in London', in Grell, O.P., Cunningham, A. and Jütte, R. (eds), *Health Care and Poor Relief in 18th and 19th Century Northern Europe* (Aldershot, 2002)

Green, D.R., 'Pauper protests: power and resistance in early nineteenth-century London workhouses', *Social History*, 31 (2006), pp. 137–59

Grell, O.P. and Cunningham, A. (eds), *Health Care and Poor Relief in Protestant Europe, 1500–1700* (London, 1997)

Grell, O.P., Cunningham, A. and Jütte, R. (eds), *Health Care and Poor Relief in 18th and 19th Century Northern Europe* (Aldershot, 2002)

Hardy, A., *Health and Medicine in Britain since 1860* (Basingstoke, 2001)

Harris, B., 'Unemployment and the dole in interwar Britain', in Johnson, P. (ed), *Twentieth-Century Britain: Economic, Social and Cultural Change* (London, 1994)

Harris, J., 'From poor law to welfare state? A European perspective', in Winch, D. and O'Brien, P. (eds), *The Political Economy of British Historical Experience, 1688–1914* (Oxford, 2002)

Harrison, B., *Drink and the Victorians: The Temperance Question in England, 1815–1872* (London, 1971)

Hatzfeld, H., *Du Paupérisme à la Sécurité Sociale, 1850–1940* (Nancy, 1989)

Henderson, J. and Wall, R. (eds), *Poor Women and Children in the European Past* (London, 1994)

Hendrick, H., *Child Welfare: England, 1872–1989* (London, 1994)

Hennock, E.P., 'The origins of British National Insurance and the German precedent, 1880–1914', in Mommsen, W.J. and Mock, W. (eds), T*he Emergence of the Welfare State in Britain and Germany, 1850–1950* (London, 1981)

Henriques, U.R.Q., 'Bastardy and the New Poor Law', *Past & Present*, 37 (1967), pp. 103–29

Henry, R.A., *The History of L'Ancresse Common* (Guernsey, 2008)

Hervey, N., 'Advocacy or folly: the Alleged Lunatics' Friend Society, 1845–63', *Medical History*, 30 (1986), pp. 245–75

Hickey, D., *Local Hospitals in Ancien Régime France: Rationalization, Resistance, Renewal, 1530–1789* (Montreal, 1997)

Hillam, C. and Bone, J.M. (eds), *The Poor Law and After: Workhouse Hospitals and Public Welfare* (Liverpool, 1999)

Himmelfarb, G., *The Idea of Poverty: England in the Early Industrial Age* (London, 1984)

Hinde, A. and Turnbull, F., 'The populations of two Hampshire workhouses, 1851–1861', *Local Population Studies*, 61 (1998), pp. 38–53

Hindle, S., *On the Parish: The Micro-Politics of Poor Relief in Rural England, c.1550–1750* (Oxford, 2004)

Hirst, D., 'Lunacy and the "Islands in the British Seas"', *History of Psychiatry*, 18 (2007), pp. 411–33

Hitchcock, T.V., 'Paupers and preachers: the SPCK and the parochial workhouse movement', in Davison, L., Hitchcock, T.V., Keirn, T. and Shoemaker, R.B. (eds), *Stilling the Grumbling Hive: The Response to Social and Economic Problems in England, 1689–1750* (Stroud, 1992)

Hitchcock, T.V., King, P. and Sharpe, P. (eds), *Chronicling Poverty: The Voices and Strategies of the English Poor, 1640–1840* (Basingstoke, 1997)

Hocart, R.P., 'Elections to the Royal Court of Guernsey, 1821–1844', *TSG*, 19 (1979), pp. 494–514

Hocart, R.P., 'A Guernsey merchant and his family in the reign of George II', *TSG*, 21 (1983), pp. 360–78

Hocart, R.P., *An Island Assembly: The Development of the States of Guernsey, 1700–1949* (Guernsey, 1988)

Hocart, R.P., 'Health services for children', in Jeffs, D.A. (ed.), *One Hundred Years of Health: The Changing Health of Guernsey, 1899–1999* (Guernsey, 1999)

Hocart, R.P., 'Review of *St Peter Port, 1680–1830* by Gregory Stevens Cox', *TSG*, 24 (1999), pp. 740–2

Hocart, R.P., 'Jean Guille of St George: an extended view, 1711–1721', *TSG*, 26 (2008), pp. 402–13

Hocart, R.P., *Guernsey's Countryside: An Introduction to the History of the Rural Landscape* (Guernsey, 2010)

Hodgkinson, R.G., *The Origins of the National Health Service* (London, 1967)

Holderness, B.A., 'The origins of high farming', in Holderness, B.A. and Turner, M. (eds), *Land, Labour and Agriculture, 1700–1920: Essays for Gordon Mingay* (London, 1991)

Hopkins, E., 'The urban working classes in England, 1880–1914', *The Historian*, 74 (2002), pp. 17–24

House, M., Storey, G. and Tillotson, K. (eds), *The Letters of Charles Dickens*, 12 vols (Oxford, 1965–2002), 4

Howells, G., '"For I was tired of England Sir": English pauper emigrant strategies, 1834–60', *Social History*, 23 (1998), pp. 181–94

Hufton, O.H., *The Poor of Eighteenth Century France, 1750–1789* (Oxford, 1974)

Humphreys, R., 'Bygone charity – myths and realities', *LSE Working Papers in Economic History*, 23 (1994)

Humphreys, R., *Sin, Organized Charity and the Poor Law in Victorian England* (London, 1995)

Humphreys, R., *No Fixed Abode: A History of Responses to the Roofless and the Rootless in Britain* (Basingstoke, 1999)

Hunt, E.H., *Regional Wage Variations in Britain, 1850–1914* (Oxford, 1973)

Innes, J., 'Prisons for the poor: English bridewells, 1555–1800', in Snyder, F. and Hay, D. (eds), *Labour, Law and Crime: An Historical Perspective* (London, 1987)

Innes, J., 'The "mixed economy of welfare" in early modern England: assessments of the options from Hale to Malthus (c.1683–1803)', in Daunton, M. (ed.), *Charity, Self-Interest and Welfare in the English Past* (London, 1996)

Innes, J., 'State, church and voluntarism in European welfare, 1690–1850', in H. Cunningham and J. Innes (eds), *Charity, Philanthropy and Reform in Europe and North America, 1690–1850* (Basingstoke, 1998)

Innes, J., 'The state and the poor: eighteenth-century England in historical perspective', in Brewer, J. and Hellmuth, E. (eds), *Rethinking Leviathan: The Eighteenth-Century State in Britain and Germany* (Oxford, 1999)

Innes, J., 'The distinctiveness of the English poor laws, 1750–1850', in Winch, D. and O'Brien, P. (eds), *The Political Economy of British Historical Experience, 1688–1914* (Oxford, 2002)

Irvine, R.E., 'Health services in Guernsey', *The Review of the Guernsey Society*, 46 (1990), pp. 19–21

Jackson, D.G., 'Kent workhouse populations in 1881: a study based on the census enumerators' books', *Local Population Studies*, 69 (2002), pp. 51–66

Jackson, D.G., 'The Medway union workhouse, 1876–1881: a study based on the admission and discharge registers and the census enumerators' books', *Local Population Studies*, 75 (2005), pp. 11–32

Jamieson, A.G. (ed.), *A People of the Sea: The Maritime History of the Channel Islands* (London, 1986)

Jamieson, A.G., 'The return to privateering: Channel Island privateers, 1739–83', in Jamieson, A.G. (ed.), *A People of the Sea: The Maritime History of the Channel Islands* (London, 1986)

Jamieson, A.G., 'The Channel Islands and smuggling, 1680–1850', in Jamieson, A.G. (ed.), *A People of the Sea: The Maritime History of the Channel Islands* (London, 1986)

Jamieson, A.G., 'The Channel Islands and British maritime strategy, 1689–1945', in Jamieson, A.G. (ed.), *A People of the Sea: The Maritime History of the Channel Islands* (London, 1986)

Jamieson, A.G., 'The Channel Islands and overseas settlement, 1600–1900', in Jamieson, A.G. (ed.), *A People of the Sea: The Maritime History of the Channel Islands* (London, 1986)

Jamieson, A.G., 'Island shipowners and seamen, 1700–1900', in Jamieson, A.G. (ed.), *A People of the Sea: The Maritime History of the Channel Islands* (London, 1986)

Jamieson, A.G., 'Voyage patterns and trades of Channel Island vessels, 1700–1900', in Jamieson, A.G. (ed.), *A People of the Sea: The Maritime History of the Channel Islands* (London, 1986)

Jeffs, D.A. (ed.), *One Hundred Years of Health: The Changing Health of Guernsey, 1899–1999* (Guernsey, 1999)

Jeffs, D.A., 'Through the eyes of the MoH', in Jeffs, D.A. (ed.), *One Hundred Years of Health: The Changing Health of Guernsey, 1899–1999* (Guernsey, 1999)

Joerger, M., 'The structure of the hospital system in France in the Ancien Régime', in Forster, R. and Ranum, O. (eds), *Medicine and Society in France* (Baltimore, 1980)

Johns, R.A. and Le Marchant, C.M., *Finance Centres: British Isle Offshore Development since 1979* (London, 1993)

Johnson, P. (ed), *Twentieth-Century Britain: Economic, Social and Cultural Change* (London, 1994)

Johnson, P., 'Risk, redistribution and social welfare in Britain from the poor law to Beveridge', in Daunton, M. (ed.), *Charity, Self-Interest and Welfare in the English Past* (London, 1996)

Johnston, P., 'The cholera and smallpox epidemic of 1849', *The Review of the Guernsey Society*, 54 (1998), pp. 84–5

Johnston, V.J., *Diet in Workhouses and Prisons, 1835–1895* (London, 1985)

Jones, A., 'The community nursing service', in Jeffs, D.A. (ed.), *One Hundred Years of Health: The Changing Health of Guernsey, 1899–1999* (Guernsey, 1999)

Jones, K., *A History of the Mental Health Services* (London, 1972)

Jones, M.C., *The Guernsey Norman French Translations of Thomas Martin: A Linguistic Study of an Unpublished Archive* (Leuven, 2008)

Jütte, R., *Poverty and Deviance in Early Modern Europe* (Cambridge, 1994)

Kahl, S., 'The religious roots of modern poverty policy: Catholic, Lutheran and Reformed Protestant traditions compared', *European Journal of Sociology*, 45 (2005), pp. 91–126

Kelleher, J.D., *The Triumph of the Country: The Rural Community in Nineteenth-Century Jersey* (Jersey, 1994)

Kellett-Smith, S.K., 'The Guernsey cholera epidemic of 1832', *TSG*, 20 (1980), pp. 643–55

Kidd, A., *State, Society and the Poor in Nineteenth-Century England* (Basingstoke, 1999)

King, F.H.H., *Survey our Empire! Robert Montgomery Martin (1801?–1868), a Bio-bibliography* (Hong Kong, 1979)

King, P., 'The rise of juvenile delinquency in England, 1780–1840: changing patterns of perception and prosecution', *Past & Present*, 160 (1998), pp. 116–66

King, S.A., 'Poor relief and English economic development reappraised', *The Economic History Review*, 50 (1997), pp. 360–8

King, S.A., *Poverty and Welfare in England, 1700–1850: A Regional Perspective* (Manchester, 2000)

King, S.A., 'Welfare regimes and welfare regions in Britain and Europe, c.1750s to 1860s', *Journal of Modern European History*, 9 (2011), pp. 42–67

King, S.A. and Stewart, J. (eds), *Welfare Peripheries: The Development of Welfare States in Nineteenth and Twentieth Century Europe* (Bern, 2007)

King, S.A. and Stewart, J., 'Welfare peripheries in modern Europe', in King, S.A. and Stewart, J. (eds), *Welfare Peripheries: The Development of Welfare States in Nineteenth and Twentieth Century Europe* (Bern, 2007)

King, S.A. and Tomkins, A. (eds), *The Poor in England, 1700–1850: An Economy of Makeshifts* (Manchester, 2004)

Kingdon, R.M., 'Social welfare in Calvin's Geneva', *American Historical Review*, 76 (1971), pp. 50–70

Kümin, B., 'The English parish in a European perspective', in French, K., Gibbs, G. and Kümin, B. (eds), *The Parish in English Life, 1400–1600* (Manchester, 1997)

Land, N., *Victorian Workhouse: A Study of the Bromsgrove Union Workhouse* (Studley, 1990)

Lane, J., *A Social History of Medicine: Health, Healing and Disease in England, 1750–1950* (London, 2001)

Langford, S.R., 'Paying for health', in Jeffs, D.A. (ed.), *One Hundred Years of Health: The Changing Health of Guernsey, 1899–1999* (Guernsey, 1999)

Laqueur, T.W., 'Bodies, death and pauper funerals', *Representations*, 1 (1983), pp. 109–31

Laslett, P., *The World we Have Lost – Further Explored* (1965; Cambridge, 1983 edn)

Lawton, R. and Lee, R. (eds), *Urban Population Development in Western Europe from the Late-Eighteenth to the Early-Twentieth Century* (Liverpool, 1989)

Lawton, R. and Lee, R. (eds), *Population and Society in Western European Port-Cities, c.1650–1939* (Liverpool, 2002)

Lawton, R. and Lee, R., 'Port development and the demographic dynamics of European urbanization', in Lawton, R. and Lee, R. (eds), *Population and Society in Western European Port-Cities, c.1650–1939* (Liverpool, 2002)

Le Cornu, N., 'Brothels and houses of ill-fame in Jersey, 1790–1918', *Bulletin of the Jersey Society in London*, 7 (2001), pp. 9–11

Lees, L.H., *The Solidarities of Strangers: The English Poor Laws and the People, 1700–1948* (Cambridge, 1998)

Lenfestey, G.M., 'Medical practices at the Town Hospital, 1743–1850', *TSG*, 23 (1992), pp. 378–95

Lenfestey, G.M., 'The story of the Town Hospital, 1900–1987', in Jeffs, D.A. (ed.), *One Hundred Years of Health: The Changing Health of Guernsey, 1899–1999* (Guernsey, 1999)

Lenfestey, J.H., 'Extracts from books of the Town Hospital regarding Daniel Morris', *The Review of the Guernsey Society*, 46 (1987), pp. 34–7

Léonard, J., 'Women, religion and medicine', in Forster, R. and Ranum, O. (eds), *Medicine and Society in France* (Baltimore, 1980)

Levitt, I., *Poverty and Welfare in Scotland, 1890–1948* (Edinburgh, 1988)

Lindert, P.H., 'Poor relief before the Welfare State: Britain versus the Continent, 1780–1880', *European Review of Economic History*, 2 (1998), pp. 101–240

Lis, C. and Soly, H. (trans. Coonan, J.), *Poverty and Capitalism in Pre-Industrial Europe* (1979; Brighton, 1982 edn)

Longmate, N., *The Workhouse: A Social History* (London, 1974)

Loveridge, J., *The Constitution and Law of Guernsey* (1975; Guernsey, 1997 edn)

Lowe, R., *The Welfare State in Britain since 1945* (Basingstoke, 1993)

Lowe, R., 'Postwar welfare', in Johnson, P. (ed), *Twentieth-Century Britain: Economic, Social and Cultural Change* (London, 1994)

McCord, N., 'Poor law and philanthropy', in Fraser, D. (ed.), *The New Poor Law in the Nineteenth Century* (London, 1976)

McCormack, J., *Channel Island Churches* (Chichester, 1986)

MacKay, L., 'A culture of poverty? St Martin in the Fields workhouse, 1817', *Journal of Interdisciplinary History*, 26 (1995), pp. 209–31

McKee, E.A., *John Calvin on the Diaconate and Liturgical Almsgiving* (Geneva, 1984)

MacKinnon, M., 'English poor law policy and the crusade against out-relief', *The Journal of Economic History*, 47 (1987), pp. 603–25

McLellan, J., 'The strange case of the Maladies Secrètes ordinance of 1912', *Jersey and Guernsey Law Review*, February 2013

Macnicol, J., 'Family allowances and less eligibility', in Thane, P. (ed.), *The Origins of British Social Policy* (London, 1978)

Makower, H., Marschak, J. and Robinson, H.W., 'Studies in mobility of labour: analysis of Great Britain, part one', *Oxford Economic Papers*, 2 (1939), pp. 70–97

Marett Godfray, H., 'The early protestant refugees in the Channel Islands', *Bulletin of the Société Jersiaise*, 10 (1923–7), pp. 325–34

Marr, J., *The History of Guernsey: The Bailiwick's Story* (1982; Guernsey, 2001 edn)

Marr, J., *Guernsey People* (Chichester, 1984)

Marshall-Fraser, W., 'A history of printing, of the press and of publications in the Channel Islands', *TSG*, 15 (1954), pp. 59–72

Martel, E., 'Philological report', *TSG*, 17 (1965), pp. 708–10

Martin, E.W. (ed.), *Comparative Development in Social Welfare* (London, 1972)

Mason, T., 'Women in Germany, 1925–1940: family, welfare and work, part one', *History Workshop*, 1 (1976), pp. 74–113

Meldrum, T., 'London domestic servants from depositional evidence, 1660–1750: servant–employer sexuality in the patriarchal household', in Hitchcock, T.V., King, P. and Sharpe, P. (eds), *Chronicling Poverty: The Voices and Strategies of the English Poor, 1640–1840* (Basingstoke, 1997)

Mignot, A., *Mignot Manoeuvres: An Alderney Genealogy* (Alderney, 2013)

Mitchison, R., 'The making of the Old Scottish Poor Law', *Past & Present*, 63 (1974), pp. 58–93

Mitchison, R., *Coping with Destitution: Poverty and Relief in Western Europe* (Toronto, 1991)

Mitchison, R., *The Old Poor Law in Scotland: The Experience of Poverty, 1574–1845* (Edinburgh, 2000)

Mitchison, R., 'Poor relief and health care in 19th century Scotland', in Grell, O.P., Cunningham, A. and Jütte, R. (eds), *Health Care and Poor Relief in 18th and 19th Century Northern Europe* (Aldershot, 2002)

Mitchison, R. and Roebuck, P. (eds), *Economy and Society in Scotland and Ireland, 1500–1939* (Edinburgh, 1988)

Mommsen, W.J. and Mock, W. (eds), *The Emergence of the Welfare State in Britain and Germany, 1850–1950* (London, 1981)

Moullin, E.B., 'Josué Le Roy, 1647–1709, youngest child of Pierre Le Roy, the diarist', *TSG*, 12 (1951), pp. 119–25

Mowat, C.L., *The Charity Organisation Society, 1869–1913: Its Ideas and Work* (London, 1961)

Mumm, S., '"Not worse than other girls": the convent-based rehabilitation of fallen women in Victorian Britain', *Journal of Social History*, 29 (1996), pp. 527–40

Murdoch, T. and Vigne, R., *The French Hospital in England: Its Huguenot History and Collections* (Cambridge, 2009)

Murray, P., *Poverty and Welfare, 1830–1914* (London, 1999)

Neeson, J.M., *Commoners: Common Rights, Enclosure and Social Change in England, 1700–1820* (Cambridge, 1993)

Neeson, J.M., 'Gathering the humid harvest of the deep: the midsummer cut vraic harvest in nineteenth-century Guernsey', *TSG*, 26 (2009), pp. 521–38

Nord, P., 'The welfare state in France, 1870–1914', *French Historical Studies*, 18 (1994), pp. 821–38

O'Brien, G., 'A question of attitude: responses to the new poor law in Ireland and Scotland', in Mitchison, R. and Roebuck, P. (eds), *Economy and Society in Scotland and Ireland, 1500–1939* (Edinburgh, 1988)

Ogier, D.M., *Reformation and Society in Guernsey* (Woodbridge, 1996)

Ogier, D.M., *The Government and Law of Guernsey* (Guernsey, 2005)

Ogier, D.M., 'The origins of Guernsey's parishes and the ownership and maintenance of their ancient church buildings', *The Jersey Law Review*, 9 (2005), pp. 315–45

Olson, J.E., *Calvin and Social Welfare: Deacons and the Bourse Française* (London, 1989)

Oxley, G.W., *Poor Relief in England and Wales, 1601–1834* (Newton Abbot, 1974)

Page, S., 'Pauperism and the Leicester workhouse in 1881', *Transactions of the Leicestershire Archaeological and Historical Society*, 63 (1989), pp. 59–97

Pallot, S., 'Le connétable et sa paroisse', *The Jersey Law Review*, October 2003

Paterson, A., 'The poor law in nineteenth-century Scotland', in Fraser, D. (ed.), *The New Poor Law in the Nineteenth Century* (London, 1976)

Patriquin, L., 'Why was there no "Old Poor Law" in Scotland and Ireland?' *The Journal of Peasant Studies*, 33 (2006), pp. 219–47

Patriquin, L., *Agrarian Capitalism and Poor Relief in England, 1500–1860* (Basingstoke, 2007)

Payne, M. and Shardlow, S.M. (eds), *Social Work in the British Isles* (London, 2002)

Persson, K.G., 'The seven lean years, elasticity traps, and intervention in grain markets in pre-industrial Europe', *The Economic History Review*, 49 (1996), pp. 692–714

Phelps Brown, H. and Hopkins, S.V., *A Perspective of Wages and Prices* (London, 1981)

Phillips, M., *Poor People* (Jersey, 2001)

Platt, C., *A Concise History of Jersey: A New Perspective* (Jersey, 2009)

Porter, R., *Disease, Medicine and Society in England, 1550–1860* (1987; Cambridge, 1995 edn)

Pounds, N.J.G., *A History of the English Parish: The Culture of Religion from Augustine to Victoria* (Cambridge, 2000)

Priaulx, T.F., 'Les pauvres', *Quarterly Review of the Guernsey Society*, 21–4 (1965–8), pp. 32–5

Priaulx, T.F., 'Secular parish administration in Guernsey', *Quarterly Review of the Guernsey Society*, 21–4 (1965–8), pp. 49–52

Priaulx, T.F., 'Monnaie tournois', *Quarterly Review of the Guernsey Society*, 21–4 (1965–8), pp. 57–9

Priaulx, T.F., 'The De La Court Fund', *Quarterly Review of the Guernsey Society*, 25 (1969), pp. 67–71

Prochaska, F.K., *Women and Philanthropy in Nineteenth-Century England* (Oxford, 1980)

Prochaska, F.K., *The Voluntary Impulse: Philanthropy in Modern Britain* (London, 1988)

Raban, P., 'War and trade in the mid-eighteenth century', *TSG*, 22 (1986), pp. 131–63

Raban, P., 'Clandestine trade in the mid-eighteenth century', *TSG*, 22 (1987), pp. 303–26

Rankilor, B.A., 'Three gentlemen at Geneva', *The Review of the Guernsey Society*, 39 (1983), pp. 66–8

Richardson, R., *Death, Dissection and the Destitute* (London, 1987)

Rimlinger, G.V., *Welfare Policy and Industrialization in Europe, America and Russia* (Chichester, 1971)

Rivlin, J.J., 'Getting a medical qualification in England in the nineteenth century', *Bulletin of the Liverpool Medical History Society*, 9 (1997), pp. 56–63

Roberts, M.E., *The Cottage Hospitals, 1859–1990* (London, 1991)

Robin, A.C., 'Notes on population of Guernsey', *TSG*, 14 (1947), pp. 181–7

Robin, A.C., 'Some impressions of the census of 1961', *TSG*, 17 (1962), pp. 550–3

Robinson, R., 'The finance and provision of long term care for elderly people in the UK: recent trends, current policy and future prospects' (http:www.ipss.go.jp/webj-ad/webjournal.files/socialsecurity/2002/02dec/robinson.pdf)

Rose, C., 'The origins and ideals of the SPCK, 1699–1716', in Walsh, J., Haydon, C. and Taylor, J. (eds), *The Church of England, c.1689–c.1833* (Cambridge, 1993)

Rose, M.E., 'Settlement, removal and the New Poor Law', in Fraser, D. (ed.), *The New Poor Law in the Nineteenth Century* (London, 1976)

Rose, M.E., 'Introduction: the poor and the city, 1834–1914', in Rose, M.E. (ed.), *The Poor and the City: The English Poor Law in its Urban Context, 1834–1914* (Leicester, 1985)

Rose, M.E. (ed.), *The Poor and the City: The English Poor Law in its Urban Context, 1834–1914* (Leicester, 1985)

Schwartz, R.M., *Policing the Poor in Eighteenth-Century France* (Chapel Hill, 1988)

Scull, A., *The Most Solitary of Afflictions: Madness and Society in Britain, 1700–1900* (New Haven, 1993)

Sebire, H., *The Archaeology and Early History of the Channel Islands* (Stroud, 2005)

Seth-Smith, B., 'The post-war period', in Jeffs, D.A. (ed.), *One Hundred Years of Health: The Changing Health of Guernsey, 1899–1999* (Guernsey, 1999)

Sharp, E.W., 'The shipbuilders of Guernsey', *TSG*, 27 (1970), pp. 226–66

Slack, P.A., *Poverty and Policy in Tudor and Stuart England* (Harlow, 1988)

Slack, P.A., *The English Poor Law, 1531–1782* (1990; Cambridge, 1995 edn)

Slack, P.A., *From Reformation to Improvement: Public Welfare in Early Modern England* (Oxford, 1999)

Smith, F.B., *The People's Health, 1830–1910* (1979; London, 1990 edn)

Smith, N., Davis, A. and Hirsh, D., *A Minimum Income Standard for Guernsey* (Loughborough, 2011)

Smith, R.M., 'Social security as a developmental institution? Extending the Solar case for the relative efficacy of poor relief provisions under the English old poor law', Brookes World Poverty Institute Working Paper 56 (2008)

Smith, T.B., 'The ideology of charity, the image of the English Poor Law, and debates over the right to assistance in France, 1830–1905', *The Historical Journal*, 40 (1997), pp. 997–1032

Snell, K.D.M., 'Parish registration and the study of labour mobility', *Local Population Studies*, 33 (1984), pp. 29–44

Snell, K.D.M., *Annals of the Labouring Poor: Social Change and Agrarian England, 1660–1900* (Cambridge, 1985)

Snell, K.D.M., 'Pauper settlement and the right to poor relief in England and Wales',

Continuity and Change, 6 (1991), pp. 375–415

Snell, K.D.M., 'Settlement, poor law and the rural historian: new approaches and opportunities', *Rural History*, 3 (1992), pp. 145–72

Snell, K.D.M., *Parish and Belonging: Community, Identity and Welfare in England and Wales, 1700–1950* (Cambridge, 2006)

Snyder, F. and Hay, D. (eds), *Labour, Law and Crime: An Historical Perspective* (London, 1987)

Solar, P.M., 'Poor relief and English economic development before the industrial revolution', *The Economic History Review*, 48 (1995), pp. 1–22

Solar, P.M., 'Poor relief and English economic development: a renewed plea for comparative history', *The Economic History Review*, 50 (1997), pp. 369–74

States of Guernsey, *Guernsey Census, 1991* (Guernsey, 1992)

States of Guernsey, *Guernsey Census, 1996* (Guernsey, 1997)

States of Guernsey, *Report on the 2001 Guernsey Census* (Guernsey, 2002)

States of Guernsey, *Managing Guernsey's Population: A Consultation Document* (Guernsey, 2011)

States of Guernsey, *Guernsey Facts and Figures, 2011* (Guernsey, 2011)

States of Guernsey, *Guernsey Facts and Figures, 2012* (Guernsey, 2012)

States of Guernsey, *Guernsey Facts and Figures, 2013* (Guernsey, 2013)

States of Guernsey, *Public Consultation on Personal Tax, Pensions and Benefits*, Part B (Guernsey, 2013)

States of Guernsey, *Guernsey Financial Services: A Strategy for the Future* (Guernsey, 2014)

Stevens Cox, G., *St Peter Port, 1680–1830: The History of an International Entrepôt* (Woodbridge, 1999)

Stevens Cox, G., *The Guernsey Merchants and their World* (Guernsey, 2009)

Stevenson, W., 'The Middle Ages, 1000–1500', in Jamieson, A.G. (ed.), *A People of the Sea: The Maritime History of the Channel Islands* (London, 1986)

Strange, J.-M., *Death, Grief and Poverty in Britain, 1870–1914* (Cambridge, 2005)

Styles, J., *The Dress of the People: Everyday Fashion in Eighteenth-Century England* (London, 2007)

Styles, P., 'The evolution of the law of settlement', *University of Birmingham Historical Journal*, 9 (1964), pp. 33–63

Tampke, J., 'Bismarck's social legislation: a genuine breakthrough?' in Mommsen, W.J. and Mock, W. (eds), *The Emergence of the Welfare State in Britain and Germany, 1850–1950* (London, 1981)

Tate, W.E., *The Parish Chest: A Study of the Records of Parochial Administration in England* (1969; Chichester, 1983 edn)

Taylor, J.S., 'The unreformed workhouse, 1776–1834', in Martin, E.W. (ed.), *Comparative Development in Social Welfare* (London, 1972)

Taylor, J.S., *Poverty, Migration and Settlement in the Industrial Revolution* (Palo Alto, 1989)

Temple-Patterson, A., *Southampton: A Biography* (London, 1970)

Thane, P. (ed.), *The Origins of British Social Policy* (London, 1978)

Thane, P., 'Women and the poor law in Victorian and Edwardian England', *History Workshop*, 6 (1978), pp. 30–51

Thane, P., 'Non-contributory versus insurance pensions, 1878–1908', in Thane, P. (ed.), *The Origins of British Social Policy* (London, 1978)

Thane, P., *Old Age in English History: Past Experiences, Present Issues* (Oxford, 2000)

Thompson, E.P., *Customs in Common* (London, 1991)

Thomson, D., 'Workhouse to nursing home: residential care of elderly people in England since 1840', *Aging and Society*, 3 (1983), pp. 43–69

Thornton, T., *The Charters of Guernsey* (Bognor Regis, 2004)

Thornton, T., *The Channel Islands, 1370–1640: Between England and Normandy* (Woodbridge, 2012)

Tierney, B., *Medieval Poor Law* (Berkeley, 1959)

Timmins, N., *The Five Giants: A Biography of the Welfare State* (London, 1995)

Tomkins, A., *The Experience of Urban Poverty, 1723–82: Parish, Charity and Credit* (Manchester, 2006)

Tough, K., 'Health in the Occupation', in Jeffs, D.A. (ed.), *One Hundred Years of Health: The Changing Health of Guernsey, 1899–1999* (Guernsey, 1999)

Townsend, P., *Poverty in the United Kingdom: A Survey of Household Resources and Standards of Living* (Harmondsworth, 1979)

Treble, J.H., *Urban Poverty in Britain, 1830–1914* (London, 1979)

Underdown, D., *Fire from Heaven: Life in an English Town in the Seventeenth Century* (London, 1992)

Valenze, D., 'Custom and humanity: changing attitudes towards the poor in eighteenth-century England', in Garnett, J. and Matthew, C. (eds), *Revival and Religion since 1700* (London, 1993)

van Leeuwen, M., 'Histories of risk and welfare in Europe during the 18th and 19th centuries', in Grell, O.P., Cunningham, A. and Jütte, R. (eds), *Health Care and Poor Relief in 18th and 19th Century Northern Europe* (Aldershot, 2002)

van Leuven, J.N., 'History and practice of parochial taxation in Sark and Guernsey', *Guernsey Law Journal*, 24 (1997), pp. 111–22

van Leuven, J.N., 'Constitutional relationships within the Bailiwick of Guernsey – Alderney', *The Jersey Law Review*, June 2004

Vorspan, R., 'Vagrancy and the new poor law in late-Victorian and Edwardian England', *English Historical Review*, 92 (1977), pp. 59–81

Walsh, J., Haydon, C. and Taylor, J., *The Church of England, c.1689–c.1833* (Cambridge, 1993)

Walter, J. and Schofield, R. (eds), *Famine, Disease and the Social Order in Early Modern Society* (1989; Cambridge, 1991 edn)

Ward, M.A., 'Guernsey's insurance history: an initial essay', *TSG*, 22 (1989), pp. 659–78

Wardley, P., 'Edwardian Britain: empire, income and political discontent', in Johnson, P. (ed.), *Twentieth-Century Britain: Economic, Social and Cultural Change* (London, 1994)

Warren, M.D., *A Chronology of State Medicine, Public Health, Welfare and Related Services in Britain, 1066–1999* (London, 2000)

Weinbren, D., 'Supporting self-help: charity, mutuality and reciprocity in nineteenth-century Britain', in Brigden, P. and Harris, B. (eds), *Charity and Mutual Aid in Europe and North America since 1800* (Abingdon, 2007)

Wheadon, E.A., 'The history of the tomato in Guernsey,' *TSG*, 12 (1935), pp. 338–50

Williams, C., *From Sail to Steam: Studies in the Nineteenth-Century History of the Channel Islands* (Chichester, 2000)

Williams, K., *From Pauperism to Poverty* (London, 1981)

Winch, D. and O'Brien, P. (eds), *The Political Economy of British Historical Experience, 1688–1914* (Oxford, 2002)

Wolfe, J., 'Guernsey: social work on a small island', in Payne, M. and Shardlow, S.M. (eds), *Social Work in the British Isles* (London, 2002)

Wood, P., *Poverty and the Workhouse in Victorian Britain* (Stroud, 1991)

Woolf, S., *The Poor in Western Europe in the Eighteenth and Nineteenth Centuries* (London, 1986)

Wrigley, E.A. and Schofield, R.S., *The Population History of England, 1541–1871: A Reconstruction* (1981; Cambridge, 1989 edn)

Unpublished Theses and Dissertations

Bennett, A., 'A history of the French newspapers and nineteenth-century English newspapers of Guernsey' (unpub. MA dissertation, Loughborough University, 1995)

Charlesworth, L.R., 'Salutary and humane law, a legal history of the law of settlement and removals, c.1795–1865' (unpub. PhD thesis, Manchester University, 1998)

Finch, G., 'The experience of peripheral regions in an age of industrialisation: the case of Devon, 1840–1914' (unpub. PhD thesis, Oxford University, 1984)

Hitchcock, T.V., 'The English workhouse: a study in institutional poor relief in selected counties, 1696–1750' (unpub. DPhil thesis, Oxford University, 1985)

Richmond, T.V., '"No finery": the dress of the poor in nineteenth-century England (unpub. PhD thesis, London University, 2005)

Salazar Gourley, I.C., 'A survey of the history and development of education in the Bailiwick of Guernsey, Channel Islands, pre-Reformation–1976' (unpub. MA dissertation, University of British Columbia, 1976)

Seal, C.V., 'Poor relief and welfare: a comparative study of the Belper and Cheltenham poor law unions, 1780 to 1914' (unpub. PhD thesis, Leicester University, 2009)

Index

Sherwill, Sir Ambrose (Bailiff)   251
Shipbuilding   15
Shipping   11–12, 13, 15
Shoesmith, Thomas   193
Shortt, Francis   157
Sir William Collings Fund   107
Slate clubs *see* box clubs
Sleque, Judith   203
Smallpox   77, 152-3, 156
Smiles, Samuel   277
Smith, George   105
Smith, Minnie   208
Smuggling   12, 14–15
Social Insurance (Guernsey) Law, 1964   254, 255, 258, 265
Social Insurance (Guernsey) Law, 1978   255
Société Charitable de l'Ile de Guernesey   106
Société de Secours Mutuels   100
Société Fraternelle de l'Ile de Sarnia   101
Society of St Vincent de Paul   106
Soup kitchen   86, 104, 212
Southampton County Penitentiary   199
SPCK   116–7, 227, 271
Squires, Sophie   193, 224
St Andrews (parish)   58 n.93, 59, 74
States
    Board of Health   149, 153, 176, 238, 257, 259, 261, 262, 263
    Central Poor Law Board   69, 72, 174–5, 197
    Children's Home   196–7, 206
    composition and functions of   9–11, 22
    Health Insurance schemes   256, 257, 259–61, 266
    Health Service Fund   258, 260
    Homes for Workers Committee   242–3
    housing   242–3
    Insurance Authority   245, 248, 250, 251, 252, 253, 254, 255 n.95, 257, 259–60
    Insurance Fund   254, 267
    Long-Term Care Insurance Fund   263, 267
    Medical Officer of Health   153, 216
    Mental Health Services Board   176
    Old Age Pensions Authority   246, 248
    Public Assistance Authority   69, 72, 79, 197, 255
        Central Outdoor Assistance Board   69, 72, 237 n.233
        Children Board   69
        Hospital Board   69, 72, 79, 122, 177
    Review of Benefits and Taxation (2015)   266–7
    role in poor relief   67–9
    Social Security Authority   255, 260, 262, 263
    Social Security Department (SSD)   255, 256 n.97, 266

Stephens, Mary Ann   188
Stevens, Margaret   208
Stevens, Rev. J.D.   231
Stigma (associated with poor relief)   94–5, 111
St John Ambulance Association   109, 110, 150
St Julian's Hospital   46, 51, 115
St Julian's House   144 n.205, 237 n.233, 261
St Martins (parish)   58, 70, 73 n.87, 74, 98, 100
Stocking-knitting   12, 27, 51
Stokes, Sophie   203
Stone trade   16, 38
St Peters (parish)   58 n.91, 74, 75, 282
Strangers
    Constables' responsibility for   61, 67, 71, 72, 78, 82, 206–7
    deportation of   65–7, 82–3
    eligibility for relief   57, 62–5, 82–3
    in Town Hospital   206–10
    relief expenditure on   68, 74
St Sampsons (parish)   11 n.37, 16, 58, 74
St Saviours (parish)   28, 57, 59, 74
Strickland, Dr John   149
Suffrage
    parochial elections   21, 22
    States elections   22, 80, 264
Supplementary Benefit (Amendment) Ordinance, 2005   256, 283
Supplementary Benefit (Guernsey) Law, 1971   254, 255, 256, 257 n.106
Symons, Ann   207
Symons, John   207
Syphilis *see* sexually transmitted diseases

Tax, income *see under* income tax
Tax, parochial *see under* poor rates
Taylor, Frederick   195 n.164
Tea   218, 220
Thornton, William (economist)   277
Thoume, Elizabeth   135
Thurstan, Louisa   105
Todd, James   225
Torteval (parish)   58 n.93, 70
Tourism   16, 265
Town Hospital (St Peter Port)
    admission and discharge policy   124, 127 n.91, 187
    as a geriatric hospital   237–8, 261
    buildings   119, 122–3
    bullying   157
    chapel   228–9
    closure   238
    clothing   221–3
    daily routine   211–13
    directors   177–81